The Church and Economic Life

A Documentary Study: 1945 to the Present

Malcolm Brown
and Paul Ballard

EPWORTH

British Library Cataloguing in Publication data

A catalogue record for this book is available from the British Library

07162 0600 5
978 07162 0600 2

First published in 2006
by Epworth Press
4 John Wesley Road
Werrington
Peterborough PE4 6ZP

Printed and bound in Great Britain by
William Clowes Ltd, Beccles, Suffolk

Contents

Acknowledgements

In our research for this book we have been fortunate to be able to draw on the enthusiastic interest and valuable help and encouragement of a large number of people. Our gratitude goes, therefore, to all who have been so supportive over a considerable period, and of a project that in many ways proved more elusive than originally anticipated. We hope that the result is worthy of the expectation. At the risk of omitting many who deserve mention, however, there are some who were more formally caught up in the process of our researches whose help ought to be recorded, but who are, obviously, not responsible for the results. Not all contacts yielded directly suitable material for this volume, but all contributed to the overall acquisition of information and understanding.

These can be categorized into three groups. The first stage in testing out the initial outline was to write to a number of key individuals who had been, over the years, engaged in the field, especially in relation to industrial mission and social responsibility policies of the churches. Out of this came a fruitful correspondence with a number of people. Some of these were also included in exploratory visits made to London and Edinburgh.

At the same time contact was made with the major denominational headquarters and the ecumenical instruments, usually through their social responsibility officer. Again useful insights and material were forthcoming, which in several cases was fruitfully supplemented by subsequent visits. These two visits, over several days each, therefore, in the Autumn of 2002, were mainly, on the one hand, to the church and ecumenical offices and, on the other, to a number of relevant para-ecclesial organizations. This enabled us, through personal contact, to discuss the aims and needs of the project more widely and to get to know something of current practice.

The third group of contacts were a number of libraries, archives and collections, which provided access to material relating to our subject. We are grateful to the librarians and keepers of these collections for offering us access and providing back-up services.

We would, therefore, here like to record our thanks to the following, among many others, who were visited in their capacities as described:

Chris Beales, of Employment Forum UK and former Secretary of the Board for Social Responsibility of the Church of England.

Andrew Bradstock, Social Responsibility Secretary of the United Reformed Church.

Donald Bruce, Director, Science, Religion and Technology Project, Church of Scotland.

Erik Cramb, Co-ordinator, Scottish Churches' Industrial Mission.

John Ellis, Secretary, Business and Economic Affairs, Methodist Church.

Duncan Forrester, New College, Edinburgh.

Kristine Gibbs, Social Interests Officer, Church of Scotland.

Malcolm Grundy, formerly in industrial mission.

Alastair Hulbert, Centre for Theology and Public Issues, New College, Edinburgh.

John Kennedy, Social Responsibility Secretary of Churches Together in Britain and Ireland.

John Lovatt, of the Industrial Christian Fellowship.

David Lyall, New College, Edinburgh.

Marjory McLean, Acting Clerk to the General Assembly, Church of Scotland.

Andrew Morton, formerly Secretary for Social Responsibility, British Council of Churches.

Douglas Nichol, General Secretary, National Mission, Church of Scotland.

Geoffrey Platt, Secretary, Rural Theology Association.

Peter Sedgwick, Secretary of the Board for Social Responsibility of the Church of England.

Norman Shanks, Leader, The Iona Community.

David Sinclair, Secretary, Committee on Church and Nation, Church of Scotland.

Charles Wookey, Assistant General Secretary, Catholic Bishops' Conference of England and Wales.

Also the following libraries and archives:

John Rylands University Library, Manchester.
Archives of the William Temple Foundation.
Archives of the Industrial Mission Association and some local teams.
Archives of the Methodist Church.

Archives of the Church of England, Battersea, London.
Board for Social Responsibility.
British Council of Churches.

The Library, Friends' House, London.

The Church of Scotland.
Minutes of the National Assembly.

The Arts and Social Sciences Library, Cardiff University.
Research facilities and Inter-library loans.

Cambridge University Library.

Finally, but by no means least, thanks are due to those who have patiently yet firmly helped us take the project through to publication:

Acknowledgements

Barbara Clayton, Administrator for the Eastern Region Ministry Course.

Natalie Watson and her colleagues at Epworth Press.

John Atherton for his very helpful Preface.

Angela and Gerrie, longsuffering wives, without whose determination nothing would happen.

Foreword

Why Developing Tradition is a Matter of Life or Death

Since 1945, Britain and the world have experienced the greatest period of change in economic history. It has been a story of increasingly extensive and intensive change, gathering pace particularly since the 1980s, and showing no signs of slowing down. (*The Church and Economic Life* rightly and valuably addresses this whole context, focusing especially on the last twenty years.) My current research on global religion and capitalism strongly confirms this judgement. Indeed, I am increasingly aware of the great gap even between the later 1990s and 2005, and what went before, and what that means for our living. For example, these intensive changes are bringing to the fore two series of interacting realities which are likely to dominate the next few years. On the one hand, we are becoming more and more aware of the impact of globalization, including the growing interdependence of economies and their interlinking with political, social (including demographic), technological, environmental and cultural changes. On the other hand, we are witnessing, outside the decline of mainstream churches in Britain and Western Europe, the rise of furious religion, again interconnecting with every other sphere of life. And, because this is a global phenomenon, it is increasingly intruding into the West, and generating change through interaction with the churches. For example, Christianity is being reminded that the exception in world history and in contemporary global experience is the current western practice of dividing religion from public life.

For the churches in Britain to address economic life in such an emerging context will mean accepting the realities of globalized localities. What this book does is to provide tools and resources from recent church experience for facing up to that task. It will not deliver success, because the emerging agenda is too new and disconnected from even the recent past. Yet there are sufficient connections for it to provide real help. For example, the book's account of British endeavours recognizes the profound impact made at a local level of the mission to places of employment, spearheaded by industrial mission. For that was certainly to people, often in profoundly alienating contexts, but also to the structurings that so shaped their lives. Equally, there were always links, often tenuous, with other nations and experiences, industrially and theologically, from Nigeria and Japan, to the USA, Germany and France. For churches now compelled to address global localities, these sources provide invaluable incentives and support for the new task. And not least, it will remind them that any renewal of what it means to be Church and to engage in mission has to be rooted in a profoundly public and practical theology. Old past friends and colleagues of industrial mission, like Mark Gibbs, rightly and critically wrote and spoke of the Christian tendency to project a God who was too small, too domestic and too unconnected with a world created, redeemed and supported by him. That is possibly the most important lesson for the British churches, and especially the Church of England, to learn from these texts, given their current over-absorption with church decline (and therefore, their inevitable missing of the mark as to why these things have happened, and therefore what can best be done about them).

Yet what I have observed in the most recent period of change, from the late 1990s to the present, should also provide some real comfort to those of us concerned to reconnect the churches to economic life. For example, in terms of official national church reports, I have been struck by a sudden outburst of real church interest in political economy, ecumenically from *Unemployment and the Future of Work* (1997) to *Prosperity with a Purpose*

(2005), and denominationally from *The Common Good* (1996), 'Prosperity with a Purpose' (1999[1]), (Roman Catholic), *The Paradox of Prosperity* (1999) and *The Responsibility Gap* (2004), (Salvation Army), and the report of the *Church Urban Life and Faith Commission* (2006), (Church of England.) And, once again, following the tradition elaborated in *The Church and Economic Life*, I have seen the significance of church engagement with the economy in the regions (a new form of the local). For example, in the North West we have seen, from regional government, *Faith in England's Northwest: The Contribution Made by Faith Communities to Civil Society in the Region* (2003) and *Faith in England's Northwest: Economic Impact Assessment* (2005), and from Christian NGOs like the William Temple Foundation's Year Two Research Report, *Telling the Stories: How Churches are Contributing to Social Capital* (2005), and the Manchester Centre for Public Theology's initiation of a conversation, and likely agreed statement, between Muslims and Christians on faith-based finance programmes and theologies. These reports underline the emerging importance of religious capital and its contribution to human and community well-being, not least for the emerging agendas of government, business and civil society, itself a recognition that the new Christian task transcends any particular sector. The Muslim–Christian conversation also points to the likely emerging significance of the evolution from intra-faith (ecumenical Christian) social ethics to interfaith social ethics, of profound importance for global localities. In teaching and research for over twenty years at Manchester University, I have also observed a growing interest in the tradition of relating economics to ethics. From Adam Smith and Malthus, through Marshall and Keynes, ethical economics is currently generating renewed interest through, for example, the work of Sen on human development and Layard on human happiness. Both stress the central role of ethics in a multifaceted interpretation of human welfare. And this emerging significance of ethical economics is confirmed by its centrality to the great global problematics, say, of environmental crisis, gross inequalities between and within nations, and technological innovations. Clearly, the churches need to encourage the contribution of Christian social ethics to such ethical economics as a way of promoting the fruitful interaction between churches, academies and faithful practitioners, itself part of a fruitful interaction between Christianity, other faiths, governments, business and civil society nationally and increasingly globally. That would be a strong endorsement of the character of Christianity as promoting a public theology and Church for the common good of all.

To that end, *The Church and Economic Life* makes an important and timely contribution, as essentially an 'extended seminar' on applied theology (as public and practical theology). And, it does so in three strategic ways. First, the substantial commentaries that introduce each historical period can be usefully read together as an extended essay on economic change from 1945 to 2005. It is a rich source of interpretation, argued with conviction. Second, the introductions to each of the readings are, in themselves, an informative history of the rich, multifaceted nature of Christian involvement in economic affairs. Third, the readings are the heart of the book, but only providing they encourage us to consult the sources and, equally important, to address what has necessarily been omitted.

Taken together, these three provide one of the best sources for engaging recent tradition and are central for its development in the emerging contemporary context. Given the problematics shaping that context, particularly as they impinge more and more on every global locality, and the centrality of Christian social ethics to addressing all that, it is therefore a timely reminder to the churches that they will increasingly and rightly cease to count unless they think far more. That means promoting a public Church with a public theology. And that will continue to be tested on the anvil of economic affairs, the central determining reality of contemporary society. That is why developing this tradition is so important.

John Atherton

1

The Economy as a Site of Christian Mission

One finds strange things in secondhand shops. One of the authors recently discovered a children's book of British history in pictures – undated but, from internal evidence, produced in the mid-1930s. It doesn't even have a title as it appears to be a part-work, amateurishly bound. Every page contains a series of pen-and-ink drawings which together illustrate a theme, topic or moment in history. There is almost no written text. However, it was not the early sections on cavemen, or even the splendid sketch of 'The Recantation of Cranmer' that attracted our attention, but the very final page entitled 'Social Problems'. It is a most eclectic assembly featuring a 'traffic robot' (traffic lights to us), condemned dwellings and the council houses that replace them, 'wood-cutting for the unemployed' and a hunger march – all significant issues in the mid-1930s. But at the centre of the page is a head-and-shoulders sketch of the only named individual – Dr Temple, Archbishop of York.

The fascination is that Temple's presence apparently required no explanation. His inclusion clearly signals his status as a leading figure addressing the social problems of the age, and his office as Archbishop seems to undergird that role in the name of the Church. But while Temple's contribution to Christian social ethics between the 1920s and the 1940s is still well known, it is very much harder to bridge the conceptual gap between our world today and a world where the social role of the Church, and the contribution of a particular churchman, is so obviously recognizable as to require no further explanation.

This study covers the engagement that the churches in Britain have made with economic issues and ethics since the Second World War. The war brought about a degree of social dislocation which took some time to be recognized in its full seriousness. The world of the 1930s, whether in church, in society or in politics, could never be recaptured, yet the legacy of Christian social engagement, forged in the uncertain and nervous 1930s, contributed in no small way to the shaping of the post-war world and to the subsequent directions taken by the churches' ministry and mission.

Another noteworthy feature of that page of the children's history book is that 'Social Problems' are conceived in very strongly economic terms: public housing replacing slums; unemployment and hunger marches; a 'free café for the destitute' – even the problems of road safety and traffic congestion reflect the growing prosperity and mass production methods that were bringing motoring within the reach of millions, although the unequal distribution of that prosperity was clearly disturbing. And the perennial concerns of healthcare, childcare and education (which feature here as 'a modern hospital', 'a day nursery' and – somewhat bizarrely – 'open-air lessons') required, then as now, extensive public investment and political direction of resources. So Temple's presence confirms not only the churches' social involvement but, implicitly, its concern for the ordering of the economy and the participation of all in economic dimensions of life.[1]

It is thought-provoking to imagine what a similar page illustrating social problems might look like today, and to try to interpret the underlying social changes that they represent. The reader of the 1930s clearly did not expect to see anti-social behaviour, racism, binge-drinking, youths with weapons on the streets, graffiti, terrorism, or even crime in general (to select headlines from just one day's newspaper in 2005) listed as immediate causes of social concern. And while all these contemporary phenomena can rightly be seen to have economic dimensions, the patterns of public debate do not easily allow connections to be made between the social problems of our day and the structures of the economy.[2] Indeed, questions of how the economy is ordered, as opposed to the minutiae of how it is managed, have not figured high on the list of public concerns for some time. However, this book is not intended simply as a retrospective examination of a period when the churches pursued ethical issues that have now fallen away from public concern. It is our contention that the ordering of economic life, the moral questions that inform the workings of the economy and the ethical questions that arise as consequences of economic life, are all matters to which Christian theology has things to say. And if there is a fruitful dialogue to be had between theology and economics, the practice of the churches in their ministry and mission is the location where that engagement is made manifest.

Why the economy?

During the post-war period, the churches' practical and theological engagements with economic issues tended to reflect the relative salience of economics within the political and public life of the nation. Thus in periods of prosperity such as the later 1950s (when, as Harold Macmillan didn't say, 'You've never had it so good!' – although the misquote captured the public mood succinctly) the churches tended to reinforce the prevailing social consensus, often with an assumption that it was essentially a Christian consensus, and to regard problems of poverty and inequity as transient issues to which solutions could quite straightforwardly be found. But the more confrontational politics of Margaret Thatcher in the 1980s, which aimed to achieve a major reorientation of economic institutions and concepts of economic justice, made the churches' interventions more self-consciously controversial. These are generalizations, of course, as our subsequent chapters will show, but the interesting point is that Christian social theology and practice have taken a very distinctive flavour from the prevailing social and economic climate and have not, on the whole, suggested the unwavering application of eternal doctrinal truths. Economic issues create a context in which the direction and emphasis of ministry and mission are essentially reactive, often without awareness that this is so. It is important, therefore, to turn to those parts of the churches that kept economic questions at the forefront of their thinking in order to see what the churches were saying and doing about the context that had such a profound effect on their activities.

One could argue long and hard about why the economy has always held such an ambiguous role as a topic for Christian reflection, Christian practice and Christian ethics. Simple – perhaps simplistic – arguments would be that the churches have never quite woken up to modernity (and the market economy is the supremely modernist institution); that the churches have historically held a highly individualistic approach to responsibility and morality with little awareness of structural sin or social ethics; that economics, being as contentious as politics, risked dividing Christians and weakening the Church; or that the churches knew, subliminally or otherwise, that they were deeply implicated in the workings of an economy which, were they to scrutinize it, might not exhibit many recognizable Christian traits. William Temple began his hugely important book *Christianity and Social Order* (1942) with a ringing rebuttal of the 'entirely modern and extremely questionable' heresy that religion and politics (including economics) are concerned with separate worlds. But Temple was arguing from assumptions about the social role of the Church which have been further eroded as modernity has tightened its grip, and ideas about the nature of Christendom have come to seem far less easily recoverable. The case for a Christian engagement with economic issues needs to be made afresh for the twenty-first century.

Why a 'Reader' on the Church and the economy?

In one way, this book is something of a prolegomenon to that task. It approaches the questions facing the contemporary churches through revisiting the churches' own contributions to the dialogue with economic issues over the last sixty or so years. Too many of the texts that we have included here are to be found only in ephemera or in archived materials, so part of our purpose is to bring the very considerable work of the churches in this field back into the light of day. Daylight, however, implies openness to scrutiny. It is not our intention to offer data from the past as if it contained unambiguous solutions for the present. While we retain a considerable admiration for the determination, insight and creativity of many of those who have worked at the interface between the Church and the economy, we will also explore critical perspectives – not only critiques that were offered contemporaneously, but also critiques that can be made with the benefit of hindsight.

Nevertheless, we believe very strongly that the neglect of the economy as a location for practical theology and Christian ethics has been, and remains, an omission that diminishes the ability of the churches to witness to the claims of the gospel in the contemporary world, and so it is incumbent upon us to set out the framework of our argument for why this is the case.

Moral aspects of the economy

First, and perhaps most obvious, is the observation that the workings of the economy embroil every citizen within their structures. We are all 'players', caught up, for good or ill, in the same game. From the moment we begin to exchange goods and services with one another, questions of value arise and mechanisms for agreeing value are inescapable. In practice, it is almost impossible to live outside the structures of the prevailing economic system. Relatively small human groupings, motivated perhaps by common beliefs and particular values, may order their internal economy in ways that do not conform to the dominant models in the wider society. But at some point – usually at many points – there has to be an interface with more extensive markets. An example here might be the Amish communities of North America who seek to live according to highly distinctive ethical principles that contrast with those of the communities around them. However, even the Amish are driven to engage with the wider economy in ways that have entailed immense ethical debate and some interesting and surprising compromises.[3]

Although we are all involved in the economy at one level or another, there remains an interesting debate about whether our economic participation is a matter of moral import or not. Apologists for the purest forms of market economics sometimes argue that the nature of the market itself, as the agglomeration of millions of discrete personal decisions, means that the outcomes of market processes cannot be regarded as moral or immoral since they cannot be manipulated with any expectation that intervention will lead to desired outcomes. Market forces, it is argued, involve neither agency nor intention – if it works out that I become rich while you do not, no moral judgement can be made against me since I neither intended you to be poor nor acted in ways that brought your poverty about.

If this argument were uncontroversial, the interventions of the churches in matters of economic life would be superfluous or misguided. However, there are two major challenges to be made to the market theorists here. First, their own arguments can be confronted on empirical and theoretical grounds. While the majority of economists would agree that the impact of any attempt to influence market outcomes is extraordinarily hard to predict, economists are not (contrary to popular impression) wedded to a single interpretation of human motivation. If numbers of individuals start to alter their economic behaviour, this will be mirrored in the workings of the market and in its outcomes, in complex, but not wholly unpredictable, ways. Therefore the market apologists' desire to uncouple human agency from market outcomes is called into question and, with it, the claim that the market itself is an amoral structure.

Second, it is not at all clear that moral claims on an individual apply only where the person has directly brought a situation about. Simply stated, where there is an opportunity for us to remedy an ill or to promote a good, there is at least some moral claim on us to do so however the situation was caused. The extent of personal responsibility in this respect is, of course, a matter for debate, but it is not self-evident that the very restricted version of personal responsibility which underlies the claims of market apologists is sustainable.[4]

So there are good grounds for regarding the operations of a market economy as legitimate subjects for moral enquiry, and therefore appropriate topics for Christian theological reflection and church intervention. But there are further reasons why a Christian engagement with economic questions should not be neglected; in particular the argument that economics offers a rigorous 'test case' that can illuminate the effectiveness or otherwise of the churches' public theology.[5]

The economy as a test case for a public theology

In the last twenty years or so, the study of Christian ethics in the British and US academic context has become one of the most exciting areas of the theological curriculum, largely because the generally liberal approach that characterized the first thirty years after the Second World War has come to seem tired and unequal to the challenges posed by the stage of modernity in which the world finds itself. (We are cautious about using the term 'postmodernity' since it embraces a multitude of positions, not all of them compatible with each other – but we are agreed that the modernity that we thought we understood no longer provides a viable framework for understanding how the world works.) In place of a weary liberalism, academic theology has taken a turn towards confessional and communitarian stances which re-emphasize the distinctiveness of Christian values and beliefs, focus afresh on the centrality of the Church as the harbinger of new ways of living, and sit light to concepts such as 'relevance' or the desire to engage in a search for common meanings. The uniqueness of the Christian message, comprehended through God's self-revelation and not through the powers of human reason, draws the theological and ecclesiological focus away from what Christians hold in common with all people and stresses instead the surprising and counter-cultural impact of the gospel.

It would be hard to argue that this return to a confessional focus in theology is not, in many ways, welcome and timely. It has breathed new life into the discipline but, perhaps, more importantly, it is openly addressing key issues of human identity at a time in history when religion – far from withering on the vine as many secularization theories predicted – is becoming intensely significant in a realigned world politics. However, the problematics of economics continue to raise the question of how disparate cultural groupings can establish shared values. One may concede that the old liberal attempt to make universal human reason the foundation for common values has lost its way (although many believe there is life in that project yet). But it remains that the confessional theologians face a choice when it comes to economic affairs: to retreat into faith-based cells focusing on their internal economy and regarding cross-cultural exchange and agreement about value as elusive; or to treat economics (covertly or otherwise) as a topic of little interest. It is noteworthy that the few theologians of a strongly confessional bent who have tackled the problems posed by economics have tended to promote a return to medieval structures such as guilds, to be opposed to the concept of extensive or global markets and to be sceptical of the claim that economics can be understood as a discrete discipline that can set the terms of debate.[6] It is not necessary to be an enthusiast for economic globalization and markets, or to regard economics as a new Queen of Sciences, to suspect that such phenomena, and the forms of knowledge that sustain them, are extraordinarily difficult to un-invent.

A vitally important aspect of market economics is that it is a system designed, as Jeremy Bentham put it, for a society of strangers. In other words, the market is a device that establishes the value of things independently of local custom or tradition, and is therefore a mechanism that both enables and responds to the ability of human beings to engage in commerce (in every sense) across the divisions of geography, culture and faith. If we believe that the market is a deeply flawed institution whose outcomes frequently offend against the demands of justice, we still have to answer the question of how a better version of economic justice is to be established which will command assent from people very different from ourselves. This is an area where Christian writings on economics are notoriously weak, often underplaying the extent of disagreement about the nature of justice and tending to assume that most people will assent to a version of justice that will be conformable to the tenets of Christian faith. Too often, the supposition that Christians know what they mean by justice is taken to imply that the concept of justice is not problematic. In a world where contact between faiths and cultures – not least economic contact – cannot easily be undone (short of a major catastrophe), such easy agreement seems unlikely.

So the confessional strand in Christian ethics has still to give a comprehensive answer to the problem of moral plurality which the market economy believes itself to address. But, far from validating the older liberal theological responses, the problem of plurality simply raises new and difficult questions for that tradition.

The classic liberal project sought to overcome cultural and tribal difference through the search for universal foundations that transcended the particularity of traditions. To that extent at least, liberal strands in theology may be said to share something of the genealogy of the market economy, for both sought to offer a basis for human values that was not constrained by local and accidental factors – in other words, to establish an ethic for a global society. But two difficulties follow from this for the liberal theologian. First, the search for common values and shared stories makes it difficult to give much salience to the particular values and narratives of Christian faith. Both in theory and in practice, liberal theologies, while strong on engagement with the created order and human society, have been weak in exploring the specifically Christian element in such ethical engagements. This is not to say that Christian distinctiveness must always be of such a high order that no non-Christian could possibly share the same position. But Christian authenticity, in the sense of knowing how one's values, patterns of living and political or economic commitments are grounded in the specifics of the Christian tradition, is surely an essential element in any practice that calls itself Christian. While the liberal theological tradition has, at times, sought to explore its own grounding in the specifics of the tradition, on the whole it has neglected this aspect of the theological task rather badly, leaving the high ground to the confessional and communitarian theologians who have (not surprisingly) a much more highly developed sense of rootedness in tradition and, often, a more developed ecclesiology.

Second, liberal theologians have frequently found themselves on the opposite side of the political fence to the apologists for market economics – and it is at this point that the limitations of labels such as 'liberal' begin to make themselves felt. The radical free-market agenda of the economic neo-liberals clashed stridently with the corporatism of the theological liberals whose liberalism had led them to stress shared human values and to support structures for sustaining a common life. In this, the theological liberals showed that their liberalism was far less thoroughgoing than the 'liberal' economics being pursued by the policies of Thatcherism. Ronald Preston from the left and Michael Novak from the right are both examples of theological liberals whose work was strongly tempered by an element of communitarian thinking which was generally absent in the work of economic liberals of the time. But because of the amount of shared territory, theological liberals struggled to develop a tough critique of the underlying philosophy of the free market. Swingeing criticisms of the effects of markets were frequent – but because both varieties of liberalism were discernibly part of the same project, it was hard to make the charges stick at a more profound level. Moreover, there was a strange hubris apparent in many theologically liberal interventions. It was as if the social and political consensus, of which liberal theology had been a part, could not countenance the idea that other ways of thinking were now in the ascendancy. The ideas that once appeared to serve the Church and the world well – ideas that had seemed to give a definitive understanding of how the world worked – were under challenge and frequently failed to recognize the instability of their intellectual foundations. The sense in which the free-market economy represented the apotheosis of the liberal project was not easily understood when liberal theologians generally found themselves so profoundly in opposition to its character and effects. Nor did a theology grounded in a search for shared human values find it easy to give a coherent account of why the consensus that had been achieved (at least within hitherto relatively homogenous western societies) was now breaking down.

If the interesting divide within the study of Christian ethics today is that between liberal and confessional or communitarian positions, then it is clear that the economy as a subject for ethical enquiry asks profound questions of both protagonists. Giving attention to the ethical questions raised by market economics reopens some of the human problems that will not go away – the necessary dialogue between diverse communities and the necessity for communities and cultures, in all their particularity, to be recognized as the places where ethical foundations are laid and sustained.

And the economy serves as a test case for Christian ethics in another way also. It has often been too easy for Christian ethics to confine itself to those moral problems that are essentially personal or familial in their scope – in other words, to confine ethical debate to the spheres where individual responsibility is the paramount concern. As a result, the aspects of the moral life in which the individual acts within social structures, and cultural institutions where the impact of the individual conscience is proportionately slight, have not been given much attention. To put the case strongly, the churches in the West have been woefully inadequate in offering a moral discourse that could inform people's participation in wider civil society, in political life or, of course, in economics. The early years of the twenty-first century are witnessing some gradual redressing of this imbalance, with significant new work on topics such as global conflict and political theology. But the study of the ethics and theology that can engage with questions of economic life continues to be an important entry point into this more socially alert and structurally informed approach to Christian moral teaching.

Economics, mission and practice

So far, we have focused mainly on the theological and theoretical arguments that place economics firmly within the proper ambit of the churches' concern. But the main focus of this book is on the churches' practice in ministry and mission directed to the economy and its human consequences in the labour market and the workplace; so we move now to consider how theology and practice connect.

It is hard to say whether new emphases, whether in theology or in other disciplines, begin in the academy and move to the practical sphere, or vice versa. Often it feels like a strongly reciprocal relationship in which the condition of the Church and the state of the world prompt new directions in academic theology which, in turn, generate new approaches to practice. But whatever the main direction of the flow of ideas, it remains that the worlds of practitioners and academic theologians have not always perceived their need of one another very clearly. (And here it is interesting that the institutions created by the churches to engage with economic issues have frequently included practitioners who were among the best read and most reflective, alongside others who held the deepest suspicions about the 'ivory-tower' irrelevance of academic theologians in general.) Too frequently, those engaged in the churches' ministry and mission have privileged the 'view from below' and the authenticity of practical experience in ways that fail to recognize that no experience is perceived unmediated by some ideological or philosophical framework of meaning, however unconscious and taken for granted. And there have also been times and places where the theology of the academy has been driven too much by its own internal concerns with very little interest in or engagement with the life of the empirical Church itself.

The divorce between theology and practice remains an ever-present danger, and one that this book is, in part, designed to address. By pointing the spotlight on the economy and on those in the churches who have pursued the questions raised by economics through the last sixty years or so, we offer an extended case study of practice and theology in conversation. True, it is a conversation that we have, at times, had to draw out and extrapolate from the available evidence, but it remains that practitioners whose ministry and mission has been directed towards the economy have rarely been able to utilize a ready-made church theology which could be applied without further thought and development to the questions which ministry in economic affairs threw up. The economy, as we have argued, exemplifies some intractable but central problems of Christian ethics which rarely emerge so strongly in Sunday-by-Sunday church life. Those who face the pastoral, ethical and missiological complexities of the economy and the workplace usually needed to be practical theologians themselves. Yet their perception of what constituted ministry and mission in those contexts was inevitably shaped by their own theological formation within a church that had not made the economy a prime site for theological reflection. The story of ministry and mission that this book seeks to tell is thus a complex web of relationships in which the state of the churches has often been a significant but overlooked partner and where the state of academic theology and the state of political life have woven together a rich tapestry of insight into the nature of mission itself.

Misunderstanding the economy

Our reasons for revisiting the churches' missiological engagement with economic issues are not only about returning that theme to the prominence we believe it deserves. The churches may have been historically inclined to neglect the moral and social issues arising from economic affairs, but the churches have never been entirely persuaded to remain quiet on matters of which they know little. In other words, if we accept that, even infrequently, the churches will wish to engage publicly with matters that have an economic dimension, it is best if they do so from a position of understanding rather than one of ignorance. And it is only through the hard work of regular contact, wide-ranging conversation and focused study that ignorance can be overcome. The churches' historic neglect of the economy has meant that there is a great deal of ground to be made up before a sensible critical engagement can be made between Christian theology and the complexities of economic life. For a relatively short period after the Second World War the British churches made a concerted attempt to enable such learning to take place. This work is the subject matter of our book. But it remains that the churches, and Christian theologians and commentators generally, are very frequently unable to hit the targets they are aiming for because they fail to understand how economic matters really work.

Two examples may suffice. First, it is very common to find Christian commentators berating economists for the sins of politicians. This is, to some extent, understandable given the unhelpful elision between matters political and economic in much media coverage and in the discourses of politicians themselves. But speak to any reputable economist and one will find a very clear distinction made between the role of politics in determining the direction of policy and the contribution of the economist in working out the consequences of specific changes. Nor is it true, as often claimed, that economics as a discipline works with a highly attenuated account of human motivation which renders altruism and self-sacrifice invisible. If the dominant economic model of human behaviour is that of self-interest it is, perhaps sadly for Christian consciences, because the overall aggregate of innumerable human decisions suggests that altruism is not common enough significantly to influence outcomes. While economists may, at times, use self-interest as an excessively dominant model to the extent that the subtleties of human behaviour are inadequately represented, their objective is to work with as realistic a model as they can devise. Much ill-informed Christian writing about economics cuts no ice at all with professional economists precisely because it makes this fundamental error about the nature of economics as a discipline (and, one is tempted to add, because Christians do seem to be impatient with anyone who points to the gap between the world as it is and the world they want to live in).

Second, Christian commentators often mistake the meaning of words when they are used technically. A good example is the term 'scarcity', which is popularly used to mean an insufficiency or a state of not having enough to go around. It is therefore frequently claimed that the world's resources are not scarce so much as ill distributed and that if the rapaciousness of the developed world could be contained there would be sufficient food and other resources to serve all people's needs. This may well be so. However, the argument is too often extended to embrace the claim that the economists' practice of defining all goods as scarce by their very nature prevents us from perceiving their abundance and creates the conditions for maldistribution. A further claim is often made to the effect that God's gifts in creation are marked by abundance and sufficiency and so the idea that goods are, of their nature, scarce is profoundly heretical. But this is to make a fundamental error in interpreting the notion of scarcity. As used in economics, scarcity is about finitude. Something is scarce if its use for one end precludes its use for another. Scarcity in economics is the condition that necessitates choices about end use. A good remains scarce so long as it can be applied to competing ends. The question of distribution is a vitally important one, but distinct. So, through a remediable error of interpretation and meaning, Christian commentators have all too often made their ignorance of economic matters rather blatantly manifest. This is not a new phenomenon. A similar misunderstanding, dating back many decades, led Christians to castigate the centrality of competition in economic theory, and to promote instead an idealized economy based on co-operation. However, to an economist, the antithesis of competition is not co-operation but monopoly. Interestingly, the document from the Church of England's Board for Social Responsibility on *Faith in a Global Economy*

(1998 – see Chapter 5) makes use of the economists' view of scarcity with no reference to the neglect of this perspective by so many Christian commentators. This perhaps reflected the involvement of practical economists in that working group – a methodology typical of the BSR at its best, but not especially reflective of contemporary theological trends.

The churches and the economy today

One theme which will emerge more strongly later in the book deserves to be highlighted briefly here. We have already referred to the churches' mission without unpacking that word. We have, perhaps, given a clue to our overall approach in the passing references to conversation and dialogue between persons, communities and cultures that differ acutely. But a crucially important part of the story of the churches' engagement with economic issues in Britain has been the sense in which – whether actively and consciously or only in lingering historical memories – mission has been understood as a process by which God's world can be called upon to reform the Christian churches and not merely vice versa. Thus, deeply embedded in the story of the Industrial Mission movement is the account of the analysis that gave it birth – the perception that the churches had mistaken middle-class values for Christian virtues and had thereby abdicated their vocation to identify God at work in a world of work and productive industry. The Industrial Mission movement was conceived as a programme to identify and celebrate the prevenient grace of God in such places as steelworks and railway yards and to articulate a theology – to discover how God may be spoken of – in the lives and experiences of working people whose alienation from the institutional churches was more about the churches' narrow self-righteousness than working-class apathy or godlessness. The initial intention was not to extend the churches' pastoral oversight to those beyond its usual reach, nor to 'Christianize' the godless world of manufacturing and commerce, but to call the churches back to their proper vocation by listening to perceptions of God and godliness emanating from sources which the churches, in their class-bound captivity, had failed to recognize. The mission, in other words, was to bring the Kingdom of God closer to the life of the world by reforming the churches so that they could more closely appreciate the fullness of their divine calling to mirror that Kingdom.

But missing from this missiology was a sufficiently nuanced understanding of how institutional power operates and how structures resist reform. Radical reformers require powerful patrons, and when the imaginative and energetic Leslie Hunter retired as Bishop of Sheffield in 1962, the experiment in Industrial Mission in that city fell foul of those in the Church who saw it as a cuckoo in the nest. And as Industrial Missions proliferated across Britain, their rationale was quietly institutionalized and their missiological foundations made subtly more acceptable to the structures of the churches that sponsored them. Although the Industrial Mission movement was never widely perceived as a trustworthy arm of the institutional churches, the urge to reform the churches became muted and so the underlying theology became more conformable to church theology. Mission became defined in ways that restored the perception that God was the churches' possession to be generously shared with others. The emphasis on the importance of structures – and of structural understandings of sin – remained, but the theology was rarely applied to the churches as institutions rather than to the world of corporations, companies and unions.

A broader understanding of mission

The point of this brief excursion into the history of the churches' engagements with the economic sphere is that it offers a timely corrective to the current ascendancy of the concept of mission in the lives of the British churches. As the twentieth century drew to a close, the decline of church membership, the waning of ecclesial authority in public and private spheres alike, and the increasing self-confidence of secularism (even overt atheism) in the media and public life conspired to undermine the assumptions of permanence and stability in all aspects of church life. The response was a new energy for mission – but mission interpreted as the building up of the Church. The new mission-oriented Church of the twenty-first century had a distinctly iconoclastic flavour. 'New ways of being church' are promoted as a kind of elixir for a declining institution, and in some ways it might seem as if the will to reform the institutional churches is as strong as anything that Leslie Hunter and the Industrial Mission movement could have desired.

But the critique that the reformers apply to the Church today differs profoundly from that which saw working life as a source of authentic spiritual insight and the churches' salvation to lie in a humble listening role. New models of church being promoted today frequently accept the dominant consumeristic culture of the West and seek to create a church that responds to what the US Lutheran theologian Cynthia Moe-Lobeda has called *homo economicus, consumens et dominans*.[7] To be sure, the churches are seeking to listen to what the surrounding culture has to say, but it is impossible to avoid the conclusion that a more sophisticated economic analysis, and an appreciation of the ethical implications of the economic context, would be helpful. For the culture of consumerism – the stress on the chosen rather than the given; on the ability of people to choose, rather than be given their own fundamental identity by God; and the dominant motifs of commodification and manipulability – all these things are facets of the current phase of capitalist economics in the West. As such, the consumeristic mentality may come to understand being human as chosen rather than given and highly manipulable and, indeed, manipulative. Just as the early Industrial Missioners listened carefully to working-class culture instead of preaching in the tones of an alien caste, so the churches of today aspire to learn from the surrounding culture. But the early Industrial Missioners were not passive recipients or uncritical devotees of the cultures they encountered. They brought with them, not a pre-packaged gospel, but a spirituality that was inherently sceptical of the claims of any culture (secular or ecclesial) to offer a total world view. They sought to reform the Church, but they did so, not primarily to expand the earthly Church, but to strengthen its authentic gospel nature. Nor was theirs a mission to bolster the capitalism of their day through any implicit ecclesial benediction. Rather they sought, in a dialogue between the gospel and the reality of working-class experience (rather than the middle-class myths about industrial life), to identify and celebrate the coming Kingdom of God. Perhaps that kind of social optimism seems naive and shallow in a more cynical age or in the light of a different eschatological emphasis. But it remains that taking the workings of the economy seriously gave a cutting edge to those mid-twentieth-century missioners who (as was said of the writer George Orwell) went native in their own country. They may have seemed enviably at ease among overalled workers and in the grimy mess-rooms of steelworks, but part of the authenticity of their mission can be measured in the discomfort of their relationships on many fronts: with the institutional churches, with the structures of industry and politics, with the theories of capitalism and with the mores of popular culture. The current re-emphasis on mission in the British churches feels altogether too much at home in the bland cultural assumptions of contemporary market-led politics and market-shaped human aspirations.

When analysts of all kinds fail to acknowledge the significance of the economic dimensions of life, whole swathes of human experience become essentially invisible to them – and this is demonstrably true of Christian mission. A concern for the way the economy works requires an alertness to the condition, not only of the broad generality of humankind, but of the poor and the marginal. Economic relationships, of their nature, transcend the personal and face-to-face dimension in which fellow-feeling is generated by proximity. Neglect of the economic dimension risks making invisible those on whom we rely but whom we do not encounter as autonomous persons – the new servant class, the cleaners, the shopworkers, the easily blamed and scapegoated. Neglect of the economic dimension risks a false accounting when it comes to establishing moral concepts such as worth, obligation and interdependence.

It is, in our view, one of the tragedies of the contemporary churches that their concern for their own flourishing has narrowed their understanding of mission and allowed them to slough off uncomfortable ventures which, however tired or rough-edged, might have held out a more challenging and effective missiology. The last few decades have seen the rapid withdrawal of church resources from Industrial Missions, Social Responsibility Councils and other agencies that have served to hold the claims of the economy as a site of mission before the institutional churches. True, no institution is comfortable with the idea that it should pay for licensed critics, but where now are the voices that will require the churches to take the economic context seriously as a determining reality in peoples' lives and that will see the churches as prophetic bodies whose dialogue with economic realities gives them something of import to say on behalf of others and not just in response to their own tightened purse strings? It sometimes seems as if, once the churches found themselves victims of economic stringency, their desire to offer a critique of economic institutions faded overnight. True, the same period in history saw a more general political apathy as the dominant global economy appeared to be not only unchallenged but unchallengeable. But it remains that the churches' ability to offer a structured and coherent ethical engagement with economics has all but disappeared in the last few years.

We are not contending here that the old structures – Industrial Missions, Social Responsibility and others whose writings form the bulk of this book – were ready or able to respond adequately to the context of a complex global economy in the twenty-first century. Our own commentary on many of the texts will be critical of the often reactive, timid or theologically ill-formed work that characterized the post-war period. But the fact is that this period saw the churches and their representatives thinking hard about economic issues and attempting to put into practice the missiological implications of their analyses. The fact that these texts have often had to be rescued from relative obscurity demonstrates that they were always somewhat marginal. But they are evidence of a period of theological seriousness that should not be forgotten. Indeed, it may be that while the fate of recent history is often to be untrendy and hence temporarily invisible, the time may now be ripe for the economic concerns of the post-war Church to be revisited for their exceptional intrinsic interest, their potential for illuminating big issues and for the practical missiological lessons – positive and negative – that they offer to today.

The shape of this book

Our aim has been to tell the story of the churches' involvement with economic issues through the documents of the times. Although the quantity of such material known to exist is not immense, we have, inevitably, had to be selective, not only in choosing which material to use, but in selecting extracts from within larger documents, many of which contained far more material of interest than we had space to include.

Over the sixty years since the end of the Second World War the context within which the churches have been operating has changed enormously – not least in the rate of change itself. As churches, like other institutions, have struggled to make sense of their political, social and economic context, it is not surprising that it becomes difficult to speak of distinct eras and movements within our period. We have sought to distinguish our material according to chronology but do not pretend that arbitrary dates can adequately delineate discrete trends. There is therefore a degree of overlap between the periods covered by our chapters but we have striven to allow each section to tell a distinctive part of the overall story.

For similar reasons, there is a shift of gear and a change of approach between Chapters 3 and 4, with the pivotal date being 1979. As explained later, we are not alone in seeing that year as one that marks a very clear 'before and after' in the political and social life of Britain and, indeed, much of the world. This is, of course, to view the period with the benefits of hindsight.

Nevertheless, we have taken that date to indicate the beginning of a period of radical reordering of the nation's economic life – a development that coincided with the churches' public realization of their marginalization from everyday life, declining membership and growing uncertainty of role. The tone of the churches' engagement with economic issues therefore changes noticeably at this time. The economy had been pushed to the forefront of national consciousness and a Christian response could not be avoided, yet the resources on which a response could be based – both in terms of a theological critique and an alternative social or economic model – were not immediately apparent. Indeed, this is a situation that continues to pertain, in slightly different guises, today.

As a result, it felt best to allow the texts from this period to be quoted at greater length and to allow a stronger sense of the churches' struggle for coherence to emerge. Whereas, in the earlier periods, it was easier to weave the texts into the story of the times, after 1979 we have tried to epitomize the wider context and then to use extensive extracts from a number of texts to illustrate the responses of the churches. It is, perhaps, inevitable in a time of radical social upheaval that the story is not capable of presentation as a single linear narrative. Maybe a future generation will have distilled the history of the last twenty-five years to the point where such a story may one day be told, but it will have to be told in ways that lose much of the immediacy, the sense of conflicting analyses and approaches, and the sense of how institutions and practitioners evolve while continuing to engage with shifting contexts. If, then, Chapters 4 and 5 lack some of the narrative flow of the earlier parts of the book, that is, we think, not only inevitable but a more accurate representation of the times, and in our concluding section we attempt to draw the story together in ways that not only evaluate the past but offer some lessons and pointers to the future.

2

Heritage and Response 1918–45

Part 1 The inherited tradition

This chapter is intended to set the scene for the main story of the churches' engagement with the economy and the world of work since 1945 in the UK. It therefore does two things: it briefly outlines the situation in 1945, after two world wars and the depression; and it tries to indicate how Christian thought and action had responded to the industrialization of society and the emergence of modern Christian social thought. The starting point for the churches from the end of the Second World War is illustrated by two excerpts from documents formative for their socio-economic thinking. The chapter ends with a note on some of the theological methodologies that have supported church engagements with economic issues in the period covered by the book, starting with the fundamental methodology that emerged from the creative pioneering work done before, during and just after the Second World War, and that to some extent still carries influence.

The legacy and challenges

In 1945, Britain emerged out of the Second World War victorious but bankrupt and exhausted. The war had only been won through the dogged tenacity of the people, symbolized and sustained by Winston Churchill, and the costly price of world alliances. But that hard-won peace was also seen as the opportunity for new beginnings, for there were memories of what had happened since the last time. There was bitterness after the First World War when the 'land fit for heroes' did not materialize. This was followed by the depression of 1929–31, which had exposed the extent of poverty and had driven unemployment to unacceptable heights, especially in the north of England and South Wales. So, in order to appreciate the events of the latter half of the twentieth century it is necessary to have a brief overview of what had previously been happening to Britain economically in relation to the wider world and domestically.

In 1914, Britain was still the major trading country in the world, though already feeling the impact of the industrialization of Germany and the USA and to some extent France and Japan. The great industries on which so much wealth depended were coal, which fuelled the steam age on land and sea; textiles, both wool and cotton, drawing raw materials from across the globe; and engineering, creating and sustaining the infrastructure of the new world civilization. London was the financial capital of the world, supporting out of its great wealth the modern enterprises that exploited the riches of the world's natural resources. This was supported through the largest empire the world had ever known, which included, alongside the colonies and protectorates, the new Dominions. All this was disrupted by the Great War (1914–18), which not only tore Europe apart but also changed the pattern of global relations. Britain was able to sustain the war effort on the basis of this great wealth but inevitably emerged dramatically poorer. The decline in world standing, already visible since the 1880s, had accelerated. There was no longer a safety margin by which economic downturns could be cushioned. There were also other changes. The patterns of world markets had changed. New suppliers had filled the vacuum created by diverting industries into the war effort and it was not going to be easy to regain those markets. Indeed, especially in textiles and most significantly in India, manufacturing went to the countries supplying the raw materials, often undercutting costs. Thus what used to be exports became imports. At the same time, through the decades after the war, the price of raw materials, which had been rising before, went into decline. The effect of this is well illustrated by the fall in wheat prices to which the British farmers were exposed by the repeal, in 1921, of the 1920 Agriculture Act that had guaranteed stability through import duties, thus undermining domestic producers. The result was agricultural depression. At the same time, as in other cases, such as wool from Australia and copper from Rhodesia, the fall in prices, while it lowered manufacturing costs, also meant that there was less money out there to purchase British exports.

The break up of the German, Austrian and Turkish empires also had adverse effects. The turmoil in Eastern Europe, including the Russian Revolution, disrupted important markets. In the Middle East and Africa imperial responsibilities expanded, demanding greater military and administrative expenditure. This was compounded by the acceleration of demands for independence, especially in Ireland, India, Egypt and Iraq, with all that meant in unrest and added policing. The Palestinian problem had also been set alight by the Balfour declaration of 1917 concerning a Jewish homeland.

There were also changes in the financial markets. The USA became the dominant creditor nation. Britain had to borrow to cover deficits in the current account, which included some drain on gold reserves. Moreover, an increasing proportion of international borrowing was short-term, which exposed debtors to the vagaries of the market. As a result the world's economic system was threatened with greater instability.

The major economic incident in the inter-war years was the Wall Street crash (1929) and the ensuing world slump. For Britain this came on top of the financial strain caused by lending, for reconstruction, to the central European countries created by the Treaty of Versailles. The collapse of the Austrian financial system not only dragged Germany into the abyss but also threatened to undermine the credibility of the Bank of England. The repercussions were deep and widespread.

All this has also to be seen in the context of the policy dilemmas facing the British government since the Great War.

There was a determination to return to the free-trade practices that had been dominant since the nineteenth century. This was, by and large, the creed of the British Liberal Party, but such a policy exposed the country to the unpredictability of the open market. The second desire was to return to the 'gold standard'. The pound had been allowed to float against the dollar as an emergency measure but it was assumed that it would return as soon as possible to its previous stability. This was done (apparently reluctantly) by Winston Churchill as Chancellor in 1925; but the rate of exchange was unfortunately set at the pre-war level, which overvalued the pound by approximately 10 per cent. This put additional strains on the currency. One of the effects of the slump was the eventual abandonment of the gold standard in 1935 after costly and determined defences. This immediately eased the strain through an effective devaluation of the pound.

If the Liberal tradition favoured free trade, there was a strong pull among many Conservatives towards protectionism. This was designed to maintain domestic employment by keeping out foreign imports. The argument against this was that it would create a tariff war and would slow down international trade and, domestically, raise the cost of living. One variation that had considerable support in this period was imperial preference, which opened the British market to colonial goods, especially food, but ring-fenced the sterling area. This was indeed the policy of the late 1930s.

Domestically there were two policies available in response to the depression. The first, and normal orthodoxy, was to introduce deflationary pressures. Notably, this was done by curbing public expenditure and having a balanced budget. The most notorious example from the inter-war period was the so-called 'Geddes Axe', a report prepared in 1922. The budget for that year has been called 'the most striking example of reduction in public spending in a single year'. Both the armed forces and welfare budgets were slashed; but it was also accompanied by a cut in income tax. This downward pressure was also exercised on wages as a means of making industry competitive. Indeed, the

1926 coal strike, which spilled over into the short-lived General Strike, was primarily against wage cuts in the threatened coal industry.

The other possibility, then being advocated and gaining acceptability, was to spend the way out of a depression, especially by improving the infrastructure of society (roads, power services, housing stock etc.). Keynesianism (so called after the economist J. M. Keynes) was more acceptable to the Labour Party and among some Liberals. This, too, had its dangers: of stimulating imports to satisfy the demand and of effectively mortgaging the future. There were indeed some small investments in public works, mainly in building roads to cater for the rising popularity of the motor car. The politician in the Labour ranks who most strongly championed stimulating the economy in this way was Oswald Moseley, later to break away and found the New Party and to become the leader of the British Union of Fascists.

In fact Britain weathered the Great Depression surprisingly well. In part this was due to a cautious and conservative financial sector that was therefore not drastically overstretched. There were no major banking collapses. Gradually the storm subsided and by 1937 recovery was clearly on the way. By then, production was up by 24 per cent on 1929 levels. Unemployment fell from a peak of 15.6 per cent of all workers in 1932 to 7.8 per cent in 1937 and, after a blip in 1938, to 5.8 per cent in 1939. But there were wide discrepancies. It was the traditional heavy and staple industries that suffered most, especially in the industrial north and west (South Wales and Cornwall). There unemployment was far greater. So, for Jarrow in 1934 it was 67.8 per cent as compared with Coventry's 5.1 per cent (11 per cent nationally). Shipbuilding was very badly hit. There were also industries being squeezed by competition from elsewhere or through product supercession, such as with coal being replaced by oil and electricity. But at the same time there were new industries coming on stream – usually in the areas of consumer goods such as the car or the radio. The first electronic revolution was making production cleaner and quicker. Labour patterns were changing: less heavy manual and more production-line manufacturing. There was also a decided shift southwards, creating new industrial areas such as the west of London. Above all there was the housing boom, starting in the 1920s but accelerating, in both public and private spheres, in an attempt to clear slums, renew stock and meet the changing demands. It reached its peak in the mid-1930s (1934 saw the production of 350,000 units). All this was aided by the expansion of public transport, most notably with the electrification of the South London rail network and the expansion of the Underground north of the Thames. London more than doubled in area in the inter-war years and suburbia sprawled out from every conurbation. Despite, therefore, the desperation epitomized by the Jarrow marchers (1936), the period overall was a time of growth. Real incomes rose and prices fell. Consumer goods were increasingly available. Over the period 1924–37 there was an average rise in the Gross National Product (GNP) per annum of 2.2 per cent, as high as almost any such period since 1856.

The Second World War broke, therefore, at a time of growing prosperity, despite many severely depressed areas. Indeed rearmament was a form of Keynesian public works and revived much waning industry as the country geared itself for war. Rearmament was a slow process, partly because of the reluctance to overheat the economy but partly because, since the First World War, there had been a running down of the military in the face of a lack of a perceived enemy. But in the event, in the second war, the British war machine dominated the domestic economy to a much greater extent than any other economy, including Germany. There was, in effect, a level of social control and a drive towards self-sufficiency that would hardly have been imagined. This brings out an important difference between 1918 and 1945. At the earlier time the ideal of liberal individualism was dominant and it was assumed that a return to laissez-faire practices should be as swift as possible. In 1945, in the wake of the depression of the 1930s, the growing political acceptability of socialist thinking, followed by the wartime experience of social control, which for many included a better standard of health and guaranteed work, collectivism was not something necessarily to be feared but to be cherished.

It is not surprising, therefore, that care was taken to prepare for the peace even as the conflict was in progress. There was no appetite to go through the same debacle as greeted the end of the earlier war. So plans were laid for a very different society. The Beveridge Report (1942) pledged that the 'five giants' of 'Want, Disease, Ignorance, Squalor and Idleness' must be defeated. This was to be the basis of the modern welfare state. So, well before the cessation of hostilities, plans were being laid for a revised benefits system, comprehensive social services and a National Health Service. All this was a radical enlargement of the welfare provision that went back to Lloyd George's introduction of the state pension in 1909. At the same time, R. A. Butler steered the Education Act (1944) through Church and Parliament, giving secondary education to all, which reshaped the educational expectations of subsequent generations.

Nevertheless, by the end of the second war Britain was virtually bankrupt. Overseas assets had almost disappeared and there was a colossal debt with the USA from lend-lease agreements. Industrial plant and infrastructure were in urgent need of modernizing. Moreover, as in the earlier conflict, international trade had been disrupted and displaced, but even more drastically. Normalization of the economy was going to be an uphill struggle despite the readiness of the people to try to rebuild for a new era.

The churches

As the Second World War drew to a close and the nation moved into a period of reconstruction the churches were in many ways similarly poised. Within the Church of England, but also commanding wide respect almost without parallel in the nation at large and among the other churches, this was in no small way due to the towering personality of William Temple, the 'people's' Archbishop who, sadly, had died in 1944. He had constantly been concerned for the condition of those at the bottom of the socio-economic heap. A man firmly of the Establishment, he was a known supporter of the Labour Party. He was involved with the plans put forward by his friend Beveridge for the welfare state. His vision was of a nation bound by mutual respect and responsibility. He had also been instrumental in negotiating the 'religious clauses' that were to shape religious education in the state schools, on the basis of locally agreed syllabi, for a generation and in forging a new alliance between the church-based schools and central Government in the Butler Education Act (1944). His ecumenical commitment helped found the British Council of Churches (BCC, 1942), enabling the growing collaboration between many non-Catholic denominations. Temple was at the heart of the work of the Malvern Conference (1941), which met when Britain's war fortunes were at their lowest ebb but which was already planning for a renewed society after victory had been achieved. He also set up the commission that produced the key report *Towards the Conversion of England*, which, in its notion of evangelism, included a concern for the socio-economic structures of society as well as personal faith and commitment, which was to have a quiet but real influence on the post-war churches.

It is necessary, however, in order to appreciate the post-war developments, to trace some of the factors that shaped both thinking and practice prior to 1945. While, inevitably, this story is going to be dominated by the Church of England as the established and largest church in the four nations of Britain, there are parallel and significant strands in which the other denominations play their part and which will be picked up from time to time as the story unfolds.

The Enabling Act (1919) can be understood as a formative moment in the history of the Church of England. The Life and Liberty Movement, into which the young William Temple put so much energy, argued for and obtained freedom for the church to take responsibility for its own policies and practices, albeit under the authority of the Sovereign in Parliament. The National Assembly of the Church of England, the precursor of what today is the General Synod, met first in 1920. This was a concrete expression of the process that had been going on over previous centuries of the increasing differentiation in society between the secular and the religious, which is a definitive characteristic of modern western culture. This process had meant, argued R. H. Tawney, in his influential *Religion and the Rise of Capitalism* echoing much that Max Weber was saying about Protestantism more widely, that the influence of the Christian perspective on thinking and practice in economic affairs had been eroded so that the two were thought of as being in two separate spheres. As a result the emergence of industrialism and industrial capitalism had been almost unchallenged by the Christian tradition and had taken on a life of its own. The Church, therefore, largely went along with and bought into the assumptions and ways of society at large, unable to offer any prophetic critique.

While this can be argued as a general case it is not the complete picture. The rise of industrialism and especially the appalling conditions of the new industrial cities were not without effect on the conscience and lives of many church persons in every tradition, ordained and lay. They had, however, given the situation of the time, to act as individuals and form societies or pressure groups and evolve their own charitable or co-operative or other structures. Few would have access to the corridors of power. From the early part of the nineteenth century, therefore, parallel to the rise of working-class politics, there slowly emerged expressions of Christian concern about the economic and social conditions found in industrial Britain. This can be illustrated, in the first instance, by three examples from the Church of England.

Lord Shaftesbury represented the growing evangelical concern for human welfare that was a feature of the nineteenth century. As a Tory peer he acknowledged the responsibility of those with power and possessions for those in their care. For him this extended beyond those who worked on his estates. From his investigations into the conditions of the London poor he concluded that, since there was no one else to take responsibility, the governing elite had to act on their behalf. So, through

Parliament, introducing laws that regulated employment, and by setting up agencies such as the Ragged Schools Union and the YMCA, he fought to improve the conditions of the poor, especially women and children. He was not alone, as others also developed societies and institutes in the tenements and rows of the new cities.

F. D. Maurice stands out as the theological giant among those who were socially concerned. His emphasis on the doctrine of the Kingdom of God provided the foundation for a vision of a corporate society in which all are mutually responsible to each other. This was the basis for a Christian version of socialism, a social theory that was beginning to surface in various forms in the mid-nineteenth century. With his companions, including Charles Kingsley, he tried to express this practically, setting up schemes of employment and founding the Working Men's College (1854). While this expression of Christian socialism lasted a comparatively short time, it has had a lasting impact down to this day, appeal frequently being made to Maurice and his companions as formative for this tradition.

In some ways it can be argued that Maurice's heritage was taken up most strongly by the Anglo-Catholic movement that was burgeoning in the latter part of the century and into the twentieth century. The Guild of St Matthew (1877) and the Christian Social Union (1889) sought to reinforce and support Christian social thought and action. Between the world wars this strand of the tradition continued and deepened and produced a disproportionate number of church leaders, such as Bishops Headlam and Gore. Its most notable expression was possibly to be found in the Christendom Group, which sought to establish a Christian sociological perspective that could inform the working of a Christian society. Though often criticized for its appeal to medieval concepts and a simplistic elision of theology and sociology, it was nevertheless influential from the late 1920s to the 1950s, and included such contributors as V. A. Demant and Maurice Reckitt. There were also noted examples of High Church parishes, settlements and monastic foundations, both Anglican and Catholic, to be found in the slums of the major industrial cities. After the First World War the Christian Social Union amalgamated with the 'Navvy Mission' to form the Industrial Christian Fellowship. This brought together an activist tradition, represented by the 'Navvy Mission' which had been formed to minister to the travelling camps of men creating the canals and railways, with a movement that concentrated on critical research. The new organization, using priests like Studdert Kennedy and Dick Sheppard and numerous lay leaders, combined a programme of study and publication, challenging people about their Christian social responsibility through open-air preaching or conferences, together with organizing training centres or soup kitchens for the unemployed. This is one of the main precursors of Industrial Mission as it emerged after the Second World War.

With the setting up of the Assembly, the Church of England could act nationally in ways not previously possible. It is, therefore, not surprising that the growing pressure to take the socio-economic dimension seriously meant that there was set up in 1923 a Social and Industrial Commission that was, through a number of changes, the predecessor of the Board for Social Responsibility. Its task was to monitor and advise the church on matters of public, social and economic concern.

In the years between the two world wars three key symbolic events need to be noted. The first was the Conference on Christian Politics, Economics and Citizenship (COPEC, 1924) in which William Temple had a leading role. While the proceedings did not produce any startling insights they marked the clear commitment of the Church of England to take economics seriously and became a landmark returned to time and again in subsequent discussions. The second is the Malvern Conference (1941), meeting under the pressure of wartime conditions. The preparatory thinking for this national and ecumenically aware conference had been done by the Christendom Group. Its purpose, according to Temple, was to propose a methodology whereby the Church could apply the imperatives of the gospel to the complex and technical issues that bedevil society. The key to Christian reflection and judgement was thought to be found in 'middle axioms', a feature of Christian sociology, which are, to quote the report, 'maxims for conduct which moderate between fundamental principles and the tangle of particular problems' (see below). This intention allowed Malvern to be more theological and, perhaps, more sober than COPEC had been, reflecting, too, the greater realism, or pessimism, of the 1930s and 40s and the emerging influence of the, then recent, Neo-orthodoxy of Karl Barth and Emil Brunner from Europe and the Christian Realism of Reinhold Niebuhr from the USA. This was, however, the foundation that was to provide the churches with a working tool for a generation and to set the tone for their attitudes to post-war reconstruction. Its most popular expression is to be found in Temple's bestseller, *Christianity and Social Order* (1942).

The third event takes us on to the world canvas in the shape of the second conference of the Life and Work Movement, which met in Oxford in 1937. This was a pivotal meeting of one of the streams of the then embryonic Ecumenical Movement. Life and Work, like its parallel developments Faith and Order and the International Missionary Conference (IMC), was rooted in the great World Mission conference in Edinburgh in 1910. Largely through the efforts of Archbishop Söderblom of Sweden, the first conference was held in Stockholm in 1925 around the assumption that the churches could express their unity better through the consideration of their common task in and with society rather than in 'Faith and Order' discussions that concentrated on the divisions in Christendom. This second conference met under the shadow of the impending Second World War and in the aftermath of the threatened collapse of capitalism in the Great Depression. Under the guidance of Joe Oldham, the influential lay missiologist and ecumenical pioneer, the Oxford Conference began the process of outlining modern Christian ecumenical social ethics around the concept of the 'just society', which became a dominant theme for ecumenical thinking in the post-war years. It also laid the foundation, with the Faith and Order Conference which met in Edinburgh in the same year, of the World Council of Churches, which came into being in

1948, its inauguration having been delayed by the war. Thus Oxford provided both a stimulus and a resource for developing Christian social theory in Britain.

North of the border, the Church of Scotland has a history of secession and reunion, culminating in the union of 1929. The details do not concern us here. Suffice it to say that in some ways the history of the Church of Scotland in relation to the modern economy reflects a path parallel to that taken by the Church of England. Here, too, the growth of industrial society stimulated a reaction in the church. This was especially true of the more evangelical wing and contributed to the Great Disruption of 1843. The civil law that bound the church was deemed by those who sought to make the Kirk more responsive to the needs of the time to have hampered the freedom sought in the field of charity, education and poor relief. Conversely, it was the reunions of 1900 and, in particular, of 1921 that secured for the church its present status of independence from the civil authority, thus securing the church's right to work to its own agenda in relation to civic affairs. As a result, the General Assembly, as we shall see, has provided for the Scottish nation a public forum for debate apart from the British Parliament in London.

Of particular interest in relation to Scotland, parallel to the Malvern Conference, is the Commission for the Interpretation of God's Will in the Present Crisis (1940–45), known as the Baillie Commission, after the eminent theologian, John Baillie, who was its chairman. The brief was to take up the issues that had shaken the world in the years before the war and in the conflict through which they were presently living and to seek to respond with faith and hope and commitment to the possibilities of the future. Thus the Commission started from a theological base, looking at every aspect of life in the light of the gospel. Here, too, the idea of middle axioms was seen as a way of bringing general ethical principles into relation with the demands and minutiae of concrete living.

For the Free Churches the nineteenth century saw their emancipation from being marginalized and penalized minorities to becoming a considerable force in the land. This was, in no little part, due to the Evangelical Revival of the eighteenth century and the subsequent secession of Methodism from the Church of England, which increased their numbers considerably. It was also part of the liberalizing process found in society at large. Against this background the Free Churches have their own contribution to the Christian response to industrialization.

First, many of the new industrialists and entrepreneurs were Free Churchmen. This produces a certain political and social ambiguity. As capitalists they were free-traders but also had strong roots in the lower classes from which they often sprang. There was often a real affinity with the working classes, especially for the hard-working, deserving poor. They were more likely (but not exclusively) to have regard to the welfare of those they employed and the community in which they lived. It is not surprising, therefore, to find a considerable representation of Free Churchmen in the civil politics of the new industrial cities, working for the enhancement and amenities of the urban environment. In Birmingham, for example, there is the work of R. W. Dale, Congregationalist minister of Carrs Lane Chapel, and Joseph Chamberlain, its Unitarian Lord Mayor.

Second, the chapel, as the alternative to the church, often provided the working and the new middle classes with a religious home. It was also the location for self-education, the relief of poverty, the base for co-operative enterprise, and a political and cultural centre that was a training ground for the rising democracy. The minister, often the most educated person in the community, was teacher, pastor, mentor and social voice. In the South Wales valleys, in parts of the north and Cornwall there was, for a period, what can only be described as a Nonconformist culture, politically liberal in the radical sense, gaining strength through adversity. It has in fact been argued that it was the politicization of the chapels that saved Britain from violent revolution. It has also been pointed out that it was the chapel, not least Methodism, that contributed largely to the formation of the trade unions and to some extent to the Labour Party. However, the rise of the Labour Party shifted the socio-political centre out of the chapels and the two tended to drift apart, certainly in the twentieth century.

Third, the high point of the so-called Nonconformist conscience was from the 1870s to the First World War. The pulpit could command respect and the Nonconformist preachers, such as the Methodists Hugh Price Hughes, from his base in the West London Mission, and Scott Lidgett, in Bermondsey, and the Baptist John Clifford, at Westbourne Park in Paddington, sought to raise the moral consciousness of the nation, speaking out on public issues and influencing public policy. Weekly papers, such as the *Christian World* and the *British Weekly*, commented on current affairs. Outstanding individuals contributed to reform and social relief, such as Thomas Barnardo and George Mueller with their work with children. Other organizations sprang up in the inner city. Most well known was the Salvation Army, with its mixture of popular evangelism and impressive social service programmes, but there were various other city missions in London and elsewhere. Community centres and settlements were established in the industrial areas, such as the Baptist West Ham Central Mission and the Central Halls in London, Manchester and Stepney of the Methodist Forward Movement.

Thus, from the turn of the century, the Free Churches were able to play an increasing part on the national stage alongside the Established Church. The emerging ecumenism of the inter-war period, pioneered by such organizations as the Student Christian Movement (SCM) and the YMCA, drew them further into the mainstream. Thus they were fully part of the newly formed ecumenical instruments established in and after the war and partners in evangelistic and other initiatives such as the Christian Commando Campaigns.

British Catholicism, too, went through a process of emancipation in the nineteenth century. In 1850 the Catholic hierarchy was restored. Even so, the Catholic Church tended to remain in comparative isolation until Vatican II in 1963. This marginal role reflected the ultramontane and anti-modernist tone of the Church at large.

Catholicism, however, was naturally caught up in the industrialization process. Large numbers of Catholics from Ireland, but also from mainland Europe, migrated into the new industrial cities, notably Liverpool and Glasgow, and also provided a pool of manual labour that dug out the canals and laid the railways. This meant a considerable amount of pastoral energy was devoted to the poor, not least through the newly formed charitable and teaching orders. Cardinal Manning mediated effectively in the London Dock Strike of 1889. Catholic thought in relation to the modern world, however, took its lead from the teaching of the Popes notably Leo XIII (*Rerum Novarum,* 1891) and Pius XI (*Quadragesimo Anno,* 1931), which will be discussed in the next chapter.

What we have traced here in a brief and eclectic way have been the responses that emerged out of the Christian community to the massive and rapid transformation of British society into the greatest industrial complex in the world of its day. A number of things emerge. First, it can be argued that it was little, and often tardy. But it could also be suggested that the churches were in no worse a position than the politicians and society in general. All had to adjust to a new world. Nor was there then a culture of social intervention. Individuals and like-minded groups had to take up their causes and use the means to hand – influence, associations, campaigns or sheer dogged hard work on a project. Nor, second, should we expect a clear answer to the complexities and ambiguities of society's development. Nevertheless, for all its faults and weaknesses, it is a story that has many unsung and forgotten heroes, men and women who spent their time, energy and often wealth in serving the needs of the poor or who struggled with the intractable issues of understanding this new and strange world. We are the heirs of that story.

Part 2 Readings

1 Oxford Conference on Life and Work, 1937

These passages come from the Report of the Oxford Conference on Life and Work (1937) that was so formative on ecumenical thinking. It sets out the notion of the 'just society', a theme that was to be retained and enlarged in the deliberations of the World Council of Churches down to our own day, as 'the just and participatory society' and, more recently, as 'justice, peace and the integrity of creation'. The background of the thinking is the triple global social issues posed by the emergence of Russian Communism, the rise of Nazism and Fascism and the great recession of the 1930s. The discussion, however, primarily addresses the capitalist international economy. The report (Part 1) first establishes the basis for Christian social ethics. It then goes on to offer a general, critical analysis of the then current situation. We return to the text (Part V) with the guiding principles that should inform Christian judgements at a practical level. These are examples of 'middle axioms' that are intended to provide guidance without being prescriptive and that allow those engaged in the day-to-day decision making to use their judgement.

PART 1. THE BASIS OF THE CHRISTIAN CONCERN FOR THE ECONOMIC ORDER.

[. . .]

The Kingdom of God, as proclaimed in the Gospel, is the reign of God which both has come and is coming. It is an established reality in the coming of Christ and in the presence of His Spirit in the world. It is, however, still in conflict with a sinful world, which crucified its Lord, and its ultimate triumph is still to come. In so far as it has come, the will of God as revealed in Christ (that is, the commandment of love) is the ultimate standard of Christian conduct. . . . [I]n so far as the Kingdom of God is in conflict with the world, and is therefore still to come, the Christian finds himself under the necessity of discovering the best available means of checking human sinfulness and of increasing the possibilities and opportunities of love within a sinful world.

The relevant and departmental standard for all the social arrangements and institutions, all the economic structures and political systems, by which the life of man is ordered, is the principle of justice. Justice, as the ideal of an harmonious relation of life to life, obviously presupposes the sinful tendency of one life to take advantage of another. This sinful tendency it seeks to check, by defining the rightful place and privilege which each life must have in the harmony of the whole and by assigning the duty of each to each. Justice does not demand that the self *sacrifice* itself completely for the neighbour's good, but seeks to define and to maintain the good which each member of the community may rightfully claim in the harmony of the whole.

The principle of justice has both a positive and negative significance.

Negatively, principles of justice restrain evil and the evildoer. They must therefore become embodied in systems of coercion which prevent men from doing what sinful ambition, pride, lust and greed might prompt them to do. This necessary coercion is itself a root of new evils, since the exercise of coercion involves power, and power tempts the possessor to its unrighteous use. Furthermore coercion may arouse resentment among those coerced, even when its purpose is a necessary social end. The use of power and coercion cannot therefore be regarded by Christians as ultimately desirable. Criticism against its abuses must constantly be maintained. On the other hand, it cannot be assumed that the practice of Christian love will ever obviate the necessity for coercive political and economic arrangements.

The laws of justice are not purely negative. . . . Forms of production and methods of co-operation may serve the cause of human brotherhood by serving and extending the principle of love beyond the sphere of purely personal relations.

The commandment of love therefore always presents possibilities for individuals beyond the requirements of economic and social institutions. . . . Institutional requirements necessarily prescribe only the minimum. . . .

The love which is the fulfilment of the law is, however, no substitute for law, for institutions, or for systems. Individual acts of charity within a given system of government or economics may mitigate its injustices and increase its justice. But they do not absolve the Christian from seeking the best possible institutional arrangement and social structure for the ordering of human life.

[. . .]

PART V. CHRISTIAN TEACHING IN RELATION TO THE ECONOMIC ORDER.

[Guidance to be offered concerning the economic order on the basis of faith would be found in three areas.]

(A) *Christian teaching should deal with ends, in the sense of long-range goals, standards, and principles in the light of which every concrete situation and every proposal for improving it must be tested.*

[. . .]

(i) Right fellowship between man and man being a condition of man's fellowship with God, every economic arrangement which frustrates or restricts it must be modified – in particular such ordering of economic life as tends to divide the community into classes based upon differences of wealth and to occasion a sense of injustice among the poorer members of society. To every member of the community there must be made open a worthy means of livelihood. The possibilities of amassing private accumulations of wealth should be so limited that the scale of social values is not perverted by the fear and the envy, the insolence and servility, which tend to accompany extreme inequality.

(ii) . . . [E]very child and youth must have opportunities of education suitable for the full development of his particular capacities. . . . In this connection, the protection of the family as a social unit should be an urgent concern of the community.
(iii) Persons disabled from economic activity, whether by sickness, infirmity, or age, should not be economically penalised.
. . .
(iv) Labour has intrinsic worth and dignity, as being designed by God for man's welfare. The duty and the right of men to work should therefore alike be emphasised. In the industrial process labour should never be considered as a mere commodity. In their daily work men should be able to recognise and fulfil a Christian vocation. . . .
(v) The resources of the earth, such as the soil and mineral wealth, should be recognised as gifts of God to the whole human race, and used with due and balanced consideration for the needs of the present and future generations.
[. . .]

[Closely connected with the foregoing paragraphs is the whole question of property.]
(i) . . . [A]ll human property rights are relative and contingent only in virtue of the dependence of man upon God as the giver of all wealth and as the creator of man's capacities to develop the resources of nature. . . .
(ii) . . . [E]very argument in defence of property rights which is valid for Christian thinking is also an argument for the widest possible distribution of these rights.
(iii) . . . [P]roperty rights must never be maintained or exercised without regard to their social consequences . . .
(iv) . . . The property which consists in personal possessions for use, such as home, has behind it a clearer moral justification than property in the means of production and in land which gives the owners power over other persons. . . . Industrial property in particular encourages the concentration of power; for it gives the owner control over both the place and the instruments of labour and thus leaves the worker powerless,

so far as property relations are concerned, allowing him only the organised strength of his union and his political franchise to set against the power of ownership. . . .

(B) *The message of Christianity should throw a searchlight on the actual facts of the existing situation and in particular reveal the human consequences of present forms of economic behaviour.* It is this which saves statements of principles from being platitudes. . . .

The expert may have to supply statistics, but the meaning of the statistics can be known only to those who see the particular results of an economic situation in the lives of persons. . . . Christian insight ought to enable men and women to see more deeply into the effects of an economic situation. . . .

(C) *The searchlight of the Christian message can also make clear the obstacles to economic justice in the human heart, and especially those that are present in the hearts of people within the Church.* It is not enough that individual Christians should become good in their intentions or become changed in their conscious motives. What is needed is the kind of self-knowledge which will help Christians to understand how far their attitudes are moulded by the position which they hold in the economic order. Self-knowledge is no less important than knowledge of external conditions, and more important than the knowledge of the sins of others.

The Churches Survey their Task; Report of the Oxford Conference on Church, Community and State, London, George Allen and Unwin, 1937, pp. 92–5, 115–21 (italics original).

2 *Christianity and Social Order*

William Temple's seminal book came out in the Second World War and was an immediate best seller. It set out in direct and careful terms the reasons for the Church's interest in social and economic affairs and enumerated the principles and beliefs that should govern that interest. It was for many the inspiration for the social reconstruction that came in the welfare state and contributed to the consensus that was to be characteristic of post-war politics.

> [The Church] may declare the proper relation of the economic to other activities of men, but it cannot claim to know what will be the purely economic effect of particular proposals. It is, however, entitled to say that some economic gains ought not to be sought because of the injuries involved to interests higher than economic; and this principle of the subordination of the whole economic sphere is not yet generally accepted. We all recognise that in fact the exploitation of the poor, especially of workhouse children, in the early days of power-factories was an abomination not to be excused by any economic advantage thereby secured; but we fail to recognise that such an admission carries with it the principle that economics are properly subject to a non-economic criterion.
>
> The approach to the problem in our own time is to be made along four distinct lines: (1) the claims of sympathy for those who suffer; (2) the educational influence of the social and economic system; (3) the challenge offered to our present system in the name of justice; (4) the duty of conformity to the 'Natural Order' in which is to be found the purpose of God.
>
> [. . .]
>
> In this enterprise we shall be censured for departure from our own contention that the Church is concerned with principles and not with policy. For the framing of policy knowledge of contemporary facts, and that power to estimate tendencies which comes only from specialist study, are indispensable. But a statement of principles will carry us onto ground commonly left during the last three centuries to purely secular forces; it is bound to seem like an intrusion into practical politics even when it scrupulously stops short. And the line of demarcation is not very clear. It may be possible to draw it with more definiteness when we have reviewed the history of the Church's enterprise or lack of it in this field, and have set out some of the principles concerned. The aim, however, is clear throughout. The Christian citizen is required in his civic action (e.g. voting)

to promote the best interests of his country, with a Christian interpretation of the word 'best'; the aim of any formulation of Christian social principles is to provide that Christian interpretation or at least the means of reaching it.

So we answer the question 'How should the Church interfere' by saying: In three ways – (1) its members must fulfil their moral responsibilities and functions in a Christian spirit; (2) its members must exercise their purely civil rights in a Christian spirit; (3) it must itself supply them with a systematic statement of principles to aid them in doing these two things, and this will carry with it a denunciation of customs or institutions in contemporary life and practice which offend against those principles.

There remains the question whether the Church should ever interfere in a particular issue, such as, for example, an actual trade dispute which has broken out. It can be answered with almost complete assurance that the Church acting officially, should stand aside. It has its own witness to give; and if this were heeded, no dispute would arise. It is very seldom that Christianity offers a solution of practical problems; what it can do is to lift the parties to a level of thought and feeling at which the problem disappears.

[. . .]

[Christian social principles.]

The Primary principle of Christian Ethics and Christian Politics must be respect for every person simply as a person. If each man and women is a child of God, whom God loves and for whom Christ died, then there is in each a worth absolutely independent of all usefulness to society. The person is primary and not society; the State exists for the citizen, not the citizen for the State. The first aim of social progress must be to give the fullest possible scope for the exercise of all powers and qualities which are distinctly personal; and of these the most fundamental is choice.

[. . .]

No man is fitted for an isolated life; everyone has needs which he cannot supply for himself; but he needs not only what his neighbours contribute to the equipment of his life but their actual selves as the complement to his own. Man is naturally and incurably social.

[. . .]

Liberty is actual in the various cultural and commercial and local associations that men form. In each of these a man can feel that he counts for something and that others depend on him as he on them.

[. . .]

The combination of Freedom and Fellowship as principles of social life issues in the obligation of Service. No one doubts this in so far as it concerns the individual . . . all groupings of men must do the same. The rule here should be that we use our wider loyalties to check the narrower. A man is a member of his family, of his nation and of mankind. It is very seldom that we can render service directly to mankind as a whole. We serve mankind by serving those parts of it to which we are closely connected.

[. . .]

It is possible that my discussion of Christian social principles in the last two chapters may be criticised for omitting the two most important of all – Justice and Love. But these are principles of another order. They have their place in this field chiefly as regulating those which I have already described. It is axiomatic that Love should be the predominant Christian impulse, and that the primary form of Love in social organization is Justice. . . .

These two great principles then – Love and Justice – must be rather regulative of other principles than taken as immediate guides to social policy. But they must constantly be borne in mind as checks upon policy. As we must use our wider loyalties to check the narrower, so we must use these higher principles of all to check our application of the lower. Freedom must not be pursued in ways that offend against Love, nor must service be demanded, or fellowship in any actual instance promoted, in ways that offend against Justice.

In earlier time, Christian thinkers made great use of the notion of Natural Law. . . . In practice the Natural Order or

Natural Law is discovered partly by observing the generally accepted standards of judgement and partly by consideration of the proper functions of whatever is the subject of enquiry. This is a task for human reason; but so far as reason enables us to reach the truth about anything in its own essence and its relationships, it enables us to see it as it is in the mind of God. Thus it is a Natural, not a Supernatural, Order with which we are concerned; but as God is Creator, this Natural Order is His order and its law is His law. . . .

But the believer in Natural Order has another shot in his locker. For he refuses to admit that the economic activity of man may be thus isolated and judged by its own canons alone. Certainly there is a real technical autonomy in this as in every other department, and neither theology nor ethics can determine the probable economic effects of any proposed economic reform. In the region of causes and effects, economic science is autonomous. But according to Natural Law the economic process is not an end in itself; it and all its parts are primarily a means to something that is much more than economic – the life of man. . . .

It is wholesome to go back to this conception of Natural Law because it holds together two aspects of truth which it is not easy to hold together in combination – the ideal and the practical. We tend to follow one or other of two lines: either we start from a purely ideal conception, and then bleat fatuously about love; or else we start from the world as it is with the hope of remedying an abuse here or there, and we have no general direction or criterion of progress. The conception of Natural Law will help us form a conception of the right or ideal relation between the various activities of men and of the men engaged in them.

William Temple, *Christianity and Social Order*,
Harmondsworth, Penguin, 1942,
(SPCK, 1976), pp. 32, 43, 67, 68, 69, 73, 79–82.

3 *Towards the Conversion of England*

This report was commissioned by William Temple, when Archbishop of York, in order to set out the tasks the Church of England faced in the challenges of the post-war period. The leading members of the Commission were Henry Wilson, Bishop of Chelmsford, Chairman, and Christopher Chavasse, Bishop of Rochester, both from the evangelical wing of the church. But the report takes a broad understanding of evangelism, as more than the proclamation and acceptance of personal faith. It includes the life of discipleship, which, by implication, means the whole of life in society. In fact the definition offered in the report is that evangelism is 'so to present Jesus Christ in the power of the Holy Spirit, that men shall come to put their trust in God through him, to accept him as their saviour and serve him as King in the fellowship of his Church'.

The analysis given of both the opportunities and threats in modern society and of the Christian task may ring as somewhat antiquated, authoritarian and even naive. However, it is clearly recognized that industrialization and the economic order were to be included in the Church's purview and are a proper field of ministry and mission. While the report was not taken up wholeheartedly (the call for a Council for Evangelism went by default) it nevertheless stimulated a number of initiatives and has become a benchmark frequently referred to.

135. Evangelism in the working world means more than bearing personal testimony . . . It also means claiming for Christ the whole of the particular occupation in which we are engaged, and the doing of our work to reflect his likeness. . . . [T]o extend God's Kingdom . . . includes the bringing of our every activity, and our performance of it, into harmony with God's sovereign law as revealed by Christ.

136. This involves, as *The Oxford Conference on Church, Community and State* pointed out, a two-fold Christian witness.

First there is the continual witness to Christ's law of love as the criterion which governs all human relationships, not excepting those of the economic order of society. . . .

137. There is, also, the other, and complementary Christian witness, of acting like Christ in the economic order as it now exists. 'Christians are under constraint to carry their faith and loyalty into concrete situations, the daily business and the personal relationships of life.' . . .

138. This being so, the Christian laity should be recognised as the priesthood of the Church in the working world, and as the Church militant in the mission fields of politics, industry and commerce.

Towards the Conversion of England,
Report to Church Assembly, 1945.

A note on theological methodology

As a preliminary to telling the post-war story of the churches' engagement with the economy, it is important to consider some of the main strands of thinking that have offered a framework for theology to determine its relation to secular matters. We have selected four distinct approaches, which will make their appearances again as the story unfolds.

1 Middle axioms

One of the legacies from the pioneering work of the Christendom Group, as well as Joe Oldham, William Temple and others has been the idea of 'middle axioms'. This was their answer to the problem as to how to relate in a creative and practical way the universal assertions of the gospel to the particular and concrete issues of the time. This is finely described in the following passage taken from the introductory documentation for the Life and Work Conference in Oxford in 1937.

The Gospel is not a code of morals or a new law. But the new mind which is formed in those who have responded to the revelation of a new reality in Christ must express itself in new forms of behaviour. It belongs to the prophetic and teaching office of the church to expound the implications of the Christian understanding of its life and to make clear the kind of behaviour to which belief in the Gospel prompts.

Such broad assertions as that Christians are bound to obey the law of love or strive for social justice do not go far towards helping the individual to know what he ought to do in particular cases. On the other hand, there is no way by which he can be relieved of the responsibility of decisions in concrete situations. To give him precise instructions to be literally carried out is to rob him of his moral responsibility as a person. It is not the function of the clergy to tell the laity how to act in public affairs, but to confront them with the Christian demand and to encourage them to discover its application for themselves. Hence between purely general statements of the ethical demands of the gospel and the decisions that have to be made in concrete situations there is need for what may be described as middle axioms. It is these that give relevance and point to the Christian ethic. They are attempts to define the directions in which, in a particular state of society, Christian faith must express itself. They are not binding for all time, but are provisional definitions of the type of behaviour required of Christians at a given period in given circumstances.

W. A. Visser t'Hooft and J. H. Oldham,
The Church and its Function in Society, 1936, pp. 206f.,
quoted in R. H. Preston, *Church and Society in the Late Twentieth Century*, London, SCM Press, 1983, p. 144.

This subsequently became the guiding principle for preparing reports or statements on socio-economic issues among the British churches, certainly in the first half of the period covered by this book. It is, therefore, one of the classic methodologies of Christian social ethics that still has considerable influence. The churches, having to make their case in competition with other interested parties, would need to be seen to be firmly based in the actualities of the situation and the sociological, economic and scientific understanding of the issues involved. Thus in a working party or in the writings of a particular author, it was important to show the necessary range of expertise and/or resources. Similarly the theological reflection, to avoid vague generalizations, must be directed towards the particular concern addressed and, while not being too prescriptive, point towards and give reasons for the options offered. These must also be socially and politically reasonable, capable of being the basis of workable political decisions. In this way it was hoped that the churches could make, and sometimes did, a significant contribution to the national debate, whether through particular spokesmen or a report. It was also intended to provide a way of educating the Christian constituency and offering support to those who, as Christians, had to make concrete decisions within the limitations of their particular circumstances.

Such a methodology must inevitably be somewhat open-ended and flexible. This will mean that reports and statements will vary in the distinctiveness and clarity afforded to the guidance given. Critics have suggested that the weakness of this approach is that it does not really ensure the interlocking of the theological imperative with the concrete and particular situation. The Christian commentary can still feel bland and generalized and somewhat tacked on to an otherwise detailed discussion. The obverse of this is that the real decisions are made by the experts and practitioners who find it difficult to take account of external theoretical and moral arguments. They can, by their very position and knowledge, dominate any discussion. It can, however, be pointed out in reply that middle axioms should not be seen as a set of clear directives but a methodology that insists, on the one hand, that it is a genuinely inter-disciplinary process that holds together all the relevant contributions to the discussion while, on the other hand, allowing due respect and autonomy to the different expertises, each of which functions in its own way. Arriving, in any particular case, at a Christian comment is always a matter of informed judgement based on the exercise of wisdom and patient reflection.

2 The regulated market

More recently, in the 1990s, with the collapse of Eastern European communism and the apparent triumph of neo-capitalism there has been a further change in the approach to Christian social ethics. This is to accept the market and globalization but to recognize its weaknesses and to press for the humanization of the market. This both recognizes the effective strengths of the market and the diversity and plurality of the transactions in which it consists that are impossible to regulate in detail, but at the same time to recognize its dangers and propensity to favour the powerful and create an underclass that necessitates appropriate intervention and regulation. The market is not an invincible force but a human invention that is there to serve the well-being of humanity. Thus John Atherton:

> To so regard the market economy as the least harmful economic option reflects two affirmative affirmations about the market in the interactive process: the positive and the constraining.
>
> It is important to begin by acknowledging the positive character of the concept. It is not simply about identifying the market as the 'best of a bad bunch'. Three features of the market substantiate this conclusion:
>
> 1. As we have seen, the market economy is the most effective way of operating a modern economy known to us. Given the basic economic problem of the allocation of scarce resources, and the problems which flow from that, the market appears to be best able to deal with them. . . .
> 2. The concept is a recognition of the positive value of the untidiness of reality: 'The nature of man is intricate; the objects of society are of the greatest possible complexity.'
> 3. Affirming the market as least harmful is a rejection of any commitments to blueprints, whether of a Marxist, libertarian, Christian kind, or any other type. No human design or planning capacity has the 'degree of wisdom and

foreknowledge' to meet the economic needs of large modern populations. . . .

The other principal affirmation emphasizes the constraining character of the least harmful concept. . . . On the one hand, it is a recognition that the market economy has harmful tendencies because if its intrinsic defects and its inability to deal completely with the great challenges. . . .

On the other hand, the concept is also an acknowledgment of the structural as well as personal nature of the deep strain of imperfection in reason and morality. Essentially, it represents what Christians have described traditionally as original sin . . .

The understanding of the market as least harmful that is beginning to emerge from these insights is essentially constructive. Its empiricism and pragmatism contribute to this positive nature and, in doing so, warn against two misapprehensions. First it stands against the use of theological realism, or original sin, to support conservative reaction rather than progressive justice. The relative autonomy of the economic order does not reduce the importance of the political order as democracy and modern state, and their obligation to contribute to the socialization of the market. . . . Secondly, the understanding of the least harmful also questions the too-simple use of theological realism to deny the power of Christ to transform even the economic order.

John Atherton, *Christianity and the Market: Christian Social Thought for our Times*, London, SPCK, 1992, pp. 226–8.

3 Liberation theology

From the mid-1960s, however, a new voice was beginning to be heard coming out of Latin America. Liberation theology, which first made its mark on the global scene at the Life and Work Conference of the WCC at Geneva in 1966, advocated working with the rather different tools of analysis found in the Marxist tradition. Here practical truth emerges out of reflection on the structures and motivations of practice. Action is not deduced from right belief and correct information but from *praxis*. This is set out by Bevans as follows:

> When we speak of the praxis model of contextual theology, we are speaking about a model, the central insight of which is that theology is done not simply by providing relevant expression of Christian faith but also by commitment to Christian action. But even more than this, theology is understood as the product of the continual dialogue of these two aspects of the Christian life. The praxis model employs a method which 'in its most profound sense is understood as the unity of knowledge as activity and knowledge as content'. . . . It is reflected upon action and acted-upon reflection – both rolled into one. [. . .]
>
> Practitioners of the praxis model that stress Christian action as one of the key components of theology will inevitably come up against the fact that such action takes place within a sinful world and a world of sinful structures that condone the sins of those that support them and oppress those who do not. True Christianity, it becomes clear, must work against such oppressive structures not just by seeking to change certain features, but by seeking to supplant them completely. Liberation and transformation, not just gradual development or friendly persuasion, is the only way men and women can fulfil their call to be genuine children of God.

Stephen B. Bevans, *Models of Contextual Theology*, Maryknoll, Orbis (revised and expanded edn), 2002, pp. 72–3

There has been much debate about the strengths and weaknesses of liberation theology, not least from the Vatican. It has also been a problem as to how far it is possible to translate it into the British context. Nevertheless it has permeated in indirect ways into the working style of much British theology. Its most pervasive expression has been the adoption of the 'pastoral cycle' into practical theology, a methodology widely used among the 'base communities' in Latin America. It has also introduced a number of principles which, in one form or another, have tended to colour Christian social ethics. First, there is the recognition of power and the necessity to recognize its use and misuse. There is always the need to ask the subversive questions: who benefits? who controls? Second the key guiding principle of the Gospel is 'God's option for the poor'. The thrust of Christian action must be to offer liberation for those who are in different ways disadvantaged. The approach tends to be more confrontational than conciliatory. Third, there is an emphasis on equality and solidarity. This tends to challenge the individualism and competitiveness of capitalism. It was interesting that this style of theologizing should come to the fore in the 1970s and 80s, just at the time when neo-capitalism was to dominate the political scene.

4 Radical orthodoxy

A further approach that also recognizes the marginalization of religion in modern society and the pluralism of the postmodern world is found in various forms of what has become known as 'radical orthodoxy'. Here Christian thought and practice seeks to reassert its distinctive understanding of the nature of creation and human existence and to release it from the trammels of contamination by secular modernism. In socio ethical terms this means basing practice firmly and directly on the perspectives and precepts of the gospel. The Christian community, therefore, has primarily to be the witness to the Kingdom as found in Jesus. Its life, corporately and through its members, is first informed by the virtues of the Kingdom, which gives both content and direction to action. While the term 'radical orthodoxy' was coined by a group of theologians associated with John Milbank, the approach has become wider and new alliances have begun to emerge between Milbank and the US, Mennonite-influenced, theologian Stanley Hauerwas. It is from Hauerwas that the following extract is drawn.

> For the church to *be* rather than to *have* a social ethic moreover means that a certain kind of people are required to sustain it

as an institution across time. They must above all be a people of virtue – not simply any virtue, but the virtues necessary for remembering and telling the story of a crucified saviour. They must be capable of being peaceable among themselves and with the world, so that the world sees what it means to hope for God's kingdom. Such a people do not believe that everyone is free to do whatever they will, but that we are each called upon to develop our particular gifts to serve the community of faith.

[. . .]

But that does not mean that what is meant by faith, hope and love is the same for Christians as for other people. For Christians, the sense of what it is in which they have faith, in which they hope, and the kind of love that must be displayed among them derives from the tradition that moulds their community. Indeed, because of the character of that story, the nature and the meaning of the virtues are essentially changed. For Christians are the community of the new age which must continue to exist in the old age. Because of their existence between the time, because they are a people 'on a way', they require, or perhaps better, make central, certain virtues that other communities do not.

[. . .]

The church must learn time and again that its task is not to *make* the world the kingdom, but to be faithful to the kingdom by showing to the world what it means to be a community of peace. Thus we are required to be patient and never lose hope. But hope in what? Specifically, hope in the God who has promised that faithfulness to the kingdom will be of use in God's care for the world. Thus our hope is not in this world, or in humankind's goodness, or in some sense that everything always works out for the best, but in God and God's faithful caring for the world.

Stanley Hauerwas, *The Peaceable Kingdom,*
London, SCM Press, 1984, pp. 102–4.

By contrasting the Christian perspective with the assumptions and presuppositions of wider society or alternative thought systems, the argument is not about what line to follow or which policy to adopt, but about the values and meanings that compete. Perhaps, however, theological and ethical consistency and integrity can be held at the cost of the possibility of shared action and of shaping, if only partially, some aspects of the world.

3

Consensus 1945–79

Part 1 Britain in the post-war world

1945–51 Post-war recovery

Britain emerged, as we have seen, from the Second World War exhausted and virtually bankrupt. In waging the war its economy, even more than Germany's, had been completely diverted to the immediate end of defeating the enemy. This meant, paradoxically, full employment, including the greater use of female employment, reprieve for the major heavy industries such as coal and shipbuilding, and agricultural prosperity. But it also meant diverting resources away from the normal channels, a massive lack of investment, the deterioration of the housing stock and industrial plant, as well as in community resources and infrastructure, not least through enemy action. Financial assets were run down and immense debts were incurred, most significantly with the United States, not always on favourable terms. Meanwhile trading partners had found alternative means of supply or developed local industries. So when hostilities ended there was a massive task to bring things back to some semblance of normality but little or no resources with which to do it.

At the same time there was a determination not to repeat the experience after the First World War (1914–18) when the 'land fit for heroes' never materialized. Already, in the war years, plans and proposals were being laid down to establish improvements in education, health and welfare. Full employment, one of the objectives of the Beveridge Report, was high on the agenda.

Moreover the experience of a highly managed economy in the war gave credibility to the possibility of building and regulating a fairer and more equitable society in peace time. The churches, too, were actively engaged. In England, Temple's influence was still strong and the Malvern Conference a resource. In Scotland the Baillie Commission was to hand. The embryonic structures were in place, such as the British Council of Churches (BCC). And there was the sense of partnership between the churches and the state that had been built up. There was, therefore, a real sense of consensus, not only politically but, more or less, throughout society.

The Labour government under Clement Attlee, elected by a landslide in July 1945, had the unenviable task of rebuilding a country that had high expectations. Its great achievement was to implement and develop the structures of a modern welfare state, notably the National Health Service and other welfare structures in support of the disabled, elderly and disadvantaged. At the same time there was a programme of nationalization of key elements of the economy's infrastructure, including the Bank of England, the railways and the utilities. In some cases this meant consolidating already existing wartime regulations. While this move towards state socialism was controversial, the Conservative opposition, in its *Industrial Charter* (1947), accepted the mixed economy and nationalisation as a socio-economic tool. This meant that political argument was not over the principle but over the extent and appropriateness of the nationalization programme. Some industries, however, notably steel, had to live with uncertainty as they were over the years nationalized and denationalized. A further aspect of this socialist tendency was the introduction of the Town and Country Planning regulations (1947). These measures provided the framework for government action for over thirty years.

The country had to clamber out of bankruptcy. This was done at a price. At home austerity measures (rationing was more stringent than in the war) were patiently borne. Industry was gradually brought back to peacetime tasks, though any modernization was slow. To save imports, tariffs were high and agriculture heavily subsidized, a policy that in various guises still continues to this day. By 1960, some 50 per cent of our food was home grown, compared with 30 per cent pre-war. A concerted effort was made to divert goods into exports. But it would have been impossible without enormous loans from the USA and Canada and, as a consequence of the emergence of the Cold War (the Berlin blockade and setting up of NATO was in 1948–9), the implementation of the Marshall Plan (1948–50). Even so the pound was devalued from the pre-war exchange rate of US$4.03 to US$2.88. Meanwhile British overseas commitments had to be met. At the same time, an Empire and mandated territories had to be ruled and their future determined. The first stage in dismembering the Empire was to give India and Pakistan independence in 1947. British troops were expensively engaged in Palestine (1945–48) Malaya (1948–60) and elsewhere. Then came UN action in Korea in the face of North Korean and, subsequently, Chinese aggression (1950–53), which conflict also created an international recession. Despite all this Britain was able gradually to reassert itself in the world, albeit as a lesser power.

This was the context for the churches' developing engagement with the socio-economic sphere. Broadly it may be said to have taken two, but interrelated, directions. Continuing the momentum begun before the war, the mainstream denominations, together with the newly constituted BCC, set up committees to monitor and be concerned with social affairs, usually subsuming economics into the wider brief that worked across the board from welfare to defence; though some, such as the Church of England and the Methodists, also had additional bodies responsible for industrial and cognate issues. Thus these concerns were to be found at the heart of the life of the churches. But for some, such as the Anglicans, the Church of Scotland and the Methodists, there were also regional bodies and networks of social responsibility officers, whether full- or part-time. This provided the basis for responding to economic issues as they developed, normally in three ways: first, as a resource for briefing church spokespersons, such as moderators or bishops in the House of Lords, or for compiling press releases; second, as a means of informing and educating the Christian constituency through such activities as publications, conferences or conscience-raising activities; third, as a way to contribute to the public debate on key issues, usually through working parties and reports commended by the relevant bodies.

The other major development was the emergence of Industrial Mission (IM). This had roots in the activities of the Industrial Christian Fellowship (ICF) and other specialized ministries such as the seamen's missions. But there had been, in the war, a move to provide chaplains to the large munitions factories, where people were working long shifts under intense pressure. This harked back to the Navvy Mission and was, interestingly, to be taken up again by the Church of Scotland in relation to the large camps in remote places associated with the building of nuclear power stations. Second, in the immediate post-war years the Christian Commando Campaigns had conducted meetings in many venues, including factories and other places of work. A new field was potentially opened up. Third, there was overwhelming evidence of the alienation of the working populace in the industrial cities from the Church. It was Leslie Hunter, Bishop of Sheffield, who made this a primary concern and deliberately challenged his diocese, and the Church of England generally, to act.

So, in the decade from 1945, numerous, often uncoordinated, initiatives emerged. We can perhaps discern four main strands. Industrial Mission, in Britain, in its modern form, has usually been traced back to Bishop Leslie Hunter's initiative in Sheffield. In an episcopal letter to his diocese Hunter challenged the church to overcome the rift between it, with its predominantly middle-class ethos, and the world of industry and the urban working classes. To this end he appointed Ted Wickham as his chaplain to industry. For Wickham this was clearly seen as 'cross-cultural mission'. It was necessary for the church to recognize its failings and to listen to those outside its normal constituency. Those engaged in this mission were thus crossing a real cultural divide and moving into a new world of industry.

It involved learning afresh what it meant to encounter the gospel in unknown ways; to discover the shape of the Kingdom where God was at work in that world; and to challenge the Church to renewal. Out of this, patiently and perhaps painfully, might emerge new models of church and worshipping communities, parallel to the accepted inherited structures.

A few, somewhat tentatively, followed the path set by the 'worker priests' in France (see Mantle, 2000). These identified themselves with the world of work by taking up employment and seeking to find ways of exercising a ministry from that base. It was later, in the 1960s, to be one of the inspirations for the Bishop of Southwark, Mervyn Stockwood, to introduce non-stipendiary ministry. The hope was that such priests would remain in and structure their ministry in relation to their secular work.

Third, others (and this strongly coloured Methodism's engagement) wanted to talk about industrial evangelism. The base here was the local congregation, which through chaplaincy work and active commitment to the local community, would build bridges between the community of faith, the community of work and the residential community. This was well typified by the Industrial College in Luton, which was attached to the local Methodist congregation, founded under Bill Gowland's ministry. Essentially, on this model, IM was to be seen as an adaptation into new and flexible ways of the one ministry of the Church.

The fourth pattern became the dominant one. With the growth of many different initiatives across the country there were pressures to seek to form some kind of identity and coherence. This was further stimulated by the suspicion of what appeared to be radical innovations and a certain critical independency shown towards the churches by some in IM. Conversely IM felt itself to be marginalized from the mainstream life of the churches. Such were some of the issues at the heart of the major crisis that hit Sheffield IM in the 1960s and that shaped IM from then on. Hunter's successor Bishop John Taylor, and the team leader Michael Jackson, felt that IM was creating a semiautonomous endeavour that was claiming authority for what they regarded as dubious approaches to mission and the understanding of the gospel. They saw it as their priority to assert that IM was essentially part of the community of faith, part of the one mission of the Church, though working in a specific and important field. But the tendency they saw in IM to create its own ethos and structures opened up all sorts of theological and ecclesiological problems. The effective outcome in IM was to try to redefine the relation between the churches and IM by emphasizing the mediating role of IM between the Church and the world of industry. The task of the chaplain was henceforth to be the visible presence of the Church in the workplace and in the structures of commerce and industry, supporting the laity and offering such pastoral action as possible, not least within and towards their structures of power and corporate functioning. By negotiation, the chaplains were guests in the world of work and, by trial and error, found ways and means to relate creatively to the constituency. On the other hand, it was their task, as those with a special ministry, to represent the world of economics and work in and to the Church, shaping the life and policies of the community of faith. This, however, could lead to an uneasy tension and split loyalties. There is always some suspicion between the two poles. This issue was to be revisited in a different form in the 1980s with the report *Industrial Mission: An Appraisal.*

Not surprisingly, as a sign of both its increased influence and recognition and its growing body of expertise and practice and its desire to secure its freedom and identity, IM began to forge its own structures. The Industrial Mission Association (IMA) was formed in the mid-1960s, providing the majority of those engaged in IM across Britain with a common forum and support structure. It published the monthly journal, formerly the *Industrial Mission Newsletter*, currently *IMAgenda*, and holding biennial conferences. The greater sense of coherence also facilitated the growth of national networks. In some industries, such as coal, electricity and later retailing, this meant that IM had contacts with the central structures, usually based in

London, as well as with the local plants. Also, in the 1960s, international contacts grew both in Europe as the UK moved towards and into the Common Market (now the European Union) and worldwide through contacts facilitated through the Urban and Rural Ministry desk at the World Council of Churches in Geneva.

The IMA is also engaged with the question of standards and norms for this ministry that arose haphazardly in response to opportunity and need. Both the Church of Scotland and the Methodists, with their more centralized systems of governance, have licensed clergy for this special ministry and provided induction training courses, which for the Methodists were at the College in Luton. Training opportunities were also available through the William Temple College at Rugby, which subsequently moved to Manchester as the William Temple Foundation.

IM has also been one of the pressure points for ecumenical development. Management and unions are, not unreasonably, unwilling to negotiate with more than one body. They are suspicious of the fragmentariness of the churches. This has forced IM to develop ecumenical structures both nationally and locally. In Scotland all industrial chaplains from whatever denomination come under the one managing committee. Local teams are usually based in an industrial region or city and co-ordinate the use of resources mission strategy. Nationally the Churches' Consortium for Industrial Mission was set up as the liaison committee between the denominations and the BCC. This is the body that issued the national guidelines that helped shape the appointment and working of chaplains.

IM, therefore, emerged in the decades immediately after the war as a small but not insignificant sign of the renewal of the churches, which has had a steady and valuable influence. Unfortunately the promises were not fulfilled: either in relation to industry and the industrial classes, or in relation to the churches, for whom IM remained an interesting, specialized sideline. Nevertheless, in its heyday most industrial centres of any size had teams, some of which continue to this day.

1951–70 Prosperity

On the national stage, the 1951 election brought the Conservatives, under Churchill, back into power. By this time the post-war recovery had begun to take hold. After the Korean War Britain began to find its feet. Rationing disappeared in the mid-1950s. By 1957 Harold Macmillan could imply that the majority of Britons 'had never had it so good'. Indeed the Gross National Product (GNP) grew from between 2.5 per cent to 3.4 per cent over each of the business cycles 1951–73; a rate that represents as good a sustained period of growth as any in recent times.

All was not, however, as comfortable as it seemed. There was concern that Britain's economic performance was not as strong as its industrial rivals, including Germany, Japan and France, each of which had suffered more greatly in the war. The relative decline that had been a feature of the whole twentieth century was still steadily eroding away Britain's world position. By the mid-1960s the cumulative evidence gave cause for alarm as the country entered into 'stagflation' and a balance of payments crisis that led to the devaluation of 1967 (to US$2.40). The question was how to halt the so-called 'British disease'.

A number of strands can be found, each of which has been named (usually by those who want to point the finger) as the primary cause. Clearly external events have a considerable impact on a frail and vulnerable economy. From the mid-1950s the process of trade liberalization, under the General Agreement on Tariffs and Trade (GATT), had begun. This exposed the UK to greater competition, which had the effect of sucking in imports while not sufficiently stimulating exports. Trade cycles, such as the 1957–58 world recession, had an even greater impact. Events in the Middle East, not least the invasion of Egypt and the associated oil crisis (1956), and others, such as emergencies in Cyprus (1959), Kenya (1952), Rhodesia (1968) and South Africa (from 1961), all demanded attention and resources. This was the time of Britain's rapid withdrawal from imperial obligations, typified by Macmillan's 'winds of change' speech and Wilson's withdrawal from 'east of Suez'.

The balance of the British economy was also changing. Continuing trends already noted, there was a decline in heavy industrial activity and a shift towards newer industries, lighter and electronically based. Above all was the growth in the service sector. This was to accelerate throughout this period. In terms of the balance of payments, therefore, increasing reliance was placed on 'invisible earnings', such as banking. But this itself was vulnerable to the flows of money in and out of the country in pursuit of capital growth. It was also affected by the increase in overseas travel that counterbalanced the developing tourist trade. Indeed the Wilson government imposed limits to the amount of sterling that could be taken out of the country (1966–67).

One of the factors often referred to was the apparent power of the unions and their ability to command wage increases well above inflation. Britain's levels of productivity were also below those of its competitors in Europe as well as the USA. There were anxieties about the numbers of strikes and restrictive practices that seemed to symbolize resistance to progress. This could be exaggerated, however. The most dramatic episode was the miners' strike and the three-day working week that was imposed by the Heath government, arguing that the issue was 'who governs Britain' (1973–74). It meant, though, that trade union reform was in the air from 1965. The first abortive attempt to bring in a negotiated reform was Barbara Castle's *In Place of Strife* in 1968. Conversely, accusations, by the unions and others, were made about the levels of investment in British industry and the competence of management, coupled with criticisms of investment in the infrastructure and training. The favoured way of facing such issues was to find ways and means of arriving at collaborative agreements between the government, the unions and the Confederation of British Industry (CBI) concerning industrial practices and wages. The Attlee government set up mechanisms to deal with restrictive practices, monopolies and retail prices. In 1961 the Conservative government set up the National Economic Development Council (NEDC, or Neddy). Both Wilson and Heath instituted periods of wage restraint backed by varying levels of legal enforcement.

Above all, it was hoped that decline could be countered by planning, moving resources from older industries to newer enterprises. Wilson's pledge in the 1964 election to harness 'the white heat of technology' envisaged a new era of expansion driven by training and imaginative innovation. George Brown was given the task, from his new Department of Economic Affairs, to draw up a national plan. There were also many initiatives from monetary inducements to training boards to try to encourage new enterprises to replace waning industries. All was not, however, doom and gloom. There were indeed growing economic activities and a positive shift in manufacturing. As domestic consumption rose there was a demand for 'white goods', the petro-chemical industry flourished and the automobile industry became the measuring stick of the economy.

By the early 1970s, however, a new phenomenon arose. Unemployment was steadily rising, to grow exponentially from 1975. The post-war expectation had begun to break down. Moreover it was coupled with high rates of inflation. 'Stagflation' (stagnation coupled with inflation) went against the expectations of Keynsian economics which had, by and large, been accepted as the basic framework of economic policy. Keynes had argued that the economy is best regulated through the 'demand side', that is, by creating demand, whether by planned expansion, especially of the infrastructure, or by increasing the purchasing power of people (by cutting taxes or increasing the money supply). Thus a depression in economic activity could be countered by a regulated boost. But there was a balance to be sustained. Unemployment would tend to drive wages and prices down, that is, to produce deflation. On the other hand, too much purchasing power would send prices up, producing inflation. The new factor in the 70s was the simultaneous rise in both unemployment and inflation. The received orthodoxy was breaking down. The search was on for both a theoretical and a practical solution. The era of consensus was drawing to a close.

1970–79 A twilight zone

This brings us to the turbulent years of Edward Heath's Conservative government (1970–74) and the Labour governments of Wilson's second term (1974–76) and James Callaghan (1976–79) when the British disease seemed to be about to be terminal.

With Heath there came the first espousal of monetarism as an alternative to Keynes. Milton Friedman, in the USA, had forcibly reasserted the perspectives of classical economic theory that had been dominant up to the Second World War. This suggested that the key mechanism to control the economy was through the control of inflation rather than creating employment. This was to be done through restricting the money supply so that there should not be too much money chasing too few goods and thus pushing up prices. Otherwise everything could be left to the workings of the market. Such a policy would have the effect of deflating the economy. Heath's 1970 manifesto proposed policies that closely followed such a theory. Dubbed 'Selsdon man', after the place where the manifesto was drawn up, there was now a clear clash of principle between the two major parties. 'Butskellism', named after the two chancellors R. A. Butler (Conservative) and Hugh Gaitskell (Labour) in the 50s, was over.

In fact Heath's policy was jettisoned because of a number of industrial failures and the ensuing threat of civil disorder, notably in the face of the threatened closure of John Brown's shipyard on the Clyde. This was followed by a miners' strike (1973–74) against pit closures. All this was politically related to the first effective moves to reform the trade unions. The 1971 act began the process of restructuring the laws concerning the rights and freedoms that had been won, often painfully, since before the First World War. In it Heath had taken up many of the proposals previously set out by Barbara Castle but abandoned by the Labour government.

Heath's major political legacy was the accession of Britain to the Treaty of Rome by which Britain joined, with others, the

European Economic Community (now the European Union) in 1973. This was the third time of asking. De Gaulle had vetoed approaches by Macmillan (1961) and Wilson (1967); but he was no longer occupying the Élysée Palace in Paris. Economically this was a recognition that trade with Europe had steadily grown and was, by 1970, something like 33 per cent of Britain's market, to rise to well over 50 per cent by 1980. Proportionally, trade with the sterling area had diminished from about 50 per cent in 1950 to about 30 per cent in 1970 and about 20 per cent in 1980.

In 1973, associated with the Yom Kippur War in the Middle East, came the second major oil crisis. This immediately threw world trade patterns into chaos and suddenly increased import costs, and thus the cost of living. It threatened to undermine the fabric of the western, including the British, oil-dependent economies, in which oil had replaced coal as a cheap source of power.

The 1974 Labour government inherited a massive trade deficit and an overheated economy. Unemployment, already moving upward, soared, reaching 1.6 million in 1977. There was a severe run on sterling. In 1973 sterling, in line with the gradual collapse across the world of the post-war Bretton Woods fixed exchange agreement, had been allowed to float against other currencies. Since then it had fallen sharply. Meanwhile inflation was moving higher. By 1975 it was briefly running at 26.9 per cent. High inflation pushed up wage demands. Industrial efficiency did not seem to improve. Industrial unrest seemed endemic. The government had to react and slammed on the economic breaks. A significant loan from the International Monetary Fund (IMF) was negotiated in 1976, carrying with it harsh deflationary conditions. Government spending was reined in, contrary to the Labour Party's tradition of social spending. Wage and price restraints were imposed. All this spilled out in to the so-called 'winter of discontent' of 1978–79 when, in the popular imagination, a series of public service strikes threatened to bring the nation to a standstill.

In point of fact, however, the economic measures were

effective and the crisis, as opposed to the political aftermath, was fairly quickly under control. It was, however, significantly helped by the introduction of North Sea oil and gas. The first landing of oil, after long years of preparation, was in 1975. From then on, Britain was increasingly able to benefit not only from being an oil producer but from becoming an oil exporter. So, by 1979, when the ailing government finally called a general election, prospects were reasonably bright again. But that did not save it from a crushing defeat, allowing Margaret Thatcher, by now leader of the Conservatives, to take up residence at 10 Downing Street, ushering in a very new era.

The gradual demise of the post-war consensus also posed questions to the churches and Industrial Mission. It is apparent that the churches were in no better position than the wider community regarding what was happening and how to respond. On the whole the reaction was to support such measures as the government was proposing on the understanding that this was the best way to sustain full employment and to make the transition to new patterns of industry and work. Reports published at this time, therefore, tended to accept greater control and higher public spending. There was very little critical analysis of either the economic situation or of the social issues involved. At the same time, Industrial Mission found itself heavily involved with the declining heavy industries, resulting from a policy of working with the key, influential points of economic power. Here there had been developed national networks, such as with coal and electricity, as well as local links. Now, in the new situation, it was necessary to diversify, to relate to the new industries, including, as they arose in importance, retail, service and leisure industries. However, there was, as we have already noted, another and perhaps more immediate task of working with the emerging army of the unemployed. At this stage the hope was that a transition could be worked through by planned measures. So, many Industrial Mission teams became pro-actively involved with government schemes for retraining and providing temporary employment through, for example, the Manpower Services Commission. Chaplains found themselves working as managers to and sponsors of such schemes. Nationally this led to the formation of Church Action with the Unemployed (CAWTU).

At the same time there was a theological shift. The collapse of political consensus called into question the consensual theological approach represented by 'middle axioms'. From the late 1960s an alternative was beginning to be available. Liberation theology had come onto the world stage at the WCC conference on development in Geneva in 1966. Thus a Latin American radical theology, based on a Marxian conflictual analysis of society, and especially of world economics, appeared to lend itself readily to the new situation, even if it was not easy to see how such a culturally determined theology could adequately be translated to the British scene. But the attraction of liberation theology was reinforced by a European political theology that was emerging from the Lutheran Jürgen Moltmann and the Catholic Johannes-Baptiste Metz and others. So the emphasis shifted towards an emphasis on justice as 'bias to the poor', which has permeated much theological discourse since.

Part 2 Readings

Here, through annotated extracts from selected documents, the aim is to fill out the outline previously given as to the churches' response to the situation they found themselves in over the period under review in this chapter. This will be done under four headings.

1 The churches' voices

The denominations and the BCC developed central structures whereby they could monitor and respond to particular issues. These will be presented under the names of selected churches. This is done partly to draw attention to the different ways the traditions approach the task, reflecting their history and ethos.

2 Industrial Mission

Here the emphasis is on the practice of IM through comparing and contrasting different approaches, and recording something of its story and the debates concerning policy and theology.

3 Centres for enquiry and study

A small number of specialist institutes or study circles have been set up over the years. These have made their own contribution to the overall enterprise and deserve to be noted.

4 Individual authors

Scholars and practitioners have, as individuals, contributed to the broad debate through their writings.

1 The churches' voices 1945–79

This section is concerned with three things. First, it is interesting to see something of the different styles of working. These relate to the historic place a denomination has had in relation to the state and society in general and to the theological understanding of the nature of the Church and its place in the world. Second, there are the actual issues taken up and the comments made. Third, it is possible to observe how the methodologies discussed elsewhere (pp. 49–57) are used in addressing these issues.

The Church of England

As the Established Church of by far the largest part of the UK, the Church of England has been the dominant and sometimes controlling ecclesiastical force, certainly south of the border. Its traditional place within the governance of the realm, exemplified by the presence of bishops in the House of Lords, gives it considerable access to the corridors of power. However, through the twentieth century there was a gradual loosening of the ties of establishment. This has meant that the church has increasingly become a separate institution, speaking to the nation alongside other voices. This is embedded in the emergence of synodical government.

In response to the report *Towards the Conversion of England* (see Chapter 2) the Church Assembly set up a Social and Industrial Council (1951), replacing the earlier Social and Industrial Commission (1923). The new body exhibited its determination by issuing two reports: *The National Church and the Social Order* (1956) and *The Task of the Church in Relation to Industry* (1959).

Justification for the concern with the world of industry

This is the first of two excerpts from the second of these foundational documents. The other is under the section on Industrial Mission (pp. 109–13). Indeed the thrust of the document as a whole is to propose the management of IM as it was emerging in the early days. This extract, however, sets out briefly the justification for the Church's responsibility, which applies to the whole of the socio-economic sphere.

> That justification, or at least explanation, can be logically argued in the following syllogism:-
>
> > The Christian Church is concerned with the quality of human life, both of men individually, and of their society.
> > Industry, the industrial organisation of society, determines to a very large degree the quality of human life, both of men and of their society.
> > Therefore, the Church should be concerned with industry and the industrial organisation of their society.
>
> We think it unnecessary to argue the truth of these two premises; they should be evident. But a number of things should be noted about this explanation and justification of the Church's concern, out of which her objectives should become clearer. The explanation refuses to restrict the concern of the Church to what is called 'industrial evangelism',

that is to say, the conversion of individual men and women to the Christian faith. Of course this is very important. . . . But it also insists that the organisation and goals of industrial society itself (and therefore of industrial institutions) should be the proper consideration of Christians, for men are shaped by their environment and by what happens in society, and can be damaged and stunted, or on the other hand, increased in human stature, by their material environment.

This brings out an objective of the Church's task, namely, that she should shoulder her proper responsibility for the well being of our society by becoming more deeply involved in the life of society, and not contract out of the world into a narrow interest with 'religion'. For Christianity, as is so frequently and rightly insisted, is a way of life as well as a religion, and a way of life is something that should extend into all the different areas of society. . . .

Christianity, the historic faith of our country, has always provided moral and social principles that in any age a society claiming to be Christian must seek to embody, and in the light of which society should be scrutinized and judged. This has often happened even where the church as an institution has failed to recognize the social implications of her own message. The fact is that the great Christian and Biblical axioms and insights concerning justice and fair dealing, community and brotherhood, responsibility and human status, the social meaning of work and wealth, the very meaning of life and history. These remain relevant to our world and nation, and to the institutions within them; and the basic institution of our modern society is industry. And lastly, we cannot fail to note how often in these days, when the most intractable problems of industry are discussed, the discussion is led into the imponderable questions of human relationships, personal and social ethics, human and social motivations and behaviour – all of which are the very stuff of the Christian concern and insight.

The Task of the Church in Relation to Industry,
London, Church Information Office, 1959,
pp. 10 and 12.

The emergence of 'stagflation' in the mid-1970s

In the mid-1970s the British economy was showing signs of strain and there were fears of collapse and conflict. The Board for Social Responsibility, under its then dynamic leadership, set up a series of working parties to study and advise on a range of issues. Here the problem is the slowing down of economic growth and the rise of inflation; the emergence of 'stagflation'. This report was one of a group of three, the others of which are quoted below, which were produced out of the deliberations of a working party set up to consider the deteriorating economic situation. Unusually they were published under the name of a given author as a personal contribution. Ted Wickham, the author, was the doyen of IM, as the founder of the Sheffield Industrial Mission, and at this time Bishop of Middleton.

> In the short term it now appears that standards of living in our country must fall, either through unchecked inflation or the measures required to hold inflation within tolerable limits. Without doubt the latter is to be preferred. The question then is whether we shall be poorer in strength, laying the foundations for real growth, or poorer in weakness, leading to prostration or even social breakdown. It is surely clear how that question should be answered. Taking the longer view it appears there are promising factors in our energy, fuel and oil resources. Among our national resources we should also determine to count our human potential and our capacity to respond to crisis. It is the task of government to take the necessary steps to deal effectively with our economic crisis, and we need a government courageous enough to do that. But there are limits to what a government can do in a democracy. As individuals, as industrial organisations, as social and economic groups, we all have a part to play.
>
> And it is properly a task of the Christian Church to encourage our leaders to do the things that have to be done, and to encourage fortitude and mutuality among the people, for there are deep spiritual aspects to the economic questions that are

posed to the nation. There is the question whether we can have the corporate will required . . . and whether we can do it in a good spirit, without falling apart. . . . Underlying them are all the old questions of how you gain the world, or a good living in the world, without losing your soul, how you care for your neighbour, and what are the things that really belong to our peace?

E. R. Wickham, *Growth and Inflation*,
London, Church Information Office, 1975, p. 13.

The struggle for industrial democracy and issues of power

The growth of union power, the desire to enrich the concept of work and the emergence of the corporate social responsibility of industry raise questions about the rights and interests of different parties in the structures of industry.

The search for meaning and fulfilment from one's work is basic and is thrown into sharper relief when considered in the context of the Christian view of man.

The challenge for change increasingly includes the concern to be more fully involved in the decision making process within industry. This concern can cover a wide spectrum from the individual who believes his own skill and experience can and should be brought to bear . . . through to those who claim the right to be involved when the decisions are likely to affect their work or security of their group.

[. . .]

The past decade has seen within industry both an increase in power for the shop floor and its elected representatives and because of the growing complexity and interrelationship of industry an increased ability to forge the power that is always inherent in the work place into a cogent bargaining weapon. . . . It is vital, therefore, that this new-found power at the grass roots of industry is used responsibly – for the common good and not simply for the advantage of narrow sectional interests.

[. . .]

If past experience is to be relied upon, the problem will not be solved at a stroke, and in the last analysis will require the development of imaginative and pragmatic initiatives which enjoy the support of all powerful interests – Government, management, unions, shareholders, employees and the community in general.

It is the underlying assumption of this paper that cataclysmic confrontation can and should be avoided; that the existing structures can be modified and developed to meet the powerful demands for change.

Geoffrey Gilbertson, *Powersharing in Industry*, London, Church Information Office, 1975, pp. 2–3.

Responsibility in business – shareholders and stakeholders

The third of the papers published in 1975 by the Board for Social Responsibility continued the themes of wider responsibility of industry for society as a whole by looking at the legal and moral obligations of business beyond making a profit for the benefit of shareholders.

The CBI [Confederation of British Industries] has stated that business has responsibility for five interdependent relationships. These are the relationships between a company and its customers, employees, financial stakeholders, suppliers and society at large. . . . The developed debate in the area of the responsibility between a company and its employees will be enlarged by the debate now beginning in the whole area of employee participation. But that debate will be enormously hindered unless there is a common acceptance and affirmation expressed by all parties concerned and accepted by our society, regarding the responsibility of business and the public companies that fulfil that responsibility.

[. . .]

The public responsibility and corporate behaviour of a company in the UK today requires to be expressed in amended law but also, and most importantly, in a non-statuary code of corporate practice in business having status in law and thus national recognition. In the difficult and rapidly changing industrial conditions of today all engaged in business – employers, employees and professional people involved in the business of this land – need every help that can be given them in the vital task in which they are engaged, so that they know for what society holds them to be responsible and the principal ways in which society believes that that responsibility should be exercised, reviewed and developed.

Kenneth Adams, *Ethical Choice and Business Responsibilities*, London, Church Information Office, 1975, pp. 7 and 9.

Trade unions and the closed shop

A closed shop is a place of work where employees, as a condition of employment, must hold membership of a union recognized by the agreement that pertains to that place. As part of the turmoil of the 1970s trade union reform was high on the agenda. The 1971 Act had abolished the closed shop but the subsequent Labour Government, as part of its attempt to draw the unions into economic agreements, controversially restored it.

57. We have tried to argue for an informed understanding of the demand for closed shops, within the context of the historical growth and the present position of trade unions in Britain. With the safeguards for individuals described above, we judge that closed shops may be legitimately negotiated in our society.
58. . . . The major Christian Churches do not teach that association with others who do not hold the Christian faith . . . is wrong and so cannot recommend the exclusive view which leads some to refuse to join unions on religious grounds. Indeed the churches encourage positive participation in responsible social organisations. But where exclusive groups do exist, the mainstream Christian position should be to ensure that their views are respected. We therefore welcome the exemption clause in the 1976 Act.

59. . . . We approve of the existence of the Industrial Tribunals, the Employment Appeal Tribunal, the Advisory Conciliation and Arbitration Service and the TUC Independent Review Committee. Such bodies as these, strongly established, provide a necessary safeguard against certain possible abuses of power in the world of industry.

60. Finally the Christian Church should be constantly aware of the natural human tendency of power to corrupt and should continue to keep a vigilant eye open to what is happening in society.

Understanding Closed Shops,
Church Information Office, 1977.

Work under threat – the end of full employment

The late 1970s also saw the inexorable rise of unemployment that did not seem to respond to any fiscal or planning measures. This caused considerable anxiety, signalling the end of full employment. Several reasons were advanced: wage inflation, imposed by the unions, was not matched by productivity, thus putting unit cost up; the advance of technology that replaces labour, especially unskilled and routine jobs; overseas competition from cheaper sources. There were also several reactions, each of which questioned the place of work in a capitalist society. Not to work was to be marginalized and impoverished. So, either ways have to be found to get people back into work; or remuneration has to be offered for a broad notion of work that includes, for example, housekeeping, caring for children or the elderly and voluntary community work; or to recognize that we are entering the leisure society and to distribute work evenly. Here an attempt is made to pinpoint the core requirements necessary for meaningful human existence.

59. There is a profound interplay between all these ideas which belong to the Christian tradition of thought about work. Just as one writer points to creative and fulfilling aspects, so another calls attention to a more degrading and

alienating side. When contemplation is held in higher esteem than labour, another strand emerges to maintain that the two cannot properly be separated. When man's dominion over the environment turns into exploitation and waste, another strand in the tradition begins to point to a more responsible stewardship of human and material resources. This tradition needs to be further expanded today. As the introduction of new technology and the development of world trade on a more equitable basis change accustomed patterns of work, a new opportunity emerges to shape the future in accordance with the insights that are held into what ought to be done. In contemporary society, however, there is little widely-held vision of this nature which could help to guide the choices and decisions which will have to be taken.

60. In our view, there are within the Christian tradition a number of moral insights into the place of work in life which seem to us to be relevant to the formation of such a contemporary vision. They form, as it were, some points from which bearings can be taken and 'navigation' in the future made more possible. They are summed up, in particular, in the concepts of humanization, of creativity and of responsible dominion. . . . Whatever is done in the future needs to be so arranged that it serves the greater realisation of these three ideas. Together they form a basis of moral perspective on work and its future.

76. . . . The challenges themselves lie in the need to find a more genuine motivation to work, to adapt patterns of employment to cope with the introduction of new technology, to create new jobs and to devise economic policies which will enable this country to play a larger part in world development. . . . We have also argued that considerable experiment is necessary in order to develop new products and services, new companies and new forms of industrial organisation. It is also necessary in order to develop new opportunities for other activities outside paid employment and new opportunities for leisure.

Work and the Future,
Church Information Offices, 1979.

Methodism

In Methodism, by far the largest Nonconformist or Free Church, responsibility for ministry and mission in society is vested in the Home Mission Division. Each year the division reports to Conference on its work. As a further contribution to public awareness and discussion it has, over the years, published, usually under the name of a specific author, a series of Occasional Papers, taking up an issue or expounding good practice. Ministry and mission, however, has traditionally been seen as based on the local Society, or congregation, and therefore on its place in the wider community. As a result there has been a long tradition of concern for the inner city and community development rather than for economics or industry as such, even though the two cannot be separated. To illustrate this, in this extract, Clifford Hill reports on developments in London's docklands in the 1970s.

> Emphasis has already been laid upon the necessity of a proper understanding of the inner-city as the social environment for mission. Christians cannot expect to meet effectively the needs of an area they do not understand. The complexity of social issues and social forces that are at work in the inner-city cannot be overstressed. The inner-city requires careful analysis using the insights available to us through the disciplines of sociology and social anthropology.
>
> [. . .]
>
> 21. INDUSTRY
>
> The industrial boom of the 1960's that produced full employment and a rising standard of living for most workers in Britain has petered out into the frustration of the 70's. In East London the docks that stretch from the Tower of London to North Woolwich have been closing one after another since 1970. . . .
>
> With the rundown of the docks has come the closure of one industry after another. Recent Government policy has encouraged the expansion of industry in the North-East of England. But this has led to an increasing run-down of industry in the

South-East. Hardest hit has been the East End of London with its high dependency upon the docks and associated industries.

Newham and Tower Hamlets are boroughs that depend heavily upon the income derived from industry to support social services and rent and rate subsidies needed for an aging and dependent population. This has resulted in cut-backs in services that inevitably affect the poorest and most needy in the community.

Redundancies and sackings have revived East-Enders' memories of the bad old days of the 1920's and 30's – of unemployment, poverty, dole queues and the hated means test. East London, once in the vanguard of industrial expansion and the development of world trade, is today probably the foremost area in Britain suffering from all the social malaise resulting from the experience of advanced industrial and urban decay.

Clifford Hill, *Renewal in the Inner City*,
Occasional Paper 27, Methodist Home
Mission *c.* 1977, pp. 14–15.

The Religious Society of Friends (Quakers)

The Quakers have had an enviable reputation for commitment to social welfare. One only has to name Elizabeth Fry (prison reform), Joseph Lancaster (education) and Joseph Rowntree (factory reform and housing). They are, however, unique in their approach to their corporate responsibility. They work through personal concern and community consensus. This is illustrated by the book of discipline, *Quaker Faith and Practice*. It is largely a compendium of sayings, drawn from every part of Quaker history, representing the growing and changing attitudes to behaviour and responsibility. Here is set out a path to walk and a focus for meditative commitment as the individual discovers his or her vocation and joins with others of like mind. The following two examples stress the awareness that social responsibility includes a willingness to affect fundamental structural change.

23.19 Are you working towards the removal of social injustices? Have you attempted to examine their causes objectively, and are you ready to abandon old prejudices and think again? Do you as disciples of Christ, take a living interest in the social conditions of the district in which you live? Do you seek to promote the welfare of those in any kind of need and a just distribution of the resources of the world?

Queries, 1964.

23.53 It was once possible to argue that economic affairs might, like total abstinence, slavery, spiritual healing, be a field of particular interest to groups of Friends. We can now see that the economic order is not a peripheral concern, but central to the whole relationship between faith and practice. This is not a claim that, say, the interests in peace and international relations ought now to take a secondary place in our thoughts and prayers. Still less is it a demand that the Society should cease to be first and foremost a religious body, or to say that it should in any way neglect its spiritual foundations in favour of more good citizenship. It is rather that economic affairs are now so central to our whole existence that no other aspect of personal relationships or individual life-styles can now be looked at without first understanding what it means in terms of our national wealth, incomes, and their distribution.

David Eversley, 1976.

The British Council of Churches

Set up in 1942 under the influence of William Temple and other early British ecumenical leaders, the British Council of Churches (BCC) drew together into a consultative forum most of the mainstream churches, the greatest exception being the Roman Catholics. Its aim was to promote the unity of the Church through consultation and collaboration in diverse areas, including the socio-economic life of the country. From the start there was a division for social responsibility. Here we give three examples of reports illustrating these concerns.

The Church and industry

As with the Church of England, the BCC was concerned for the work of the churches in relation to industry. In this seminal report it noted the need to address the gap between the Church and the world of work. It recorded the emergence of various initiatives both abroad in France and Germany, and across the British Isles and various denominations. Its plea was to harness the new ecumenical enthusiasm of the post-war years for greater co-ordination and inter-church collaboration in entering what was in effect a new field of mission.

> As in the national, so in local situations, there is a new opportunity for Churches to be articulate together about the concern, on the bases which have been proposed. It is hoped, therefore, that locally as well as nationally, much prayer, study and discussion may take place before any action is embarked upon. It would be vital that responsible leaders of local industry, management and trade unions, Christians and others, should be brought into these consultations. For the problem is how best the Church *and* industry together can think about this concern and take responsible action.
>
> Meanwhile, individual ordained ministers or others in a local situation, whatever their differences about ends and means, should weigh the misunderstandings which arise if they decide 'to go it alone' without serious regard to the points which have been made in this document and in advance of further consideration by the Churches, especially if they propose to do this without consultation with others locally or regardless of their activities. The Social Responsibility Department of the British Council of Churches recently, considering difficulties which had arisen because of such individualistic action, has been concerned to emphasise the clear need for common courtesy to be exercised between denominations in this matter.

The Church and Industry, London,
British Council of Churches, 1958, p. 31.

Britain today and tomorrow

In the mid-1970s, partly as a response to the fiftieth anniversary of the COPEC Conference of 1924, the BCC embarked on a programme of study of different aspects of British life of the time where events were challenging the churches to find a voice. This resulted in a number of publications, usually in the form of reports. Two of these directly impinged on the socio-economic.

The first picks up the growing anxiety concerning work and unemployment. One of the issues was the possible disappearance of work for large numbers of people and what might be put in its place. Were people to be faced with useless lives wasted in idleness or were there alternatives such as the development of community service and creative leisure?

Work and employment

> 64. We have stressed the importance of a close relationship between our beliefs and our actions. . . . We believe this because our Christian faith bears witness to the presence of God in all his fullness in the historical person of Jesus. . . . So it is that our proposals must move forward from ideas to action that is feasible in the world as it is. . . . But action must also be related to a vision of what should be. The end to which our faith bears witness is one of perfection, completeness and fullness. Man's potential for being a creator and a decision maker sharing with God in carrying responsibility for the world needs to be kept before our eyes as the goal to which we strive. Of course, we may never reach that goal. It is the common human experience that we are prevented from such attainment. Theologians call that sin, both in its individual expression and in its expression in the behaviour of organisations and in the structure of society. . . .
>
> 65. The vision of what should be is revealed, in a practical way, in our values. . . .

i. First we value *truth* and the realism in policy making which comes from facing it squarely. In the employment situation in Britain today we have detected deep seated structural changes. . . . We believe that fundamentally new thinking is needed if we are to respond adequately. We applaud the variety of schemes devised at great cost to alleviate the short term effects of unemployment, but we must recognise that on their own they are not enough.
ii. Secondly we value a *concern for the disadvantaged* and the poor. . . . We cannot be a society motivated by Christian values if we fail to pay special attention to those who suffer most among us. . . .
iii. Thirdly we value *human fulfilment.* We see that this takes place chiefly in community, and we value work as a creative opportunity to this end. . . . At the same time, we recognise that some work is dehumanising and that there is a need for certain aspects of the work experience to be radically changed. . . . We place a high value, therefore, on a policy of full employment.
iv. Fourthly, we value *human equality.* We have discovered that unemployment is a deeply divisive element in modern society. . . .
v. Fifthly, we value *world brotherhood.*
[. . .]

67. We would like to go beyond the scope of some recent reports on employment and unemployment, which have rightly, concentrated on specific proposals for immediate action. We do this as well, but we also pay attention to certain matters of fundamental importance in the longer term. . . .
i. First, we propose that *the facts* of our changing economic situation should be more widely known and should be honestly faced. . . . These facts are: the increasing rate of technological change; the emergence of structural unemployment in most advanced countries; the transition from manufacturing to service employment; the significant movement of married women into employment; the special disadvantages encountered by certain groups; the continuing reality of poverty; the unequal

sharing of available work; the persistent regional inequalities; and potentially most seriously of all for the future, the considerable increase of labour supply that is projected. . . .
ii. Secondly, we propose that there should be *further substantial selective measures* to help those groups which suffer most as a result of unemployment. . . .
iii. Thirdly, we propose that there should be research into the development of a *new 'life ethic'* to give significance to our common productive process. . . . Today a new social purpose is needed. It should be rooted in the fulfilment of the potential of human beings and should build on an understanding of our common interdependence. . . .
iv. Fourthly, we propose that there should be greater investment in *the development of alternatives* to the dominant industrial products, methods of working and organisational styles of today. . . .
v. Fifthly, we propose that these objectives should always be considered in their *international context.*

Work or What? London,
British Council of Churches, 1977.

Taking poverty seriously

The second comes from the Community Resource Unit, which challenges the churches to take poverty seriously, not least in response to the gospel imperative, learned from the liberation theologians, of God's option for the poor.

. . . It is the local congregation, the gathered Christian community, living, worshipping and witnessing to its Faith in a specific local situation. It is with this third way of relating to society that this section is concerned. . . . almost all local churches have a quite unique contact with families in their neighbourhood . . . . It has also sponsored a great deal of social work with certain sections of the community . . . This needs to be recognised, and it ought to be spelled out. . . .

An identification with the poor would mean that the

churches begin to see poverty and deprivation through the eyes and experiences of those who are poor and deprived. This is incarnational living, and this is the responsibility of the local church. We are so often blind; just as the hungry need to be fed and the oppressed liberated, so the blind need to see.

We also need to recognise that the poor and the oppressed are not necessarily the same people. Nor is economic poverty the only form of poverty.... There are so many poor people all around us, waiting, perhaps longing, for an authentic Christian Community to share their experience and stand alongside them on their road to fullness of living. *Why are churches so reticent to identify and be identified with the poor and oppressed?* Surely this is a question that demands urgent attention.

Understanding Inequality, London,
British Council of Churches, 1977.

The consumer and consumerism

The BCC responded to a request by the Church Leaders' Conference (1972) for some work to be done on understanding the economic and financial structures of British society by setting up a Directorate of Economic Studies in 1974. A series of local study groups was commissioned to look at various aspects of the problem, out of which came the report *The Consumer Goods Society*. This outlined the nature of the market economy but paid most immediate attention to the notion of 'growth', which was seen to be driving contemporary understanding of economic well-being.

The Western economies, certainly in the last thirty years or so, have experienced a fairly steady rate of economic growth. There have been deliberate government policies to encourage growth. . . . There seems, however, to be a continually rising standard of expectation on the part of the mass population. There has been much debate in recent years about both the desirability and the possibility of continued growth. We need only to refer to the 'no-growth' debate and the studies to the 'limits to growth' made topical by the Club of Rome and responded to in this country by W. F. Beckerman and other economists. Also, whereas the bulk of the tradition of economic thought, since Adam Smith, has been concerned with the best use of a given amount of resources, since the second world war, while concern for efficiency has remained great, the study of the *growth* of resources has become an increasingly important part of economic analysis.

[. . .]

We . . . speak of a 'hopeful and critical realism' as the appropriate attitude to man and his possibilities, as illuminated by our understanding of God; 'realism', since we are dealing with what really is, not with ultimately unfounded aspirations; 'hopeful', since our belief in God as creator and over-ruler, and our human experience, lead us to believe in the possibility of real change, the purpose of which is to 'make and keep human life human' (Paul Lehmann); 'critical', since it takes full account of that deep-rooted tendency in man to fail to reach or even turn away from, his perceptions of the good, which in the Christian tradition is called sin.

These considerations suggest to us the following detailed bases for judging our economic system:

(a) How much opportunity does it give people for exercising real choice in the use of resources available to them, and thus for developing as autonomous beings?

(b) Does it depend upon the belief that the worth of a person is to be derived from his possessions or his income?

(c) Does it enhance or weaken the sense of inter-dependence between one person or group and another?

(d) Does it encourage a short term view in the use of raw materials and other resources?

[. . .]

We have identified a number of features of the consumer goods society which appear to us to be beneficial: the widening of the range of choice of goods and services and of occupation: the contribution it has made to increasing people's sense of being responsible persons: the way in which, as public

expenditure is largely financed out of public taxation, it has produced a convergence of public and private interests in the health of the economy: the sensitivity to consumer preferences and the efficient use of raw materials in mass production.
[. . .]

There is the danger that men and women may be valued not for who they are but for what they possess. Some producers stimulate conspicuous consumption by advertising that emphasises status and social esteem and they encourage the desire for goods by playing on people's greed, envy or insecurity. There is a threat to minority tastes from the spread of mass production. There is a danger that the really poor in our society may be overlooked amidst the general affluence and finally there is a weak sense of interdependence at a world level.

The Consumer Goods Society,
London, British Council of Churches,
1978, pp. 10, 20, 22, 24, 25.

The Church of Scotland

The Kirk, state and society

Despite being the Established Church, the relationship between the Church of Scotland and the Scottish people and the body politic is very different from that in Erastian England. This article brings out the historic difference and the unique place of the General Assembly of the church. What will happen under devolution and the restoration of the Scottish Parliament will only be known as events unfold. In this next excerpt Duncan Forrester describes this relationship.

The overall stress in the *Article Declaratory* [part of the 1929 union] is on the Church of Scotland as a *national* church, 'representative of the Christian Faith of the Scottish people' with a distinctive call to bring the ordinances of religion to the people of every parish. It is only in this context that establishment, meaning simply the legal recognition of the

Church by the state, and a mutual commitment to reciprocal responsibilities, is to be understood. . . .

The democratic or populist self-understanding of the Kirk, its national character, its Calvinist theology, its insistence on its own spiritual independence and responsibility *for* (rather than *to*) the state, together with its social and geographical distance from the main power centre in the UK have all influenced the way the Church of Scotland contributes to public debate on issues of politics, social policy and the economy. . . .

A generally acknowledged high point in the Church of Scotland's contribution to public affairs was the Commission for the Interpretation of God's will in the Present Crisis which met during the war years from 1940–45. . . . The task was therefore seen as primarily an evangelical one: how to understand and proclaim the Gospel in the current circumstances. . . .

The gospel, the Commission argues, cannot be separated from Christian values, nor can either be presented in abstraction from the problems of the world. But how may Christian values and principles be made operational in relation to public issues? The Commission affirms emphatically the relevance of New Testament ethics, but recognizes that there are technical decisions in which Christian theology can give no precise guidance.

Nevertheless, in *every* problem there is a spiritual and ethical dimension. In dealing with such matters theologians and secular experts between them must develop 'middle axioms' or 'certain secondary and more specialised principles which exhibit the relevance of the ruling principles to the particular field of action in which guidance is needed'. . . .

Sadly it would be misleading to suggest that the Baillie Commission provided an approach which shaped several decades of the Church of Scotland's contribution to public debate. . . . After 1945 the Church was not slow to advise or criticise government but did not commonly give much attention to the theological or ecclesiastical grounding of statements, or to the promotion of 'active citizenship'.

The Church and Nation Committee

The annual debate in the General Assembly on the report of the Church and Nation Committee is the most obvious and well publicised interface between the Church of Scotland and public affairs. The Assembly is crowded, and the Lord High Commissioner is invariably in his place in the gallery, often accompanied by leading politicians, ministers and public figures. The media usually give more attention to this debate than to any other part of the Assembly's proceedings. . . . After the sitting the committee's report and the deliverances are sent to Government ministers, to all Scottish MPs and to a wide range of public bodies. . . .

As a creature of the Assembly the committee does not have unfettered control of its own agenda. In practice it decides that it wants to study certain questions, but the Assembly can, and often does, add issues that are sometimes unwelcome . . .

This unevenness makes it an unrewarding experience to work through a series of Church and Nation reports. So much is ephemeral, or ill-thought out; so little seems to present a distinctive Christian and Calvinist social teaching, clearly grounded in Christian and theological premises. Only too often the committee and the Assembly have apparently seen their task as articulating Scottish opinion, or Scottish Christian opinion, or Kirk opinion at a particular moment in a rather diffuse fashion.

Duncan Forrester, 'The Church and Public Policy',
Scottish Affairs 4, Summer 1993,pp. 69–74.

Reports of the Church and Nation Committee

Reports from the various divisions of the Assembly are contained in the compendious Annual Report of Assembly, which is really a set of extended minutes. There are comparatively few published reports for the wider public. To hear the voice of the church it is necessary to work one's way through these rather dense records. Over the period being covered, however, there were comparatively few major economic issues debated:

1954	Atomic energy.
1956	The Church and industrial society.
1962	A response to the Toothill Committee on the Scottish economy.
	Railway and colliery closures.
1970	The struggle for the quality of life – ecology and technology.
1973–74	The oil industry.
1976	Urban deprivation.

Excerpts from four examples will illustrate the way of working.

1956 Church and industrial society

The main foundation of progress and prosperity in the industrial realm lies in the attainment of new and happier human relationships, a new spirit of understanding, trust and partnership. . . .

A truth that has become clear is that industry has developed its organisational structures without reference to the basic need of human nature. . . . Not only is he given a purpose which has little relationship to himself as a man, he is in all probability given a task which has no relation to anything he can see or understand. He must simply carry out the task to its predetermined rhythm . . .

The structure of human relations in industry is founded upon and takes its shape and quality from an economic principle, and until this foundation is relaid, adjustments of the structure above it and attempts to inject a new spirit will amount to little more than tinkering with a matter of the most vital importance. The economic principle is the ownership of the income of industry, or in other words the distribution of profit among the factors in production – capital, management and labour.

. . . To be real and therapeutic, profit sharing must be based on justice, upon the civic entitlement of members of a society which claims to be democratic, and must be the foundation of a structure in industry which gives expression to the common interest of capital, management and labour, and in particular creates and fosters a conscious awareness of partnership in the minds of employees.

Here we find ourselves with our non-Christian fellow-men in a fabric of human relationships, and the most crucial ones are in industry. In these industrial relationships men spend the greatest part of their waking hours throughout their stay in this world. Here each gets his picture and estimate of himself and his place and value in the human scheme of things. Here he should find God and brotherhood as experienced realities.

. . . In this field the influence of the Industrial Chaplain has been a factor of inestimable value in creating a new atmosphere of interest and concern. . . . Responsibility [primarily] rests upon the laymen of the Church in industry. The door is open to them only, and they must combine study and action. Through the Scottish Christian Industrial Order the Church of Scotland has offered a means for this dual function. Men of all grades of industry are invited to take their stand together on the common ground of their Faith and their loyalty to the Christian ethic, and to combine their experience, their knowledge and their faith for their common illumination and guidance, so that individually and collectively they may make their convictions and influence effective at all levels within the existing structures in the places where they are employed, in joint-consultation organisations, in trade unions and managerial societies.

1973 and 1974 North Sea oil

In response to a motion (deliverance) of the General Assembly, John Francis and Norman Swann presented a report in 1973 commending research set out in a report *Scotland in Turmoil,* which found that church people of all denominations, at both

Presbytery and parish levels, had been among those most actively concerned about the quality of life. Areas of concern were divided into two.

1) At national level, issues such as: government offices; research in underwater technology; jobs for local personnel; planning decisions; public discussion; environmental impact; compensation, especially for accidents; and housing costs.
2) At local level, issues such as: welcoming and integrating newcomers; community structures; medical facilities; young people and education provision; and ecumenical co-operation.

> . . . North Sea Oil and Gas are only a short term and partial solution to long term unemployment in Scotland. They could be a springboard; not a featherbed.
>
> For the comparatively short period of intense oil and gas related activity the relevant coastal communities, however, can expect not only to have minimal unemployment but also to experience influxes of workers, temporary and permanent. . . . Considerable employment will also be generated temporarily in the creation of large scale improvements to the Scottish infrastructure. Other jobs will be generated in relation both to the initiative of management in Scotland taking advantage of oil and gas opportunities and also to the state of industrial relations on which, to a major extent, depend quality and delivery dates. . . . Long term stability, however, could benefit materially from using the improved infrastructure.
>
> As employment of the right type is such an important factor in the well being of communities, the churches in the oil related areas are requested to concern themselves openly and actively at both Presbytery and parish level. Not only with the short term fluctuations of employment, but also with the long term issues.

Church and Nation report, 1973

The following year a second report, *Scotland's Pipedream*, presented a study of Peterhead as a case study.

> There is cause, however, for considerable concern about the husbandry of the fishing resources of the North Sea. . . . It seems important that the sustainable fishing yield should be recognised and enforced since otherwise overfishing will quickly reduce the viability of the industry.
>
> The lack of housing has been strangling any orderly development in Peterhead. . . . Decisive official intervention to retrieve this situation became urgently necessary, since otherwise the houses would simply not be built.
>
> Money in increasing quantities has brought almost universal problems to Peterhead as underage drinking, increased betting and gambling, some prostitution, a significant malaise that land and property deals have been realising undue profits, mistrust, envy, greed, unhappiness in apparently comfortable homes, more alcoholism. On the credit side the poverty of a generation ago and unemployment, the greatest social and moral polluter of them all, have been banished, possibly for a long time, industrial relations and fish permitting. Nevertheless, the materialistic philosophy that 'money can buy it all' may mean that the spiritual scars of prosperity will be deeper and more permanent than any physical abuse of the environment.
>
> A sense of responsibility to the groups, community and society which make prosperity possible seems to be much less general. It would seem that parents, schools and colleges throughout the country might do much more . . . to encourage a greater sense of responsibility between the individual and his groups, community and society.
>
> There would seem to be a case for the application of scheduling techniques that are commonplace to most industrial operations. This might take the form of a Project Group of mixed disciplines. . . . By analogy with the New Town procedure, a single decision centre at a community level would have major advantages quite apart from streamlining the planning

controls and expediting the almost inevitable modifications to the Development plan for the area.

. . . all credit is due to those Christians who give of their time and talents to the common good, whether as elected officials or in any other capacity. A broadening of this interest and effort, however, is required in almost any community faced with sudden industrial prosperity. . . . It would be worthwhile for all Christian groups regularly to ask themselves whether they have become exclusive or do open their ranks effectively to newcomers to the area. . . . The Church can also help in immediately practical ways by working together with other denominations in flexible community groups to try to meet any pressing social, moral or spiritual needs which seem to be within the range of their talents and resources.

1976 Urban deprivation

This was the response of the Church and Nation Committee (in its annual report) to a Scottish Office report on deprivation, *Census Indicators of Urban Deprivation.*

[T]here are other areas of deprivation which require to be identified and their causes discovered. Basically there is a moral and spiritual malaise which is a cause both of the conditions themselves and of the discontent engendered by them; the Church has a function in overcoming both the deprivation and the malaise.

. . . [There is an issue of] depopulation in the rural areas. Country dwellers have been deprived of local schools and of schoolmasters, of doctors, and now in many parishes of ministers. . . . [R]ail and bus services have been withdrawn.

Within both urban and rural communities there are many in new houses who find themselves strangers among strangers. This applies particularly in urban areas to people who have moved to high-rise flats where difficulties are magnified, for adults by lack of communal meeting places and for children by lack of play areas. . . . [T]here is a great opportunity for

> the Church to introduce that sense of community which is its particular function as a fellowship, provided that the congregation is prepared to be the agent of pastoral concern in the community.
>
> It [the report *Protection against Vandalism* (Home Office 1975)] pays no attention to the underlying malaise, the deprivation which drives these young people to vandalism. In this matter there are two vital features, one being the unacceptably high rate of unemployment amongst school leavers, and the other the quality of family life. . . . Here the Church should become the supportive community for the Christian family.
>
> The Church with its Gospel is called to give to areas of deprivation and disadvantage a sense of community, to family life a new vitality, and to the individual a new sense of responsibility. It can in essence become the heart of the community stimulating it to a new kind of life and serving it in the name of Christ. But it can only do so if its members accept the challenge of the situation. . . . It is one of the difficulties of the local Church in some areas that they are communities where leaders and potential leaders move out and not in. . . . It must be contended, however, that the Church has a duty not only to serve the community, but to change it. Attitudes must be changed, and attitudes cannot be changed either by a process of legislation or by a multiplication of social workers.

Roman Catholicism

The fourth approach to the discussion of social ethics comes from the Roman Catholic Church. This focuses on the function of the magisterium, or teaching function of the church. The pope and the bishops, assisted by their advisors in the Vatican and elsewhere and through theological discussion, have the pastoral task to guide the church and to witness before the world in the understanding and practice of God's will for human persons and society. This takes the form of an evolving tradition of teaching, reaching back to and interpreting the apostolic faith in the New Testament. This teaching is expressed in two ways:

the pronouncements and documents of the universal councils of the church and the encyclicals of the popes as *pastor pastorum*. National bishops' councils and individual bishops interpret this in the local situation.

The modern phase of Catholic social teaching is normally understood as stemming from Leo XIII's encyclical *Rerum Novarum* (1891), the first significant attempt to react to the rise of socialism and democracy in the nineteenth century. It has been followed, especially since the Second World War, by a remarkable series of encyclicals, of which John XXIII's *Mater et Magistra* (1961) and *Pacem in Terris* (1963), Paul VI's *Populorum Progressio* (1967) and *Octogesima Adveniens* (1971) and John Paul II's *Redemptor Hominis* (1979) are the most significant to fall in the period with which this chapter is concerned. To this must be added *Gaudium et Spes* (1965) from the Second Vatican Council (1962–65).

The general thrust of this teaching can be summed up in the frequently used phrase 'the common good'. This implies, regardless of faith or race, a universal mutuality and responsibility both between individuals and within the structures and forces in society. For our present concerns three themes recur: the place of the state in ordering society; the nature of work; and social justice. There was something of a shift from an assumption about natural justice to the more radical approaches of liberation theology from the mid 1960s. The key Medellin conference (1968), which Pope Paul VI attended, claimed the 'option for the poor' as the centre of social justice; followed by Puebla, attended by Pope John Paul II (1979). While the thrust of the new perspective was broadly welcomed, Rome was also wary of the possibility of a surrender to Marxism. The following extracts are designed to indicate something of this way of working and the relevant themes.

However, in Britain Catholicism was still emerging from its position as an alien faith whose disabilities had only fairly recently been removed. Reinforced by Rome's traditional suspicion of the modern world, the Catholic Church tended to eschew participation in public affairs. But the new vision engendered by

Vatican II, with its ecumenical and worldwide vision, allowed the growing pressure to enter into the mainstream of ecclesiastical and political life to express itself. Nevertheless it was not until the 1980s, when Cardinal Hume was Archbishop of Westminster, that Catholicism came to centre stage. This development will be discussed in the next chapter.

Work and unemployment

> 54. The present advance in scientific knowledge and productive technology clearly puts it within the power of the public authority to a much greater degree than ever before to reduce imbalances which may exist between different branches of the economy or between different regions within the same country or even between different peoples of the world. It also puts into the hands of public authority a greater means for limiting fluctuations in the economy and for providing effective measures to prevent the recurrence of mass unemployment. Hence the insistent demands on those in authority – since they are responsible for the common good – to increase the degree and scope of their activities in the economic sphere, and to devise ways and means and set the necessary machinery in motion for the attainment of this end.
>
> 55. But however extensive and far reaching the influence of the state on the economy may be, it must never be exerted to the extent of depriving the individual citizen of his freedom of action. It must rather augment his freedom while effectually guaranteeing the protection of his essential personal rights. Among these is a man's right and duty to be primarily responsible for his own upkeep and that of his family. Hence every economic system must permit and facilitate the free development of productive activity. [. . .]
>
> 65. . . . Moreover, we consider it altogether vital that the numerous intermediary bodies and corporate enterprises . . . be really autonomous, and loyally collaborate in pursuit of their own specific interests and those of the common good. For these groups must themselves necessarily present the form

and substance of true community, and this will only be the case if they treat their individual members as human persons and encourage them to take an active part in the ordering of their lives. . . .

[. . .]

71. We therefore consider it our duty to reaffirm that the remuneration of work is not something that can be left to the laws of the market place; nor should it be a decision left to the will of the more powerful. It must be determined in accordance with justice and equity; which means that workers must be paid a wage which allows them to live a truly human life and to fulfil their family obligations in a worthy manner. Other factors too enter . . . the effective contribution each individual makes. . . the financial state of the company . . . the requirement of the general good . . .

Mater et Magistra (1961).

Production and people

64 . . . [T]echnical progress, an inventive spirit, an eagerness to create and to expand enterprises, the application of methods of production . . . must be promoted. The fundamental purpose of this production is not the mere increase of products nor profit or control but rather the service of man, and indeed of the whole man with regard for the full range of his material needs and the demands of his intellectual, moral, spiritual, and religious life. . . . Consequently, economic activity is to be carried on according to its own methods and laws within the limits of the moral order, so that God's plan for mankind may be realised.

65. Economic development must remain under man's determination and must not be left to the judgement of a few men or groups possessing too much economic power or of the political community alone or of certain more powerful nations. . . .

67. Human labour which is expended in the production and exchange of goods or in the performance of economic services

is superior to other elements of economic life, for the latter have only the nature of tools.

68. In economic enterprises it is persons who are joined together, that is, free and independent human beings created in the image of God. Therefore, taking account of the prerogatives of each – owners or employers, management or labour – and without doing harm to the necessary unity of management, the active sharing of all in the administration and profits of these enterprises in ways properly to be determined should be promoted. Since more often, however, decisions concerning economic and social conditions, on which the future lot of the workers and their children depends, are not made within the business itself but by institutions on a higher level, the workers themselves should have a share also in determining these conditions – in person or through freely elected delegates.

Gaudium et Spes (1965).

The common good

The year 1979 saw the election of Karol Wojtyla as Pope John Paul II, a Pole who broke the Italian monopoly of the post-Renaissance papacy. It also ushered in a new era within the church, in which the radical hopes engendered by Vatican II began to fade and a new conservatism entered. This, Pope John Paul's first encyclical, was written on his return from Puebla (Latin America). It reveals both the desire to consolidate what he sees as the gains of the Council with a suspicion of external ideologies and conflictual philosophies. Nevertheless, although the central theme is redemption in Christ, he is concerned to show that the challenge to create social justice is part of that redemption process. To do this he reaffirms the concept of the common good.

16.2. If we make bold to describe man's situation in the modern world as far removed from the objective demands of the moral order, from the exigencies of justice, and still more from social love, we do so because this is confirmed by well-known facts and comparisons that have already on various occasions found an echo in the pages of statements by the popes, the council and the synod.

[. . .]

16.4. So widespread is the phenomenon that it brings into question the financial, monetary, production and commercial mechanisms that, resting on various political pressures, support the world economy. These are proving incapable either of remedying the unjust social situations inherited from the past or of dealing with the urgent challenges and ethical demands of the present.

[. . .]

16.6 . . . The principle of solidarity, in a wide sense, must inspire the effective search for appropriate institutions and mechanisms, whether in the sector of trade, where the laws of healthy competition must be allowed to lead the way, or on the level of a wider and more immediate redistribution of riches and of control over them in order that the economically developing peoples may be able not only to satisfy their essential needs but also to advance gradually and effectively.

[. . .]

17.3. The Declaration of Human Rights . . . had as its aim . . . to create the basis for continual revision of programmes, systems and regimes precisely from this single fundamental point of view, namely the welfare of man – or, let us say, of the person in the community – which must, as a fundamental factor in the common good, constitute the essential criterion for all programmes, systems and regimes.

[. . .]

17.5. The essential sense of the state, as a political community, consists in that the society and people composing it are master and sovereign of their own destiny. . . .

17.6. The Church has always taught the duty to act for the common good and, in so doing, has likewise educated good citizens for each state. Furthermore, she has always taught that the fundamental duty of power is solicitude for the common good of society; this is what gives power its fundamental rights.

> Precisely in the name of these premises of the objective ethical order, the rights of power can only be understood on the basis of respect for the objective and inviolable rights of man. The common good that authority in the state serves is brought to full realization only when all the citizens are sure of their rights.
>
> *Redemptor Hominis* (1979).

2 Industrial Mission

Perhaps the most significant response to the challenges of the economic and industrial world in the second half of the twentieth century has been the emergence of Industrial Mission (IM). This section attempts to fill out something of the story and activities and thinking of IM. By its very nature it has been a diffuse and changing activity. The fragmented structures of the Church have meant that initiatives can be very local and sometimes ephemeral. The world of industry and patterns of employment have been changing, calling forth different responses. There are also differing theological positions each with its own evaluation of the challenges offered.

The changing Industrial Mission scene

This excerpt is taken from the first paper in a collection published in 1985 when the Theology Development Group (TDG) of the Industrial Mission Association (IMA) was engaged in a review of IM strategy in the mid-1980s. However, it conveniently summarizes the first phases of IM with which this chapter is concerned. It also shows how IM in the late 1970s and into the 80s was able to respond to the shift in British industrial life.

> We are aware of the great changes that have taken place in both society as a whole and in our economic life in particular. The Britain of 1984 is different from the Britain of 1944. The decline of manufacturing industries, with which IM has been particularly associated, has been strongly marked. We

are becoming a service economy and, perhaps, we may indeed speak, in Galbraith's phrase, of a 'post-industrial state'. . . . In this changing scene members of the TDG were clear about two basic points for IM: (1) that IM should stay with the changes and not be locked into some order that is passing away; and (2) that IM should stay with the victims of change and not leave them alone because IM is concerned with the 'broken heart'. . . .

It would be odd, if in the context of the changes of the last 40 years, the Industrial Mission had itself not changed; at any rate in emphasis, interests and even organisation. . . . To that may be added the simple point that there never was a 'classic theory' of Industrial Mission. No style was ever common to the churches, even in the earliest days. There was never a thought out theology and strategy. But there was a deep concern for industrial life. . . . The major written contributions from Sheffield did not emerge until the mission there was well over a decade into its work and the Church Assembly working party was busy with plans for a national policy. Even after this time a visit to Ralph Stevens in Birmingham or Bill Gowland in Luton was a very different experience from a stay with Ted Wickham in Sheffield or with Colin Cuttell in South London. Furthermore those chaplains who left Sheffield to lead other pieces of work, together with those who went there for 'training' all developed their own style. It was not only a matter of Sheffield training but of understanding the actual industrial situation into which they were now put, to say nothing of their own insights, economic and theological. It was also a matter of the nature of diocesan policy, both then and now. One important thing to bear in mind throughout is the fact that resources available to Industrial Mission from the churches have remained virtually static for some twenty years. . . .

In those early days of expansion, there were, however, fairly broad agreements. Of these, perhaps the greatest was the need to get inside places of employment. This was what had never been satisfactorily achieved in earlier attempts to engage the world of work. No longer was it deemed useful to stand at the factory gates and hail the passing throng. There must be some closer and steadier relationship with the industrial culture and the people, in particular, who led in shaping it. . . . It was thus a matter of 'getting into industry'; and that meant places of employment and thereafter the building up of a great network of relationships. . . .

We should be wrong in thinking, however, that because such a style of IM started from a baseline of visitation inside places of employment that it was, in fact, merely factory centred. . . . [B]ut it was also an important springboard for extremely crucial pieces of work outside factories: the study groups, the management groups, attendance at trade union meetings, involvement in a variety of industrial activities promoted by other bodies. These were major projects and they were issue centred. There was, in particular, a good deal of both formal and informal adult education concerned with industrial issues, problems in social ethics, biblical and theological studies and general discussion groups. . . .

Next, in those days, the alienation of ordinary working class people from the churches was clearly recognised. The literature of the *Christian Newsletter* may have been influential. . . . The books about developments in France almost certainly reached a wider public. . . . There was a good deal about the relationship between the church and people in England for the student to read and understand the nature of the abyss but in IM circles two books clinched the argument once and for all: Wickham's book and Michael Jackson's translation of the work of the sociological consultant to the French Church, Canon Boulard. . . . There must be a correlation of the Christian Gospel with them all. The theological method of Paul Tillich appeared at just the right time.

Overall, too, there was a fairly distinctive style, whatever the *modus operandi*. Chaplains did not front movements. . . . The chaplain was not seen as an executive instrument; rather he was seen as a person who encouraged others to discharge what was implicit in their roles and also discover others who should take part in the processes of industrial life in all their variety and complexity. IM did not aspire to be a clerically dominated movement. . . . Against the more confrontational style of parts of churchly activity today this must seem rather bland. Indeed I have heard it argued that we accepted the injustices and deprivations of the time. I do not think that this is the case. A distinction has to be drawn between accepting something and tolerating it. . . . Since we were agreed that most of all we wanted access to the works we tolerated what we could not avoid. After all this was no more than some of us had done in urban parishes and in family pastoral work. . . . What we realised, as people in later time have recognised, is that crusading within factories is rather different from campaigning outside them. If the chaplain is the recipient of industrial hospitality, when visits are willing to be received then there must, of necessity, be a style which though it may be candid cannot easily be confrontational. . . .

Regardless of style, however, IM was criticised then, as it is criticised now, for being political. This is a generalised term often meaning no more than not seeming to support the view of the critic. On other occasions it is more serious and relates to the way in which the whole Church does its work. [Also] there are managers who seem to suspect a conspiracy every time a chaplain is seen talking to a trade union official and there are union men who consider time spent with managers is merely toadying to the agents of capitalism. . . . We shall deal with it most satisfactorily by arguing the case for Christian ministry among all men whom God has created and redeemed. All the rest savours of nitpicking defensiveness.

. . . It always takes time to get established because it depends upon the quality and confidence of the relationships that come into being. After their firm foundations then explorations into other aspects of industrial life can follow: the development of projects, the extension of contacts into various industrial and economic projections, the taking up of particular causes, and involvement in a number of practical activities.

Of all those extensions the most ambitious was the marking out of a national policy. [Report, *The Task of the Church in*

Relation to Industry. See next excerpt.] . . . It was a forlorn hope. In the first place neither the Church of England nor a whole industry operated in such an executive framework. Secondly the resources could never be deployed. . . . The liaison with London centred industry was much more rewarding and a network of sorts did develop which involved, for some time, the larger companies and the industrial chaplains in post at that time.

Industrial mission, of course, took some colouration both from the theological and industrial thinking of the times. William Temple's activities and writings were influential in the immediate post-war period. The outlook of Reinhold Niebuhr was also known. As the chaplains themselves became more familiar with the industrial landscape they branched out into various aspects of industrial theory and practice. These were investigations into prophetic religion, God speaking to man and not simply man aspiring to the infinite God. . . .

. . . [T]he development of an appropriate religious life for a secular based laity may need to be tackled afresh. For example, not enough attention was ever paid to the regular eucharists held in Sheffield Cathedral in earlier times, nor the number of people who were confirmed in the Anglican Church or prepared for full membership of other churches in the area. There was a very religious side to the old Sheffield Industrial Mission which never got any publicity and never got written up. (We regarded it as part of Bonhoeffer's secret discipline.)

On the other hand we have to ask ourselves how much development was there ever going to be in the contact made in work places which were sustained by regular visits. . . . It was rather like routine parish visiting. It sustained a simple relationship and oiled parts of the total activity. . . . But if visits became expected then their abandonment, particularly without explanation, could lead to feeling of rejection. . . .

Originally the hope was that large numbers of lay people would ally themselves with IM and exercise an apostolate from their role occupancy in industry. . . . Now attention is drawn not to this kind of *corps d'elite* but to all who are concerned with issues and are victims of change. The concern to do something for the many people who are unemployed and deprived as a result is causing a major shift in the outlook, practice and sympathies of chaplains. . . .

[Also] due weight must be given to the considerable IM programme of the Church of Scotland, with the minority churches associated with it. There is a great deal going on there which includes a large amount of factory visitation, conference work, social and political lobbying for Scottish industry and causes and a steady stream of publications. Again the development of ecumenical co-operation and planning has been a considerable achievement.

The ecumenical note is not explicitly struck in the following papers but it is implied throughout; and indeed is fundamental to all the work. . . .

Industrial Mission is changing but, now it also has a history, in which pledges were given. The chaplains and their appointing churches asked the leaders of industry to 'take us seriously'. In order to encourage them to do so we offered them a stable and continuous relationship. . . . It was to be part of a permanent strategy. Those who did not proceed in this fashion found to their cost that casual or stop–go work reaped little reward and each attempt at renewal became harder and harder.

Above all, perhaps, we offered a commitment to ordinary working people; those who had never had any consistent relationship with the Church. . . .

Now we are faced with an endemic social evil in the form of unemployment. . . . [W]e, as chaplains have thought it right to respond to this both by participation in worthy schemes with and for the unemployed and also by attending to the intractable issues that beset our society.

Changing Industrial Mission: Models and Hopes,
William Temple Foundation, 1985, pp. 1–11.

The vision for Industrial Mission

The report *The Task of the Church in Relation to Industry* (1959) came from a study inaugurated by the Church Assembly of the Church of England to suggest a coherent policy in relation to the growing range of experimental ministries started since the Second World War. It therefore maps a threefold pattern of supporting and developing industrial concerns within and through the church. This is the second extract from this report which was so influential on subsequent policy, even though some of its recommendations were not able to overcome diocesan independency.

> The overall picture is a very mixed one, both encouraging and discouraging. As an aggregate, the Church's work in industry adds up to a very sizable programme, though in relation to the size of British industry it is, of course, small. [Dioceses vary,] some have little directly industrial work in hand, others have made it a matter of high priority. Nor is it easy to assess accurately the quality of work in any area for many reasons, though it is clear that among the difficulties are the very different presuppositions behind the work, the different expectations of what might be accomplished, and the different standards about what should be attempted. Nonetheless, we can attempt a summary of what is going on, and distinguish different categories within it.
>
> First there is the work in industry done in the course of normal parish work. . . . [I]n many parishes the parish priest has a close contact with one or more factories in his parish, in which he knows the people, visits particular individuals, and may regularly visit throughout the works. . . . [T]he parish in which the incumbent has the easiest and most natural contact with the factory of the area, is the small town parish set within a larger rural area. . . . [T]hey nonetheless have rarely had special training for what is a complex field, and also that the work, once undertaken, is so easily terminated when a man leaves . . . [I]f there is to be any extension of this work, cer-

tainly among the vast number of *small* works and factories, the burden must largely fall on the parish clergy. It raises the question of the appropriate theological, sociological and practical training of men for competence in this work.

Falling within the work radiating from the parish [is] the Industrial Christian Fellowship. The Fellowship was formed as long ago as 1920 by a fusion of two older social agencies of the Church – the Christian Social Union and the Navvy Mission. . . . [T]here is a small general staff in London responsible for the organisation, its field work is carried by a number of lay missioners who are lay readers deployed to visit industrial establishments in the localities where they are situated. . . . The ICF has other activities . . . the arranging of Industrial Sunday . . . the annual service before the Trades Union Congress, and . . . the publication of literature . . .

Since the second world war, an entirely new pattern of industrial work has been developed in various industrial centres of the country. The new projects are very different from one another for many reasons and all bear the imprint of the men who have pioneered them. But there are also similarities . . . They are all localised projects and all of them owe their existence directly to particular bishops who have appointed men to act on their behalf in establishing relationships with the industrial institutions in the diocese. . . . [T]his new pattern of work has had greater status in the eyes of both the Church and industry than earlier work of the Church in this field, for a variety of reasons – the bishop has been clearly identified with it; men have been specially selected for their likely competence in this field, and the work, through concentration, has been able to 'go deep'. . . . The new pattern developed from the wartime precedent when one or two bishops appointed full-time chaplains to large Government Ordnance Factories . . . but it was a short step . . . to an appointment to a steel or automobile city. . . . There has been a loose but fairly regular relationship between these various pieces of work maintained through the men directing them. Undoubtedly they have stimulated one another, and some have grown directly out of others.

A great range of work is in hand in these centres, with full-time staffs, though sometimes supplemented by part-time assistance from parish ministers. The kind of things done are . . .:

A concerted attempt to know the *personae* of the basic industry and the larger works of the area . . .

Frequently the regular visitation of the works where the productive process permits, and always after agreement both with management and Trade Unions, shop stewards' committees and works councils, etc.

The organisation of informal groups of men at work for study and discussion . . .

Pastoral work, that inevitably arises . . .

Education and Training work in company schemes . . .

'Learning to earning' conferences for boys and girls.

Introductory courses.

Day Continuation School for the local authorities.

Study groups for apprentices and junior operatives.

Foremen courses.

Management Courses, both at plant level and in schemes provided by Employers' Federations, professional management associations; etc.

Visiting Trades Union meetings and conferences and professional associations.

Organising residential courses.

Representing a point of view within the councils of the diocese, assisting junior clergy training; . . .

Training laymen in industry to make a responsible contribution through their jobs and within their associations and assisting them to take full responsibility for running projects within their own works and in their own groups.

All the men directing these initiatives would testify to the welcome given . . . where it has been done with sensitivity, respect for the works' community in its own right and not merely as a pool for fishing for converts and where intelligent respect for the works' primary purpose, to produce, is shown.

. . . [There are] weaknesses . . . that should be fully recognised and which any overall policy of the Church must be designed to meet.

. . . [W]ork can weaken and fall down, not only through the departure of a man in the field to pastures new, but also through a change of bishop . . . Experience suggests that there should always be a board of clergy and laity, industrialists and Trade Unionists, to carry responsibility for maintenance and continuity of Industrial Mission, though there are clearly factors in man power that are beyond its control.

. . . [S]ome [problems] can only be dissolved by planning *within a context larger than the diocese*. . . . [E.g.] recruitment, training and deployment of suitable men . . . finance. . . . Industrial Mission projects can become self-supporting, even with considerable staffs – but it is also clear that financial help for their first few years must be a charge on the Church, and not every diocese is able to meet this. . . . [There are] problems of communication associated with the efficient development of the work . . .

. . . [There exists] the need for some kind of national structure of Industrial Mission that can accept responsibility for the development and extension of the work from one area to another, across diocesan boundaries . . .

Among the weaknesses we are also bound to take note of the differences of theological and sociological presuppositions behind the various industrial projects. . . . At its service it needs a theology compounded of distinctive insights, with a secular cutting-edge and clear social orientation. . . .

[T]he men engaged in this work have an ecumenical outlook, dictated not least by the realities of the work they are engaged in. This cannot be a field for ecumenical narrowness. . . . [T]he leaders of Churches and the appropriate boards of denominations have a duty to face this problem, not leaving it just to the purely advisory role of the British Council of Churches.

'It is very desirable that the Church should, at national level, have good contacts.'

It remains to be said – and it cannot be said too often – that the work of the Church in industry is essentially the day to day, unseen work of the laity in their secular jobs. If we have dwelt so largely on the contribution of the ministry of the Church, both parochial and specialised, it is because theirs is a catalytic role to stimulate the body of the Church . . . but their role is ancillary, as servant of the servants of God, and the final test of the industrial mission of the Church will be the quality of men and women, and the quality of their thinking and actions, within the world of industry.

The Task of the Church in Relation to Industry,
Church Information Office, 1959, pp. 14–25.

The manifesto of Industrial Mission

E. R. Wickham's book *Church and People in an Industrial City*, a study of Sheffield, served for many practitioners and others as the manifesto for industrial mission. Its foundation was the discerned alienation of the working classes and industrial culture from the Church. This was argued for through a sustained examination of the data available on Sheffield. Wickham then propounded a theological and missiological strategy. He was also one of the influential pioneers of post-war Industrial Mission. The Sheffield Industrial Mission became the primary model and source of training and recruitment for work elsewhere. In these paragraphs he sets out his theological perspectives that underline his vision. Surprisingly to us today this included a hope that there could emerge a Christian community from within the industrial world that would take on its own shape and activity. His premise is that Christianity is concerned for the life of this world in a radical secular way. The Kingdom of God impinges on and should shape the day-to-day world not only of individuals but also of institutions and cultures. William Temple is clearly one of his theological sources but so were Dietrich Bonhoeffer, whose *Letters and Papers from Prison* were making at that time their first impact on British theology, and Martin Buber, the seminal Jewish philosopher. Later Industrial Mission was also strongly influenced by Reinhold Niebuhr's *Moral Man and Immoral Society* (1932, reprinted by SCM Press, 1963) and from the mid-1960s liberation theology was further to radicalize IM thinking.

A secular understanding of the Gospel

Christianity is about the meaning of human life and history, of ordinary secular history which is the only kind there is, and if true, true for every man . . . which not only means God has wrought mighty works in history, but also that all secular history permits a unique interpretation in relation to which those acts themselves have meaning. This is not to dispense with the concept of revelation; on the contrary it is to insist that among the various interpretations that men can put on the meaning of life and on the sequence of events that make up history, Christianity gives us a certain interpretation which is no less than the situation as God himself sees it. . . . [Y]et not merely to be accepted because it is Biblical, but because ultimately, when discovered through all those devious ways in which it is disclosed to us, it is found to be profoundly adequate, not just as it were to a religious instinct, but to our experience of life. . . .

The major theme of that revelation and interpretation is that there is a potential in history that God wills to realise, and an end for which the whole creation groans and travails . . . Men make their history, and it is written in blood, sweat and tears, ever on the verge of greater possibilities of good and evil . . . God too is at work in his creation, confronting men, calling them, inspiring them, and in ways we may not define – only leaving them men, with some remnants of His image and likeness. . . .

Men are making their history, and in every generation and epoch there are lesser ends, modest ends to be realised, by hard means, all of which are to be tested by the meaning of history and the greater purpose to which the creation travails. And here the qualities of the Kingdom are demanded, to do justly, to love mercy, to walk humbly, to realize good law, good political and economic organisation, good relations, and a second mile to pull the law on to a higher level. . . .

. . . [T]he Church is subservient to the kingdom. . . . [I]t enables us to recognise that there are those who are 'not far from the Kingdom of God'. . . . [I]t demands that the Church be continuously under judgement . . . It roots Christian obedience in the world, from which it so easily escapes into 'religion', and it demands that Christian men seek God's will for the world, with which the Christian faith is seen to be patently concerned. And the hard facts of a scientific and technological organization of society, and the welter of social revolution the world over, can be seen, not as awkward difficulties that we must somehow live with, but as the raw material of which our age has to be built, and through which the Living God confronts our century. . . .

. . . [Christ] is God revealed in history in the only way that man could understand Him, in whom the Kingdom is supremely established, who wills to incorporate all men into Himself making them instruments of his Kingdom, who will subdue all things and subject them to the Father. . . . The Church becomes the conscious instrument of the Kingdom, and the ordinances of grace take on a new relevance as the dimensions of the Christian concern lift us from a narrow pre-occupation with one's own soul. Prayer is energised with work. The sense of sin is widened to include man's corporate guilt – with all the creative consequences that follow. The Eucharist is illuminated in a score of ways. . . .

This mode of understanding the Christian faith, wilfully related at all points to the secular order, forces us to engage the world, work and converse within it in ways that compel our faith to relevance. . . . We need to prise people's eyes open to see how community has collapsed in the urban society leaving man a stranger to his neighbour. . . . Again, we need to expose how men on such a wide scale are seduced by distraction, activism, and the purely pleasurable, and show the high stakes in more purposeful living. . . .

In no area of life is it more crucial for us to learn how to communicate Christian truth than in the field of politics and industry . . . since it is in the broadly industrial context that the technological and social revolutions join hands. . . . There are no neat solutions or Christian blueprints, but there are social principles of the Bible, 'middle axioms', a moral and dynamic view of history, and an understanding of man's nature, which bear upon the problems. Nor is prophecy impossible, for prophecy is not crystal-gazing or clairvoyancy; prophecy is the reading of the present through a profound discernment of the past, and a realization of the possibilities, even the certainties that lie ahead, in the light of our handling of the present.

E. R. Wickham, *Church and People in an Industrial City*, Lutterworth, 1957, pp. 232–8.

Lively debate

This group of articles appeared in a single issue of *Theology*, an Anglican journal, and are here excerpted in the order published.

It is important, however, to recognize that they were published at a crucial time for IM (1966). IM had begun to establish itself on the national scene but had not yet consolidated its position. At that point a major crisis was precipitated at the very heart of IM in Sheffield by the then Bishop, John Taylor, and the Senior Chaplain, Michael Jackson. It reflected a profound clash of perspectives as to the nature and purpose of IM. Ted Wickham had seen this in terms of re-establishing the Christian presence in 'the strange new world' of industry and the working classes. The successors to Bishop Hunter and Wickham saw it in terms of extending the Church's presence. IM was to be an arm of the Church proclaiming the faith, albeit in difficult and unknown territory, requiring specialist insights and skills. This reverberated round IM and, indeed, the churches.

We cannot know how these articles were put together: whether, having received Jackson's contribution the editor gathered others in a kind of response; or whether they had been planned as a thematic issue. However that may be, Jackson's contribution is key. The others read as descriptive and to some extent as apologetic, showing that IM has a theological basis and sound practice. They in fact provide a good introduction to the best of IM as it was at the time, showing the variation and self-understanding.

Jackson offers a sustained attack on what he sees as the heretical weaknesses of IM, all of which appear to stem from the supposed separatist tendencies of IM to act as an extra-ecclesial, or semi-independent, activity. This results in a loss of rootedness in the classical Christian tradition and the emergence of esoteric and dangerous insights and practices. Such a thoroughgoing critique could only flow from profound disagreements with the direction that IM had taken over the years. There is a missiological difference, because IM, following Wickham, sought signs of the Kingdom in the life of the world, including industry, that had to be appreciated by, and corrective of, the life of the Church, rather than a proclamation of the gospel from and through the Church. There is an ecclesiological difference in the focus of Christian life, because IM does not seem to value the traditional marks of the Church of word and sacrament. There is a theological difference in that IM appears to play down the need for grace freely given in a fallen world. And there is a sociological difference in trying to make industry a special case.

Len Dryden, 'Industry a segment, the mission not a sect'

> The Social and Industrial Team in Bristol has understood its work primarily in terms of a ministry to an 'industrial society', and not simply to 'Industry'. Our church base and work centre, the church of St Thomas-the-Martyr, makes explicit our conviction that Industrial Mission is the Church's work. We have no intention of becoming a sect or para-church. Neither are we concerned to find a theology for industry, but rather to relate Christian theology to the community in which we live.
>
> The technological age is a fulfilment of God's word . . . an inevitable consequence of man's potential becoming actual, and we see this as part of God's purpose for the world. We could not accept, however, that every technological achievement is necessarily 'progress'. . . .

Man created in God's image is therefore a creative being, and work is God's gift to man in order that through it man's creativity may be expressed. . . . Today there is emphasis on leisure, right use of leisure, the need for leisure, and so forth. Man's greatest need, however, is for work, not freedom *from* work but freedom *within* work. Unemployment is evil because it inhibits the growth of man to maturity, and so obstructs God's purpose for man. Work is not meant to be creative only, but also to have a purpose. Contemporary industrial society, however, is geared to the departmentalising and division of labour and skill. Economics demands this. Hence, although much of work in modern society is boring and cannot be creative, it nevertheless ought to be seen to have a purpose, and thus meet a need. . . .

Christ's commission to his Church was to go into all the world and proclaim the Gospel. Historically this has been interpreted in a geographical sense. Industrial Mission must interpret this in a functional sense. We are to go into the world of education, the world of industry, the world of the social services, and proclaim this gospel. Conversion, the acceptance of Christ's lordship, is to become a co-partner with Christ. . . . However, God's purposes for the world will be accomplished not only through the Church, but through the structures of society, for God's sovereignty extends beyond his own community. . . .

Secularization means a change of responsibility from the religious to the worldly authority. Such a loss of authority or administration does not necessarily imply a loss of spiritual content. The secularization of social responsibility was inevitable, and why should it not be part of God's purpose for his world?

The social and industrial work in Bristol is expressed both through the local base and through the central base. . . . [Following Paul] to the Church at Filton we commend to you the industrial conurbations of B.A.C. and Bristol Siddeley Engines; to the Church of Christ at Avonmouth the ships and dock industries in your locality; and so forth. . . . There is no room for any denominational differences to assert themselves;

and by 'the Church' we mean, of course, not simply the clergy and ministers but all God's people. . . .

Our method of penetrating the world of education, industry and social services will illustrate our theological thinking. In the School Leaver Conferences, Youth Employment Officers, industrialists and educationists are brought together by the local churches. . . . The theme and pattern of the four-day residential conferences for apprentices illustrate our conviction that God's lordship and sovereignty extend throughout his world. . . . The Filton lectures . . . allow our team and local clergymen to engage with men of Christian conviction in their own work environment. . . . Christian groups already exist in the Filton industries, and we encourage their participation in our work. . . . Shop floor visiting is based on local church grouping, corresponding to industrial grouping. The purpose of this kind of visiting is a simple one, namely, that the clergyman or minister should become an accepted part of the factory pattern. . . . [B]y his presence he emphasizes God's concern for factory life. There is a pastoral need in such a situation. . . .

Those engaged in Industrial Mission need the *koinonia* and the prayerful support of a worshipping community: that which epitomizes Christian worship in an act, expressed in material forms, bread and wine.

Bill Dudman, 'Onward from an apology'

My belief about industrial mission is based on my belief about three things; contemporary society; the things of the New Testament; the Church. I want the Church to be the instrument of that divine love which leaps out at us from the pages of the New Testament and which is empowered by the presence and dynamism of the Risen Lord.

[. . .]

My belief about industrial mission is that by making the attempt to understand society at depth our work enables us to have some insights into the contemporary situation which, in their turn, could, can, and in some cases do, inform not only our own work but the whole concept of mission. . . .

I see industrial mission as a sort of two pronged fork. It attempts to interpret, and helps others to interpret, the things of the New Testament in ways and places from which the Church has long been an absentee: it also has a work of interpretation in bringing the Church to understand the world. . . .

. . . [O]ur work stands in continual help from every and any theologian who is prepared to see mission as the Church's first priority. We need help in working out a Christology for today. . . . We need great help, and a good deal of sympathetic understanding, in helping the Church itself to be restructured in such a way that it may be capable of understanding and supporting mission. . . . Industrial mission is not on its own in all this. Every good piece of work that has emerged in the world Church during the last two decades has been asking exactly these same questions.

Michael Jackson, 'No new Gospel'

The aims of Industrial Mission do not differ from those of the Christian Church as a whole. Industrial Mission is a sociological term to describe one sphere of the Church's work. The task of theology is to make sure that the Church's work in this sphere is that of the Christian Church as a whole, which is to be a faithful witness to the risen Lord. . . . Orthodox theology summarised in the Catholic and Reformed doctrine of justification by faith rules out certain trends which have already had time to appear in Industrial Mission. It rules out gnosticism, the intellectual heresy, which selects certain concepts, doctrines and theologians to form the real truth about Industrial Mission. Those admitted to these secrets know and base their work on the correct theological assumptions. . . .

It also rules out a certain Judaism. The Old Testament is held to be normative scripture for Industrial Mission because it has much to say about social order and because it was the Bible for Jesus of Nazareth. . . . The Lord and Saviour of the world is more than a social reformer with insights into man and society. . . . It forgets the close link of the law and the prophets with the cult. This selectivity in the scriptures as a whole leads to an

Industrial Mission form of Marcionism. Selection produces a God who does not judge but is kind, willing to reconcile good and evil, truth and falsehood, and to promote good human relationships within the present framework of society. . . .

Under the patronage of a weak, absent or dying God the British heresy of Pelagianism has full play. We are saved by our own efforts, our dialogues and healthy relationships, our planning, principles of management or trades unionism. We create the good society by the skilful application of science and technology, which may after all be the first signs of that new creation begun by Jesus Christ.

[. . .]

Existentialism is not always open to theological objection, but a certain line of thinking in Industrial Mission has encouraged an inhuman and atheistic form of it. . . . Where God is not outside the human situation and there is no objective gift of grace the discovery of need drives to despair. Men are plunged deeper into the mire, into atheism and into the arms of the impotent but indispensable counsellor. . . . Industrial Mission has had long enough to grow its *syllabus errorum*. . . .The corrective is objective theology summarized in the great assertion of *sola fide*. . . .

Industrial Mission is a sociologically defined area of the Church's mission. . . . Christianity cares about society and therefore it must care about what is decided in industry and the Church must set on foot a special programme of work to put this care into action. . . . There is also a political issue. . . . In every society, including industrial society, politics under God is paramount. . . . There is a theological danger in the sociological argument. It may put a social institution, industry, into the centre of society. This place belongs only to God in any form of society. . . . The Church sees all situations from the point of view of eternity; a sociological analysis cannot. . . .

The sociological argument for Industrial Mission has drawn support from a historical one. There is a view of history which sees the Church as an institution failing and receding since the Industrial Revolution. . . . This is an area of study where the facts are not self-evident but at the mercy of the propagandist, who may play up or play down according to his intentions. . . . The argument has conditioned the approach to people in industry – by assuming they are pagan. Another argument . . . is that men in industry are of a new kind. Religious concepts are dead to them. . . [and] men come of age don't need them. . . . It is nonsense because the evidence is far from supporting it. Belief in God and prayer are widespread. . . .

How far can a special agency of the Church not do those things in its corporate life which the Church as a whole does? . . . Can it, therefore, exclude worship, sacrament and catechumenate? If it does, will it not allow other and lesser activities to usurp the place of these? . . .

What is the Church's mission and ministry in industry? . . . [T]he work of the Church in industry goes before and comes after what is done elsewhere. It prepares the ground for faith and it works out the consequences of faith. If the industrial plant by its nature cannot be a church, then a parochial or congregational organisation of the Church holds a key place in mission. . . . Industrial Mission is the body of Christ dispersed in its occupations. Laymen are witnesses to the risen Lord at their work. . . . There is a task of mission to call out such Christians, and of ministry to support them in their discipline of life and in their thinking and behaviour. The Church has set aside clergy for this work. . . , men of God who are not tools of the various pressure groups in industry, but humble servants of their Master.

Bill Wright, 'The reality and the dream'

Industrial-urban issues can't be left to industrial chaplains alone. They are the concern of the whole Church and involve it in the political and economic debates out of which social change comes. . . . What we call the secular world is, in fact, God's creation. God is described as Love, Justice, Truth, Reconciliation, Wisdom; Christlike obedience to him means establishing these values in the concrete situations of each generation. . . . Our worship too must reflect this intimate link between Christian profession and secular involvement. The symbol of bread in the eucharist speaks both of the co-operative offering of the whole world of work and also our failure to distribute justly the rewards of work (bread hints at near poverty). . . .

One of the consequences of such a theological understanding of life will be a demand for forms of ministry and methods of 'lay' training dealing in detail with the issues raised by secular involvement. Most ministry is 'lay' and expressed through work, social responsibility, voluntary service and individual acts of caring. . . . We need often to be reminded that the ordained minister is the servant of the 'layman'. . . . If 'laymen' are not offering Christian service in the main streams of twentieth century life, then there is no mission. . . .

From the experience of existing industrial chaplaincy work some things are clear about the new role for the ordained ministry. The offering of full-time service gives a freedom and flexibility that most laymen tied to a job never can achieve. . . . [H]e can take a more dispassionate view of things. His interested neutrality and increasingly well-informed opinion give him an opportunity to bring together the numerous specialists who work on common problems often without much contact with one another. He still has astonishingly free access to people and doesn't have to wait for an invitation before getting involved.

In his prophetic role – only when he has earned respect for his impartiality – he can help to have highly controversial issues raised, encouraging 'laymen' to initiate creative criticism within existing organisations. . . . His role as 'confessor' is universally understood and appreciated. There are many occasions, especially in big organizations, when people feel the need to speak to a non-aligned person who none the less appreciates the background problems.

Nowadays, of course, the basic elements of this kind of ministry have been shared with a host of state and voluntary agencies . . . the traditional Christian demand for a unifying factor becomes more urgent. The priest remains an obvious symbol of that need. . . .

The Church [in Teesside] is engaged in FOUR quite distinct kinds of ministry – to residential, voluntary, statutory and occupational groups. Each one of these demands a highly specialised ministry in modern conditions. It is quite silly to talk of general practitioners in the parish ministry and specialists in the others. . . .

This, and nothing less, is how I see the bare bones of 'industrial mission' – the mission of all the Churches in one of the fastest growing industrial-urban areas in Britain. It is more demanding and all-embracing than either parish ministry or industrial mission as each is practised at present. This wider industrial mission is the care of the Church of God as a whole for people in every aspect of their modern lives.

Gordon Hopkins, 'The vicar'

During a long number of years in Pallion (Wearside), it has been possible, gradually, to get to know a very large number of people engaged in varying kinds of work in local industrial life. At no time has life for most of them been plain sailing or easy for very long, and people are glad of the chance to talk informally about a great many different facets of industrial life, with its problems and difficulties. . . .

[In the early 1940s] quite a considerable number of young workers were trained in Pallion along these lines [as Jocists], and they are the people who have since been most effective and faithful in Church life, and have, in almost every case, pursued extremely interesting and worthwhile careers in industrial life. . . . The essential point of Jocism and kindred movements is that the whole structure of a man's working and domestic life must be spread out before God, and caught up into the action of the eucharist. This was seized upon, and emphasized, by 'Parish and People' and the liturgical movements in England and on the Continent. . . .

. . . [I]t is still a fairly tightly knit community, in which people know each other very well. . . . This makes it possible for the parochial clergy to make ready contact with the works, and to be accepted as such within the local set-up. . . . The parish priest, like the industrial missioner, if he remains in the same place over a good long period of time, is able to get together groups of people who are prepared to meet and discuss outside working hours. . . .

Experience suggests that, although a man ought not to be tethered to the parish pump, yet if he is to survive effectively as a focus of Christian influence, he will need a strong sacramental life as the background to his existence. It looks as though the Roman Catholics do much more for the spiritual life of the industrial worker than we do in the Church of England. . . .

There are dangers and drawbacks. . . .The parish priest can only do a mere fraction of the work that cries out to be tackled. There is the appalling problem of the rapid mobility of the parish clergy in these days . . . a great deal of this kind of work is intimate, intangible and personal in character. He knows that his successor may not be at all at home in this kind of field, or he may be succeeded by someone who will rush in and make blunders. . . . [C]uriously little [is] available in the nature of training for this work in most large industrial towns. . . .

. . . [There is] a widespread impression that there was a wedge driven in between industrial mission and the parochial clergy . . . particularly about the implied suggestion that the parochial clergy were tinkering about with an outworn institution, while the specialist practitioners in the field were getting to grips with the secular world, or the 'real' world. The parochial clergy have tended to identify industrial mission with 'South Bank' attitudes, and to sheer away from this whole field.

Tom Chapman, 'The Layman and the Priest'

The great failure of industrial mission, as I see it, has been the inability to utilize the vast potential of lay man power. It would be a grave reflection on the teaching of the Church, if it were true that a churchman is of little use to the Church in industry. I do not believe this. In the last analysis the laymen must carry the main burden of responsibility, because they alone are dispersed throughout and entrenched in the life of industry. . . .

. . . [A] Christian layman must above all be a good workman

... he keeps the larger purpose of his work in mind and knows how his part fits into the whole product . . . He must know that he serves those with whom he works and with this in mind will want to participate in those activities which also serve the larger causes of mankind, for instance his trade union. . . . The training of the layman is therefore of vital importance. He requires theological reasoning as part of his competence in the skills of his vocation.

[. . .]

. . . [A] very special training is required for the clergy who participate in industrial mission. . . . [I]ndustry is the fulcrum of the nation's economic structure and – this nation being what it is – a determining factor in the economy of the world. . . . He must be a specialist. His training must include experience within industry, . . . the study of social ethics and economic theory . . . [and] at least twelve months as an industrial labourer. . . . [T]he brotherhood which may exist between workers is one of the great leavens in society; and the missioner must nourish it by using it, rather than cut across it. . . . [Furthermore] the labourer's status will give the missioner humility . . . to remind him constantly that God is no respecter of persons, but put him in a position where he will ask rather than dictate.

Theology vol. XIX no.538, December 1966.

Worker priests

Another attempt to enable the Church to reconnect with the urbanized and secularized working classes was the worker-priest movement. This was strongest in France, stemming from the experience of priests who aligned themselves with the enforced migrant workers in occupied Europe in the Second World War. A number of Catholic priests were allowed to move out of the parochial system and to enter into secular work in factories and elsewhere, where they sought ways of exercising a new style of ministry. This created considerable interest. However, after initial enthusiasm, the experiment was suppressed.[1] This model never really took on in Britain but there were some, especially Anglicans, who set out to follow such a vocation.[2] Nevertheless the idea of having a ministry immersed in the secular culture has never been lost. One of the hopes for developing the non-stipendiary part-time ministry, not least in the mind of Mervyn Stockwood, Bishop of Southwark, was that clergy would be free to create new forms of ministry in their work context and communities. Also there are those who deliberately move into the inner-city areas, sometimes as a small commune or as religious. This article describes part of the English experience in the early days.

> There are four worker-priests of the Church of England at the present active in this country, and one worker-deacon. . . . They are part of a movement which had its beginnings some nine or ten years ago, but our movement is not primarily one of priests. We are a group of Christian men and women who are committed to the industrial wage earners of this country by sharing as fully as we can in their life and work, and living on the earnings of our work as they do. . . .
>
> 1. We believe that if we seriously intend to get over the Gospel to the people of our time, we must live it in the materialistic terms of money and work which they most easily understand. . . .
> 2. We wish to proclaim the Gospel visibly 'free of charge'. . . .
> 3. Some of us in doing this work are responding to a modern vocation to 'poverty'. In England today most wage-earners are not very poor in material things, but as a class they suffer a form of poverty determined by the wage-status itself, the impersonal, indeed, soul destroying nature of much of their work, insecurity of employment, and still, to some extent, educational under-privilege. . . .
>
> Our group is not a formal movement, but for some years now we have met together every summer to exchange news and ideas. . . .

The worker-priests do not go out of their way to make themselves known as parsons, but the fact inevitably comes out before long in conversation, and the news spreads a certain amount. . . . Isn't all this a waste of a priest's training. . . . [B]ut as a shop steward commented, 'There are 13,000 heathen in this factory, and if that isn't enough for one man, I don't know what is.' As to the query whether this work might not be done more fittingly by lay men . . . two practical points. One is the fact that a number of priests have felt an unanswerable call to the work. The other is that certain developments of our work are only conceivable if they are led by an ordained man. There is a distinct possibility that small discussion groups may develop into 'house churches', alongside the parish structure. . . .

In the factory, worker-priests tend to get asked their opinion on various moral issues, and receive a few confidences. . . . Some have been interested to come to church, others to visit our homes for an evening, or to welcome an occasional visit in their own homes. Our main business is to 'be' rather than to do. . . .

All of the group who are eligible do in fact belong to Trade Unions, and three of them are Shop Stewards. . . . The type and extent of our involvement in Union and political affairs does not spring in the main from theoretical beliefs, but is determined by the needs of the human situation in which we are placed. . . .

It is certainly true that we are not giving them many of this world's goods: . . . However, our children will almost certainly benefit from being brought up in closer contact with 'real life' than their parents were. . . .

We are thankful that part of what we have done and hope to do is now being sponsored officially, notably by the Bishop of Southwark. If our work is distinct from that of others, it is in this, that it is not part of a policy, it is not an 'experiment': for us it is a way of life.

Anne Grubb, 'English Worker-Priests',
Frontier, 3: IV, Winter 1960.

Scottish Industrial Mission

The first thing to say about Scottish Industrial Mission (SIM) is that it is clearly integrated into the structures of the Church of Scotland, though it was widened to include chaplains from other denominations that accepted representation in the SIM management structures. SIM has also consistently been an active participant in the IMA, thus ensuring a UK-wide dimension for IM. As a sector ministry it reports to the Church and Industry Committee where it is lodged under the Home Board, which curiously separates it organizationally from the Church and Nation Committee that deals with national social issues. The annual report of the Church and Industry Committee is presented to General Assembly within the Home Board report. It is substantially an account of events and personalia from the previous year. Chaplains are appointed by the Board and this procedure has been accepted and recognized by the other denominations so that there is, effectively, a single co-ordinated structure. Standards of training are set. There is also a closer relationship between the local parish and SIM as the great majority of chaplains operate part-time out of their parochial ministry; but even so this ministry has to be properly authorized. The Church and Industry Committee also acts as the national forum in dealing with socio-economic issues and its deliberations are summarized in the annual report. It is only possible to indicate briefly some of the concerns to which it has turned its attention. It, on occasion, sponsors publications from leaflets to more substantial booklets. The following excerpts from the Board reports give some idea of how SIM is organized and the work it does.

1. *History and structure*

(1958) The Scottish Christian Industrial Order is an organisation for laymen sponsored by the Church and Industry Committee on behalf of the Home Board, its aim being 'to advance the knowledge and understanding of the Christian Faith and its practice; to promote the best human relations in industry on the basis of that Faith; and to further the application of its principles throughout industrial life and society'. The Order is given a wide measure of autonomy.

(1962) 1962 marks the twentieth birthday of the Home Board's Industrial Chaplains scheme. For thirteen years it has been under the direction of a full-time organiser and now the twentieth year brings the appointment of the first full-time Industrial Chaplain to work in the shipyards of Port Glasgow and Greenock. . . . [There has been a] change of attitude of working men generally towards the Church and its ministers. Several factors account for this . . . but no small credit must be allowed to the faithful service of Industrial Chaplains who have been in close contact with the men at their work, acquainting themselves with the conditions of work in different branches of industry, discussing all manner of subjects with individuals and groups and serving them in a variety of ways, particularly in times of trouble, sickness and bereavement.

(1971) The number of Industrial Chaplains has risen slightly to 112, of whom 67 are members of teams within the six areas now served by [local] Church and Industry Committees. Our three full time chaplains continue to operate in Greenock, Motherwell and Glasgow. . . . Altogether there are seven Methodists, five Congregationalists, four Episcopalians and one Baptist acting as Industrial Chaplains, whose work is coordinated by the Committee (which itself contains representatives of these denominations). . . . The Committee has given some time to the consideration of the training of Chaplains in industry. It has agreed that the minimum training should consist of (a) a half day with a full time Chaplain, (b) an induction programme arranged by the firm . . . (c) attendance at a three day course at Chesters Management School, and (d) an annual two-day refresher course for all Industrial Chaplains.

2. *Issues*

(1958) [Enquiries were made concerning placing] an Industrial Chaplain at the atomic electricity generating station under consultation at Hunterston, West Kilbride. . . . [In relation to Dounreay and Chapelcross] at both places construction work is now almost complete and it is possible these Industrial Chaplains will cease to be necessary. [However in] view of the scale of the construction work, which according to Government statements, was to be undertaken in the Islands of North Uist, Benbecula and South Uist in connection with the proposed Rocket Range [the Committee] conferred with the Presbytery of Uist on the question of providing assistance . . . but the announcement of the drastic curtailment of the Government's plans brought [that] to an end. . . . [Also] the large-scale hydro-electric projects in the Highlands has passed its peak and that in future Chaplaincy services in camps will be within the capacity of parish ministers.

(1958) March 1957, the constituent Unions of the Confederation of Shipbuilding and Engineering Unions called their members out on strike. . . . [A] meeting of the Presbyteries was called . . . as it was feared that the strike might be prolonged and give rise to much hardship. . . . Before further steps could be taken it was announced that the Minister of Labour would appoint a Court of Enquiry . . . [and it was agreed] that the Church and Industry Committee should submit a memorandum with comments on the causes of the disputes when the Reports of the Court of Enquiry were published. . . .

(1959) Men at work are now involved in a network of interlocking and interacting organisations – from the informal organisations of working groups, to the formal organisation of the shop floor, of the shop stewards committee, the trade union branch, the national organisation of the trade union to the Trades Union Congress. Nor is this confined to the employees' side of industry; there are interlocking and interacting formal and informal organisations on the management side. . . . In this situation strongly organised minority groups can and do easily seize and wield enormous power . . . and the methods of democracy can be used to destroy democracy.

This has been seen in the activities of financial manipulators and also of members of the Communist Party in certain trade unions. . . . Christian men must combine to guide and support each other and produce their own leaders who will further the ends of the Gospel and democracy.

(1961) For several years the Church and Industry Committee has given considerable thought to the problems of the transition of young people from school to industry and to the provision of adequate training for employment which would prevent their entry into 'dead end' jobs.

(1976) In relation to the serious redundancy situations which face Scottish industry, chaplains have found themselves drawn into the discussion both on the shop floor and with management, as those who have a serious contribution to make. The publication of the booklet *Redundant? A Personal Survival Kit,* along with the St Andrews Press, has underlined the Church's concern and established the chaplain's right to be heard.

Methodism

Among the Free Churches, the Methodists were best placed to contribute to the development of IM (though all the mainstream traditions put in resources). The Methodists, however, also brought a distinct slant to the enterprise, which arose out of their revivalist, evangelical tradition.

Christian Commando Campaigns and Industrial Evangelism

The Christian Commando Campaigns were inter-church evangelistic initiatives that often included open-air preaching and visits to and meetings in factories and other places of work. Out of this grew the realization that there was a need for a more permanent relationship between the institutional church and the world of work. As a result many Methodist ministers began part-time chaplaincies. This was known as 'Industrial Evangelism' and the emphasis was on personal conversion as well as pastoral contacts. There was always, therefore, a strong emphasis on building up the congregation alongside a growing recognition of the wider social issues involved.

Out of this came Methodism's expression of IM. This had as its focus the College for Industrial Evangelism at Luton, founded in 1954. At first it was all part time, with well over a hundred circuit ministers involved. The proposal to second ministers full time came in 1954, though these were always reasonably few in number at any one time. In 1956 a national committee was set up under the auspices of the Home Mission Department and in 1962 districts were asked to form Committees for Industrial Evangelism across the country.

The following comes from the Report of the Home Mission Department for 1954.

> Industrial Evangelism is a form of Christian service which was closely allied to the Christian Commando Campaigns. The experience gained in those Campaigns revealed a field of great opportunity for evangelism in industry, and one that was sadly neglected. A number of ministers, on their own initiative, followed up the openings made in places of industry by the Christian Commando Campaigns, and became Industrial Chaplains.
>
> The Home Mission Department, foreseeing that Conference of 1954 would accept the recommendation 'That the Methodist Church should extend its work of Industrial Evangelism' as part of its policy supported the appointment of the Rev. William Gowland to Chapel Street Church, Luton, and expressed the hope that this church would become the headquarters of the Department's experiments in Industrial Evangelism. Part of the premises there have been transformed to make this work possible, thanks to the help of the Joseph Rank Benevolent Trust, the Chapel Committee, and the efforts of the local Church.
>
> The Home Mission Department and the Christian Citizen Department have collaborated in forming a strong committee on which ministers already engaged in this work, represen-

tatives of Trade Unions and Industrial Management, and Members of Parliament consented to serve. This Committee was officially appointed at the June meeting of the Home Mission Committee.

The Luton Industrial College

The Luton Industrial College was founded by Bill Gowland, a Methodist minister, in 1954, as part of his industrial chaplaincy work around the then major employer Vauxhall Motors and as the centre for Methodist research and training in IM. It provided neutral ground, locally, where those in industry and the community could meet to thrash out issues; a venue for courses run for industry for groups such as apprentices, skilled craftsmen, shop-floor foremen or managers; and an educational facility for Christians struggling with their faith in the context of work. Nationally, it provided courses for ordinands, clergy and lay people in industry and a centre for numerous consultations. The college was closed in 1996. Here was, perhaps, the best example in Britain of the model of a church-based centre as the focus for industrial mission, a model that is normal in (e.g.) the French Protestant Industrial Mission. This report is found in the Home Mission Report for 1956.

> For many years now, many Ministers have been working as factory Padres, but there has been little continuity, and they have received little guidance. . . . The College at Luton will provide a meeting place for such men and thus assist in forming a nation-wide network, with all the sense of unity and strength which that implies. They will also meet and hear outstanding figures from the industrial world and thus gain a better appreciation of the principles that underlie the managing of a factory and the processes of production.
>
> The aims of the College were stated by Dr. W.E.Sangster in his address at the Dedication of the College last Easter.
> They are:-
>
> 1. To make the Christian Faith real to the world in which we live.

2. To meet that need in industry which is beyond even the finest welfare work.
3. To train people in Industrial Evangelism, not only in theory but in practice as well.

Dr. Sangster added the three following explanatory points:-

1. While Methodism is glad to lead here this is not for Methodists only.
2. While this is a Christian enterprise, it is not for Christians only. Anyone willing to *consider* the claims of Christ is welcome.
3. This is not for ministers only. It is for the laity first and mainly.

[. . .]

One of the most valuable features of the College is that it is based on a Church which is committed to this work. Students are thus able to . . . meet laymen and women who are carrying the College programme to the factory floor.

[. . .]

Reports of those who have had the privilege of spending a week at Luton are unanimous in their glowing appreciation. . . . The course, they say, has given them new ideas and a new confidence in tackling the job. . . . [W]hile the first courses have been primarily for ministers, future courses will be primarily for laymen.

Percy Scott, Home Mission Report, 1956, pp. 50–1.

The Doncaster District Coalfields' Mission

This initiative sought to make an impact on an industrial area through the local churches by concentrating resources and modifying the structures of the Church. Thus local congregations (societies) were released into a special community-based programme. While the emphasis, in accordance with the tradition, was on evangelism and building up the Church, there was also and integrally much social work and community involvement. Notably in the 1960s concern was shown for miners being moved from the northern fields to the more profitable areas. This included helping to provide housing as well as social support. The following is part of the report of the Home Mission Department for 1954.

> The Conference of 1949 directed the Home Mission Department to prepare plans for an experiment of 'prolonged and intensive evangelistic work in one of the large coalfields'. South Yorkshire coalfield was selected for the experiment, and the Doncaster District Coalfields' Mission began in 1950. . . . We pay tribute to the work of the Ministers, Lay Pastors and Deaconesses who have shared in this enterprise.
>
> During the past year there has been much to give encouragement. Conversions have taken place, and there have been new ventures in fellowship.
>
> Although the results of the experiment during the six years have been gratifying, there has been a growing conviction, both locally and Connexionally, that a regrouping, on a geographical basis, of our Churches in the areas covered by and adjacent to the Coalfields' Mission, would make for greater efficiency in our work. A beginning to implement this policy was made at the last Conference . . .
>
> . . . [T]he Societies brought into the Mission are blending well. As part of the Forward Movement, a Monday Night Cinema Club, at Thurnscoe, is attracting hundreds of children each week. Two of our mobile ministers with the Caravan 'Evangel' and a Mobile Cinema are missioning in the area.

The Methodist Approach to Industrial Mission, 1968

This was a policy document, prepared by the Committee for Industrial Evangelism as a contribution to the discussions then going on about the ecumenical regulation of IM and published as Home Mission Occasional Paper 5. It shows how Methodism, while keeping its distinctive ethos, has also been assimilated into the mainstream of IM thinking and practice.

3. *The Theological Basis of Mission to Industry.*

There is no specific theology of industrial mission, for industrial mission is only part of the total mission of the Church. . . . Mature thinking no longer talks about industrial evangelism or even industrial 'mission' but industrial society . . . The Gospel is about the wholeness of man and the purposes of God in the totality of life in his world. . . .

To the question, does the Church participate in Christ's mission *in* and *for* the world, or does the Church perform a mission *to* the world, we reply that God has direct relationships with the world, and with the Church. He is not limited to working in the world by what the Church will permit him to do; on the other hand, he does work through the Church as well as through other agencies. The Church is in the world for the sake of the world, to bear witness to the fact that God loves the world and seeks to reconcile it to himself. . . .

Industrial mission means that the Church must be available within industry, but available in the skilled and competent sense. . . .

Again, does reconciliation mean that conflict must disappear and that everybody must agree? Industrial conflict is often fantastically destructive and wasteful, but at other times it may be creative. Does not reconciliation rather mean establishing the kind of relationship between individuals and groups in which men can live and work together, even though they may disagree, creative tension being one of the ways of getting at new truth? And how can this struggle be contained within the framework of industrial relations? Mission which avoids these issues is in real danger of reducing itself to an ambulance service, yet failing at the real point of testing.

4. *Industrial Mission; Chaplain and Layman.*

The term 'industrial mission' is usually identified with the work of industrial chaplains. . . . But industrial chaplaincy is only a small part of industrial mission. Even the finest chaplain working all day in the factory is, in one sense, still only a visitor. The clerical view of mission is theologically unsound and dangerous in practice. The layman is the resident missionary . . . Industrial mission is, of necessity, primarily a layman's movement. The Church is in the factory in the layman who must often make decisions on specific problems within industry and carry the responsibility for those decisions in a way the chaplain never can, for he must remain in some respects unaligned. . . .

. . . [I]t is the chaplain who seeks to minister to and serve the layman by helping to make his contribution to industrial society. This means, in practice, encouraging men to live and work in a *creative* and *responsible* way and helping them to discern just what are the factors within the complex life of modern industry which make for, or militate against, these qualities. Where the structures of industry are bad, or inhuman, it is the duty of the chaplain, and indeed the whole Church, to support the layman as he seeks to change them. . . . This calls for a new partnership between chaplain and layman, in which the layman will bring his specialist knowledge of industry, whilst the chaplain will seek to contribute relevant insights from his knowledge of the Christian faith and theological training. . . .

5. *Church-Based Industrial Mission.*

Methodism has always believed that industrial mission could and should be Church-based. . . . Industrial mission is an integral part of the total mission of the Church. At the same time, it is vital that our approach remains flexible and that room is allowed for responsible experimentation. Some laymen who do not attend church and have at present no intention of so doing, nevertheless find industrial mission a form of the church with which they are ready to identify themselves. Church-based does not mean that the ultimate goal is that all activity shall be centred in traditional church buildings.

The Methodist Approach to Industrial Mission,
Home Mission Department, Occasional Paper 5, 1968.

The Roman Catholic approach to IM

The Roman Catholic Church was not a participant in the Industrial Mission movement, preferring to see ministry and mission at work as a lay apostolate. In this, there is some echo of the view expressed by Shigeko Masumoto (see Chapter 4) that IM was in some danger of falling into an unexamined clericalism.

Nevertheless, the Roman Catholic Church maintained a very practical interest in social developments including the workings of the economy in the lives of individuals and communities and, at a time when the Roman Catholic Church was starting to show a stronger interest in ecumenical co-operation, many in IM and the social action agencies of the Protestant denominations were keen to share experiences and to understand Catholic perspectives.

As one of its working papers on Industrial Mission, the Anglican Board for Social Responsibility published Kevin Muir's exposition of a Catholic approach to economic and industrial questions from which the following extract is taken. The style is distinctive when compared to most written materials emanating from IM circles as is the focus on the local and personal and on small Christian groupings as the structures for support and what became known as conscientization among lay Christians. It remains an important reminder that engagement with economic issues is not the sole preserve of the Anglican and Free Churches operating through institutional models.

> The main thrust of the Catholic Church's mission to the world of work has found expression in and through lay organisations. . . . The most significant of these movements have been the Young Christian Workers, the various adult Christian Worker movements developed by former YCWs and the organisations for employers, managers and professional people grouped under the umbrella of the International Christian Union of Business Executives (UNIAPAC). And the most significant shifts in thinking relate to the indispensable role of the laity in

the mission of the Church and the development of liberation theology.

How to describe mission to the world of work in practice? Its method is based on reflection on life situations in the light of the teachings of Scripture and the Church. What follows is an account of a review of her life [Jean's life as a District Nurse] by a member of an adult Action in Work group.

[Jean's story; analysis follows]

The Gospel and the Particular

The emphasis on the particular, on the detail, at each level of our analysis is crucial; the Gospel response can only emerge in response to the real. The real problems, evils, have to be identified if a true judgement is to emerge. This is true at every level of our review. If Jean had had more time she could tell of the detailed questions we asked about, who sat where in the office, about the relationship between State Enlisted Nurses and the State Registered, about the relationship of the white middle class management to her black West Indian colleagues. She could tell of the detailed comparison we made between her first union, the Royal College of Nursing, and her second, NUPE. She could tell of the gradual picture we built up on the relationship of the plight of the Health Service to other services like Housing and Education, in her District.

The Kingdom of God, which was another way of speaking of the nearness of God, of God in action, was revealed in the particularity of Jesus' life. His judgements of the Temple and its priests, on Pharisaic tendencies, on the rich, did not come ready made. His was not the accepted opinion of the time. If you read the Gospels carefully, you can see Jesus' attention to detail. He observes the different styles of work; the fishing industry around Galilee, the new large estates the Roman taxes were creating with their rich absentee landlords away in Jerusalem, their stewards under pressure to make profit, and the new class of landless day workers they used. Our Lord's teaching is full of such observed detail. That's why it hit home.

The Emerging Gospel

Brought up as racially prejudiced as any other good Jew, we see our Lord gradually changing his mind through his own observation (cf Matt 15:21, the story of the Canaanite mother). Early in his ministry he avoids travelling through Samaria, the land of heretics, but later the Good Samaritan becomes part of his critique of the falsehood around him. Eventually, in John's account he is able to be free to speak to, and open up life for, the Samaritan Woman at the well. Our Lord wasn't born with a Gospel, the Gospel *emerged* from his detailed attending of the reality around him. This attending was done in the midst of tensions and unrest, some of which we looked at last year:

- the hidden presence of occupying forces;
- exploited masses of day workers;
- political control over Temple and Religion;
- collaboration of the highest Jewish authorities;
- scandal of the opulence of the Temple and poverty of the masses.

Jesus' critique of the hypocrisy and corruption of those in power emerges as he participates, takes up position, sees more and more clearly what is at stake: the true image of God and the true life of men and women. It all comes gradually through participation, observation, judgement and action all in the midst of tension. Our way is not likely to be any simpler.

In the same way the Christian judgements we make as a group emerge slowly. But always as we attend to the details, we look for the signs of hope. Our faith in the Resurrection leads us to expect them. The hope is sometimes just one other workmate who is half aware.

In Jean's review the signs of hope were the colleague who was strong enough to refuse overtime to bring attention to how bad things were, and the three who eventually went in deputation.

As we look to the details, the Gospel response, the way

forward gradually emerges; often in ways we could not have anticipated at the start.

For example, it took us a long time to realise that Jean had to withdraw her gifts, her ability to improvise and keep up morale, things good in themselves but which were being used to sustain an evil situation. She had to withdraw them if real, long-lasting good could emerge. That was not at all clear at first.

Gospel Confidence

We work towards a judgement in confidence. The confidence our Lord seems to have had in men and women's ability to recognise within themselves the action of the Kingdom, as it happens, and to respond positively to it, the confidence that the project of Jesus has power to generate conviction in others. . . .

Jean was able to do the same. She drew her sister nurses into greater solidarity, enabling them to identify the problems that faced them, what we might call naming the evil, then focusing on the ways forward. In doing this Jean released a new confidence, a new potential for more positive life. As she says, 'They were on cloud nine!' That was after the delegation, their first act of solidarity. That potential for more life is the dynamism of the practice of Jesus in the Gospel: the emergence of solidarity where there was isolation, generosity where there was fear and suspicion.

Our own experience as a group has echoed that of the Gospel where so often the Kingdom is revealed in Jesus' table-fellowship with the twelve, revealed in solidarity. In our World of Work group we have helped each other identify the evils besetting us as workers. In Jean's case mainly lack of management and bad conditions. We have provided solidarity in facing those evils, which then enabled Jean to be an agent of solidarity in her own work situation, enabling her to speak and act out of the clarity that the shared review of life made possible. Our own solidarity as a group has enabled us to be agents of solidarity in our various workplaces. We have helped to put our fellow workers in touch with each other as the first step towards becoming in touch with their reality. Hundreds of years ago the prophet Jeremiah said:

> 'They will say: "No use! We will follow our own devices, each one of us will behave according to the stubbornness of his evil heart."' (Jer 18:12)

Experiencing the Living God

That attitude is very common today, and just as destructive. Whole sectors of Society and of the world of work have ceased to expect participation, have ceased to look for a more equitable distribution of resources or a sharing of goods and benefits. As Christian workers we believe, in the light of the foul death of Christ and of his Resurrection, that things are never past hope. It is out of that basic Gospel hope that we confront the Antithesis – the Idols of our time – in the name of the living God and for the sake of the life of men and women. The idols are clear enough. They are identified in our recent conferences. Among others they are:

- emphasis on a rising standard of living, on increased personal affluence and possessions;
- emphasis on the individual as an independent consuming being;
- acceptance of untried theoretical or ideological economic solutions;
- emphasis on sectional interests: my group, my Union, etc.

Such false idols destroy the dignity of the human person, society, true community, real progress. Where these idols are the motivating forces, God is absent and the image of God in man and woman is destroyed.

Kevin Muir, *Industrial Mission – Catholic Style*,
Industrial Mission and the Churches in Britain Today,
Paper 4, Board for Social Responsibility, 1987.

Industrial and business ethics

The 1970s not only saw a deterioration in British industry with mounting redundancies but also a sharpening of conflict within the world of business. This was exacerbated by some notorious scandals such as the Rachman affair in property speculation. Such events raised questions about the ethical assumptions lying behind the capitalist system as to ownership and responsibility. Who are the 'stakeholders' in an enterprise? How are they related together? The short answer was that the company is owned by and exists for the benefit of the shareholders. But it was increasingly being asked, do not the workers, management, customers and the wider context, including the local community and the environment, have legitimate claims? So the process was begun for responsibility to be more inclusive. This was most usually tackled through the evolution of codes of ethics that outline the principles and objectives that control a given company. This is a process that still continues, having become in various ways legal requirements. Here Jack Keiser, an Anglican lay man and engineer, who was on the staff of William Temple College and subsequently of the William Temple Foundation, sets out a Christian reflection.

> Over recent years, industry and business have tended to acquire a bad name. There is an unacceptable face to capitalism, to quote Mr Heath, and nationalised industries do not escape criticism either. . . . Much of the public criticism and disquiet may be unjustified, but it is there and it constitutes a threat to those who run our business enterprises. . . . The responses to this situation have been many and varied. There has been a growth of legislation to regulate corporate behaviour. Individual companies have taken steps to publicize the breadth of their concern about social responsibility. Most significantly, there has been a proliferation of codes of business ethics and management ethics.
>
> Employers . . . have gone to considerable lengths to improve their public image. Consultation with the workforce over

such matters as redundancy and relocation of production has increased considerably and there is now more disclosure of information over a wide range of topics. . . . Annual reports increasingly comment upon the company' efforts in the direction of consumer protection, pollution monitoring and environmental improvement. . . . Some companies and industries even buy advertising space to inform the public of their good intentions. . . . Nevertheless each company and each industry decides itself what it prints and what it leaves out. . . .

We now turn to one of the most interesting developments over the last few years which has been the publication of numerous Codes of Business Conduct. Individual members of professional bodies, such as doctors, lawyers and engineers, have always been more or less bound by codes of professional behaviour, though the detailed content of these has varied considerably. The efficacy of sanctions has also varied. . . .

With the founding of the British Institute of Management in 1947, an attempt has been made to make management itself a profession. . . . Nevertheless, many managers in industry and business do not belong to such organisations. It is interesting, too, the British Institute of Management only published its Code of Conduct and made it obligatory for its members in 1974. . . . One of the most significant was the Conservative Government's Industrial Relations Code of Practice which, although it did not have the force of law, could be taken into account in legal proceedings under the Industrial Relations Act of 1971. . . . At about the same time, the Trades Union Congress issued its own code, which in some parts was almost identical with the government publication. Since then, many of the provisions in these codes have been given the force of law. . . . The Confederation of British Industry also gave much consideration to the possibility of drawing up an overall code for implementation in British industry and commerce. In the end, it decided against the idea, but nevertheless in 1973 published *The Responsibility of the British Public Company,* which included in an appendix a list of guiding principles. . . .

An equally carefully prepared document was *A Code of*

Business Ethics, published by the Christian Association of Business Executives in the following year. . . . A company has responsibility to employees, customers, suppliers, shareholders and other suppliers of capital, to society in general, and to local and national government . . . Another approach is that of the social audit, a concept developed by Humble as an outcome of his employment as an industrial consultant. . . .

The Code of Business Ethics suggests that individual companies should produce their own codes, and a recent British Institute of Management publication includes many extracts from such codes. . . .

Industry is very well aware that under present circumstances it will not survive unless it responds in some measure to the pressures which consumers, employees and community are now able to exert upon it and increasingly do. It is perhaps as clear an indication as any that the free market economy is at an end. . . .

The real test of codes is whether they are able to help those who make decisions in industry and business to meet the various and increasing social pressures to which they are subjected. . . . The codes provide the [manager] with a useful check list on his wider responsibilities and, at the same time, remind him of the complexity of managerial decision-making. . . . There is a sense in which the code may be as much, if not more, a symptom of the managerial dilemma than a means of its resolution. . . . The codes have a second limitation in that most of them, though admittedly not all, tend to regard social responsibility, even if important, as something peripheral to the main aim and purpose of the enterprise. Business exists to make a profit, and social responsibility would seem to be a kind of ethical bonus which gives the whole exercise a moral tone. . . .

Functioning profitably and making an appropriate return to investors is as much a social responsibility as concern for consumers, employees and community. To look at enterprise in this way is to raise questions about the structures of industry and business – questions which, for the most part, the codes avoid. . . .

[. . .]

[S]ome attempt must be made to indicate the type of model which might help those involved in decision making and initiating change. . . .

The production of wealth is the first essential feature of such a model. Making a profit is part of wealth production, because it is essential to produce more than the total input in order to build wealth into society, but it is by no means all of it. The provision of goods and services which satisfy needs in terms of design, quality and price, the rewarding of those who invest their capital and who give their labour, and the meeting of community needs through the provision of employment and in other ways are also part of the process of producing wealth. . . .

The second feature is the arena of group reaction or the group dynamics of the situation. It is the groups within the organisation, particularly the informal groups, which both provide stability and security and at the same time offer resistance to change. It is through effective action within and between these groups that meeting new situations becomes possible. The human relations situation is clearly affected by wage rates, working conditions and types of organisation, but the groups which come into existence of their own accord are part of the total scene. . . . Thirdly the model must take into account each employee's need for self-fulfilment. . . .. Repetitive, tedious and boring work which is utterly alienating should probably be eliminated, but most work includes an element of alienation, and only acquires meaning and purpose through the total context in which it is performed. . . .

Christians have no particular skill to contribute to the task of building models. They insist, however, that no research for an industrial and business ethic is possible without an appropriate method for looking at the total situation. . . . Christians, for instance, are aware that there is a perversity in human nature as a result of which the best intentions never reach complete fulfilment. . . . It is downright foolish to ignore the fact that people's motives are always mixed. There is an element of self-interest in any bargain . . . however much they may try to convince each other that they are serving common ends. Christians want to bring honesty and integrity to business transactions and to build up trust in relationships. . . . Christians are committed to the imperative of love, but in the knowledge that, human nature being what it is, love is never completely expressed in any order of society, or for that matter any particular business organisation. Some measure of justice on a temporary basis is the closest approximation possible. . . . In the conflict situation, the Christian finds himself faced simultaneously with the issue of self interest and the imperative of love. . . . Love demands that solutions be found in the interests of those who are served by and depend upon business and industrial output. It also demands that solutions do justice to both sides of the conflict or, in other words, that there should be an element of reconciliation between them. . . . Little will be accomplished without the use of power. . . . At the same time, we have to be clear that power is always liable to misuse and abuse. . . . Without becoming involved in this way, there are limits to their effectiveness as agents of change. To be thus involved, however, is to run the risk of sharing in the irresponsible use of power. Even so belief in an incarnate God demands the taking of risks. . . . To accept the incarnation is to accept that God is at work in his world as it is and that Christians are called to co-operate with him there. . . . To be gripped by an incarnational religion is, on the one hand, to be inspired by the possibilities which arise from man's control over nature, his ability to plan and to organize, and the efforts he puts in at the workplace, in the office and in the boardroom. On the other hand, it is to be immersed in the struggles, frustrations and disappointments, both individual and collective, which are part of the work scene. . . .

There is a desperate need for the churches, together with those who work in the industrial and business situation, to arrive at a new ethic for work and for the whole of life, and to proclaim it boldly. Men and women have to be liberated to express their humanity through their work and through their non-working activities without feelings of guilt, and to be helped to accept change as a challenge rather than as a threat. . . . Above all the message of hope should feature prominently in the churches' mission. . . . Technology has made affluence possible and yet has not provided the hoped-for satisfactions. Business and trade have opened up the world for fruitful interchange, and yet have subjected millions to living at near starvation levels. Industry has provided employment on a gigantic scale but has alienated workers and managers alike in the process. It is a wilderness situation. . . . For Christians there is a hope in business, industry, finance, government and all that go to make the city what it is. . . . God is to be found in the city as it is, and invites us to co-operate with him in the building of the new and better city.

Jack Keiser, *Men at Work: A Christian Approach to Business and Industrial Ethics*, London, Epworth Press, 1978, pp. 106–27.

IM under review

The most complete study of IM was published as a major review in 1988, and we examine it further in the next chapter. However, its importance, apart from offering critical sympathetic support, lay in its comprehensive survey within a strong theology of mission, thus asking about the relationship between God, Church and world, and it also contained an insightful account of IM's development and history. We have therefore placed the following extract at this point as a way of summarizing the IM tradition, drawing together the strands of thought and practice that it embodied, and setting the scene for the next period of political, economic and social change. In Chapter 4, a further extract explores IM's relationship with the institutional churches and its changing theological rationale.

A Pioneering Industrial Agency

From its earliest days, Industrial Mission has conceived of itself as being a pioneering industrial agency of the Church, with a distinctive vocation to interpret and apply Christian faith in the secular arena of industrial life and work.

As a purposeful organised involvement by the Churches in industrial life and affairs, IM owes much to the vision and inspiration of people like Bishop Leslie Hunter of Sheffield, who, in his diocesan letter of November 1941, called for 'a new evangelism', looking forward to a new order both in Church and society. Appalled at the gulf between the Church and the working classes, he called for a 're-evangelisation of Britain', through the co-operation of all Christian communities, and by means of a partnership between clergy and lay people.

An essential instrument in such a vision was to be Industrial Mission, and its beginnings are full of a very particular passion.

The distance of the Church from vast numbers who worked with their hands, from wage earners, from the 'man's world' of the shop floor was immense. There was no easy way that the residentially based ministry of the parish Church was going to be able to bridge that gap, and therefore no easy way in which the gospel was going to be proclaimed to working-class people, unless the Church crossed the gap and engaged with the dominant reality of people's lives, the world of work.

As with other great missionary forays into an unknown culture, those industrial missioners who made the journey, as they saw it, on the Church's behalf, also found that their consciousness was being shaped by the new environment in which they found themselves. The industrial world, so alien to the experience of most clergy, quickly became a stimulating and rewarding place to be. More than that, it came to be a place where many of the values associated with the Kingdom of God, such as solidarity and community, seemed more readily visible than in the middle-class world where the Church is most instinctively at home. The belief that the chaplain's task was not to take Christ into the world of industry but to go there in order to find Him where He had gone ahead, found support in the vibrant conversations and negotiations in which chaplains were involved on the shop floor, in the boardroom and in the canteen. Not surprisingly, the more domestic concerns which appeared, from the new vantage point, to occupy the parochial ministry not only figured less, but came to be thought of as obstructing the main task.

Chaplains might, and did, assist those with whom they came in contact, with personal problems and matters of individual religious questioning; but IM was always wary lest such matters should become diversions from the main task of 'finding Christ in industry', relating to an estranged working-class world, and speaking of what a good industrial world would be.

A Quest For Reconciliation

An important theological theme which IM took up with vigour was that of reconciliation. In various ways it sought for real understanding and true co-operation between management and unions, bosses and workers. IM was a child of the post-war consensus, and sought to translate Christian concepts and ideas into practical industrial goals. Hence its enormous commitment during the '60s and '70s to humanising work organizations through industrial relations projects and organisational development (OD) techniques.

There was a problem here. IM's missionary aims and hopes had become too closely identified with the chaplaincy model of working. And through the '60s and '70s, chaplains, in their involvement within the organisations in which they ministered, often felt more at home among those in positions of influence through whom change could occur. The danger of identifying with management became apparent, and the question arose: had engagement *for its own sake* become IM's equivalent to 'mission'? What was IM's gospel?

This matter was hotly contested in 1979–80 in the pages of *Crucible* between Bill Wright of the Teesside Industrial Mission and Michael Northcott, then a research student examining TIM and other patterns of ministry in the North East. Wright called for a revival of the Church's prophetic ministry, 'earning the right to be creatively critical of those powerful institutions in our world which make or mar the lives of us all, including, of course, the Church'. He then went on to describe the various stages through which the partnership between industrial lay people and industrial chaplains develops.

In stage I, a chaplain enters the life of a works, getting to know people, processes and structures. In stage II, he/she draws people together from different sides of industry, off-site, to explore the issues that have arisen in the welter of on-the-job conversations. In stage III, discussions develop into practical suggestions for application back in the works. Stage IV sees the chaplain being drawn into new management-union relationships in industrial relations, in initiating and enabling change, and in helping ideas and experiments to be tried elsewhere too.

Michael Northcott criticised Wright for thinking that this enabling role, which requires impartiality and trust, could also be prophetic, inevitably involving partiality on the side of those who are the recipients of injustice. He wrote:

> '. . . the necessary tension between the affirmation, in the Incarnation, of all that is truly human, and the judgement of God upon oppression and idolatry – this tension is absent'.

'Earning the right to be creatively critical', or 'prophesying from the inside', is an approach still favoured by many industrial chaplains in their factory visiting, though rarely with the clarity of purpose described by Wright.

[. . .]

Running through IM from its earliest days have been two contradictory strands. On the one hand, industrial chaplains – paid officers of the Churches – have spearheaded mission in and to the world of work . . . and have described their work as learning and researching on the Churches' behalf, and bringing to bear on the secular realities of industry and commerce a Christian and theological perspective. . . . On the other hand, IM has been noticeably unsuccessful in becoming a lay movement, and a great deal of agonising goes on about this.

Seven models of lay involvement in IM.
The seven models [identified in a report *Laity in Industrial Mission*] are as follows:

1. Respond! . . . bringing together Church leaders and members with community leaders and members, industrialists and trade unionists, to work on issues.
2. Grindstone . . . developed in Scotland, involves an individual Christian working with another single individual at the factory base, the aim being to create a spiritual and theological 'tool' strong enough to be of use to people in their work situations.
3. Christian discussion group in a Norwich firm. . . . analysis and working life is combined with theological reflection.
4. The Seefar programme . . . a participative programme of lay equipment and training that will provide fellowship and confidence for those engaged at the centre of secular life.
5. The Leeds Industrial Mission Lay Development Programme . . . two strands, one a 24-hour event in which a common experience is [explored]. The second strand is the development and use of programmes for group discussion.
6. The Industrial Christian Fellowship . . . to link work and faith (expressed in particular in corporate worship). It promotes this through regional and local Church 'world of work' representatives.
7. Luton Industrial College. A Methodist foundation, a lay training centre.

It can be seen that Industrial Mission is working hard in the field of lay training and involvement, with some success.

The Roman Catholic Approach.
. . . The field of economic and industrial affairs is the field of the lay apostolate, it was said; the priest 'leaves his people at the factory gates', and the relationship of clergy to industrial and economic mission must be through the enabling, formation and animation of the laity for this work. On that view, the

appointment of industrial chaplains as such would represent a retrograde step in the development of the 'new ecclesiology'. This position was further amplified by reference to two movements, the Young Christian Workers and Family and Social Action.

IM – a Pioneering Ministry.

IM describes itself as a pioneering ministry, operating on the frontier between Church and world. Its missionary approach has been 'dialogical' – a willingness to listen and learn as well as to give and share – and its technique of engagement has of necessity been flexible and adaptable; industrial chaplains have learned to be opportunists.

Three models:

1. THE LONE MISSIONARY.

The chaplain goes out from the Church into the world. This implies firm roots in the Church, but does not imply an attempt to form or plant a congregation in the industrial world. . . . Some of the best examples of this model are team ministries with an industrial chaplain member, or the 'deanery industrial chaplain' idea.

2. THE CONGREGATIONAL BUILDER.

. . . [The chaplain, here, aims] to establish a gathered congregation in the world of industry or amongst those with whom he or she is working . . . to establish worship and study in the secular setting, and from that base seeking to establish any work with the structures. Some non-stipendiary ministers have attempted this . . . some Industrial Missions, such as South London IM and Sheffield, have encouraged lay people to become 'members' or 'friends'. . . . Missions to Seamen and Railway Missions are examples of spiritual and pastoral sustenance being provided for particular groups of workers, though rarely with the intention of developing and mission to the structures of their industries.

3. THE DESERT VENTURER.

The chaplain goes out into the world of industry and secular concern to find God. It is a contemplative and demanding vocation, which has to contend with the possibility of the loss of faith . . . and of any contact with the life of prayer. . . . Strong and understanding networks from the Church are vitally important and missioners should not be left 'out there' for ever. . . . [This] is easily drifted into and may actually become preferred by people. How often have chaplains, deliberately or otherwise, found themselves, in conversation with those outside the Church, having to distance God's Kingdom from the apparent irrelevance and introvertedness of the Church round the corner – and by implication saying that their own work of Industrial Mission has little to do with the local Church's concerns?

[. . .]

The point has repeatedly been made that those matters with which Industrial Mission is wrestling are central to the whole Church's understanding of mission. . . . Why is IM so poor at describing and explaining itself?

[. . .]

Many industrial chaplains and missioners are seen as resources for the whole Church as it works out its missionary strategies. IM helps the Church pick up matters of which it would otherwise be unaware. . . . But there is widespread concern that IM, which has had relatively substantial resources allocated to it compared with other Church mission agencies, has had less influence than it should on the Churches. Blame for this may be laid at the door of both parties. . . .

IM takes as seriously as any Church movement the ecumenical vision of the whole Gospel for the whole inhabited earth. It has responded more keenly than most to new expressions of the ecumenical vision . . . The CCIM *Guidelines* are a model of how ecumenical co-operation can be achieved. Because the wider Church is not yet structured ecumenically, the seriousness with which IM takes its own ecumenical standpoint is in fact a drawback when decisions about wider Church priorities have to be taken. . . .

Industrial chaplains nearly all belong to teams, but these teams consist of people living and working in different places across a wide geographical area. They work with different issues and with different styles and approaches. ... Geographical factors such as these inevitably force chaplains to function on their own, though most teams meet on a weekly or fortnightly basis. ...

[D]e-industrialisation and diversification have undermined the analysis and proposals of the 1959 report, which had never really been implemented anyway. Hence the confusion about where IM should be concentrating its efforts in a far more complex scene in which the local, regional, national and international aspect have all become inextricably interwoven. And in those parts of England where the most significant industrial and economic growth is taking place, such as along the M4 corridor, and in parts of Surrey, Hampshire, Wiltshire, Sussex and Essex, IM is grossly under-resourced.

Industrial Mission: An Appraisal,
Board for Social Responsibility,
1988, pp. 37–40, 81–101.

3 Centres for enquiry and study

Alongside the official structures of the churches there have appeared a number of specialist organizations committed, as a major part if not the whole of their brief, to the study of the issues raised by the world of industry, theology and commerce. It is, therefore, worth noting here some significant examples that have played their part since 1945 to the present. Because those bodies that emerged within the period of this chapter are largely extant and constantly developing, it makes sense to include alongside the longer-established organizations some of the more recent entrants into this field, for together they constitute a contemporary network with an impressive historical lineage. They are clearly an aspect of the Christian response to the economy. Characteristically these have been set up on the initiative of a creative individual or as an extension of an institutional programme. Some, however, owe their origins to church authorities but have then been left to act, like a quango, on their own authority, managing their own affairs and building their own programme and taking their own initiative, as well as responding to the promptings of their parent body.

The Industrial Christian Fellowship (ICF) and the Ridley Hall Foundation (RHF)

As noted in Chapter 2, the ICF was an amalgamation of the Christian Social Union with the Navvy Mission. In its heyday in the inter-war period it had a national network of commissioners, clerical and lay, that sought by public meeting, small groups, publications and pastoral care to meet some of the challenges of the industrial world. Today its work has greatly reduced but it is nevertheless continuously active. It is primarily a network of individuals and local groups dedicated to the cause of relating Christian faith to life in the workplace. It advertises courses, encourages discussion groups, provides worship material, encourages research and tries to keep the churches informed of the concerns of those engaged in the business world.

The RHF, started in 1989 under Dr Richard Higginson, is based within an evangelical Anglican theological college in Cambridge. Its work is done through seminars, publications, including the journal jointly sponsored by the ICF, *Faith in Business,* research and public events. Its brief, as set out in its mission statement given below, is to work in the area of the relevance of Christian faith to business theory and practice.

> Business plays an enormously important role in today's world. It creates wealth through the provision of a rich variety of goods and services which enhance the quality of life. But business is often the target of public criticism. In today's highly competitive global economy, companies are having to face *searching questions* such as:
>
> > What balance to strike between the interests of different 'stakeholders'.
> > How to establish good relationships in industries where adversarialism is endemic.

What obligations of loyalty exist between employers and employees.

How to secure contracts honestly in countries where bribery is rife.

Whether business encourages a greedy, materialistic and divisive society. [. . .]

Christians in business often feel unsupported because of:

Indifference, suspicion or hostility to business on the part of church leaders.

The failure to include business in the church's prayer, preaching and celebration.

The Ridley Hall Foundation works to bridge the gap between business and the church.

(Introductory leaflet)

The Christian Frontier Council

The Christian Frontier Council was formed in 1942 under the auspices of the leadership of the Church of England, the Church of Scotland and the Free Churches and was placed under the purview of the newly formed British Council of Churches. This was a think-tank of about thirty eminent Christians drawn from a wide range of walks of life, civic, professional, academic and ecclesiastical, a forum for the discussion of current public issues 'off the record' and, by publication and other means, to stimulate Christian thinking. The aim was to 'explore the idea of the frontier' between faith and the world of 'social groups and natural relationships', especially the political, economic, cultural and intellectual. It worked at a number of levels. It met as a council with an agenda of current concerns; there were conversations and consultations around chosen topics into which others were drawn; it published a journal, at first the *Christian Newsletter* but subsequently the influential *Frontier,* which reached a wider audience; and there were study groups to examine in depth a given issue, providing the basis for a volume or other publication. These last included the widely recognized authoritative study on higher education, Walter Moberly's *Crisis in the University*, and a response to the establishment of the welfare state and its cultural implications, Daniel Jenkins's *Equality and Excellence*. However, as society moved away from what might be called an 'establishment model', dominated by the 'great and the good', coupled with growing financial exigencies, it appears that the Council has faded away.

The William Temple Foundation

After the Second World War, many churchpeople – not only Anglicans – began to think about a suitable memorial to William Temple who had died in 1944. Under the leadership of the Bishop of Sheffield, Leslie Hunter, funds were raised to endow a college named after Temple, with the unusual remit of training women in theology and the social sciences so that they could work out their Christian vocations within the new employment opportunities then emerging. Opening initially at Hawarden in 1947 with six students, it was not long before both the vision and the activities of the William Temple College expanded. By the 1950s, the College had moved to its own residential complex in Rugby and was running study programmes for men and women from what were then known as 'both sides of industry' and for specific professional groups. By the end of the 1960s, however, it was clear that neither the churches nor industry was willing to fund this work at an adequate level, and new approaches were essential. In 1971, therefore, the College moved into the then-new Manchester Business School, becoming the William Temple Foundation and conceiving itself as a 'college without walls', focusing on training programmes, research, publishing and teaching in the field of Christian social ethics, with a strong leaning towards economic matters. The first Director of the Foundation was David Jenkins, later to become Bishop of Durham, and he was soon joined by John Atherton who has remained one of the foremost British theologians working on economic issues and public theology.

From its inception in 1947, the College and Foundation had

strong links with the Industrial Mission movement, not least through the involvement of Leslie Hunter who had been the driving force behind both ventures. Until the late 1990s, the Foundation ran Induction Training for Industrial Missioners and almost all recruits to IM participated in this course, some going on to further studies through the Foundation's programmes run in conjunction with Manchester University. The Foundation also offered facilities and publishing outlets for the work of the Industrial Mission Association's Theology Development Group.

IM has, however, never been more than one string to the Foundation's bow. During the 1980s the Foundation took a leading role in the development of community work among the British churches and undertook many innovative projects, often from its own base in Salford, in community development and training. The Foundation was also a driving force behind many European church networks bringing together theologians, economists and activists to develop common agendas. In the 1990s, the Foundation was one of the first bodies to perceive the widening gap between developments in academic theology and the kind of theological analyses which had sustained grass-roots activists (including IM) since the 1960s. Its more recent programmes have therefore had a stronger research element and closer ties to the study of Christian ethics and practical theology. Since 2001, under the leadership of the Foundation's current Executive Secretary, Dr Chris Baker, the emphasis has been on the nature and structure of the postmodern city and the role of the churches in regeneration programmes.

Very soon after its inauguration, William Temple College realized the limitations of Anglican support for its work and understood that its key concerns were best approached through an ecumenical profile. Today the Foundation is based within the ecumenical Partnership for Theological Education at Luther King House in Manchester and works in close collaboration with the University's Department of Religions and Theology and with numerous grass-roots groups.

St George's House, Windsor

Through the vision of Robin Woods, the Dean of Windsor, and with the support of the Queen and Duke of Edinburgh, an eighteenth-century deanery was turned into a conference centre, situated in the outer baillie of Windsor Castle. It is specifically devoted to bringing together leaders in Church, industry, politics, administration and the professions to consider issues of spiritual, theological and social importance. It has a distinguished programme of consultations as well as playing host to special-interest groups. The policy is to work to 'Chatham House rules', enabling participants to take advantage of the confidentiality of the exchanges. Proceedings are not, therefore, normally published, though there have been valuable contributions from staff and others associated with the House. It is, in fact, one of the few centres in Britain that can be compared with the 'lay academies' that sprang up after the war on the continent, notably in Germany.

The Society, Religion and Technology Project (SRT) of the Church of Scotland

This ongoing project was founded in 1970 in response to a challenge set out by Willie Robertson, then Director of the Scottish Council for Development and Industry. The Church, he said, must take technology seriously if it was to be credible in modern society. Thus the Project can set out as its perspective:

> SRT affirms the idea that technology is a basic aspect of being human but its practice must be shaped within a framework of ethical values and social factors. Technology is not value free. It is developed through choices which imply value judgements. These reflect the values of its society and in turn technology reshapes society. The SRT Project, therefore, seeks to promote values which would encourage the development of responsible technology in relation to both humanity and God's creation, as a practical outworking of Christian principles.

A Unique Experiment, briefing paper, p. 1.

It carries out its mandate by taking up issues of public concern in the field of technology and creates a discussion network of those engaged in the field through correspondence, working groups, conferences and visits. An interdisciplinary perspective is brought to bear from scientists, technocrats, theologians, social scientists and ethicists, including those who may be critical or anxious about the route particular applications of technology threaten to take. This study process results in various types of publications, from substantial volumes, through articles in academic, professional and popular journals to participating in the debate at conferences, seminars and through the media. The process is cumulative as there builds up an ever widening network of contacts that are both resources and ways into new avenues of enquiry. Thus it is possible for the Project to keep ahead of the game, anticipating debates before they hit the public headlines. It also allows the Project to work with the opinion-formers as well as with scientists and others at the cutting edge of development. Winning confidence and respect means that the Project is a recognised authority. All this is reported back, informing the Church of Scotland's thinking, and through the ecumenical networks in Scotland, Europe and the wider world, made available to the wider church and beyond. This story is told in Ronald Ferguson's *Technology at the Crossroads* (Edinburgh, St Andrew's Press, 1994). Themes that have occupied attention have included:

in the 1970s, North Sea oil and gas and energy policy;
in the 1980s, land conservation and exploitation;
in the 1990s, bio-engineering and global warming.

The Centre for Theology and Public Issues

It is worth noting here another more recent innovative focus for public theology. Founded in 1986 by Duncan Forrester, then Professor of Christian Ethics and Practical Theology in Edinburgh, the aim of the centre is 'to promote reflection and research on important public issues to which Christian theology can make constructive contribution' (Introductory leaflet). Thus it is part of the Edinburgh Divinity Faculty's research activity, with a commitment to inter-disciplinary enquiry and an engagement with the experience, wisdom and needs of those living and working in the community. It claims to be doing 'public theology', which is described as working 'critically with Christian belief and practice in relation to public affairs'. At its heart, therefore, are research projects on current political and social issues, supported and augmented by study conferences, public events and the formation of interest groups. A stream of occasional papers and other publications make these enquiries available to a wider audience. Of direct interest here are studies on *Finance and Ethics* (1987) and 'Consumer Values' looking at 'the effects of the consumerist culture on children and their parents'.

The London Institute for Contemporary Christianity

This is an evangelical foundation, sited in the West End of London, which originated from the work of John Stott, then Rector of All Souls, Langham Place. Through public lectures, courses, study projects and publications it seeks to explore the relevance of Christianity to the contemporary scene.

The Capitalism Project, currently directed by Dr Peter Heslam, has more recently contributed to the debate on globalization.

> The truth is that contemporary economic globalization is a highly complex phenomenon, full of apparently contradictory trends. It can help to raise living and environmental standards for significant numbers of people at the same time as it helps to widen the gap between rich and poor and increases the destruction and depletion of natural resources. This reflects the fact that it is perfectly possible to achieve a good in some areas at the cost of creating a bad elsewhere. The challenge, therefore, is to shun the media-fostered mindset that only understands polarities, to consider all sides of the issue, and to base judgements on as full account of the available evidence

> as possible. Genuine solutions can only be found by seeking to understand the problems and opportunities in their complexity and interconnectedness.
>
> Peter Heslam, *Globalization and the Good*, London, SPCK, 2004.

Two issues need to be faced: to create places and times when those caught in the globalization process, those forging economic and political policies and theorists can meet, listen and reflect; and to explore the importance of religious and ethical thinking, in order to affirm the relevance of the Christian perspective.

The project has brought together thinkers and practitioners in many different settings, often in collaboration with other organizations with similar concerns, and has contributed to the deliberations of others. Out of it have also come publications, notably Peter Heslam's *Globalization: Unravelling the New Capitalism* (2002) and an edited volume of essays given at various seminars and consultations, *Globalization and the Good* (2004).

The 'Christians in Public Life' Programme (CIPL)

This programme of exchange and study was launched in 1991. It was the brainchild of David Clark, who became the co-ordinator, a Methodist minister and lecturer at Westhill College, Birmingham, where it was based.

> **The Christians in Public Life Programme** established by Westhill College is meant to ensure that the new commitment evident within the church to active involvement in the daily affairs of our society is affirmed and developed as effectively and as rigorously as possible. **The programme's main purpose is to enable Christians in public life to engage, share and work together with others in addressing fundamental questions of mutual concern.**
>
> It is a programme founded on the premise that Christians

are, with others of different faiths or none, called first and foremost to work for the coming of 'the Kingdom'. That it is in and through such shared endeavour that God reveals himself, often in quite unexpected ways. The mission of Christians in public life today is to be fully committed to and involved in this task, to help raise the awareness of others to its ultimate significance whilst being open to learn from and work alongside all fellow travellers.

The term **'public life'** has raised some interesting questions. All terms have their limitations. However related words such as 'the world' or 'society' were felt to be too global or too nebulous. 'Public life' in the context of this programme refers to that sphere of life and work beyond the private and the domestic. The emphasis is on the collective rather than the individual. Public life is fashioned primarily by institutions within which a good deal of human interaction is with the stranger or the visitor. Relationships are as often anonymous as personal, as often temporary as continuous. It is the sphere of life dominated by work, for a wage or a salary, but one which also embraces voluntary endeavour.

Public life is inevitably about the political, the economic and the social, as well as the religious affairs of society. It is about power, wealth and justice or the lack of these. It is an arena of constant and often discontinuous change. For all such reasons, public life extends well beyond the parish and the neighbourhood, though these remain a significant part of the larger picture.

David Clark, *Christians in Public Life: Origins and purpose*, CIPL position paper A1, January 1992 (emphases original).

There were four main strands of activity. A subscribers' list provided a basic network for the production and distribution of a series of short papers. These authored contributions discussed a wide range of issues concerning society, public life, the Church, mission and spirituality. A selection were edited into a book (David Clark, *Changing World, Unchanging Church*', Mowbray, 1997). This included attention to the economy under such topics as: the market, taxation, work, ecology and industrial mission. Second, there were seminars and consultations around immediate issues. Third, research was undertaken. The most significant was a survey on Christians and work, looking at how faith, religious practice and pastoral care related to people's public life. This was undertaken in England (published 1995) and Wales (published 1998). Fourth, the 'Human City Initiative' was centred on Birmingham, from 1995 to 1997.

> Cities are our future. To neglect them is to neglect the future of our civilisation. . . . So we need to create an urban society in which the truly human thrives and where what is dehumanising is rooted out. . . . **The Human City Initiative is rooted in the conviction that we as Christians will never discover a new way of being church until we also discover a new way of being city; that we will never find a new way of being city unless we also discover the true meaning of being church.**
>
> David Clark, *The Human City Initiative – Update,* November 1995 (project paper, emphasis original).

The whole programme closed down in 2002.

The Centre for Public Theology, Manchester

This is the latest initiative to respond to the renewed interest in public theology, stimulated, as suggested in Chapter 1, by the revival of so called 'confessional theology' and the need to learn to articulate Christian insights afresh in a post-Christian and pluralistic society. This draws on the resources of the Department in the University and of the Partnership for Theological Education at Luther King House, along with a number of community groups in the city.

Launched in May 2004 with a conference addressing 'Religious Capital in Regenerating Communities', the Centre describes itself thus:

> The Centre is concerned to identify the peculiarly urban, industrial and post-industrial context of Manchester as the

common focus of its core group: as a place which demonstrates in microcosm the major global currents of economic, cultural and demographic change associated with the rise of industrial capitalism, the birth of modernity and transition to post-modernity and their resulting human impact . . .

Centre: We hope to be facilitators and resources, as a meeting point between many and diverse participants. Our activities will be structured on a four-fold pattern:

- *Identifying issues and problems* – listening to a range of voices and data
- *Fuelling the debate* – seeking out resources, analysis, ideas, research
- *Facilitating dialogue* – convening conversations, encounters, speakers, events
- *Seeking performance outcomes* – disseminating our findings, putting ideas to the test, assisting best practice.

Public: We are concerned with 'public' in two dimensions; firstly, with the impact on communities, neighbourhoods, individuals and institutions of broad economic, political, cultural, social and religious trends – with the welfare of the public domain and the impact of public policy. But secondly, we are committed to conducting these debates *in public*: in a multi-disciplinary, open forum in which theological discourse is offered as a stimulus for common exploration and insight.

Theology: We do not believe that the values of faith can be segregated from the public domain, but equally, beliefs and values need to be integrated with practices and policies. We seek to bring reflection on the ways the received traditions of faith bear witness on contemporary experience.

Elaine Graham and Chris Baker (eds.), *Religious Capital in Regenerating Communities: Proceedings of the Launch Conference of the Manchester Centre for Public Theology, 10th May 2004*, Manchester Centre for Public Theology and William Temple Foundation, 2004, p. 34.

The Commission on Urban Life and Faith

Something of the historic impact of *Faith in the City* (see Chapter 4) can be gauged from the desire to mark its twentieth anniversary in 2005 with a renewed focus on the urban context and the role of the churches. Set up by the Church of England, but with substantial ecumenical participation, the Commission's intention is both to evaluate the changes in the urban context over the last twenty years and to make a substantial contribution to the debate on policy and priorities, in the public sphere as well as within the churches and other faith communities. At the time of writing, the final report of the Commission has not yet emerged, but the following themes are forming the framework for the group's enquiries:

1. The degeneration of towns and cities
2. The impact of diversity and fragmentation
3. Sickness and anxiety
4. Demoralised Citizens
5. Our Cities and Towns 20 years on
6. Contributions of churches and faith communities

Website of the Commission on Urban Life and Faith, http://www.culf.org/sections/key/ Accessed, 14 September 2005.

4 Individual authors

This last section to this chapter draws attention to some of the publications of key writers who have directly, in the period with which this chapter has been concerned (1945–79), addressed the question of the relationship between economics and the Christian faith. Many of these, of course, were also called upon to contribute to the deliberations of working parties and elsewhere. It reveals also the comparative lack of interest in this particular aspect of Christian social thinking compared with other areas of interest such as social conditions or family issues.

The bibliography at the end of the volume provides a much fuller list of titles, which includes many that also fall in the period 1945–79, and are thus available to any who wish to engage in a detailed survey of the material.

H. F. R. Catherwood, *The Christian in Industrial Society*, London, Tyndale Press, 1964.

A businessman, who is also a lay theologian, sets out his conservative evangelical understanding of the demands of being a Christian in modern economic life, stressing the qualities expected.

Charles Elliott, *Inflation and the Compromised Church*, Belfast, Christian Journals, 1975.

An early book by an economist and priest, an expert in developmental economics and later Director of Christian Aid.

Leslie S. Hunter, *Church Strategy in a Changing World*, London, Hodder and Stoughton, 1949.

The former Bishop of Sheffield outlines his basic perspectives on mission in society.

Margaret Kane, *Theology and Industrial Society*, London, SCM Press, 1975.

This lay woman had a long and influential career in practical social theology, starting in Sheffield and serving in Hong Kong and Durham.

George F. MacLeod, *Only One Way Left*, Glasgow, Iona Community, 1956.

The founder of the Iona Community sets out his reasons for his socialist Christianity.

Denys Munby, *Christianity and Economic Problems*, London, Macmillan, 1956.

Denys Munby, *God and the Rich Society*, Oxford, Oxford University Press, 1961.

This Oxford economist argues that God has given us responsibility to use and develop the riches of the world, but within clear moral purposes.

Owen Nankivell, *All Good Gifts: A Christian view of the Affluent Society*, London, Epworth Press, 1978.

A Methodist lay man and civil servant argues that affluence has its moral advantages but also brings responsibilities.

Ronald H. Preston and Edwin Barker, *Christians in Society*, London, SCM Press, 1939.

Ronald H. Preston (ed.), *Technology and Social Justice*, London, SCM Press, 1971.

Ronald H. Preston (ed.), *Industrial Conflicts and their Place in Modern Society*, London, SCM Press, 1974.

Ronald H. Preston (ed.), *Perspectives on Strikes*, London, SCM Press, 1975.

Ronald H. Preston, *Religion and the Persistence of Capitalism*, London, SCM Press, 1979.

Anglican priest, theologian and economist, Preston was perhaps the most significant British thinker in this field in the second half of the twentieth century. He continued the tradition rooted in Oldham and Temple. He espoused and defended the use of an approach similar to 'middle axioms', and was critical of later political and liberation theologies.

John F. Sleeman, *Basic Economic Problems: A Christian Approach*, London, SCM Press, 1953.

John F. Sleeman, *Economic Crisis: A Christian Perspective*, London, SCM Press, 1976.

This economist, based at the University of Glasgow, tries to show how economics both illuminates our understanding of the world and people and impinges on and is illuminated by faith.

Horst Symanowski, *The Christian Witness in an Industrial Society*, London, Collins, 1966.

A leading pioneer of IM in post-war Germany; this is a classic of IM thinking.

R. H. Tawney; *Religion and the Rise of Capitalism*, Harmondsworth, Penguin, 1938.

Using Britain as a case study, this classic sets out a version of the argument that the churches have been marginalized from the economic field as society has segmented, but that it is imperative to remake the connection if society is to recover a sense of social moral direction.

William Temple; *Christianity and Social Order*, London, SPCK (1942), 1976.

Temple's bestseller and classic exposition of how the Church can become engaged in social issues through providing guiding principles ('middle axioms').

E. R.Wickham, *Church and People in an Industrial City*, London, Lutterworth, 1957.

E. R. Wickham, *Encounter with Modern Society*, London, Lutterworth, 1964.

The 'father' of British IM, in his classic study of Sheffield, sets out his seminal theological reflections. The second, slighter, volume allows him to reflect on wider concerns in society.

4

Crisis 1979–90

Part 1 The end of consensus

The passing of time has made it difficult to remember whether the advent of Margaret Thatcher's first government in 1979 felt at the time like the seismic cultural, as well as political, event that it is now seen to be. While her election was generally understood to represent a widespread weariness and frustration with the Callaghan years, and it was Thatcher's image of strength and purpose to which the electorate had warmed, her early manifestos were, by later standards, distinctly cautious. Cutting government spending was to be achieved through eliminating 'waste' – who could object to that? – rather than the wholesale re-engineering of the social contract which had, hitherto, been accepted by post-war governments of Right and Left alike. The Thatcher revolution might have been schemed out in theory before she took power, but the possibility of bringing it into being only became apparent as her grasp of power became secured.

The novelist and commentator Julian Barnes suggests that liberal-minded people made two fundamental mistakes about Mrs Thatcher. First, they took her to be 'some kind of political weirdo', a right-wing Tory seeking to govern a country that had oscillated between governments of the Labour Right and Tory Left for decades. Barnes goes on to note that the 'second miscalculation was the assumption, made until quite late in the day, that what she was doing to the country could, and would, eventually be undone'.[1] Now, in the third 'New Labour' administration of Tony Blair, the 1960s and 70s seem like a very foreign country indeed, to which a return is beyond imagination. Church people, of course, were as inclined to make mistakes about Thatcher as anyone, and while there were many who welcomed her election with enthusiasm, there was real wariness among the churches' 'social action' practitioners even as they too mistook the nature of the imminent revolution. If, before 1979, there was still some truth in the old claim that the Church of England was the 'Tory Party at prayer' (and, of course, Christian – and Anglican – apologists for Tory policies have never gone away) it was perhaps the stridency of the Thatcher years that made the alliance between Christianity and Conservatism seem less and less plausible.

If the mood of Britain in 1979 could be recaptured, it would probably be recognized as a mixture of slightly truculent anger and pessimistic nostalgia. The cultural upheavals of the 1960s had destroyed many social certainties that had never quite recovered from the Second World War, and the sense of promise which the 1960s had encapsulated very rapidly faded during the following decade. Thatcher herself frequently made the 1960s the butt of her contempt, but it is doubtful whether she ever articulated a coherent analysis of their significance. But by the late 1970s it was manifestly apparent that buoyant self-confidence, and an almost unlimited faith in human progress, was unsustainable. The brief flowering of England (especially Liverpool and London) as the centre of that new phenomenon 'pop culture' had proved to be no more than a temporary interruption to the inexorable decline of Britain as a world power still coming to terms with the loss of Empire. The 'socialism' of the Labour Party and 'One Nation' Conservatism alike had failed to maintain an expectation that constant growth in prosperity could be combined with egalitarianism, while the gradual but incomplete erosion of rigid class differences and social deference had, along with growing incomes powering a consumer culture, generated resentments at both ends of the social spectrum. Not surprisingly, perhaps, the evocation of 'Victorian Values' proved seductive, although what they entailed was less well formulated at the time. Indeed, nostalgia for the Victorian era, combining as it did economic liberalism and social authoritarianism, might be seen as containing all along the seeds of the contradictions that eventually exposed the post-Thatcher impotence of the Tory Party.

Francis Wheen makes 1979 a turning point, both in the politics of Britain and in the history of ideas.[2] That year saw not only the coming to power of Thatcher in Britain but the advent of a fundamentalist Islamic regime in Iran under the Ayatollah Khomeni. For Wheen, both events marked a turning away from the Enlightenment values of rationality and the proper evaluation of evidence. He sees the free-market economics espoused by Thatcher as another, apparently secular, version of anti-rational fundamentalism. But while there is much that is persuasive in Wheen's reassertion of the virtues of the Enlightenment, there is no doubt that Thatcher and Khomeni alike were not only agents of radical change but also symptoms of a deeper malaise that perhaps they themselves could apprehend only vaguely or viscerally.

The antecedents of Thatcher's economic policies are traceable not only to Adam Smith (with whom they are perhaps most often associated) but, perhaps less romantically, to Friedrich Hayek's *The Road to Serfdom* of 1944 and that writer's subsequent thinking. Smith's writings are more nuanced and varied than the rhetoric of Thatcher and her supporters would imply, but Hayek's polemic appealed much more to the technocratic mentality of the late twentieth century. And whereas Adam Smith's thought is profoundly influenced by his Christian convictions, Hayek's commitment is to a world where religious concerns are no more than regressive anachronisms. It is interesting that Margaret Thatcher's frequently asserted Christian convictions (see, for example, her address in 1988 to the Assembly of the Church of Scotland[3]) never really went deep enough to explore the theological roots of Adam Smith's thinking but were, rather, deployed in support of policies that were far more congruent with Hayek's dismissive approach to any ethic grounded in faith.

Hayek's project, outlined most comprehensively in *The Mirage of Social Justice*,[4] was in many ways the apotheosis of classic liberalism. Where people had, historically, inhabited tribal societies in which ethical agreement was a condition of belonging, he argued, humanity was now within sight of a 'Great Society' in which the things that people hold in common have superseded tribal difference and exclusiveness. In the Great Society, people must come to recognize that ethical agreement about just ends is impossible to achieve. Until that is understood, people will fail to see that conceptions like social justice are no more than the illegitimate imposition of the interests of an elite upon everyone else. Once agreement about ends is accepted as impossible, the way is clear to order the Great Society on the basis of agreement about means. Hence the priority of the market in Hayek's – and Thatcher's – thinking. The outcomes of the market are unknowable since they are the result of the interplay of millions of individual transactions. And, if I cannot know the outcome of my own decisions within a market economy, it becomes absurd to speak as if I could, by my economic choices, promote any such concept as social justice.[5]

Hayek's thought was taken up with enthusiasm by Keith Joseph, one of Thatcher's ministers who had previously served in the government of Edward Heath. For Joseph, the philosophical and moral case for the market brought on a personal conversion and much public repentance of what he had come to see as the errors of the interventionist economics championed by Keynes and adopted by Labour and Tory governments alike since the Second World War. It is often claimed that Joseph was an unworldly academic who never foresaw (or at least mistook the significance of) the social consequences of his theories. Even if this is so, Margaret Thatcher was a consummate politician who understood that Hayekian market economics could be harnessed to a political project that could reverse the (in her view, heretical) doctrines of ever-greater material equality engineered by governments that taxed the rich and controlled increasing swathes of public life. Such heresies had, it was claimed, created a dependent underclass supported by the virtuous, hard-working middle class; they had allowed Britain to lose markets and influence in the face of international competition and had sapped the entrepreneurial spirit by destroying the incentive to take risks. It was often noted by her opponents that the practical politics of market economics in the Thatcherite mode entailed that we must all be more productive, but that the poor must be encouraged to work harder by being paid less while the rich must be 'incentivized' by being paid more.

Given Thatcher's working assumption that British society was insufficiently exposed to the rigours of the marketplace and that, as a result, the economy was marked by inefficiency and lazy thinking, it is hardly surprising that the immediate consequences of her policies, once implemented, included a startling rise in unemployment. It was noted with irony that among the most effective posters in her 1979 election campaign was one that declared that 'Labour Isn't Working' and depicted a snaking queue of benefit claimants (in fact, actors). Then, unemployment had reached something over 1 million. During the Thatcher years it rose beyond 3 million, counted according to a methodology that had been changed so often (always with the effect of reducing the total) that strict comparisons became impossible. Along with unemployment, but only recognized much later, inequality between rich and poor widened rapidly. That this was the result of Thatcher's economic policies became clear in later years when 1979 was sent to be the moment at which a gradual closing of the gap over several decades was reversed both suddenly and continuously with only a gentle slowing of the pace (but not the direction) of change through the 1990s.

The churches in the Thatcher years

How did the churches respond to the evolving Thatcher project? Some, perhaps, were reassured by her reciting the well-known prayer of St Francis in the hours immediately following her election. But if the desire to bring love where there had been hatred was sincere, then she showed little concern, through the following years, to mitigate the social divisions that her policies brought about. This opening of divisions in society, and the bitterness that emerged on both sides, as her tendency to triumphalism required that her opponents be not only defeated but vanquished, was profoundly disturbing to a majority of Christian consciences. But while many probably shared Julian Barnes's misapprehension that the more extreme policies could and would be reversed when their deleterious social consequences became inescapable, few at the time could grasp that the Thatcher government saw its task as a profoundly moral, not merely a pragmatic, venture. And, given the robust Methodist version of the Protestant work ethic within which Thatcher had grown up (the legacy of her much revered father, the Grantham grocer and alderman), it was to the vocabulary of Christian faith that she and her cohorts naturally turned when confronting their opponents. With Hayek and Joseph, she had come to see the pursuit by government of social justice as not merely a mirage but an immoral act of coercion, but, unlike them, she seemed to feel viscerally that this insight was wholly congruent with a Christian understanding of the primacy of the individual and the centrality of the family as the moral and social unit. (Famously, she was to remark that 'there is no such thing as society, only individual men and women and families'.) This conviction meant that, throughout the Thatcher years, opposition from the churches was a particular anathema, and Christian apologists like Brian Griffiths and Digby Anderson[6] were deployed officially (in the case of Griffiths) or otherwise to present the moral case for market economics and to denigrate those church leaders who dared to proclaim a dissenting ethic.

Among the best co-ordinated confrontations between the churches and the government came, not over domestic economic policy, but over nuclear deterrence. In concert with the Reagan administration in the USA, the Thatcher government had from the outset pursued a policy of military strength against the Soviet bloc. Nuclear arsenals proliferated (including the hugely controversial deployment of US missiles on bases in England) and organizations like the Campaign for Nuclear

Disarmament, hitherto almost moribund since their heyday in the 1950s, became mass movements. The rapid multiplication of nuclear warheads and delivery systems worried the churches too, and the Anglican Board for Social Responsibility compiled a report, *The Church and the Bomb*,[7] calling for the West to take a lead in disarmament. The General Synod rejected the conclusions of the report, but not by a very large majority. But the debate about disarmament, which continued to be highly contentious until the fall of the Soviet system in the late 1980s, rarely touched on the economic implications. The extent to which the UK economy relied upon armament manufacture was rarely highlighted in the moral arguments of either side. Only in Industrial Mission, and then only in some teams, did the extent of the arms industry and its economic impact feature as a cause for concern. Here, it was IM's historic links with the trade union movement that opened up the issue – in particular, the interest shown in developments at Lucas Aerospace where shop stewards had initiated an investigation into conversion and diversification of their industry to non-arms production. The Lucas project fell victim to the powerful arms lobby, but the interest in alternatives – an interest easily incorporated into theological concepts of redemption and repentance – persisted in IM for many years, though with little practical impact. There was no real sign that the enthusiasts for arms conversion projects had thought through their approaches (or their theology) in the light of the moral compass that guided the government's economic policies.

It was only in the second Thatcher administration from 1983 that the relentless and irreversible character of her so-called New Right policies began to elicit the beginnings of a coherent reaction from the churches. Hitherto, their responses had been essentially geared to pastoral care of those most affected by unemployment and social dislocation and to continuing along old ways in the expectation that something like normal service would be resumed as soon as possible. It was widely believed that the country was simply experiencing the unwelcome, but doubtless necessary, upheaval attendant upon rapid change and that in time everything would settle down again. There was some disquiet that government ministers might not be sufficiently aware of the social disruption that their policies were causing, but this was generally conceived as a matter that could be put right if the churches and others fulfilled their proper duty of caring for the victims and patiently explaining the facts to the powerful. The idea that the powerful might know all too well what was going on, but see it as an essential element in asserting a new set of social relationships, was credible only to class warriors on the left and a long way from the consensual politics in which the churches had such a strong investment and in which they continued to believe even as contrary evidence multiplied around them. However, the Falklands War and its domestic aftermath opened a new chapter.

Faith in the City

The landslide election victory of 1983, capitalizing on the victory over Argentina in the Falklands, gave Thatcher's government the impetus to press on with its project with less concern than ever for voices in opposition. With the Labour Party impotent and polarized between those who sought a return to consensus and those who urged as aggressive a class war on the rich as the Tories were thought to be pursuing on the poor, there were few credible voices in Parliament to check her. Her policies were, in her own rhetoric, so closely identified with the national interest (she persistently asserted, in private and in public, that there were no alternatives) that dissent was regarded as unpatriotic or even treasonable. The moral conviction that drove Margaret Thatcher meant that only voices that could draw upon a similar well of unshakeable morality stood any chance of standing in her way. Not unnaturally, this role became filled, more or less unwillingly, by the churches – and in particular, because of its perceived centrality to national life, by the Church of England.

The precipitating crisis that drew the churches into the fray was not, at first, a matter of economic policy. The churches' historic neglect of economic questions, and their marginalization since the time of Temple of complex questions of social morality, had left them ill equipped to challenge Thatcherism on ideological grounds. Moreover, there was a natural caution among church leaders about making public criticism of an elected government – especially one with a thumping parliamentary majority. Even when social divisions and despair overflowed in 1983 into street rioting in Brixton, Toxteth and elsewhere, with complex racial dimensions, did the pastoral imperative of church intervention become inescapable.

The response from the Church of England was an Archbishops' Commission on what became known as Urban Priority Areas (UPAs) – the inner city and outer-estate zones that had borne the brunt of unemployment and social marginalization. It is worth recalling that the impetus for the Commission came, first and foremost, from the parish clergy who lived and ministered in those areas, though with enthusiastic backing from bodies such as Industrial Mission and the Board for Social Responsibility. It was these clergy who first petitioned the Archbishop of Canterbury, Robert Runcie, urging the necessity of some kind of action and intervention from the churches.

The report which emerged in 1985, *Faith in the City*, was perhaps the most substantial flowering of the 'middle axiom' tradition of theological reflection that had characterized Anglican social thought since Temple. Many Anglican assumptions suffused the process and content of the report. For instance, the research was undertaken on the model of a Royal Commission, headed by a retired senior civil servant. The working party, which represented church interests and different areas of academic expertise, did not encompass the people who actually lived in the UPAs with no serious prospect of escape, although it drew evidence from them in its various tours of the affected regions. As part of the classic tradition, its recommendations were addressed to the state and to the church; critical of both, to be sure, but with an inbuilt assumption that, if only the true picture was made clear to government and church leaders, change for the better would naturally ensue.

But it was in its theological chapter that *Faith in the City* marked a tentative move away from the tradition and a recognition that the times were changing.[8] Despite its patrician composition, the Archbishops' Commission clearly came to recognize that expressions of Christian faith appropriate to a consensual and stable society were of limited salience in communities that had been marginalized from the benefits of economic and social participation in the country's affairs. Cautiously, the report drew on the insights of liberation theology, which, emerging as it then was from Christian base communities excluded by military oppression from democratic participation in their nations, had come to develop theologies that stood in stark contrast to the state religion of their oppressors and yet drew, with reverence and authenticity, on biblical images of communities throwing off the yokes of political and spiritual oppression. In the popular mind, however, liberation theology was tainted by its respectful grappling with Marxist analyses. In the depths of the Cold War, this alone was sufficient to damn it in the eyes of the political Right. *Faith in the City* merely suggested that a theology for the UPA might find some resonances in liberation theology, yet this did not prevent Norman Tebbit, Mrs Thatcher's most aggressively partisan minister, from denouncing the report as 'pure Marxist theology' – a convenient soundbite that he did not bother to explicate. Whether Tebbit's outburst helped or hindered the report's reception in the churches and among the public in general is a moot point. For many on the fringe of organized religion, the report was received as evidence that the church was coming to represent one of very few points of coherent institutional resistance to Thatcherism.

It seems probable that the churches – and especially the Church of England – slipped into this oppositional role almost by accident. Wedded as they were to the old understandings of social consensus and the limits of governmental power, they were not only ill prepared for the emerging creed of Thatcherism but, by acting in ways they had always done, almost inadvertently found themselves articulating the anxieties and bewilderments of a society in turmoil. A key factor with which the churches had failed to grapple was Thatcher's 'project' to denigrate and weaken the so-called intermediate institutions – bodies that played a part in national life at some level between the government and the individual citizen. Thatcher was elected in 1979 with a pretty clear mandate to 'do something' about the trade unions, which were widely perceived as over-mighty and dictatorial. What many failed to see was that the philosophy that set out to corral the unions was, potentially, no more sympathetic to any other social institution. In the ideology of the Tory Party in the 1980s, the only legitimate source of power apart from the market was that derived from the popular franchise. 'The people' elected the government, and any other institution that pretended to speak for 'the people' without that legitimating mandate was no more than a conspiracy against freedom. There was elected government and there was the market. No other expression of public feeling, justice or truth could be entertained. Thus not only the trade unions but the BBC, the conception of a non-political civil service, even local government (when it sought to implement non-Thatcherite policies) came under assault. Naturally, political expediency dictated that some targets were easier than others, and it was only rather late in the day that some of the professions such as doctors and university teachers came to realize that the antipathy to institutional power applied to them as well. But the case of the churches is especially interesting since traditional Tory sympathy with religion, coupled with Margaret Thatcher's own Methodist upbringing, meant that the charge against the Church had to be exceptionally subtle.

The Thatcherite position was that every individual must speak for themselves and their views should never be assumed by the bodies to which they might belong. Thus a trade union might vote by a majority to go on strike, but that vote must not be binding on those individuals who dissented. This was the extreme case. But while clubs and associations might, on occasion, be permitted to speak for their members in general, the notion that any institution might dare to articulate truth for all was anathema. Here, then, in the social policies of the Conservative Party in the 1980s, the whole philosophical tension between religion and modernity was encapsulated. Could there be religion without the claim to objective, religious truth? What did it mean to be a 'Christian nation'? What was the role of an Established Church? In all these things, the traditional Tory position supporting Christian faith and the Established Church was at odds with the rhetoric of the party with its strident individualism and desire to withdraw legitimacy from intermediate institutions of all kinds. This made the churches very difficult targets for Thatcherism to hit. It might even be argued that Thatcherism collapsed from the force of its internal contradictions on this very point – that, in the end, the modernist project of market economics and individuated social relationships could not be accommodated within Toryism's instinctive nostalgia for Christendom and community.

But the clash between faith and modernity was not just a problem for the government. The churches also had to face the secularization of the surrounding context, and the demise of cherished Christendom assumptions. The shifts in religious adherence since the Second World War have been ably traced and documented by Grace Davie who has not only analysed the British context (coining the helpful, descriptive phrase 'believing without belonging') but has also shown how the UK experience is mirrored in much of Europe, but is very different from that in the USA and on other continents.[9] However, in the early 1980s the trajectories of secularization were less clearly understood. Church leaders continued to exercise their responsibility to speak on issues of public concern and, perhaps because of a general assumption of living in a Christian country, few saw the necessity to place their comments within an overtly Christian rationale. This constituted yet another manifestation of the crisis in social relationships in the 1980s. Those who spoke publicly in the name of the churches had not yet understood that, as far as the government was concerned, their legitimacy lay almost solely in the extent of the active membership. It took time for people in the churches to make the link between declining church attendance and the authority of church leaders in the public realm. So there was a dissonance between the style of public church utterances and the reality of their political and social muscle. There was a mismatch between the expectation that pronouncements by church leaders would have at least some impact on government policy and the reality, as the Thatcherite project became more and more daring in its iconoclasm. And yet the churches could not quite be vilified with the vehemence directed at the unions. Their cultural significance remained (at least for the time being) just too strong to be dismissed totally. At the very least, apologists for the government had to be mobilized to make the moral and theological case. As the work of Brian Griffiths shows, this was often rather thin and selective, but there was not much theological sophistication among the clerical critics of the government either.

It was during the 1980s that the theological underpinning of the churches' social action began to wake up from a fairly lengthy slumber. Temple's legacy from the 1930s had continued to serve the churches well through the period of post-war prosperity and consensus. It had, perhaps, been an approach especially well in tune with the post-war self-image of the British (or at least the English) people as a nation where old class-bound distinctions were on the wane, being replaced by the journey towards equality and co-operation – a planned, managerial vision of social progress. The 'middle axiom' approach to theological engagement with social issues rested on some untested assumptions about the reserved place for Christian theology at the table where debate took place, about the role of the church as an 'estate of the realm' with the responsibility for 'Christianizing' national life, and about the very possibility that 'people of good will' could, and would, speak commensurate languages and achieve something like agreement. But these assumptions were to be tested, from Left and Right, both by the hard politics of the 1980s and by the deeper trends in culture, philosophy and theology itself.

In the period under consideration, some of these trends were only tentatively emerging. There was an almost tangible sense of a tradition of social Christianity under threat but not yet clear which threat to answer or how to respond. In the following chapters we will argue that, while some of these uncertainties remain, at least it has become possible to note some dominant trends – both politically and theologically – and to suggest some of the ground on which the future engagement of the churches with the economy might take place. For now, however, our focus is on the self-questioning that emerged in the churches as the struggle with change deepened.

In many ways, it was the churches' practical engagement with the economy and the consequences of economic policies that precipitated the re-evaluation of the theological task. This was for two reasons. First, ventures such as Industrial Mission had always attracted a proportion of clergy and others who were theologically reflective and alert to developments in the academy. These practitioners, though relatively few in number, kept up the intellectual task of relating social realities to academic trends – and not only in theology, for, like Ted Wickham in the early days of IM, key figures in the movement through the '70s, '80s and '90s such as Mostyn Davies read widely in the disciplines of management theory, political science, economics and philosophy as well as theology. Second, the social divisions that opened up within British society proffered an immediate challenge to the assumptions of the established theological method. To the question, 'Who is meant by the word "we"?', the churches had, for years, responded in vague terms that suggested the answer was the whole nation and, in some circumstances, the whole of humanity. But when whole working communities, whole ways of life and whole regions of the country were being treated as peripheral, redundant or even 'the enemy within' (as Thatcher dubbed the striking miners), such anodyne ways of thinking became insupportable. And it was the practitioners in fields such as IM and Social Responsibility, alongside the people and clergy in marginalized communities, for whom the issue first became inescapable.

Industrial conflict

Gradually, the Thatcher government had selected its enemies – those who opposed its policies – within industry and, later, within wider social culture. One of Mrs Thatcher's first acts on assuming office had been to approve a very large pay rise for the police. The police then played a pivotal role in the conflicts that followed as, in industry after industry, conflict between workers and management was provoked, confrontation followed, and images of lawless, violent trade unionists could be beamed around the country (indeed, around the globe) to portray the enemy who must be defeated if civilization was to survive. The steel industry and the print unions were among the first targets – the latter being of special significance since the concept of the freedom of the press could be evoked as a genuine democratic issue, and yet could be helpfully (for the Tories) elided with the more contentious question of the freedom of press barons like Rupert Murdoch to make technological changes that would facilitate the domination of the British media by Conservative-friendly global entrepreneurs.

In the country at large, the steel strike of the early 1980s, and the consequent closure of much of Britain's steel-making capacity, was seen as a sad but probably necessary response to changes in world trade. It was sad that Britain, which had been the workshop of the world, could no longer produce steel economically, but necessary, perhaps, if the future indeed lay in profitable high-tech industries. There was sympathy for the steelworkers, but it did not extend very deep. The print unions, on the other hand, were perceived as militant Luddites attempting to hold on to restrictive practices that threatened the whole concept of free speech. Of course, most people gained their impressions of these conflicts through media largely owned by the very press barons who were waging the war on the unions.

By her second administration following the 1983 General Election, Mrs Thatcher had gained the power base in Parliament, and the ideological confidence in her project, to tackle the symbolic head of the trade union movement – the miners. Her proposals to run down the once-mighty coal industry to a mere rump was not only about 'modernizing' the structures of the economy but involved a determined assertion of the authority of Government over other institutions. It had, after all, been the National Union of Mineworkers that had been instrumental in bringing down the previous Conservative administration of Edward Heath.

But Britain's self-image as an industrial power was built upon coal. The work of a miner was widely admired even as the necessity for men to delve into the bowels of the earth was deplored. The privations of deep coal mining had forged unique bonds of mutuality and community in the towns and villages of the coalfields. A whole way of life, as well as a political ethos, was at stake. Miners who had argued for years that their sons should not have to follow them down the pit realized that the government's alternative to the pit was no work at all. A market founded on a philosophy of individualism had no time for the nostalgic evocation of community solidarities. As the threat to the pits became a matter of government policy, whole communities were united in opposition and in support of the ensuing strike.

And now the gulf of imagination and experience between the old manual working class and the white-collar middle class began to be very apparent. The NUM under its firebrand leader Arthur Scargill managed the strike clumsily, enabling the media and the Tories to represent them as fundamentally undemocratic. Violence on picket lines – including the killing of a miner in Wales who was attempting to continue working – made for frightening images, while the drafting in of thousands of police threatened to bring marshal law to the coalfield communities. The miners' claim that their industry was being dismantled was widely disbelieved – the agenda purported to be one of modernization – but subsequent years proved them to be accurate. For a country whose coal reserves had not only forged the industrial revolution but had powered the way to victory in two world wars, the prospect of dependency on foreign sources of energy seemed absurd, yet the political case against the miners convinced many that the government must not lose.

Here, the churches found themselves interestingly placed. Churches and communities were wedded to one another. The Anglican parish system ensured that every community had its church and its minister, while Methodism and the Free Church tradition had vital historic links to the mining regions. The virtues of community had emerged from shared hardships and commonly borne troubles and the churches had celebrated and mourned with the people for generations. This, then, brought to the fore an aspect of Christian ministry that had rarely surfaced at national level: in contrast to the notion of the Church taking its place in the debates of the powerful, the faithful witness of local churches in hard-pressed communities came to be seen as a source of authentic theological insight. At national level, church leaders lobbied hard for a more humane approach to managing conflict. They wanted to steer a way that combined necessary modernization with consensus. They could not see why whole communities had to suffer or why the miners had to be not only defeated but vanquished. The national efforts were not well co-ordinated. In one day, three different church groups, unaware of each other, lobbied the then Secretary of State for Industry, Peter Walker. More impact was made by the newly appointed Bishop of Durham, David Jenkins (soon to become the bête noire of theological and political conservatives alike), whose enthronement sermon in Durham Cathedral challenged the government's objectives in the conflict.[10] The combination of nationally prominent leaders, well-informed practitioners (including Industrial Missioners) and local roots among the people of the coalfield communities, gave depth and effectiveness to the churches' involvement in the conflict. But it was the local rootedness and deep understanding of the dynamics of the community that gave them their authenticity at a time when old assumptions about ecclesiastical interventions in politics were called into question. This had profound theological significance.

The miners' strike of 1984 was followed by *Faith in the City* in the following year. In both, the destruction of working-class community life as a consequence of market-led policies was understood as an immeasurable loss to the social fabric of the nation and the root cause of tremendous human suffering. And in both cases, the churches were able to command a respectful audience because they were connected at ground level. The Archbishops' Commission chose the title of their report because, they said, they had found faith in the city. The double meaning was deliberate. Faithful Christian discipleship was continuing through the lives of clergy and laity in hard-pressed communities, and, as a result, it was possible to have faith that these places were capable of regeneration, physical, moral and social. Gradually, almost imperceptibly, and in ways that would not be much remarked upon for many more years, the centre of gravity of Christian social action was shifting from the centre, with leaders and a secretariat operating at national level on behalf of the churches, to the local level and the engagement of Christian people in their own communities.

In terms of engagement with the economy, however, this was both a potential strengthening and a source of weakness. It offered the beginnings of an answer to the questions about the legitimacy of church intervention in the public sphere by stressing the presence and ministry of the local church everywhere, and, especially in communities ravaged by economic change, the churches were often able to become focal points for voluntary action that both mitigated the impact of change and brokered partnerships for what was later to become known as urban regeneration. But the potential threat stemmed from the historic antipathy of local churches to regarding economic affairs as part of their pastoral or ministerial concern. Economic decision-making lay increasingly at national or supra-national level, so the activity of small numbers of people in obscure corners of the country frequently seemed utterly impotent, even when they managed to appear on the local churches' agenda at all.

But the shift of focus to the local level was theologically creative. As with *Faith in the City*, the influence of liberation theology began to be felt in an indigenously British context. It might, at times, have been applied with little contextual subtlety (the parallels and differences between British working-class communities and the base communities of Latin America were seldom explored) but it offered an established theological vocabulary which both appeared to fit the situation and overcame the increasingly unlikely stress on consensus that had characterized the middle-axiom method.

The Churches' changing self-perceptions

Once the churches started using the style and vocabulary of liberation theology, new questions began to emerge about the place of the Christian community itself. More will be said about this trend in the next chapter, but it brought to the fore the central theological questions concerning the place of the Church in a post-Christendom world. On what grounds was it possible now to speak of a 'public theology'? Was the Church called primarily to shape the structures of society in ways that reflected Christian values, or was the Christian community ultimately called to live counter-culturally as a people belonging to a Kingdom not of this earth? Was mission about infiltrating the secular world by stealth, or must Christ be named explicitly in every setting? And was the purpose of mission to save souls from damnation or to bring God's Kingdom closer in this life?

A full account of the evangelical revival of the 1980s and '90s is beyond the scope of this book. But although the roots of that revival are complex, they owe something both to the gradual acclimatization of the nation to the individualistic, even consumerist, ethos inherent in the Thatcherite project of marketization, and something to the increasing loss of confidence among the churches in their social role, their political significance and their overall viability in a secular society. Because so much of the churches' social action had been conceived in more-or-less conscious rejection of the pietist tradition, and because so much had been staked on a theological liberalism which was becoming intellectually unsustainable, Christian social action was in danger of being simultaneously high-profile (in response to social change) and perilously weakened as its energies were directed to activity rather than rebuilding its intellectual and theological foundations. The centre of gravity in the churches was shifting towards a renewed and vibrant evangelicalism.

One personal recollection may be apposite here. Harvey Cox's well-known book, *The Secular City*, appeared in 1965 and exemplified the 'secular theology' of its time with a highly optimistic reading of urban society with its anonymity and plethora of individual choices.[11] Yet, despite several decades of experience which had surely shown that there were serious downsides to urban anonymity and unbridled self-invention, Cox's book was still being read with enthusiasm in some IM circles throughout the '80s and '90s. As a number of critical essays in this period noted, IM seemed to be trapped in a theological time warp, continuing to draw on its traditional sources (only slightly mitigated by its flirtation with liberation theology) long after they had ceased to speak to the wider context. Meanwhile, a sea change in theology and moral philosophy was under way. Alasdair MacIntyre had published the first edition of his seminal study in moral theory, *After Virtue*, in 1981, with its enigmatic call for a new St Benedict to offer models of community that could endure the 'new dark ages'.[12] And while MacIntyre thus gave a whole new impetus to the communitarian approach to theology and ecclesiology, it took some time for the activists on the ground to become aware of such developments in the academy or the impact that such ideas would have on practice within a very few years.

The year 1979 ushered in a period of crisis whose reverberations were felt in every community of the country. It was as much a crisis of ideas – a crisis in the way people were to interpret their world – as in politics in any narrow sense. The political crisis, and the conflicts that followed, were both a cause and a symptom of something deeper, variously described as the end of modernity, the beginnings of globalization, and the death of tradition. But, perhaps surprisingly, it was also a brief period of flowering for Christian engagement with economic issues. To be sure, the churches had seen their memberships declining for many years, but (especially in the case of the Church of England) historic assets were cushioning the financial impact of decline. There remained widespread confidence that the churches were still as highly trusted and regarded as William Temple had been in affairs of national significance. The churches (again, particularly the Church of England) still expected to be able to speak powerfully to the powerful and to be consulted in turn by policy-makers. Paradoxically, the confrontational policies of the Thatcher governments gave the churches the opportunity to be doing something useful in the public realm. They could be the prophetic voice, the pastoral provider, the organizer of community action. At national and local levels, resources were focused on the churches' public role.

It is worth remarking here that many – even most – official church bodies took international questions seriously, reflecting, as they did, the concerns of the denominational structure rather then the neighbourhood emphasis of local church life. They were thus among those who spotted quite early on that the economy was becoming increasingly global and less susceptible to national policy-making. From the 1960s, IM had established numerous links beyond Britain, either through its association with the international trade union networks or through following up the implications of local issues. Thus in the 1980s, Industrial Missioners working in the General Motors plant in Luton had participated in longstanding links with that company's plants in Germany whose productivity was constantly held up as a target for British workers (and the British, in turn, discovered that they were held up to their German counterparts as models of cheap labour). South Hampshire Industrial Mission, its ministry in Southampton docks making the implications of international trade inescapable, built links with churches in South Africa and, later, noting the dependence of the region on arms-related production, with churches in the German Democratic Republic. But these links did not, on the whole, fit the churches' denominational perspective on internationalism, which was driven much more by the legacy of the colonial missions on the one hand and by the search for ecumenical accords on the other.

Not surprisingly, therefore, the period produced considerable internal debate about what the churches were doing – and what they thought they should be doing. Even as the agencies of church engagement with the economy flourished, they remained somewhat marginal to the mainstream of church life. To some extent, this reflected the unreconstructed assumptions, always prevalent within the churches, that the purpose of mission was personal conversion and that politics and religion occupied separate spheres (what Temple, in *Christianity and Social Order*, had called 'an entirely modern and extremely questionable assumption'). Other opposition came from those in the churches who supported Margaret Thatcher's aims and sensed (probably correctly) that the churches had a political as well as theological agenda. But within IM and the other social action agencies, the project was far from unanimously agreed. The Social Responsibility agencies had, in many cases, been formed for the purposes of social care rather than to seek social transformation. Where this pastoral and paternalist view of ministry was strong there was generally resistance to a more structure-oriented approach. In IM, it became very clear that the former focus on reconciliation between 'the two sides of industry' was increasingly difficult, but old structures geared to old aims did not adapt smoothly to new political and social realities.

Changing Industrial Mission

IM is, in this regard, an important case study of ministerial and missiological change informing, and informed by, theological change. The proliferation of IM posts in the 1960s had been resisted by Ted Wickham, the movement's founding father, on the grounds that if IM became popular in the churches it would quickly lose its prophetic mission to call the churches to repentance and renewal. Wickham feared the incorporation and institutionalization of IM, and to a degree he was right. In many places, by the late 1970s, IM had become a safe partner in a consensual industrial context. Some chaplains had developed skills in fields such as organisational development and were acting rather like unpaid management consultants to the firms they visited. Many saw their role essentially as pastor to the company's staff, simultaneously desiring to be accepted and yet conscious of the fragile position they occupied, their presence dependent upon the goodwill of the management and (in some cases) the unions. Pragmatically, IM's position within industry was rarely secure enough to risk controversy, and the expulsion of a few chaplains who had challenged management decisions in too blatant a way served as a warning to others. Many in IM were convinced that, without their privileged access to the workplace, their ministry was illegitimate.

Where this assumption was challenged, the catalyst was often unemployment. Redundant staff became non-persons in the context of their former workplace, but it went against the ministerial grain for IM chaplains to collude in this anonymity. Efforts to remain in touch with unemployed people, and a growing realization that the increasing levels of unemployment were impacting on whole communities way beyond the firm itself, drove IM into project work such as advice centres which drew as much on the model of community work as on traditional workplace visiting. IM staff were often so lightly managed by the churches (or anyone else) that they could completely revise their own activities at very short notice thus giving them an enviable ability to initiate and follow through new projects. For many, the focus of their work shifted rapidly away from workplace visiting to a more amorphous role, lobbying, fundraising, convening, servicing and managing all kinds of coalitions for voluntary action. How, then, was this new activity to be understood in theological terms? And, maybe as importantly, how was it to be explained to the sponsoring churches?

And so, the 1980s and '90s were a period of intense self-questioning and theological exploration within Industrial Mission. As already noted, liberation theology was becoming influential in the European context and IM was well to the fore in incorporating liberationist perspectives in its own thinking. But the wider question of the relation of IM's field of activity to the mainstream life and concerns of the churches could not be ignored. If IM constituted a prophetic voice addressed to the political and economic structures, from where, and with what authority, did the voice come? With the membership of the churches as divided as the country itself, in what sense did bodies like IM speak for the Church, let alone for God? IM had begun as the embodiment of Ted Wickham's desire to radicalize the churches and call them back to their proper God-given vocation. Wickham had seen the churches as heretical, mistaking bourgeois values for Christian virtues. Then, it was the world of industry that could enlighten the Church: but now the churches (or elements within them) wanted to critique the direction of the economy in the name of the gospel. IM was slow to understand the nature of this shift and, in consequence, struggled to find the theological – and especially the ecclesiological – language to locate itself in the new times.

The questions were not all in IM's court either. The churches at large were divided in a number of ways. All had their vocal supporters of Margaret Thatcher who frequently sounded as if they sought a purge of liberals in the churches to mirror the government's outlawing of traditional trade unionism. Many included a substantial caucus who were appalled by Thatcherism and lost few opportunities for public criticism (although more were, perhaps, motivated by nostalgia for a once familiar world than were driven by a coherent ideology, despite the taunts of the Right). But most church people, including church leaders, were torn between the increasing politicization of all aspects of life and a deep-seated unease at the prospect of a politicized Church. The existence of activities like IM exacerbated the nervousness.

Responses from beyond Anglicanism

Inevitably, the Church of England came under most scrutiny from government and experienced the greatest insecurity in itself. But while the tensions noted above were apparent in every mainstream denomination, some embodied a less defensive dynamic. The Church of Scotland, despite its established status, operated against the background of a nation that sensed the gap between government policy and national interest to be widening all the time. Scotland was especially hard hit by the run-down of heavy industry and especially conscious of the role of those industries in generating and sustaining viable, mutual communities. The Conservative governments gave a very strong impression of understanding the Scots little and caring about them less. The ability of the churches in Scotland to articulate both a sense of community identity and a deepening anger at the impact of national policy was evident in the scope and depth of reports to the General Assembly by the Church and Nation Committee. The Scottish Churches' Industrial Mission also flourished in this period.

Although much less well resourced than the Anglicans, the activities of the Free Churches in England and Wales were also distinctive in character. The dissenting tradition, the roots of Methodism in working-class communities, the strong bonds between the URC and Scottish people in England, all contributed in subtle ways to a mood that was distinct from Anglican concerns. The Church of England may have had the resources and staff and, often, the relatively easy access to ministers and other power-brokers, but the Free Churches were not encumbered by the desire to protect and preserve these privileges. The United Reformed Church was noteworthy for its enthusiastic focus on local communities as places where political ends could be addressed through careful, bottom-up, encouragement of the people of a locality, and the church-related community worker became recognized as an order of ministry within the URC.

Roman Catholic involvement was, as it always had been, somewhat different. Only in the later 1980s did the Roman Catholic Church begin to bury its differences with the British Council of Churches and start to participate in collective ventures through the successor body, the Council of Churches for Britain and Ireland. Although Cardinal Hume employed an economic affairs adviser, the Catholic Church had an ambivalent relationship to the involvement of the clergy in industrial life. The conflicts between the worker-priest movement in France and the hierarchy in Rome were rather too recent for comfort.[13] Catholic teaching had always emphasized that mission in the workplace was a lay apostolate rather than a priestly vocation. This raised the question of how lay people were to be trained and supported in their ministries and mission. In some places, the Young Christian Workers movement, with its characteristic 'See: Judge: Act' methodology, flourished, but its focus on the politics and economics of the workplace was rarely coordinated into anything churchwide with the authority of the Catholic Church itself behind it. The Roman Catholic Church was, nevertheless, influential. Cardinal Hume commanded considerable respect in government circles and chose the issues on which to speak carefully, partly, one suspects, to preserve his effectiveness by avoiding any impression of knee-jerk reaction. But Hume seemed to adopt a careful agnosticism on questions of economic justice, despite the tremendous effectiveness of his interventions on issues of sexual ethics and criminal justice. Justice, however, was the theme of the important document, *The Common Good*, issued by the Catholic Bishops' Conference in 1996.[14] Here was an exploration in Catholic social teaching, which, implicitly rather than directly, challenged the whole premises of the Thatcherite project. By the time *The Common Good* emerged, the government was perhaps at the high point of its hubristic triumphalism and least willing to listen to anything the churches might say, but *The Common Good* was received with acclamation among church activists, not least as a mark of solidarity from a church that had sometimes seemed politically uncommitted.

Reading the texts that follow, it is clear that they represent a period of rapid change in the social and economic life of Britain to which the churches attempted to respond both practically and theologically. But church people have no privileged perspective on change. It is always difficult to read the signs of the times and to discern what is a repeating cycle and what is an immutable trend. It took time to understand that there was to be no possibility of return to a pre-Thatcherite economy – indeed, the permanence of the change to the social landscape only became widely understood in the second Blair administration after

2001. It took time also to grasp the increasing globalization of the economy and the consequent weakening of national institutions and national politics. But some perceptions were very slow to be taken up despite the accumulation of considerable evidence. In particular, the changing relationship between the churches and the state were not just a reflection of Downing Street's ideologies but reflected the collapse in churchgoing since the 1960s. The internal weakness of the churches was barely dawning in the 1980s and the sponsorship of mission endeavours in the community and in industry was predicated upon financial resources that were dwindling rapidly. For IM, for church community work and for Christian action generally, the desire to address a prophetic word to the world left unanswered the question: 'How will this build up the people of God?' It was only in the period covered by the next chapter that this question became unavoidable and the theological tensions between holiness and survival, between counter-cultural Christian virtue and the missiological imperative to address culture, were opened up in the daily lives of the churches. Most of all, perhaps, few could predict in 1979 that, after a period of intense political controversy, the mood of the nation would lose its appetite for political solutions to ethical problems or that the collapse of the Soviet bloc would usher in an age that combined political apathy with a deep nervousness about the future.

The year 1979 did indeed inaugurate changes in the British economy – and hence in the way of life of most citizens – which appear to have proved irreversible. The churches' institutions concerned with economic life have struggled, first for a workable analysis of the context and then for adequate responses, frequently finding themselves with few fixed points as radical change and reappraisal became as much a way of life in the churches as in industry and politics. The literature of the period – at least with hindsight – thus reflects this uncertain, dislocated and often angry age. Writings that addressed the external context were frequently outnumbered by attempts to analyse and reorder the way the churches took their mission into the economic world.

This tendency toward introspection nonetheless generated some important reflections and analyses of mission. For that reason, this chapter and the next will make use of more extensive readings from the literature, allowing the analyses and arguments to unfold and to reflect the seriousness with which the churches grappled with their own role and the economic and social revolutions that they faced.

The preponderance of Anglican material in the early part of this chapter is not an accident but reflects two historical factors. First, it was the Anglicans, and especially the bishops, with their heightened public profile conferred by the Church of England's established status, who bore the brunt of Thatcherite anger and criticism. Their opposition was perceived by the political Right as a perfidy far beyond anything that other churches could commit. Second, the early 1980s was the period when Anglican resources – notably through the Board for Social Responsibility – not only outstripped those of other denominations but were used to focus (and most importantly, to publish) on economic themes as never before or since.

The contribution of other churches and denominations was far from negligible in this period, but it was offered much more through ecumenical bodies such as Industrial Mission than through publications issued in the name of a church. It is important to bear in mind that when projects and publications bear no specific denominational label they are not always to be considered Anglican by default (a frequent error in the popular press!).

Part 2 Readings

1 The churches address the issues

Although the structures of the churches' engagement with economic issues were under scrutiny from within and without – and facing up to considerable criticism, as we have seen – the denominations, especially the Church of England through its Board for Social Responsibility (BSR), continued to approach the social and economic issues of the day through its well-established method of enquiry. Derived from the middle-axiom approach which we have already explored, the processes were similar whatever the issue. This is succinctly summarized by Professor Ronald Preston, himself a staunch supporter of the BSR and contributor to reports such as *Not Just for the Poor* (1986). Preston's work includes a number of descriptions of this method of seeking responses at a middle level (Preston disliked the term 'middle axiom'). This is his last published version of that description and shows how little had changed in over thirty years.

> I have thought for a long time that the best method has three stages. (1) Identify the problem. This involves a negative judgement on the *status quo*. Christians have a radical faith. They are taught not to be satisfied with things as they are and in particular to be sensitive to all who are marginalised, so they are not likely to lack issues to take up. (2) Get at the 'facts' by searching for the relevant evidence from those involved in the problem, whether as expert witnesses or as experiencing it personally. (3) Try to arrive at a broad consensus on what should be done – first of all at a middle level. This indicates a general direction at which policy should aim. Since there are always disagreements on public policies, among Christians, no less than the general public, this puts the onus on the objector if a Church report can produce agreement on a general direction of policy. If it chooses, a Church report can go on to recommend detailed policies, though the more detailed they are the more likely they are to be affected by the inevitable uncertainties in obtaining facts; these can often be evaluated and interpreted differently. Still more are the uncertainties in forecasting the effects of any detailed policies that are advocated.

Ronald Preston, 'A Comment on Method' in Malcolm Brown and Peter Sedgwick (eds.), *Putting Theology to Work*, London and Manchester, CCBI and William Temple Foundation, 1998, pp. 36–7.

Typically, a BSR working party of the 1980s comprised half a dozen people representing a varied range of relevant experiences and areas of expertise, chaired by a bishop and serviced by Church House staff. The reports usually included a certain amount of theological reflection but the bulk of the text was devoted to a careful analysis of the economic and social context of the issue under discussion. There was a good deal of reliance on statistical information. The overall tone was usually one of seeking balanced solutions in the midst of complexity and a studied avoidance of blame for deleterious conditions. Sometimes, however, the cautious recommendations of the reports were abandoned in favour of a published symposium of diverse essays from different perspectives (*Transnational Corporations*, 1983; *Perspectives on Economics*, 1984). *Faith in the City* stood alone in this series of reports by virtue not only of its public impact but also the scale of the research that went into it and the fact that it was commissioned, not by the Board for Social Responsibility which was so often perceived as marginal to the Church at large, but by the archbishops with their much greater authority and ability to direct resources to the project. In retrospect, the BSR reports directed at specifically economic issues take for granted a very Anglican right to a public voice in political matters, assume a seamless connection between Christian theology and balanced, socially consensual approaches and show little awareness of the narrow social base from which they emanate and to which they seem to be addressed.

Winters of discontent

Industrial conflict had seemed endemic through the 1960s and '70s, appearing to culminate in the so-called 'winter of discontent' of 1978–79 when widespread strikes among public workers and others eradicated the Callaghan government's reputation for competence in managing industrial strife. The Church of England report of 1981 took a classically 'balanced' approach to conflict even as the harder line of the Thatcher administration became abundantly clear. There is no sense here that the gospel itself might be a source of conflict or even that justice might require an overt taking of sides: conflict is rather to be managed so that moderation might prevail. The churches' role appears to be as arbiter rather than champion. Few could have foreseen that, within a very few years, the trade union movement would be in chaotic retreat and the search for mediation and consensus would be regarded as a failed episode from history. As in many such reports, the extract below reveals much about the contemporary climate of opinion in the churches by virtue of what the report feels necessary to assert that it is *not* doing.

122. In this study we have been concerned to understand and to interpret our society by a reciprocal process of analysis and reflection, using both Christian beliefs and real life experience as equal elements. We have not expounded a 'Christian' platform nor claimed to discover a 'Christian' solution since it is not our understanding that such a process would provide a possible tool for living with the problems that we have identified. The Christian life is something one longs for and looks for and approximates through one's actions, and insights can arrive from many different quarters, not all of them Christian ones.

123. Thus, what we have hoped to do has been to expose some of the logical oversimplifications and ideological confusions which often darken counsel when industrial relations are being discussed. It is our understanding that there are always potential or actual conflicts between different groups in society, so that besides the question of how to adjudicate in particular cases there is the more general problem of setting up procedures for handling successive conflicts creatively (that is, so that they do not destroy). Traditional insights about the importance of such concepts as the common good, proportion, restraint, justice and fairness come in here.

124. We have been rash enough to try to discuss some immediately controversial matters . . . While not claiming any

monopoly of insight, we believe that it is legitimate for us here to offer a lead, and we are quite happy to extend an invitation to others with an equally lively claim to insight to weigh the plausibilities of our arguments, and, where they are lacking, to supply better ones.

Winters of Discontent, London,
Church Information Office, 1981, p. 46.

Transnational corporations

An early intimation of what would later be called the debate about globalization came in the symposium of essays on Transnational Corporations (TNCs), which emerged in 1983 at the behest of the BSR's Industrial and Economic Affairs Committee and the Division of Community Affairs of the British Council of Churches. Here, however, any pretension to the middle-axiom method, or even to the objective of arriving at tentative Christian moral judgements, was abandoned in favour of a series of essays, mostly by named individuals, approaching the subject from different standpoints. Thus a rather neutral description of the impact of TNCs from a senior manager of an international company, and the case for the beneficial effect of TNCs by a project worker with the World Bank were followed by critical views from a Nigerian perspective, a trade unionist and an Industrial Missioner. The following extract is taken from the concluding essay in which the editors (Tony Dyson from Manchester University and Paul Brett, Secretary to the BSR's Industrial and Economic Affairs Committee) attempt to put the essays into a theological framework.

7.32 Much of Christian concern, about the economic order in general and about TNCs in particular, can be articulated around the ecumenical concept of the just, participatory and sustainable society.

7.33 Christians need not be embarrassed by talk of justice in terms of human rights. Rights are not what we pridefully claim but what we owe to others who are made in the image of God. These rights are not abstract and ethereal; they deal first with the just distribution of the necessities of living – food, shelter, medical care. Christians have moreover a special concern for the rights of the poor, a priority which goes back, through Jesus, to the Old Testament community. Our business and economic institutions have a vital role to play in the field of social justice not simply in relation to those they employ or otherwise affect, but because we recognise that the material basis for life is essential to a dignified existence for all.

7.34 Justice and participation are closely linked because by democratic procedures we can strive to introduce and maintain those conditions which work for justice. A good deal of the concern about TNCs lies with their lack of public accountability, their uncertain relationship to democratic procedures and to trade union structures. There is some evidence both of an increased participation within TNCs (e.g., through better use of shareholders' meetings) and of external involvement in TNCs by government, trade unions, and voluntary organisations.

7.35 TNCs [. . .] are connected with a large and complex network of life. They are tied in with questions of wealth and poverty, development, war and peace, population control, political freedom. Not least, we know better than ever before that it is only at our common peril that we live outside the limits of sustainability. Thus the most careful questions have to be asked about the misuse of natural and human resources, the pollution of the earth and atmosphere, the damage to health. In such an environment the image of the swashbuckling merchant adventurer no longer holds good. Instead is a question of reasoned choice and delicate responsibility. We have come into a different world than that in which TNCs were born and corporate behaviour has to be adjusted to the new environment.

Transnational Corporations: Confronting the Issues, London, Church Information Office, 1983, pp. 68–9.

Perspectives on economics

It was as if the breakdown of consensus in society at large was creeping in on churches, but unacknowledged and not confronted. By the mid-1980s, although the BSR and other church bodies were still struggling with the kind of reports that generated consensus and ended with measured recommendations to church and state, the objective of Christian consensus was gradually giving way to a different ecclesial role – that of providing a platform from which different views could be aired. Recognizing the salience of economic ideologies and policies in the early 1980s, the Church of England BSR set up a working party to address the question of why the church did not give a 'clear lead' on matters of economic contention; not least, rising unemployment. The classic group of 'experts' – economists and theologians – struggled together for two years to produce what was described on its back cover as an 'unusual report'. In terms of Anglican social theology, its unusualness was perhaps expressed in its understated introduction:

> Our original hope was to produce a single document which we could all sign and which would set out clearly an agreed Christian judgement on the present economic state of affairs. This proved in the circumstances not to be possible. None of us approached the discussions from a fixed position or with a closed mind, but we soon discovered that individual assumptions and consequently individual perceptions were noticeably different. More importantly still, although our perceptions and understandings began to be modified as our discussions proceeded, they did not necessarily begin to merge, nor did they hold out the promise of an agreed judgement. We should have liked to write something that was prophetic as well as educational, but this double objective never came into clear focus. Moreover, the whole process in which we were participating, calling as it did for an analysis of human behaviour and institutions in a period of rapid change, turned out to be more complex and difficult than we had anticipated. . . . Furthermore, the question began to force itself upon us whether an agreed

Christian judgement was in principle possible, and if it was possible, what sort of a judgement it would be in the light of what our discussion had taught us.

After considerable heart-searching we concluded that we had sufficient of a common mind to be able to produce something more coherent than a symposium of independent essays. . . . Thus the reflections we offer are *the outcome of our interacting with each other* and exhibit a large measure of interdependence, even though the prime responsibility for each chapter remains with the person named.

[. . .]

There remains a gap, however, which still needs to be bridged, between Christian insight and moral conviction on the one hand and economic problems and practical decisions on the other. That there is such a gap in our work is undeniable. The nature of this gap – and the reason why it seems, generally speaking, to loom larger in the area of economics than in some other areas of ethical concern – itself needs further philosophical and theological analysis. It may be, among other things, that this is an area in which, as well as disagreement about practical policies, there is also a conflict of values which Christian faith as such does not immediately solve.

Perspectives on Economics, London,
Church Information Office, 1984, pp. 1–2.

Growth, justice and work

Division in society at large was, by the mid 1980s, reflected within the churches too. The search for single, authoritative, Christian judgements on economic issues was untenable in a climate where consensus was anathema to those on the political Right and, in an inevitable reaction, to many on the Left. Margaret Thatcher's second General Election victory conferred a legitimacy on her policies which an Established Church found hard to stand against with conviction. It became *de rigeur* for every working party on economic affairs to include a voice from the Right – whether representing business or monetarist economics. This attempt at representativeness must have created the worst of all worlds, with the Right-leaning members feeling outnumbered and marginalized and those seeking an alternative ethical viewpoint stymied in their search for consensus. Reports such as *Growth, Justice and Work* (1985) have an unsatisfactory and inconclusive atmosphere, struggling for areas of agreement despite the recent and raw wounds left by the miners' strike. The concern for serious engagement with data remains, but the search for moral principles has given way to a slightly desperate homiletic approach from the working party's chair, Bishop Simon Phipps.

> 5.7 The 1984–85 strike in the coal-mining industry gives us an instance of a society not responding to its future, but caught on the hop by its present, and finding no better way of solving its industrial, economic and political problems than by fighting them out when they come to the boil. It is to be hoped that we can learn its lesson. . . .
>
> HANDLING THE FUTURE WELL
>
> 5.8 But the trauma of the strike might press us to stop and think how we might handle the future well. The problem might be transformed if we saw that the future also presents us with the opportunity of a common cause. 'We are all in this together' is a phrase that could only be used about the coal-mining strike, in respect of the mess it has landed us in.

[. . .]

> BROTHERHOOD OF MAN
>
> 5.11 The teaching and living of Jesus presses upon us that the brotherhood of man is not an ideal it would be nice to aim for, if other things were equal. They press upon us that *it is a fact to be realised*. We *are* brothers and sisters. We *are* members one of another. . . . Industrial companies which have found a way of being 'us' rather than 'we and them', pull together and pull ahead. 'Us' becomes

the experience of a fact, and it is felt in terms of morale and expressed in productivity.

CROSS AND RESURRECTION

5.12 ... The value of Christian religion, marked by cross and resurrection, by costs leading to results, is its assurance that in proportion as we accept the costs of co-operation, we reach through to new realities of common life.

Growth, Justice and Work, London,
Church Information Office, 1985, pp. 46–7.

Faith in the city

Perhaps it took urban riots to push the churches into a more adventurous role than that of providing a forum for incompatible views or a pulpit for social sermons. And perhaps because social tensions had erupted in ways that transcended questions of economics, or social policy alone, the churches found a new confidence in their methods of theological enquiry into moral issues. *Faith in the City* applied something close to the old middle-axiom approach to a situation where refusal to take sides or to take refuge in platitude was no longer an option.

As we have already noted, *Faith in the City* was both the most public example of this methodological approach in practice and one of the early indicators of the difficulty of applying an essentially consensual model of enquiry to a highly divisive context. The two extracts below epitomize, first, the report's approach to theology with its explicit advocacy of a liberationist approach challenging traditional western methods and, second, the continuation in the body of the report of the measured, fact-based and moderate argument typical of a gentler era.

The Challenge to Theology

3.29 We believe, then, that there are sound theological reasons (some more apparent today than in the past), as well as solid support in many strands of the Christian (and indeed Anglican) tradition, for the Church to show its care and compassion for our disadvantaged neighbour *both* by personal ministry to individuals *and* by social comment and action; and we have drawn attention to the importance of a kind of intermediate area (often represented by a form of 'community work') embracing the two. But we must be careful not to assume that it is the wealthier and more powerful members of the Church who are always the givers, and the deprived residents of our inner cities who are always the receivers. Poverty may greatly diminish human dignity; but dignity is not necessarily restored merely by the promotion of material standards and values. There is no reason to think that the gospel is more authentically lived out in 'comfortable Britain'. On the contrary, we have again and again found evidence of a vitality and generosity in church life in deprived areas which is a challenge to more affluent congregations. Our task as a Church is by no means only to show concern for the victims of oppressive social conditions; it is also to find ways of discerning and receiving the gifts of those who have worked out a genuine Christian discipleship under circumstances of 'multiple deprivation'. The failure of the Church today is not just a failure to respond to need; it is – perhaps still more – a failure to attend to the voices, the experience and the spiritual riches of the 'poor' in its midst.

3.30 But how is this to be done? The challenge is one which raises questions about the nature of theology itself. In the West, theology since the early centuries has been understood as a deductive science. Christian truth is conceived as a system, derived both from divine revelation and human reason, and growth in understanding is aided by historical and philosophical disciplines. . . . All this has greatly favoured the life of the Church among people of above average literacy and intellectual ability; it has accorded well with the education, the reading habits and the social conventions of the upper and middle classes. But it has always been an obstacle to nurturing the Church in a working class environment. . . .

3.31 Must theology always have this deductive and academic character? . . . The vitality of other forms of theological expression in churches in the Third World, and indeed in certain congregations in our own cities, forces us to ask whether theology must always have such an academic character if it is to be authentic. . . .

3.32 An important challenge to traditional theological thinking is presented by Liberation Theology. This starts from the observation (which would be taken for granted in the sociology of knowledge but has only recently been taken account of by the churches) that the agenda and the priorities for theology have always been set, even if unconsciously, by those who have practised it – that is, those who are relatively well educated and secure. In doctrine there has been a preoccupation with intellectual consistency which has presupposed certain academic disciplines. In ethics, the questions asked have assumed a freedom of action and decision fully possessed only by the upper strata of society. In spirituality, the classic manuals assume a relatively leisured life. There has of course been a long and honourable tradition of Christian service to and ministry among the poor. But for the most part Christian theology has been created by those relatively well provided with leisure, freedom of action and material well-being. As a result, it has not much concerned itself with the perceptions and the witness of those who do not have these advantages.

3.33 In Latin America the prevailing conditions of extreme social and economic oppression have posed a challenge to these traditional theological priorities. Liberation Theology has proposed a method and a set of priorities which reflect the concerns, not of the oppressors but of the oppressed, not of the rich but of the poor. In this context, theological reasoning has seemed relevant, and in a certain sense 'true', only if it results in a determination and a strategy to liberate the poor from this oppression.

[. . .]

No Alternative?

9.38 'Unemployment', said Archbishop William Temple in the 1930s, 'is the most hideous of our social evils.' The effects of unemployment in the 1980s have been all too clear to us on our visits to Britain's UPAs. We have been confronted time and again with the deep human misery – coupled in some cases with resentment, in others with apathy and hopelessness – that is its result. The absence of regular paid work has eroded self-respect. 'Give me back my dignity' was the heartfelt plea from one man – made redundant, and with no prospects of a job – at one of our public meetings in the North-West.

[. . .]

9.46 Individual responsibility and self-reliance are excellent objectives. The nation cannot do without them. But pursuit of them must not damage a collective obligation and provision for those who have no choice, or whose choices are at best forced ones. *We believe that at present too much emphasis is being given to individualism, and not enough to collective obligation.* In the absence of a spirit of collective obligation, or the political will to foster it, there is no guarantee that the pursuit of innumerable individual self-interests will add up to an improvement in the common good.

9.47 No less an advocate of the market economy than Adam Smith accepted in his 'Theory of Moral Sentiments' that economic individualism could not be divorced from moral, religious and social obligations. The complex relationship seen by Smith has been summarised as follows: '(men) could safely be trusted to pursue their own self-interest without undue harm to the community, not only because of the restrictions imposed by the law but also because they were subject to built-in restraint derived from morals, religion, custom and education.'

[. . .]

9.48 So we must not fall into the trap of letting economics suffocate morality by taking decisions for us: economic determinism is an insidious philosophy. The role of economic science is to tell us the likely effects of choices we make on moral grounds.

[. . .]

9.52 We do not present a fully-fledged model to replace present macro-economic policies. It would be foolish of us to attempt this. We recognise, too, that there are limits to any government's freedom of action in the face of national and international economic constraints. But we must question whether, at a time when our economy is in transition to an uncertain future, a dogmatic and inflexible macro-economic stance is appropriate.

Faith in the City: A Call for Action by Church and Nation, London, Church House Publishing, 1985, pp. 61–4, 208–10.

The welfare state

Appearing soon after *Faith in the City*, but even more a product of the classic Board for Social Responsibility method, the BSR report *Not Just for the Poor* turned attention to the apparent attrition of the welfare state under the Thatcher governments. This was the era when most church reports appeared to need a witty or punning title, but this time the deliberate ambiguity of *Not Just for the Poor* made a salient and significant point about the participative model of welfare and the dangers of regarding welfare provision as no more than a safety net for the unfortunate. Among the members of the Working Party who produced the report was Professor Ronald Preston and the report, unsurprisingly, conforms closely to his way of working. The detailed enumeration of facts is painstaking, but the theological background sketched out in the early chapters is not carried through in any integrated way to the conclusions and recommendations – it is left to the reader to make the connections. There is, here, no hint of the liberation theology that informed *Faith in the City*, but the report is notable for its guiding motifs of complexity, paradox and compromise. These were difficult values to maintain in the partisan years of Thatcherism and, if they are values grounded in Christian theology (as some would claim), the grounding is not explicit here.

6.55 At the beginning of the chapter we mentioned briefly the fundamental disagreement about the impact of welfare expenditure on the economy at large. It is beyond the scope of this report to resolve such a broad and complex question, but it is important to be aware of it. It is obviously relevant to consider how the welfare state is paid for. This chapter has given a simple outline of how this is done at the moment, and made some suggestions about aspects of the present system that need to change. However, while economic policies cannot be ignored, that does not mean that economic theory must dictate the form and spirit of our welfare provision. The major decisions about the welfare state in this country were made immediately after a war which had left it drained materially. This was not, however, allowed to divert the nation from embarking on major social reforms.

6.56 The very confusion that exists about the impact of welfare expenditure on the rest of the economy shows that if the country is waiting for a united message from economists, it will have to wait for a long time. Decisions have to be made about the kind of society we want. Economic policies need to inform policy development, rather than determine it.

6.57 Of course the creation of wealth is important; of course means of reviving industrial and economic life must be sought; of course jobs need to be created in huge numbers. But the question remains: for what is that wealth to be used? The working party would argue that welfare, the well-being of all members of that society, cannot just be an incidental consequence of an economic policy but must be an integral part of the overall policy which decides in which direction our society should be heading.

Only in this way can a proper relationship be reached between economic and social policy.

Not Just for the Poor, London, Church House Publishing, 1986, pp. 115–16.

The ethics of acquisition

As an example of the BSR's work on economic issues in the late 1980s, *The Ethics of Acquisition* is not untypical and fits Preston's description of method closely. It arose as a response to a widely perceived problem. As the second Thatcher administration engineered a boom economy, it became clear that it was not enough for a company to do its job well, it had to be constantly vigilant against predatory takeover bids from rivals seeking a greater market share or from apparently unrelated enterprises seeking to diversify. Contrary to what most people had believed, the engine of economic growth was less the concern with producing and selling things than that of making money through deals which could put jobs and local institutions in jeopardy. Thus the BSR was persuaded to investigate this phenomenon with a view to offering a Christian perspective on the ethical issues.

The initial motivation for the study came through Industrial Mission. A member of the London Industrial Chaplaincy team, working in Oxford Street department stores, was concerned at the impact on staff and management of a hostile (and ultimately successful) bid for the Debenhams stores by the Burton Group. The impossibility of resisting the takeover culture at the level of the firm or even a single industry prompted a request to the BSR to investigate the issue, presumably in the hope that an intervention from the Church at national level might have more impact.

The report itself is a good example of how the method that had become the hallmark of the BSR approach now struggled in an increasingly complex world where the relevant decision-makers could not themselves be represented around the table. The issue of mergers and acquisitions clarified the sense that individuals, communities (including those in the workplace) and churches were far more distant from the levers of power than they might have thought thirty years before. As a result, the report is distinctly cautious in tone, shy even of expounding middle axioms and resorting instead to posing questions of a somewhat generalized nature. And in the extract that follows, where the report sets out five key ethical issues, explicit theology is noteworthy for its absence. Four years after *Faith in the City* flirted with liberation theology and addressed both church and government with clear proposals for change, this slighter work epitomizes the crisis of confidence in the churches as the Thatcher project reached its triumphalist zenith and the possibility that there might be viable alternatives retreated rapidly.

Five Key Ethical Issues

The following five questions arise from the previous chapters and their discussion of the issues surrounding mergers and takeovers.

1. Is it right to separate too much the wealth-creation activity from wealth distribution? This is the 'Catch 22' referred to at the beginning of Chapter Three. Many people would want to insist that the way wealth is *used* is inseparable from *how* it is created, and that the wealth creators have a greater responsibility to social wellbeing than solely the creation of wealth. How the wealth is created, by whom, for whose benefit, where, and what, are all pertinent questions.

2. Is the framework of a market economy and democratic environment sufficient to ensure that mergers and takeovers achieve the aims identified by Peter Harper (in Chapter Two) of
   a) increasing the wealth-creating capacity of the acquiring company?

   and

b) improving products, benefiting employees and satisfying customers?

3. Does the role of institutional shareholders as 'trading investors' rather than 'owners' need examining, especially in relation to small shareholders and employees? Can share price adequately measure true value? The US concept of 'stakeholder' may be helpfully explored: those with a stake in the company include not only shareholders, but also management and staff, customers and the local communities in which a company is located.

4. If mergers and takeovers can act as effective catalysts for change, how can companies exercise real care and responsibility in such situations? Should they be legally or morally obliged to consider wider interests than earnings per share?

5. Regarding the longer-term interests of employees, can the criteria [a well-run company; fairness; 'an honest contract'; loyalty; good inter-staff relations] be widely affirmed as principles which should be taken into consideration in merger situations? If so, how, and with what consequences? Is it just and proper that company directors should make provision for themselves, in the event of losing their jobs in a takeover, but nothing commensurate be provided for employees?

The Ethics of Acquisition, London,
Board for Social Responsibility, 1989, p. 23.

2 The bishops and their critics

David Jenkins, the miners' strike and Margaret Thatcher

David Jenkins came to the see of Durham from an academic post as Professor of Theology at Leeds University. Prior to this, he had been Director of the William Temple Foundation and on the staff of the World Council of Churches in Geneva, so his background was hardly that of a theological or political conservative. His appointment to the northern diocese of Durham, with a local economy deeply dependent for generations upon coal mining, came just as Mrs Thatcher's drive to break the National Union of Mineworkers and effectively close down the coal industry began to bite.

It is almost traditional for bishops to use part of their enthronement sermons to express their alertness to the local concerns of the diocese, and Jenkins was no exception. But, in the deeply conflictual context then prevailing in the North East, mild platitudes were hardly an option and Jenkins was not the man to give them. This extract from his enthronement sermon includes the passages that had an incendiary effect on Mrs Thatcher and her allies (and, if the tabloid press is to be believed, on York Minster itself which was struck by lightening, apparently as a sign of God's wrath at Jenkins's politics), in particular his remarks about Mr Ian MacGregor, the uncompromising industrial axe-man whom Thatcher had put at the head of the coal industry in place of indigenous managers who were deemed to be too soft, and too emotionally committed to the industry, to take on the miners' union.

Jenkins had already made himself notorious by openly discussing doubts about the nature of the resurrection and the virgin birth (although the accusation that he himself rejected these doctrines was the result of blatant misquoting of his words). It was often claimed that he had been too long in academe and was naive about the need for bishops to preach a simple faith to the simple faithful, but his thoughts were not only unexceptional in university theology departments, they were unexceptional in the church at large. It is hard to avoid the conclusion that the doctrinal outcry against Jenkins (who was looked upon by many radical theologians as irretrievably orthodox) was generated in order to undermine his very considerable ability to articulate local opposition to the government's economic policies, and that a number of literalist church people were, wittingly or not, co-opted to further Mrs Thatcher's cause by putting Jenkins in the Church's pillory.

Jenkins's own account of the furores that accompanied his episcopacy can be read in his autobiographical book, *The Calling of a Cuckoo* (Continuum, 2003).

This offer of freedom for newness and hope under the almightiness of God and through the down-to-earth presence of God is not, however, by any means confined to Christian churches and religious affairs. There is a power and a possibility here about hope in our present social discontents.

Here, again, triumphalism, absolutism and illusions have to be got rid of if we are to find hopeful and human ways forward. The cost of hope in our society and in our politics is a responsible readiness for compromise. Once we are clear that nobody has God's view of things or does God's will in God's way, then it also becomes clear that to insist on one's own view and nothing but one's own view, and the whole of one's own view, is outrageously self-righteous, deeply inhuman and damnably dangerous. It is to set out inevitable conflict on course for destructive fights, which no one can win, through which all will lose and which could end by destroying us all.

Until we reach the kingdom of God, responsible, mutually worked out compromise will again and again be of the essence both of true godliness and of true humanity. Anyone who rejects compromise as a matter of policy, programme or conviction is putting himself or herself in the place of God. Yet Christians and atheists can surely be agreed that, whether there is a God or not, no person or set of persons from our human race is suitable for divine appointment.

Consider the bearing of this on our most pressing current social tragedy, the miners' strike. I suggest that there must be no victory in the miners' strike. There must be no victory, but a speedy settlement which is a compromise pointing to community and the future.

There must be no victory, because the miners must not be defeated. They are desperate for their communities and this desperation forces them to action. No one concerned in this strike – and we are all concerned – must forget for one moment what it is like to be part of a community centred on a mine or a works when that mine or works closes. It is death, depression and desolation. A society which seeks economic progress for material ends must not indifferently exact such human suffering from some for the sake of the affluence of others.

The miners, then, must not be defeated, and this must be the first priority. But there must be no victory for them on present terms, because these include negotiations on their terms alone: pits left open at all costs, and the endorsement of civil violence for group ends. Yet equally there must be no victory for the government.

This government, whatever it says, seems in action to be determined to defeat the miners and thus treat workers as not part of 'us'. It also seems to be indifferent to poverty and powerlessness. Its financial measures consistently improve the lot of the already better off while worsening that of the badly off. Its answer to civil unrest seems to be to make the means of suppression more efficient while ignoring or playing down the causes. Such a government cannot promote community or give hope in the very difficult days we are faced with. It cannot even effectively promote the genuine insight it has about the need for realism in what is economically possible. To win a victory over the miners is simply to store up trouble, not to reduce it.

And there must be no victory for 'us' – that is to say society at large in our various groupings, who by our trends, tendencies and voting set up the sort of materialistic and consumer society we have. There will be no new hope for the future if all we get is the end of the strike and therefore, apparently, a quiet life again and the assurance that 'they' are dealing with things. Our problems will not go away. We shall find hope only if more and more of us are prepared to face up to what is going on, what is wrong in it, and what might be brought out of it.

Therefore a negotiated settlement which is a compromise and demands of us all further work on the problem both of the miners and of society at large is the only hopeful thing. But how might this come about?

Might it be by Mr MacGregor withdrawing from his

chairmanship and Mr Scargill climbing down from his absolute demands? The withdrawal of an elderly, imported American to leave a reconciliation opportunity for some local product is surely neither dishonourable nor improper. It would show that the interpretation of his appointment as provoking the miners to fight in order that they be defeated was false, and it would indicate that the government values the cost of hope as much as, or more than, the fruit of victory. After all, victory leads to more and more trouble. Hope has a future. But this would have to be matched by evidence that Mr Scargill, too, was not an absolutist but a compassionate and realistic negotiator who cares more for people and the future than for ideology. Without withdrawal and climbing down it looks as if we are faced with several people determined to play God. And this gives us all hell.

Meanwhile, whatever may happen in the immediate future, the direction of the life of any branch or section of the Christian church is clear. The direction is God. This is the God who has already paid the cost of hope in this confusing, risky, but potentially glorious and often enjoyable world. He it is who is as he is in Jesus, identified with our flesh and blood, ready to meet us through his Spirit wherever there is human need or despair, human creativity or joy.

What we have to do is to face up to what is going on, get involved in what is going on, and discern him in what is going on. His gift will be himself; his promise will be the growth of all that is human and his power will be hope. And in the midst of it all our anchor and assurance will be to worship him, to wait for him and to rest in him.

So 'may the God of hope fill you with all joy and peace by your faith in him until, by the power of the Holy Spirit, you overflow with hope'.

David Jenkins, Enthronement Sermon, Durham Cathedral, 21 September 1984, in David Jenkins, *God, Politics and the Future*, London, SCM Press, 1988, pp. 4–10.

Bishops in the Lords and Synod – and a riposte from No. 10

Although the churches were sometimes numbered among the more vocal critics of Margaret Thatcher's policies, the traffic was not all one way. The institutional churches may have appeared to be led by critics and doubters, but many Christians sided with her government, and some were able to mobilize theological defences of her project. The most prominent was Brian Griffiths, who was an adviser in the No. 10 Downing Street Policy Unit.

True, Griffiths's intervention was presented as a riposte to various bishops who had ventured to criticize the economic policies of the Thatcher government, but in reality this merely provided a platform from which a robust exposition of the moral case for monetarism and markets could be made. Griffiths also ventured to attack the bishops on theological grounds and, while here his thinking seems unimaginative and distinctly selective in its sources, many of the episcopal statements that he criticized were not notable for their theological depth. The exception were those of David Jenkins, whose Hibbert Lecture of 1984[15] criticized government policy in similar terms to those he had used in his enthronement sermon. Griffiths himself starts by noting some of the other statements by bishops, which became the object of his attack.

> In a recent debate in the House of Lords (13 November 1984), the Bishop of Lincoln argued that 'monetarist policies are about freeing the market. One of the obstructions to this aim is monopoly of any kind, and one of the monopolies here applied, as the Government seems to see it, is the monopoly of trade unions in the labour market. This means that building the needed climate of confidence in the nation becomes impossible.'
>
> At the time of the last Conservative Party Conference, the Archbishop of Canterbury, in a thoughtful interview with *The Times*, raised the question, 'How long can we wait for jam tomorrow?' – and answered it:

Economic growth, better living standards, higher pay for those in employment, the recovery of national pride, are all self-evidently worth aiming at; but if the human consequences of such aims mean unemployment on an unprecedented scale, poverty, bureaucracy, despair about the future of some communities, inequitable sharing of the sacrifice called for, then the objectives must be called into question.

A few days earlier, the Rt. Rev. Hugh Montefiore, Chairman of the General Synod's Board for Social Responsibility, warned that:

> If this government insists on continuing the policies of confrontation, we shall never find a national consensus on how to face the future. And so the future will continue to be a source of fear, whereas it could be a source of opportunity . . . Those in authority will never gain the goodwill of the powerless unless they begin to show a more caring face – and not only show a caring face but make it clear that they do care about others.

In the General Synod debate the following month (November 1984), the Bishop of Lincoln argued that he believed there were 'powerful influences at work in this country which have sought to raise a certain set of economic theories into an entire philosophy of life'.

Brian Griffiths, *Monetarism and Morality: An Answer to the Bishops*, London, Centre for Policy Studies, 1985, pp. 5–6.

Griffiths's pamphlet, published by the right-wing think-tank, the Centre for Policy Studies, took the argument about the morality of economics back to the bishops and others who had criticized the Thatcher project. The aim was to show them up as economically naive and deficient in their understanding of Christian theology. In so far as the churches had generally failed to grasp the moral seriousness of the Thatcherites, there were some easy points to be scored, but Griffiths's theological exposition provided a useful spur to the churches to clarify the theological content of their public pronouncements. The strong motif of individualism that lies at the heart of Griffiths's theology identifies his work as lying firmly within the liberal theological tradition, despite the general belief that it was the dissenting bishops who were the liberals. The strong commitment to consensus espoused by so-called liberal bishops is very apparent from their words as quoted by Griffiths. Thus the old typology of liberals and conservatives, which Thatcher stood on its head as she pursued liberal economic policies alongside social authoritarianism, began to break down in the churches as well.[16]

The strange areas of congruence between liberal thinkers of Right and Left was less apparent at the time than it is now. In a climate where those who were not for Mrs Thatcher in every respect were deemed to be against her, it was easily forgotten that much of the debate about faith and economics was about degree rather than fundamentals. Ronald Preston's critical essay on Brian Griffiths's work helps reveal the extent to which a liberal theologian could share ground with a market liberal from a different Christian tradition (Griffiths had grown up as a Plymouth Brethren and later become an evangelical Anglican, whereas Preston had been formed in the broader Anglican tradition of F. D. Maurice and Temple – both were trained economists, Preston having studied under R. H. Tawney).

> While it is impossible to develop a Christian blueprint for economic life, I believe it is nevertheless possible to discover certain fixed points or guidelines which hold true both for the individual and for society, however uncomfortable it may be to acknowledge them. In this respect, not the least of our problems in attempting to apply the Christian faith to social and economic life is that the fashionable words of Christian theology which are so much the currency of current clerical comment – love, peace, justice, compassion and fellowship – need to be taken alongside those unfashionable expressions which seem to be in such scarce supply – sin, judgement, evil,

lust, hell. Not only this, but in laying down guidelines we must also be very careful that our selection of themes and ideas is not simply a justification of prior opinions.

If we attempt this exercise, then I believe that one fixed point in a Christian view is the significance of the individual. The Christian starts from the profound conviction that the world in which we live is God's world and that our identity and purpose can be understood only as part of that creation. At the very centre of the created universe is man, created *imagine Dei*. It is because of this image that Christianity is a religion which attributes infinite worth to each individual, however insignificant he or she may be in the eyes of society. The commandments of Sinai, the Beatitudes of the Sermon on the Mount and the warnings of Jesus were all addressed to the individual conscience. Similarly, the compassion of the Good Samaritan was shown to an unfortunate individual, and not to some discriminated against group or disadvantaged social class. The invitation of Jesus to follow him is addressed to people as individuals, and not as representatives of a particular social class or income bracket.

[. . .]

Alongside the dignity of man, however, the Christian faith also confronts us with the tragedy of man – egotistical, proud, rebellious, uncompassionate – and the indescribable suffering and injustice which he has caused. It is because of this that the government has the important function not only of preserving property rights and maintaining law and order, but also of dealing with injustice: first, by remedying its causes, and secondly, by helping the afflicted. Throughout the Old Testament the state had a responsibility to look after the disadvantaged. It was not an indiscriminate redistribution of income to the lower paid, but was exercised on the basis of a distinction drawn between the deserving and the undeserving poor, an attempt to help those who were in real need. Again in the Gospels, our responsibility to others is something which Jesus continually emphasised, though it is in an individual and not a corporate context.

Any concept of anarchy, and of a state which is unconcerned with distributive justice, is totally alien to the Christian view. But to advocate the positive benefits which are yielded by these functions of the state is very different from statism.

For in the twentieth century we have witnessed a major assault on the freedom of the individual and the family through the growth of the state. In its most extreme form this can be seen in corporatism under fascist governments and socialism under Marxist governments. In a less extreme form it can be seen in democratic countries such as our own, in which the relentless growth of government, and the steady drift towards the corporate state, have been coupled with a loss of freedom and a growing sense of powerlessness among individuals and families – very clearly exemplified in the public sector housing projects of the inner cities of our country, the lack of parental involvement and control in state secondary schools, the complaints about the National Health Service, and the sense of frustration of ordinary members faced with militant trades union leaders.

[. . .]

I have great respect for the Bishop of Liverpool and in particular the work which he has done in two of our great cities. But if the powerlessness of individuals in the inner city is at least partly the result of large government and the lack of mediating structures, I cannot understand why he and other church leaders advocate solutions which involve more public spending, bigger government, and our continued acceptance of the increasing politicisation of our lives – all of which tend to *increase* that feeling of powerlessness which he rightly identifies as dehumanising.

It is because the Christian faith has such a high view of the dignity of man, created in the image of God, that it also has such a positive view of work and wealth creation. We have been made not only with a need to work but with a desire to be creative and productive. There is no basic dualism in either Judaism or Christianity, as there is in some other world religions, between the material and the spiritual: there is indeed an explicit reconciliation. This is not to deny that materialism as a creed is the enemy of spirituality. Our Lord's words, 'You cannot serve both God and Mammon', show the irreconcilable conflict between spiritual development and material idolatry.

Morality

The criticisms

[. . .]

[T]o the extent that monetarism is interpreted as an ideology, then it is perfectly legitimate for it to be scrutinised by the church on the basis of a Christian world-view. If it were true, as the Bishop of Lincoln has argued, that a certain set of economic theories had been elevated in this country into 'an entire philosophy of life', then I for one would accept the validity of his criticisms. The science of economics is concerned with means in relation to ends but not with ends in themselves. It can provide powerful insights into how markets work, the effects of creating money, and the unintended consequences of interference with markets and excess money creation, which we neglect at our peril. But this does not mean that the most efficient solution is always the best, or that the market should be extended into all areas of life. Because there are certain values which are by nature absolute, I believe that there are certain services which should never be placed on the free market. If monetarism is made into a religion, then the Christian has no alternative but to denounce it as incompatible with the Christian faith.

Between technical monetarism on the one hand and libertarian ideology on the other, and in the third place, is the present government's medium-term financial strategy, which is being implemented in the context of what, for lack of a better expression, I have described as economic conservatism. Because the medium-term financial strategy is frequently discussed in public by professional economists in a mechanistic way with reference to analytical models and measurements – M_0, £M3, PSL2, PSBR – it appears as if this use of monetarism is technical and mechanistic and bears no relationship to any moral concerns. Such, however, is not the case.

The morality of monetarism

In the first place, monetarism was developed to solve one of the most insidious and cancerous of economic problems – inflation. What is not commonly recognised is that inflation is at heart a moral problem, because inflation is theft. As Keynes so forcefully argued in his *Tract on Monetary Reform*, inflation is a form of concealed taxation. It is a tax levied on the holders of money balances through higher prices brought about by the excess creation of money. If the government through the Bank of England issues a £5 note with the words 'I promise to pay the bearer on demand the sum of £5', signed by the Chief Cashier for the Governor and Company of the Bank of England, but with the expectation, for example, that inflation will proceed at 20 per cent a year, it knows that in terms of purchasing power that note will be worth only £4 one year hence. Similarly, for any individual or group to support inflation – or 'reflation' – knowing (as we must now be deemed to know) that this will prove a covert means of obtaining wealth from others which they would not willingly concede, of reducing debts by cheating lenders and of giving pledges with less backing to them than appears at first sight, is morally indefensible. These are all forms of theft and deception, and their enshrinement at the very heart of the financial system exerts a disturbing and corrupting influence.

It should not surprise us therefore to find that in the 1970s inflation was both a cause and effect of our moral decline in this country. It was a cause in that it strengthened the resolve of monopolies to exercise their power (the most notable but by no means the only one on a world scale being the decision of OPEC to act concertedly over the price of oil), increased the incentive to evade taxes, and helped lead to the nationally debilitating strikes, such as those in the winter of 1973–4, and the 'winter of discontent' 1978–9.

Inflation results in a wholly capricious redistribution of income: from the weak to the strong, from the saver to the borrower, from the pensioner to those still in employment, from the cautious to the speculator. Do those Bishops who advocate substantial increases in public spending really want the present – or indeed any – government to 'cure' unemployment by robbing the weak to pay the strong, by stealing from the pensioner, and undermining the cultivation of at least two of the cardinal virtues? Surely not? Yet this in fact is what is being recommended and, as a result, both the reasonableness and the efficiency of the economic system are undermined.

[. . .]

There is a second and equally important moral strand in the government's medium-term financial strategy: it is the attempt to move away from the corporate state and to enhance the economic position of the individual in the context of the family. The government's efforts to reduce the power of the TUC and the CBI as pressure groups for large institutions, and to limit the power of the state in general in order to increase the power of the individual – by, for example, changing trade union laws; by the sale of council houses to tenants, by the privatisation of companies such as British Telecom and the sale of shares to its employees, and by providing stronger incentives to establish small businesses – all contribute to this objective.

Underlying these policies is a moral concern: to encourage and develop private ownership by families, whether of their own homes or of the firms in which they work, and to enable people to pursue their jobs free of the restrictions of monopolistic trade unions. As such they constitute a fundamental step forward in the creation of a more responsible and healthy society.

Far from being immoral, the monetarist policies of the present government are, therefore, an expression of profound moral concern. Recently the Rev. Professor Peter Baelz, Dean of Durham, described a Christian morality as one concerned with creating 'a just, sustainable and participatory society'. It is an expression which sums up admirably the belief which underlies economic conservatism.

The policy is just or fair in that it attempts to remove inflation, to allow a greater proportion of earned income to be retained by those to whom it accrues, and to remove monopolies and restrictive practices in the labour markets, in the City and in services generally. Unlike the experience of the 1970s when the growth of government spending and of money supply outstripped the growth of real output, the policy is sustainable in so far as inflation and the growth of government are now under control, the recovery of the economy is entering its fifth year and, barring external shocks or domestic monetary and fiscal mismanagement, looks likely to continue. The one element which is not sustainable is a permanently high level of unemployment. . . However, not only is the policy just and sustainable, it is also participatory. It is not participatory in the sense of accepting the politicisation of economic life, of supporting the development of the corporate state – but rather it is an attempt to encourage direct participation of individuals and families in the economy, through ownership.
[. . .]

Conclusions

[. . .]
Meanwhile, however, there is one issue on which the church is remarkably silent, yet I believe it to be one of the greatest insights of the Judaeo-Christian faith in the economic field.

Over the past few decades we have seen the secularisation of our society proceed at a rapid pace. The spirit of our age is one of creativity, spontaneity and freedom; with little acceptance of authority, tradition or rules. Religion in a traditional sense, and the traditional values of the religious person, have been set aside. The ideas that money creation should be fixed by reference to some external standard, that budgets should be balanced, that one should accumulate savings rather than borrow from banks to finance increased consumption, that saving is a good thing in itself, that in terms of personal lifestyle modesty or even frugality is the ideal, and that work should be seen as a calling, to most people seem strange, quaint and rather old-fashioned.

In many parts of our society the consequences of secularisation are all too apparent. One need think only of the statistics of family breakdown, crime, violence, drug abuse and alcoholism. There are many ways in which what the Bishop of Lewes recently described as 'the desire for more' can have an unsettling and harmful effect on economic life in the longer term. Nor can I believe that our economic problems are unrelated to our more general social problems, nor that they are unconnected with secularisation.

It is in addressing this issue that the spiritual impact of the church today seems at its weakest. We are this evening in a livery hall very close to the place commemorated by a plaque where on 24 May 1738, it says that John Wesley found his heart 'strangely warmed'. We are all, I trust, aware of the impact of that clergyman on the economic and political life of this nation. Economics is familiar with the concept of unintended consequences; if the church is really to have an impact in the creation of a just and united country, perhaps it should ask itself whether it too has not succumbed to the process of secularisation, and whether its best contribution might not be to proclaim those eternal verities which it is its unique duty and privilege to guard.

Brian Griffiths, *Monetarism and Morality: An Answer to the Bishops*, London, Centre for Policy Studies, 1985, pp. 15–28.

Griffiths examined

Griffiths' basic Christian diagnosis

The Kingdom of God is basic, and behind it is the doctrine of the created world which takes time seriously and is not fatalistic; it requires of us a responsible use of our resources, and this leads to wealth creation and a challenge to avoid its hazards. Private property (subject to some constraints) is the norm for ownership in the Old Testament, and absolute ownership is expressed in the New Testament by the Parable of the Vineyard; indeed property rights are sanctified by the Eighth Commandment and the Parable of the Talents. So we arrive at the free market and private property for each family. This is an extremely jejune use of the Bible. . . .

Griffiths, however, does stress responsibility not only for creation but for others; one of his most insistent points is that libertarians make no such demand, whilst Christians must care for those who cannot care for themselves. This leads to –

Griffiths' theological analysis of the current situation

He maintains that there has been a decline in moral standards in the last two decades, economically, socially and politically. Such comparisons are not easy to make, and Griffiths here reads very like the rhodomontade which has been the stock in trade of the evangelical preacher since the eighteenth century. He thinks that Christianity has been replaced by a rational humanism, derived from the Enlightenment . . . Here there is both error and truth. The error is to take such a negative view of humanism. It is a many faceted phenomenon, some of it crude, some of it noble. The same is the case with Christianity, for some types of Christian theology and Church strategy have led to terrible deeds. The Enlightenment saw this and was an important corrective of a defective Christianity. . . .

The truth that Griffiths perceives is that the free market and the liberal economic position is not a 'natural' phenomenon akin to something studied in the natural sciences, but a device designed by humans for human purposes, and to be judged by whether the purposes have been adequately defined and whether they have been adequately served by it. In fact it has been accompanied by an ideology which has given it a spurious overall significance. Griffiths wants to substitute a Christian for a secular one. Here he is unrealistic and mistaken. It is impossible in a plural society to bolster the social market with a Christian ideology. . . .

> Griffiths does not discuss the problems raised by the workings of the version of the free market we have actually experienced. They are formidable: the increasing inequalities of wealth and income it creates if left to itself, so that the effective demand of the wealthy for cake outweighs that of the poor for bread; the boom and slumps by which it develops which leave people's jobs at the mercy of remote, impersonal forces; the collective needs which the market can't reflect . . . the externalities, or social costs, which are not represented in market prices . . . the short term horizons of the market . . . the social limits to private consumption. . . .

Ronald H. Preston, 'Griffiths on Capitalism and the Creation of Wealth: An Appraisal', in *The Creation of Wealth*, Occasional Paper 14, Manchester, William Temple Foundation, 1985.

Mrs Thatcher faces the Church of Scotland

As Prime Minister, Margaret Thatcher made no secret of her Christian principles. Brought up a Methodist, she certainly did not regard the bishops of the Church of England as sources of theological authority to which she should defer. Amid all the tensions and friction between the churches and her policies, it was only late in the day that she made public her own version of a Christian rationale for her conviction politics and she took the opportunity to drive home two basic principles of her economic policies – individualism and choice – with a strong religious gloss.

It was, interestingly, not to the Church of England but to the Church of Scotland, at its General Assembly in 1988, that Mrs Thatcher preached (there is no other word for it) her theological message. If she thought that the Nonconformist mindset would be more fertile ground for her ideas than liberal Anglicanism she may have been mistaken. Scotland and its own established church had, as we have seen, a long and honourable tradition of political radicalism based on very different tenets – and a much more communitarian theology – than she would have found easy to stomach. Nevertheless, she would have expected her own Free Church language to be easily comprehensible in Calvinist Scotland, and there may even have been a deliberate intention to snub the Church of England bishops by gracing another denomination (and country) with her most profound reflections on faith and politics.

> Perhaps it would be best if I began by speaking personally as a Christian, as well as a politician, about the way I see things. Reading recently I came across the starkly simple phrase: 'Christianity is about spiritual redemption, not social reform'.
> [. . .]
>
> What then are the distinctive marks of Christianity?
>
> They stem not from the social but from the spiritual side of our lives. I would identify three beliefs in particular:
>
> First, that from the beginning man has been endowed by God with the fundamental right to choose between good and evil.
>
> Second, that we were made in God's own image and therefore we are expected to use all our *own* power of thought and judgement in exercising that choice; and further, if we open our hearts to God, He has promised to work within us.
>
> And third, that Our Lord Jesus Christ The Son of God, when faced with His terrible choice and lonely vigil *chose* to lay down His life that our sins might be forgiven. I remember very well a sermon on an Armistice Sunday when our Preacher said
>
> > 'No one took away the life of Jesus, He chose to lay it down.'
>
> [. . .]
>
> I believe that by taking together . . . key elements from the Old and New Testaments, we gain:
>
> a view of the universe
> a proper attitude to work
> and principles to shape economic and social life.
>
> We are told we must work and use our talents to create wealth.

'If a man will not work he shall not eat' wrote St Paul to the Thessalonians. Indeed, abundance rather than poverty has a legitimacy which derives from the very nature of Creation.

Nevertheless, the Tenth Commandment – Thou shalt not covet – recognises that making money and owning things could become selfish activities. But it is not the creation of wealth that is wrong but love of money for its own sake. The spiritual dimension comes in deciding what one does with the wealth. How could we respond to the many calls for help, or invest for the future, or support the wonderful artists and craftsmen whose work also glorifies God, unless we had first worked hard and used our talents to create the necessary wealth? And remember the woman with the alabaster jar of ointment.

[. . .]

What is certain . . . is that any set of social and economic arrangements which is not founded on the acceptance of individual responsibility will do nothing but harm.

Text of a speech given by The Prime Minister *The Rt Hon Margaret Thatcher FRS MP* to the General Assembly of the Church of Scotland in Edinburgh on Saturday 21 May 1988, Press Office, Prime Minister's Office, 10 Downing Street.

3 Reinventing Industrial Mission

The Church under Thatcher

The primary project of the first two Thatcher administrations was the reshaping of the economy with a decisive move away from the welfare priorities of the post-war settlement towards a reliance on the market in more and more spheres of life and the embracing of monetarist principles which sought to bring down inflation by severe controls on the money supply despite the concomitant rise in unemployment. Inevitably, then, out of all the agencies of the churches, it was the Industrial Mission movement that felt itself best equipped to engage with the government's policies and their outworkings on behalf of the churches. IM itself remained somewhat on the margins of the mainstream churches, frequently regarding the ecclesial institutions as instinctively conservative and unresponsive to social trends. So it was ironical that, through the 1980s, it was the Church of England itself that was widely perceived to be in strenuous opposition to the policies of Thatcherism. While the bishops were most often in the firing line from the political Right, IM was able to provide much of the ammunition for return salvos.

Henry Clark, Professor of Social Ethics in the School of Religion at the University of Southern California, visited the UK frequently in the late 1980s with the express intention of studying the Church of England's response to the government policies of Margaret Thatcher. His book, *The Church Under Thatcher*, is both a chronicle of what the Church of England did in that period and an analysis of the social and theological context. The focus of Clark's research was the Anglican Board for Social Responsibility and the Industrial Mission movement (although Clark was studying the Church of England he did note the ecumenical nature of IM).

Clark was clearly impressed by what he observed. But his book, not unnaturally perhaps, did not foresee the trajectory of either government policy or the self-confidence of the churches. He portrays a church that was self-questioning but nonetheless on something of a 'high' as its public profile grew.

Industrial Mission Activities

In order to appreciate the distinctive contribution of IM, one must appreciate the importance of *rehabilitation* as a type of *indirect reform* which has a special place on the 'relief/reform/revolution' continuum. . . .

The significance of this typology was forcibly brought to my attention during an especially fascinating conversation with several Social Responsibility Officers and Industrial Mission personnel in the Manchester diocese who obviously felt that what they were doing went significantly beyond 'relief'. They prided themselves on doing something *concrete* which would be of immediate assistance to the unemployed in their area, and for them there was a decisive difference between their area development activities and what is usually meant by 'pastoral' activities (eg visitation of the sick and the elderly, soup kitchens, providing shelter for the homeless, etc). They saw what they were engaged in as 'rehabilitation', and in explaining the difference between activities of this kind and mere 'relief', one member of the group made reference to the familiar distinction between 'giving people some fish to eat' and 'teaching them how to fish'.

On the other hand, however, it is clear that there *is* an important difference between a voluntary association's undertaking to mount special programmes to help the unemployed and that same voluntary association's attempts to get public- or private-sector institutions to take it upon *themselves* to remedy the problems of those whose lives have been dislocated by the operations of the market (and by the failure of the society as a whole, acting through the state, to regulate the market in such a way as to prevent, minimize or remedy the effects of such dislocations). It is activities of this kind – calling the megastructures of the economy and the polity to fulfil their vocations more effectively – which I consider especially worthy of being called prophetic, and it is prophetic activities that we are *most* concerned with in this study. Even so, it makes sense to recognize that rehabilitation effects reform indirectly; indeed, rehabilitation activities are a form of 'lobbying by *demonstration*'. For surely programmes which are designed primarily to give direct aid to victims by equipping the unemployed for new jobs or enabling a small business to get started have a sort of multiplier effect of their own: they not only benefit neighbourhoods (and, cumulatively, whole geographical areas) as well as the individuals and families most directly affected; they also tend to have an indirect effect upon subsequent policies. Experimental projects which are successful open up new avenues for later policy to pursue, and those who devise especially successful *means* for carrying out current policy (eg employment training) create models of action to be followed by public- and private-sector agencies which are occupied with similar tasks.

Thus it ought to be acknowledged that *indirect* reform may be just as 'prophetic' as *direct* reform, for lobbying and rehabilitation should be seen as two different tactics employed on different fronts for different objectives: lobbying directly attacks the inadequacies of structures and policies by showing how government and industry can (and ought to) operate more humanely; area development programmes affect structures and policies indirectly by demonstrating the effectiveness of new approaches and by showing the capabilities of new sponsoring coalitions. It might even be argued that the kinds of frontline work 'in the trenches' of the war against need and deprivation in Urban Priority Areas is a particularly important way of recognizing the indispensability of wealth creation, and that as such it is an absolutely essential complement to the emphasis on just distribution of economic resources reflected in the pronouncements and the lobbying of the BSR and the Bishops.

Now, to say all this is to say something important about the reasons why Industrial Mission is far too important to the concerns of this study to be ignored or set aside as peripheral. It may be true, as a generalization, that most of the practitioners of Industrial Mission like to pour their energies into 'remedial' work at the local level – but it is also true that some of the best theological and political/economic theorizing in the Church of England arises from IM circles. The movement has always seen itself as an exercise in 'action/*reflection*', and it has always promoted the kind of systematic theological dialogue which receives an appreciative hearing in the academy and in the highest circles of ecclesiastical leadership. It is hardly surprising, then, that the last two secretaries of the Industrial and Economic Affairs Committee of the BSR have come from Industrial Mission (Paul Brett and Chris Beales), and that a glance at the agenda undertaken by the IEAC and the publications it has produced in the Beales years (1983–91) shows a heavy investment in IM concerns and in the future of the IM movement.

In sum: Industrial Mission is a movement which addresses both the needs and opportunities of those in power (who formulate policy in corporations, government agencies and labour organizations) and of those who are relatively powerless (ordinary workers as well as the poor, the unemployed and the homeless). It is a crucial element in the overall social witness of the Church of England. . . .

The shift within the IM movement away from earlier emphases towards area development coalitions is the most dramatic recent development in the evolution of that exceedingly significant specialized ministry, and it is certainly accurate to highlight its significance. On the other hand, of course, it would be a mistake to overlook the fact that earlier emphases have by no means been utterly abandoned. Thus industrial chaplains still help to mount rather more conventional job-training programmes under the auspices of the Manpower Services Commission, and they still take a lead in familiar repair programmes such as neighbourhood improvement. They still carry out adult education programmes within the Churches whose intent is (at least in part) to help Christian people see their daily work as a form of Christian vocation of mission. And they still do important work in the area of labour-management relations.

Henry Clark, *The Church Under Thatcher*, London, SPCK, 1993, pp. 82–86.

The Church of England reviews Industrial Mission

One consequence of Industrial Mission's higher profile in the 1980s was that the churches which sponsored the movement became more conscious that they had neglected it for decades. Nervousness about the ability of IM to embroil the church in political controversy combined with genuine concern that the church should support this movement which had been toiling away, unheard and unsung, for so long. It was the Church of

England which put most resources into IM, so it was not surprising that it was the Church of England which initiated a major national review.

Ever since the Board for Social Responsibility had been set up by the Church of England in 1958, there had been a close, but carefully nuanced, relationship between the Board and IM. The Board's remit ran well beyond the economic sphere, but the congruence of purpose with IM was understood and reflected partly in the formal representation of the Industrial Mission Association on the Board's Industrial and Economic Affairs Committee and partly in much informal traffic of ideas and support. Nevertheless, IM jealously guarded its independence of denominational control, protesting always that it was an ecumenical movement and thus wary of growing too close to the structures of the ecclesial institutions.

The BSR itself was, of course, somewhat suspect in the eyes of rightward-leaning church people, but it was nevertheless the BSR which was commissioned to undertake the review of IM through a working party chaired by the then Bishop of Kingston, Peter Selby.[17]

The Selby report, as it became known, was indeed largely friendly, yet acute and penetrating. It discerned creative energy in IM, and yet simultaneously a sense of tiredness in a movement which still rested on dated theological assumptions. Selby also teased out the potential collusion at the heart of IM – a movement which belaboured the churches for their unconcern even as it jealously guarded its perceived independence and lack of accountability. Selby called for stronger links with the sponsoring churches but, perhaps naively, took it that the church would respond by taking IM seriously and continuing its support.

This extract begins with a review of the origins of IM – essentially telling the story the way the movement told it to itself. It goes on to explore more contemporary critical thinking and draws upon Mostyn Davies's analysis, reflecting his centrality as the spokesperson for IM at its critical best. This extract concentrates particularly on the ecclesiological implications of IM in a way which had not been explored in print before. Here is an institutional church grappling with the structural questions raised by its own desire to be open to change in dialogue with the world. It is thus a rare example of the church agonizing in public about its perceived weaknesses as well as its need to live with boundaries between Church and world. The report is also noteworthy for its ecumenical seriousness – a follow-up report[18] proposed that IM (while still funded predominantly by the Church of England) should be organized ecumenically, accountable not to the denomination but to local ecumenical bodies which were even then being debated but which did not, in practice, supplant denominationalism as hoped.

The follow-up paper was debated in General Synod in July 1989 and received without much serious criticism of IM itself. At the time it felt as if the Church of England had endorsed IM and would now rally behind its practitioners. With hindsight, the report can be seen as a document which misread the mood of the church. It is possible that the uncontroversial reception of the report was an indication more of apathy than of agreement. IM remained a marginal activity.

> For much of its life, IM's thinking and practice have been influenced by the model of the 'servant Church'. Hence the willingness of IM to allow 'the world to set the agenda', to look for God's active presence in the workplace and then seek to co-operate – the inductive approach referred to above. Hence the goal of humanisation, of helping all to realise their potential and play their proper part in contributing to the common good. Hence IM's perception of the Church as being most truly itself when actively working for social change alongside secular organisations. Hence IM's enthusiastic adoption, in 1980, of the WCC slogan identifying the goal of mission as a 'Just, Participative and Sustainable Society'. In the early '80s it became apparent that the political climate was changing significantly and a consensus society was no longer tenable. A new, harsh 'realism' had entered British political and economic life; for some, that meant recession, and with it came high unemployment. The great theological themes, which had so

influenced IM, creation, incarnation, reconciliation, servanthood, no longer seemed adequate. Now it was crucifixion, judgement and apocalypse which were more evident.

IM And The Local Church

Meanwhile, within the Church at large, IM's whole basis of work was being questioned. Those responsible for the parochial and congregationally-based ministry, with its own pressures, were profoundly unconvinced by a notion of mission without 'naming the Name', eliciting a personal response to Jesus Christ, and encouraging those who heard of Him to participate in the worshipping life of the local Christian community. Furthermore, such a notion appeared to undermine the assumptions and practice of their own ministry, even while it depended on their ministry for its financial support.

These undoubted conflicts of view between those engaged in parochial ministry and those involved in IM have their roots in the context within which each group is working. However many individual exceptions there may be, it is quite clear that there is a tendency for the activities of industrial chaplains to be seen as different not merely in their tactics, but in their basic presuppositions about what the aim of the Church should be.

What has happened, then, to that very particular passion, so conspicuous in the beginnings of IM, to cross the gap that exists between the Church and working-class people, and between the Church and the world of industry? Has IM been reduced to little more than a research project into the 'world outside', on behalf of a Church which is not really interested anyway?

Clearly, the massive industrial upheaval of the last 10 years, the growth of unemployment and the realisation of a 'new underclass' of poor people concentrated particularly in the older decaying inner cities have forced IM to change. But again and again, the working party has noticed, lurking beneath the surface within and around IM, a basic and unexplored difficulty about the nature of mission itself.

A New Theory Of Mission

Mostyn Davies describes IM's search for a new theory or theology of mission, which, he argues, is not something IM can achieve on its own; for IM is a secondary movement within the Church, 'a particular working out of the Church's primary determination to go out into the world and engage in mission'.

The reason for IM's recent struggle to articulate its purpose is directly related, therefore, to the whole Church's difficulty in responding to the changed situation in society.

IM theology and practice depend on the understanding the Church has of its own purpose in relationship to its perception of God's purposes in the world. And as new theories of mission take into account the deep divisions and injustices pervading British society, so the conclusion is reached that 'this inequity is manipulated by the affluent to favour themselves at the expense of the poor. This is not of God, so the missionary priority is to change the state of the nation.'

IM's role in all this involves detailed action in 'job-creation, training, organising and working with the dispossessed to help them get a purchase on the means of their own liberation'.

Evangelism And Witness

There is no doubt that the world of industry has offered to many engaged in IM the sense of discovery of a number of living examples of a number of Christian values. The sense of belonging and of solidarity is often in marked contrast there to the individualistic way of life often validated in the life of the average congregation. It is not rare to find industrial chaplains for whom, while the language and symbols of faith are present within the life of the local Church, the reality of faith, hope and love are to be found in the workplace, and among the community groups and others with whom they strive for change.

It has seemed at least as important to 'convert' the Church to an understanding of the values expressed 'out there' as to bring any explicit message about Jesus Christ to those with whom the chaplain works. More than that, it has appeared that to speak of Jesus Christ or to encourage membership of the local Church would be to invite a person into a world of predominantly domestic concerns and individualistic religion unconcerned with the vital issues on IM's agenda. On the other side, that has meant that, in the eyes of many local Churches, IM is not engaged in Christian mission in any recognisable sense.

Putting the matter thus, points up the issue too simply. It fails to take account of the numerous local Churches which express in their life a very strong concern for the life of the world – including the world of work – or of the numerous practitioners of IM who are as committed to encouraging a serious engagement with Christian faith as they are to examining and taking up the issues of industrial life, and have integrated the two concerns at a very deep level. Yet it is important to point up the issue starkly, even at the risk of caricature, because the difficult relationship which exists between the parochial ministry and IM arises not from personal ill-will but from a profound and unresolved theological question which the whole Church needs to struggle with, namely the character of Christian witness today.

There is no disagreement about the need to bear witness to Jesus Christ. What then are we to make of that need in a situation where vast numbers of people are so alienated from the Church and its message that the mention of Jesus Christ has no reverberations for them or, worse, arouses only the picture of a local Church apparently totally without interest in the matters of deepest concern to working people? And if we encounter in an industrial setting examples of compassion, solidarity and integrity which seem to us to be a standing witness to Jesus, what does it add to speak the name of Christ in such a setting? If we find Jesus Christ has indeed gone ahead of us in power and love within the life of the secular world, what does evangelism amount to?

[. . .]

A New Language

IM is, as this chapter has shown, the focus of intense concern about the nature of Christian witness in today's world. It has taken hold of different theological methods and tried in various ways to reflect on the way in which the gospel of Christ interacts with the world of work. It has been from its beginning, therefore, an extended seminar in applied theology, conducted in an unfamiliar setting (the workplace) and with no guaranteed audience. In the process of clarifying its own mission it has raised issues about the mission of the whole Church in the world.

Yet the intensity with which the debate has been pursued is itself a sign that beneath the surface of it there is a still deeper questioning. Behind the crucial problem of how Christianity is to be applied is the even less accessible question of what it means. As the struggle goes on about what faith involves, we find a wrestling about what it would mean for the faith to be true.

IM was born of a determination to speak of God outside the familiar setting of Church and parish, and yet in the event its practitioners have often found themselves apparently forced to choose between not speaking of God at all and speaking of God in slogans imported into the world from the spheres of preaching or academic theology. Keep silent about God, and before long the question will arise about the meaning and purpose of your missionary activity. Speak about God as the Church speaks about God, and very soon, especially in the searching environment of the workplace, the problems of that language will become all too evident. So in the early days of IM the language of 'the God who acts' seemed ready to hand as a way of speaking of the one to whom Christians witness. Yet, as Peter Sedgwick points out, language that works as rhetoric for those who are familiar with it needs after a while to be examined, and on examination is full of difficulty; for 'there is a great danger that rhetoric can cloud the continual questioning of our understanding which the life of Christ can offer'. Is

God's 'action' like 'industrial action'? Is it like the action of the board of directors? What does it add to the normal secular ways of speaking about experience?

Similarly, the language of incarnation has often been attractive to the practitioners of IM. It provides support to a 'ministry of presence' and seems to give value to human living as it is. Yet the language of incarnation was a language about Jesus; can it be used simply and straightforwardly in the City of London or a derelict shipyard?

When the Church leaves its own place and enters worldly places, as it does in IM, its language has a definite remoteness, and familiarity no longer serves to give it meaning.

As Dietrich Bonhoeffer contemplated the baptism of his baby nephew, he reflected that the Church was, like that baby, the recipient of all the great words and acts of the Christian gospel, but without understanding them. 'In the traditional words and acts we suspect that there may be something quite new and revolutionary, though we cannot as yet grasp or express it.' IM takes us to the place where we cannot avoid the loss of meaning which is the lot of the language of faith. It is not surprising that there is argument about what is an appropriate missionary strategy for such a setting. The catchphrase of 'letting the world set the agenda' or 'meeting people where they are' represents attempts to respond to the experience of being in a place where language about God does not carry immediate meaning to people. Bonhoeffer proposed 'prayer and righteous action'. Yet it is important to identify the problem for what it is, that of a Church struggling towards communication about the reality of God first with its own members and second with those outside its membership. To identify the search in that way is to name the fundamental challenge IM has to face, the challenge of discovering a new language about God. Bonhoeffer describes that language in exhilarating terms: 'It will be a new language, perhaps quite non-religious, but liberating and redeeming – as was Jesus' language; it will shock people and yet overcome them by its power; it will be the language of a new righteousness and truth, proclaiming God's peace with men and the coming of his Kingdom.' If the

Church is to have any chance of discovering that language, or rediscovering it, it needs to be in the places where that need is so clearly evident.

[. . .]

Accountability – Who Owns IM?

In most places, Industrial Mission teams and management committees are trying to develop more effective ways of relating to the various denominational structures. This is more often than not due to pressure from funding sources, and some imaginative and helpful developments are taking place. In some places, such as the areas covered by Lincoln Diocese and Derby Diocese, IM is formally constituted as a Local Ecumenical Project. In three places, an archdeacon acts as the team convenor or contact person, thus providing a link, at a senior level, with the local Anglican diocese. In Manchester, IM and community development work are now formally working in partnership, the Anglican management structure being the Diocesan Board for Social Responsibility.

More often than not, however, IM's structural relationships with funding bodies are woefully inadequate. In one diocese, for example, a Bishop has recently prematurely terminated the employment of an industrial chaplain, and no management committee, Anglican or ecumenical, exists with the power to challenge this decision.

There is a view which suggests that chaplains, though they complain about the structures and the difficulties of working them, in fact enjoy the freedom provided by their relative non-accountability. Any tighter controls would be irksome.

This epitomises the weakness of IM's position. For it has allowed a collusive relationship to be perpetuated between itself and the rest of the Church. The bargain is: IM remains a 'Cinderella' doing 'its own radical thing' on the margins, while the rest of the Church carries on with its own agenda. IM fails to challenge the Church to change, yet fails also to see that it thus neutralises its own message and mission in the world.

The belief seems to be that, if the Church knew what IM is really about, it would cease to support it at once. The reality is probably rather different. If only IM *would* take the Church more seriously and challenge it to a new engagement with the world and its structures!

Influence – Who Takes Any Notice?

Many industrial chaplains work hard to cultivate relationships with Church organisations and congregations, promoting discussion of significant issues in the world of work. Many lay people acknowledge their debt to IM for the ways in which it has helped them relate their faith and the issues of daily work, or non-work. Many industrial chaplains and missioners are seen as resources for the whole Church as it works out its missionary strategies. IM helps the Church to pick up matters of which it would otherwise be unaware. IM encourages the Church to rediscover its Monday to Saturday community role. Part time chaplains have particular opportunities for integrating faith and worship with daily life and work (though they live uncomfortably with the tension of having two demanding jobs with different expectations and emphases).

But there is widespread concern that IM, which has had relatively substantial resources allocated to it compared to other Church mission agencies, has had less influence than it should in the Churches. Blame for this may be laid at the doors of both parties. IM has not always articulated its ideas clearly. Chaplains and missioners have not been the best exponents of partnership with lay people and ministers. They have sometimes been experienced as indifferent to and arrogant about local Church life. They have appeared too 'sure' of their 'witness' theology and in some cases derogatory about 'evangelism'. Their peripheral situation has been used in an ambiguous way; it has sometimes been a cause for regret and recrimination, sometimes a joy and relief.

IM's overwhelmingly clerical makeup means that it can have an esoteric language and culture, excluding many, especially lay people, who could be its most effective participants. Has the lay apostolate model something to offer? Is IM's reputation as the least-loved form of mission deserved? Can it be countered? The best relationships are where links with ministers and congregations are cultivated with seriousness and sensitivity; the occasional well-publicised event does no harm.

IM must work harder, however, at helping local Churches see as *their* (the Churches') responsibility the things which IM believes to be important – unemployment is an example where some success can be recorded – rather than allowing the misconception to persist that, because IM exists, the Churches do not need to worry about 'doing' industry, unemployment or work.

Industrial Mission – An Appraisal: The Church's Response to the Changing Industrial and Economic Order, London, Board for Social Responsibility, 1988, pp. 43–51, 95–8.

Industrial Mission observed from outside

Radical social and economic change brought Industrial Mission into the limelight in a number of ways; not least, as a subject for academic study. There were a number of analyses of the movement by students who were closely involved or who had shadowed IM for some time.[19] But the movement also attracted attention from overseas and from the perspective of different Christian traditions. Lillemor Erlander, in Sweden, wrote a comparative study of British IM and the French worker-priest movement,[20] while perhaps the most incisive study was conducted by a Japanese Christian, Shigeko Masumoto.

Shigeko's most significant theological contribution was to develop the idea of the 'gap'. All mission activity was predicated on the existence of a gap that had to be bridged – but IM had become confused about whether the gap was theological, sociological or ecclesiological. Shigeko placed her analysis of IM firmly within an exposition of its history and this did much to enable her thinking to be recognized by IM practitioners among whom it was influential. The impact of Shigeko's study was enhanced when the BSR published an abbreviated version of her dissertation as one of a short series of working papers.[21]

Section 1. Patterns of Practice of IM which correspond to the notions of the gap between the Church and the world.

L Hunter

It is evident that British IM started from an acute sense of remoteness and separation between the Church and working-class people. Therefore, the sense of separation and the determination to close the gap between the Church and the world, particularly the world of industry, were the common factors among the ideas of the founders and their successors in IM.

Among the founders, L Hunter was exceptionally conscious of the challenging nature of mission both towards the Church and towards society when he expressed it thus:

> 'The new evangelism will be more than a recall. It will look forward to a new order both in the Church and in society.'

His radical questioning of the identity of the Church is also most suggestive from today's point of view. He asked:

> 'If the Church were God's instrument of redemption, what sort of a fellowship would it be, and what would it be at?'

This attitude of radical questioning has been inherited by some parts of IM and it is still alive as a thread, for example in M Kane's theology when she asks about the relationship between the Church and the Kingdom of God. However, for the main stream of IM, understanding of the gap has developed into a sociological notion (mainly in the 1940s and 50s) or a theological notion which is characterised by its world-affirmative attitude (mainly in the 1960s and 70s) . . .

2) Sociological notion (a)

By sociological notion of the gap, it was originally meant that the membership of the Church was highly sociologically conditioned. Middle-class people were overwhelming in the majority in the Church as E R Wickham showed through his historical investigations. His proposal was, therefore, to set up a new machinery of IM in order to meet people where they were, rather than to be waiting for people to come to the Church. At the same time he was well aware of the theological error that confines God within the Church thus narrowing the claim of God and the concern of the Church from the Kingdom solely to that of religion. His main attention was turned in a sociological direction when he established IM.

The response to this notion of the gap was the appointment of industrial chaplains, who were sent out into factories and offices to build up a network of human relationships as a link between the Church and Industry. This (sending out of the chaplains) has formed the basic structure of the work of British IM since then.

[. . .]

This is so basic to British IM in the sense that it forms its main character practically as well as theoretically that it needs a more detailed description through the following three points: firstly, in contrast to other models such as the mission model in West Germany and the centre model in France, the chaplaincy model depends on negotiation with both sides of industry. The advantage is freedom to meet anybody in the works once the negotiation has been settled so that the chaplains can approach anybody freely at their work as long as they do not disturb the process of work itself. It is a challenging task to become trusted in every situation.

The disadvantage of the chaplaincy model is its dependence on the goodwill of industry to be able to maintain the chaplaincy itself. Neutrality, whatever it actually means, is demanded as a prerequisite, whereas in the other models, there is a certain possibility of taking risks due to the fact that there is no need for negotiation at the institutional level.

Secondly, in terms of the quality of ministry, the chaplaincy model is bound to take a pastoral role as its centre. A pastoral role does not necessarily mean ministry to individuals although it is usually understood that way. Here, it means the work for reconciliation of either an individual or an institution with God and within themselves. That involves blessing, accepting, showing concern and sympathy, supporting and helping forward a better quality of individual and organisational life. In contrast with the prophetic role which emphasises the aspect of the Judgement of God, the chaplaincy model is more suitable for pastoral care.

[. . .]

The point here is that IM seems to have been dependent on this cultural background and to have done little to either challenge or change it. Another danger of the chaplaincy model must be added. For the Church, it can become a proof that it is concerned with industry and, at the same time, it can be a protection for the whole Church so that it does not have to be exposed to the complexities of secular realities.

[. . .]

3) Sociological Notion (b)

The notion of the gap caused by urbanisation and modernisation of industrial society stresses the fact that the life of modern men and women is fragmented into various parts and the basic core of self-identity is lost. People belong to different organisations among which the Christian life can become just one of the options. Different, sometimes even contradictory, principles dominate different parts of life, and the motivation to re-integrate the personal life is an important factor. Christian faith is essentially a powerful message to restore the wholeness of personality. This is based on the understanding of God and man in personal relationship, of God's love and justice which are the foundation of the unity and wholeness in the divided life of modern man. The reason I include this compartmentalisation theory in the sociological notion of the gap is that this phenomenon has been described in IM history in sociological rather than theological terms. Had there been a clearer theological understanding of this fragmentation, the response of IM might have been different.

However, in IM theory, little distinction has been made between the sociological and theological notions of the gap. The response to the sociological notion (b) was almost identical with the next pattern which I am going to describe, that of the response to a theological notion (a). Both of them focus the separation between life and faith and their response is to show the relevance of Christian faith to modern life through education and training. Theorising efforts of IMA we saw in Chapter 4 are the main feature of this response.

4) Theological Notion (a)

We saw a theological notion of the gap which led to a world-affirmative model in S Phipps' secular-based theology. It justifies the world and man's response to God within the world, rather than on the basis of the sociological observation which we have seen in the previous sub sections. The response to this theological notion of the gap is to take the public aspects of social and moral concern more seriously. At the same time, the world-affirmative stance leads to the embracing of all the interests of industry and to the chaplaincy model as the way of engagement. Thus, taking up secular issues as the subject of prayer and discussion in Christian groups has been pursued enthusiastically through the 1970s . . . As examples, industrial networks of chaplains and the consultative function of IM for the Governmental departments were examined. It was assumed that to help smoother administration and relationships, better communication, either in industries or in government authorities is undoubtedly a Christian response. Here again, hardly any radically critical attitude towards the social and industrial system could be generated.

One of the unique contributions of IM towards society has been to bring a cross-section of people into a positive collaboration which would have been difficult otherwise. This mediating function is needed in British society to become more flexibly adaptable to actual changes. School and industry liaison work is another example. Whether this is uniquely required for the Kingdom of God or for mediating a better relationship in a more general, consultative sense is questionable. But in the practice of IM, there has not been a radical questioning of this approach on the basis of the criteria of the Kingdom of God.

5) Theological Notion (b)

In the late 1970s, a more critical stance was developed around such issues as unemployment, women at work, social inequality, multi-national industries and industrial democracy (Participation). . . . I would call this response a modified pattern of the response to the theological notion (a). Here, the chief concern is with social injustice. Therefore, this stance has generally been called a prophetic model in contrast to a pastoral model which dominates the chaplaincy model. . . . [T]he current debate in IMA is between those who stand for a factory-based chaplaincy model in which pastoral ministry is emphasised and those who stand for an issue-based model in which prophetic ministry is stressed. These two models are not thought necessarily to be incompatible, and various attempts are being made to pursue both models together in balance.
[. . .]

In order to show the reason why I define the issue-based model as a modification of theological notion (a) (world-affirmative, chaplaincy model), we must examine this prophetic stance from two angles: one is the values it tries to promote, and the other is the relationship it assumes between the Church and the world. The values are indicated by the slogan 'Just, participatory and sustainable society', pointing towards the Kingdom of God. Nevertheless, those values seem to be static, to have been produced from a particular cultural value system rather than from the Christian tradition. It is limited because it is following social values rather than leading them. (For example, women at work, social equality.) As regards the second point, that is the relationship between the Church and the world which this prophetic stance implies, there is a lack of a radical self-criticism. It appears that the Church is supposed to be privileged to judge social evil and injustice without being judged itself. The fallibility of all human judgement needs to be borne in mind. The above points go some way towards explaining the morally obvious, ethically static and localised and limited nature of IM's prophetic stance.

From the fact analysed above of the practice of IM, we come to an important hypothesis that the gap which IM has been concerned with was mainly that between the Kingdom of God and the world.

[. . .]

Section 3. Some inherent dangers and weaknesses of IM

Here, we are going to focus some of the problems of IM which are recognised by many chaplains, and analyse them, from the hypothesis so far reached, under three sub-sections.

1) Clericalism

It has often been acknowledged by industrial chaplains that clericalism is one of the biggest weaknesses of IM. In the previous chapters, this subject was discussed repeatedly. Firstly, we must be clear what clericalism means. It can mean lack of lay-involvement in IM activities. It can also mean the overwhelming percentage of all the chaplains are ordained. As a result, the voice of the laity is hardly heard in IM and this causes some of the chaplains to feel uneasy, so that this subject never leaves the minds of chaplains. In a contrary way, they may feel that the industrial chaplain's job is so demanding and specialised that it is inevitable that it should operate in a chaplaincy model, and that chaplains who can act naturally and efficiently must be theologically competent.

I see clericalism as a symptom of an inadequate analysis of the nature of the gap between the Church and the world. Although IM has consciously pursued the non-ecclesiastical context in which to work, this persistent clericalism seems to show that the chaplains are not yet freed from the old model of the Church. Church-centredness in the chaplaincy model has two further implications: firstly, as a chaplain is taken as a representative of the Church by industry, the Church inevitably thinks that it can discharge its task by sending chaplains. IM has tried to communicate its experiences in industry to the Church through various occasions and channels. Nevertheless, the Church does not seem to feel any need to hear the experience of IM as something more than information. Secondly, the role consciousness of the chaplains inevitably shapes their understanding and dealing with the problems. The chaplains would think that they have to benefit the functioning of industries.

[. . .]

Secondly, through the weakness described above as clericalism, IM is challenging the whole Church to live in the tension between the Church as the institution and the Church as the event. Certainly the institutional Church is a necessity, but it is essential for Christians, particularly the laity, to experience their growth into faith as dynamics of events by building up a flexible and intimate fellowship through their particular commitment. Thus they should be able to start taking initiatives in doing theology by learning how to reflect, express and share their own experiences of faith together.

A third point is concerned with the longer-term provision of the life of the Church in today's world. If the Church is to go through a renewal to such an extent and depth, it ought to take the programme for its survival and growth, both in spiritual and material terms, absolutely seriously. If IM is to advance the issue-based mission as the prophetic ministry not only in the level of Christian insight but also in the level of strategy, it ought to be prepared to become independent from support either of industry or of Governmental bodies.

Even through its weaknesses and failures, IM is pointing to a vision of the renewed community of believers who worship God and witness to His work in and through our life in the world.

Shigeko Masumoto, 'A Critique of British Industrial Mission as a Response of the Church to Modern Industrial Society', MPhil. thesis, University of Leeds, 1983, republished in abridged form as *A Critique of British Industrial Mission*, Industrial Mission and the Church in Britain Today, Paper 1, Board for Social Responsibility, 1987. This extract from pp. 16–28.

Industrial Mission under the theological spotlight

One of the few academic theologians to maintain an interest in the Church's practical engagement with the economy was Peter Sedgwick, who, in the 1980s, was Lecturer in Theology at the University of Hull and Theological Consultant to the Churches in the North East, later becoming, successively, Vice-Principal of Westcott House theological college, staff member at the Board for Social Responsibility, and Principal of another theological college, St Michael's Llandaff.

During the mid-1980s he was also a member of the BSR's Industrial and Economic Affairs Committee on which he was able to raise questions of theological method and content in the midst of discussions on the Church of England's responses to government policies and their outcomes. Although, broadly, a defender of the classic middle-axiom methodology, Sedgwick was critical of IM's apparent willingness to stick with theological approaches that had been superseded in academic discourse.[22]

The following is an extract from his paper, published by the BSR as the second in the series of working papers entitled 'Industrial Mission and the Church in Britain Today'. Of all the papers, this was the most theologically erudite – and the most critical of current practice and thinking. In it, it is possible to detect Sedgwick's concern that any movement that exposes itself by seeking to be in the vanguard of change, and by seeking to confront the government of the day, must take seriously its engagement with ideas and the academy. Sedgwick's purpose is to build the bridge between the practices of IM and the concerns of academic theologians in a way that, although it had been an objective of Ted Wickham's, had been badly neglected by IM, which saw itself as an activist, rather than an academic, movement. Although Sedgwick's paper was not very widely read within IM, and made little discernable impact at the time, it can now be seen as an early recognition of the theological weaknesses of Industrial Mission and of the necessity for practitioners to become part of a reflective, as well as an activist, movement.

> So once again we come back to the fundamental questions of human worth. What is important is that the Church embodies or lives out the questions which ought to be put to the world. Without a living-out of the questions, it is not clear how the questions can really exist. They do not exist in a vacuum, nor are they asked by individuals apart from the Church. An example might help. An individual cannot perform the whole of a Shakespearean tragedy on their own, still less a musical symphony. The questions which ought to be put to the world stem from the Gospel. But the Gospel is a many-faceted reality, and is about the salvation of the whole human race, and the non-human creation. When the Church is true to its task, it lives out the Gospel in many ways, or 'performs the Scriptures'. An individual cannot do this alone. As the Church performs the Scriptures, or performs the text much as actors perform a play, it asks sharp questions about the life of the world. But without the living-out of that life, the performance, there can be no questions to hear at all. So the basic issue is whether questions about the nature of human worth can be heard. But it is also a religious question. In the expressions of human identity and freedom, is God present and building up the value of human life? Again can this question be heard? How do we ask these questions at all? These questions ought to be addressed by Industrial Mission.
>
> Symbols – such as the well-known images of the servant Church, God on Monday, or the Kingdom of God, all of

which resonate through the Industrial Mission literature with passionate intensity – are formed by those who wish to seek understanding about what they are speaking about. It is the beginning of a process of understanding to point to a symbol such as the Kingdom, and it does not necessarily bring clarity, though unfortunately Industrial Mission and its thinkers have often been implacably opposed to those who resisted the idea that God was at work in the world, and should be served by his followers. Industrial Mission should listen to theologians who raise questions about divine action. It is only fair to add that the dialogue with theologians and with the parochial ministry has not been easy. The preoccupations of both groups can be with their own domestic concerns of theological method or relationships within a parish. However, if these preoccupations can be avoided, a genuine dialogue about language and symbols can begin between active Church ministry and mission (including Industrial Mission) on the one hand and theologians on the other.

The question of religious symbolism is important. Symbols represent certain aspects of our experience but also set a distance between ourselves and that experience. Forming symbols allows language to develop further, so that it can represent reality more adequately. It is not as though there ever could be any consciousness which could dispense with symbols and metaphors. But religious language is particularly difficult, for it does not 'represent' a series of facts which are related in a particular theory but rather it seeks to represent the unconditioned agency on which all such facts in the world depend. One way through this difficulty is to abandon talk of God as God is in his nature, but to point to the effects of God. This theology of 'God who acts' was one which Industrial Mission adopted in the 1950s but its model of divine agency has been much criticised for being incoherent. At its simplest, this theology saw God as an active God, with the Bible as a record of His acts. The Bible is further a document written by those who responded to those acts, and it therefore logically follows that we must also respond to where God now acts . . . [O]nce passages of world history in the twentieth century are seen as the effects of God, then it is hard to know what is an effect of God's action (the Kingdom) and what is political change. All this results in a tendency to moralise Industrial Mission against those who deny God's challenge to the Church to minister and the structures of our society.

What criticism can be made of the idea of God who acts? There are two ways of developing the doctrine of divine action. In the first, which was dominant in the 1960s in the WCC, and in thinkers such as Harvey Cox, certain concepts are taken as fundamental to Scripture. So reconciliation is seen as an Old Testament concept which has to do with peace as a dynamic relationship between peoples in their public existence. This peace is not achievable by human beings, but is given by God, and is manifested by public acts of reconciliation between nations, groups, and only thirdly individuals. Yet there is a flaw in this argument. It is argued that agape in the New Testament is an idea (or concept) which comes from the Hebrew term shalom in thc Old Testament. So the theologian interested in a world-affirming theology examined all the meanings shalom could have in the Old Testament, and applied these to the Christian meaning of peace today. What is wrong with this argument is this: there is no one fixed meaning of the term shalom, or agape for that matter. Concepts do not always mean the same in each situation. Shalom could mean forgiveness or wholeness or reconciliation, and much else: the meaning is worked out from the whole context. The whole context includes the entire text under examination, and its social and cultural milieu. So the question of what it meant can mean three things: what the author intended, assuming that you know the author; what the text might be supposed to mean in the light of its cultural setting; and what it was heard to say by the original audience, which may be more than one group of people.

Under this examination the Biblical meaning of shalom simply disintegrates. There are many meanings, of authorial intention; of its cultural setting; of its reception. Each Biblical text – particular books of prophecies, or psalms, or literary traditions such as the Priestly one in Genesis where the text is reconstructed by scholars – can use a term such as shalom. Each author will use it in his or her own way, and the term, concept or idea can vary in meaning according to the passage under examination in the same text. So we cannot speak of the Biblical meaning of shalom, or any other concept.

Once it is admitted that concepts are not like boxes with the same meanings inside, then a further argument falls. For Biblical theologians in the 1950s argued that a term or concept could build up more and more meanings. First it meant x; then x and y; then x, y and z. Again, the example of peace/shalom can be given. First it meant a relationship with God, then forgiveness within the community and holiness, and then a cosmic wholeness. So the argument went. Thus a term is like an onion: it grew layers of meaning which were always present thereafter, and each layer related to the next. But why should concepts develop like this? Might they not mean different things at different times, and contradict each other, and perhaps have ambiguous meanings sometimes? Are concepts always so clear? It became obvious that concepts did not always have the same meanings, and that meaning depended on whether one was talking of author, cultural context or audience reception. (A modern example taken from the middle of the 1987 General Election: one party offers to set the people free. What does it mean – for the politician saying it; in the context of freedom as a word much debated in political circles recently; to an audience in Sevenoaks; to one in South Shields? The answer varies each time.) Furthermore, if a concept comes to mean different things across time, and people remember more than one meaning, they often do not know how to relate them. Concepts are precisely not like onion layers which form a coherent structure out of different layers of organic matter. The layers of meaning in a concept may be only seen by the Biblical scholar who knows what the concept meant a century earlier; and there may be no unity (except in the scholar's mind) between the layers so detected. It is an artificial argument.

Biblical theology came to see the Bible as made up of a whole series of concepts. The key, crowning concept was the Kingdom of God, but it was at the top of an edifice of many lesser concepts. Each was related to another, so the Bible became like an atomic diagram. It was, we were told, a scientific age. The authority of the Bible was the authority of its concepts. This gave the Bible internal coherence and reliability. These concepts had distinctive meanings not found in any other culture – and so the Bible was distinctive. It was 'the Word of God'. Theology listened to 'the Word', repeated the concepts in worked out theological systems, and applied the implications of the theology to modern life. So the theology of Industrial Mission was born. But while it is right that there should be mission to industry, and it needs a theology, the cart is before the horse here. In everyday life we learn the meaning of words by seeing how they are used in particular contexts. We look at what life is like in one culture and one workplace, say, and then learn to understand their language. Different places have different meanings for words.

Some still accept this equation of Biblical content with revelation, where the authority of Scripture is carried by the Industrial Mission chaplain into the workplace through the dynamic power of these concepts. The chaplain's job is not to sell these concepts but to be motivated by them so that he or she stands alongside the 'man come of age' and affirms him in his awe-inspiring responsibility. Yet the suspicion is precisely this. Science works with manuals which are compendia of concepts systematically interrelated, but why should scripture (or theology) be the same? In science a concept does mean the same thing on every occasion; for it is part of an artificial language. But Christians ministering to technological enterprises should not fall into the conceptual trap of assuming that their linguistic reference is also stipulated according to precise rules. Alan Richardson's *The Biblical Doctrine of Work*, and Harvey Cox's *The Secular City* span the period 1954 to 1965 when this mistake flourished. It was the great period of Industrial Mission theology. But it appears implausible with the perspective of another twenty years to see Scripture as a series of interrelated concepts, even if mediated by the presence and power of a Christian exercising loving responsibility for his fellow person. If the conceptual structure is implausible, much else must go.

Alternatively, Industrial Mission has used the notion of scripture as naming God who acts. This position stresses the uniqueness of the Biblical understanding of history, unlike other religions of the time. The understanding of history was unique because God was seen as the main agent in the history of Israel, and it was history seen as a whole, having meaningful unity. Other religions spoke of acts of God only in connection with the particular acts of heroes or kings in relation to a part of their history, or spoke of God in different ways altogether. For example, the rhythm of nature revealed the activity of God. Secondly, theologians who defended this position saw the Old Testament and New Testament as being organised around a basic proclamation of kerygma which consisted of a recital of the acts of God. The New Testament kerygma took up the Old Testament one, so that a total salvation history results (or *Heilsgeschichte*, in the technical phrase). God is therefore thirdly seen as the God who chooses or elects his people and who therefore is the rightful guardian of their laws and values and only therefore is seen as Lord of nature. Modern theology must translate the basic Biblical notions of 'act' and 'history' into the secular language of the twentieth century. Many of the great names of Industrial Mission's theological development used this technique.

There is no doubt that a world-affirming theology was necessary. . . . [C]riticism is only made because the previous constructive note has been struck by Industrial Mission. Industrial Mission needed to move the Church to see the world as a proper place for Christian existence. A dualist account of existence, with human experience being but a pale shadow of the eternal verities above, which are reflected into ecclesiastical existence, needed to be overcome. Much theological training for ordination in the 1950s and 1960s was simply inadequate and at times appallingly ignorant of the social context of the

Christian faith. Yet having said all this, there are equally problems with the school of 'God who acts'.

First, the use of scripture is ambiguous. Some features of the understanding of God are inferred from the implications of the judgements passed by Biblical writers in their narrative. Others are inferred from the history of the development of the narratives themselves. Others are inferred from the way the narratives themselves are structured. But in fact the understanding of the narrative itself is not developed as a tool for understanding God. Instead the narrative only gives us the grounds for defining Biblical concepts which are to be used by the Church today. Now it is true that these concepts are narrated in faith, as in a confessional recital, and not simply related in a technical way. The confession is what is authoritative, and not simply the concepts. Nonetheless, there is a content in Scripture which bears down on the theologian and active Christian very directly. Where the content is understandable, it is to be repeated; where it is pre-scientific, it must be given a refit and suitably adapted, put to use for the servant Church; where it is obscure, it must be explained afresh, without changing the power of the original content. The problem is in fact one of translation.

From the 1970s this position came under criticism. In America the writings of Hans Frei, David Kelsey and George Lindbeck asked what use was being made of Scripture in all this proclamation of a 'secular theology'. In Britain James Barr questioned whether a Biblical story could be seen as true because it was made up of 'historically reported events' or a narrative which used historical events to give depth to the description of human nature which it portrayed. Finally, liberal theologians asked what talk of God might mean anyway. The problem for Industrial Mission was that most of these theologians gave answers which either related Industrial Mission much more closely to the Church and its experience of worship and congregational life than had been possible for Industrial Mission to achieve given the suspicion of the Church, and Industrial Mission's dislike of the conservatism of the Church; or they made talk of divine action impossible altogether, and hence offered only renunciation of explicitly Christian activity as the way out of the problem. The answer lay in being a personnel manager, unionist, or whatever, with a Christian motivation hidden inside. The 'Christian' aspect was theologically untenable for such liberals. Yet Industrial Mission did not – or could not – move closer to the mainstream Church, and would not – to its credit – give up the 'Christian' aspect of what it was doing. Hence it preferred the theology of the 1950s and 1960s, suitably adapted to the needs of the new poor and those always disadvantaged but rediscovered in the 1970s and 1980s. By preferring a theology from its past in order to justify its position, it came dangerously close to ideology – that is, to using ideas and beliefs to justify a particular interest, which was the independence of Industrial Mission from the Churches.

[. . .]

So when we read the texts we should not seek to see God acting in the world, nor try to reconstruct what events the text is writing about. It is about God, not events. It is true that the Christian believes some events did happen and must have happened, if Christianity is true. But the Bible is not primarily a historical record, nevertheless. Nor should we try to find the key concepts or ideas either. The Bible is a narrative with profound insights into the nature of reality and of God who sustains, loves and gives new hope to all of reality. In brief, the Bible must be read as the story of God's promises to the world. Questions of revelation, historical fact and language are all subsidiary to this point. The Bible is a means for coming to understand God, through a community which is seeking to understand what belief in God means for their lives in the world. The emphasis is on 'seeking to understand', for it is a struggle and a searching.

The implications for Industrial Mission's theology are great. First, talk of God only makes sense within the life, language and culture of a believing community – and this is where Industrial Mission is often at its weakest, for whatever reasons. (There is no talk of blame here.) Secondly, talk of God being found in the world can only get under way when this talk can be earthed in the deposit of imagery, myth, rite and creed, and undergo repeated engagement with it. It is not obvious what talk of God means, still less God in the world. Often such talk can sound like the in-code of a primitive tribe. Thirdly, when such theology is joined to the mythological personification of bureaucratic structures as Biblical terms and forces there is great danger that rhetoric can cloud the continual questioning of our understanding which the life of Christ can offer. Here in the life of Christ in the Gospels is a Biblical narrative which can, when brought into relationship with our own narrative and other past and present narratives of human life, so focus talk of God that the transfiguring effect of God's mystery upon our human world begins to be understood.

Summary: The Meaning of Mission

[. . .]

My vision of Industrial Mission is . . . that it is the tool of the Church for wrestling with questions of profound human creativity and alienation in the world. It is an *industrial* mission, and this particular expertise should not be lost. It should always have a focus in industry, whatever dimensions it also includes of urban mission. This is essentially a local vision, generating a theology which speaks of God in his relation to creativity and shame. There are two enormously important contributions to mission which Industrial Mission can make here. First, it sees the nature of divine activity as given meaning by the concrete social realities of evil and creativity. What redemption means is demonstrated by the turning of shame into hope, and creativity is shown by the reality of non-order in the spontaneous abundance of technological breakthrough. Thus Industrial Mission can earth theology in the reality of evil and creativity day to day. Secondly, the nature of mission is shown by the respect which must be given to those people Industrial Mission encounters. They will be as often as not agnostic, perhaps atheist, and certainly sceptical of the Church. Why have Churches at all: why God: why talk of ultimate meaning and hope? The refusal to manipulate its audience is Industrial Mission's greatest asset, and its willingness to serve where it discerns need is again in stark contrast to much manipulative evangelism.

This paper has expressed disagreement with some of the ways Industrial Mission has argued and behaved in the past. Temple as Archbishop of Canterbury may have been a great Christian leader, but there are aspects of his ministry in the 1920s which are not impressive. Some Industrial Mission theology has not entered into dialogue with modern theology, and this means that academics and Industrial Mission need to regain contact. There are signs of this happening, but it is not easy, and the fault is not all with Industrial Mission. . . . Mission then is local; is to do with rebuilding the city; is to do with the creation of wealth and the overcoming of poverty and despair; is to do with affirming the praise of God in the centre of the city. All this is the contribution of Industrial Mission to the Church's understanding of mission.

Peter Sedgwick, *Not Ceasing from Exploring*, Industrial Mission and the Church in Britain Today, Paper 2, London, Board for Social Responsibility, 1987, pp. 18–34.

4 Facing economic change at ground level

Unions defeated by corporate and government power

It is far from the case that all good theology comes from clergy or those in the authorized ministry of the churches. The Roman Catholic Church has traditionally understood mission at work to be a lay apostolate, but faithful Christians of all churches and denominations have been involved in systematic reflection on experience and the gospel.

Few, however, have written as powerfully as Jean Sargeant who was caught up in the print unions' dispute with Rupert

Murdoch's News International Group after the latter had bought *The Times* and other papers and initiated a plan, backed by the government, to relocate newspaper production from its traditional base in Fleet Street to a new site in Wapping where new practices were to be introduced unilaterally and deliberate tactics were pursued to crush the power of the unions (principally Sogat, whose branches are, like all in the print trade, called 'chapels', the Branch Secretaries being known as 'Fathers of the Chapel' or FOC). This was one of a series of disputes that began to show the collusion between the government and the interests of multinational businesses and, although this was less clear at the time, the preparation of British society for participation in a global economy where real power lay, not with government, let alone unions, but with transnational capital.

Sargeant watched the dispute unfolding before her, including the eventual defeat of the union and its capitulation following its undermining by another trade union's members. Her theological reflections are not couched in the language of the academy, but nor are they filtered through the theological training and secure employment position of the clergy. It is, in this sense, a rare and important testimony to the politicizing environment which the Thatcher years created and the way in which, for those Christians who were not among the shielded middle class, the experience provided the occasion for a true grass-roots theology to begin to emerge.

Sargeant's pamphlet, which is structured as a diary of unfolding events illuminated by her reflections, was published by the Jubilee Group, a Left-leaning church association much associated with the radical Anglican Catholicism of Ken Leech, himself based for many years in the East End of London close to Wapping.

'Sogat admits defeat at Wapping' – *Guardian* headline February 6 1987

The more immediate outcome of the violence of the January 24 demonstration was that News International went back to the

High Court to see the resequestration of Sogat's assets, claiming the union was in contempt of the July 31 injunction.

On February 5, a week before the hearing was due, the Sogat executive met to consider the position. That afternoon, I took a phone message for the *Guardian*'s Labour correspondent, Patrick Wintour: 'The Sogat executive has voted by 23 to 9 to end the dispute, withdraw the pickets and stop demonstrations at Wapping and seek compensation for sacked members'.

I could scarcely take it in, I felt so sick at heart.

I tried to keep my morale up by reminding myself that, in T S Eliot's words, 'For us there is only the trying. The rest is not our business.' Nevertheless, defeat had a bitter feel to it.

Going home that night I remembered the night the strike began and how I had seen the police in Gray's Inn Road moving cars and erecting crash barriers, setting the stage for a play in which they would have leading roles.

It had been a play akin to a Greek tragedy in that the end had been predetermined from the beginning and everything contributed to the print union's defeat including their own past divisions. Seeing it in the consoling pattern of literature helped me a little, as did the news that the company had agreed we should get the financial compensation they had offered us in the autumn. I fortified myself further by reading Milton's *Samson Agonistes*.

Four nights later we held the last meeting of the News International Sogat clerical chapel: it had been destroyed by the Tory laws which the Government had said would give the unions back to their members.

Our members said how proud they were to be part of a chapel that had stood up to all the pressure put on us in the last year. Our FOC, George Hall, said we had come out together and we should apply for compensation together. We gave him and the chapel committee a standing ovation.

The overwhelming impression I had was of the buoyant atmosphere of the meeting and of the vitality of the people there. With all our shortcomings and human failings, we had been fighting for something bigger than ourselves which had lent our struggle a dignity and value that lifted us up as individuals. Being part of a union struggle taught me something about wholeness and that to feel depressed because I never seem to overcome certain personal failings is too individualistic a way of seeing things. We are parts of a whole and as parts, imperfect; someone else to whom I am connected has the virtues I lack through being what I am, just as I contribute to the common good in being as well as doing. As St Paul says, 'We are members one of another', a saying which for me, summarises Labour ethics (Attlee quoted it in a speech to the UN in 1945 and I heard Harold Wilson quote it in an election speech in the 1970s) – I felt it as a reality during the strike.

But, of course, our story didn't end there. The effects of Murdoch's successful offensive against the unions rippled on through the personal lives of his ex-employees and the national newspaper industry where, in the wake of Wapping, the much weakened print unions had to accept substantial job cuts and radical changes bringing worse terms and conditions for employees and a growing trend for individual contracts and union derecognition.

And the effects went beyond the newspaper industry. Our strike had been part of the broader struggle by organised labour to defend union rights and those other components of the post-war settlement that went with them – full employment and the welfare state – from the onslaught of the resurgent right. Our defeat, coming after that of the miners and followed by other union defeats – TV technicians, dockers and seamen – meant employers generally now had the whip hand and that the Tory Government could privatise, deregulate and cut jobs and services at will. One effect of the shackling of the unions was that they attached increasing importance to the electability of Labour: the Kinnockite Labour Party arose from the ashes of union, as well as parliamentary election, defeats.

What weak unions and cuts could mean for vulnerable individuals was demonstrated when a young Sogat member, Ian Corner, was sacked in 1988 by the *Daily Telegraph* for 'health reasons' after he had an epileptic fit; when Sogat colleagues protested at his dismissal by walking out, they too were threatened with the sack. Another victim was Wapping striker Keith Winfield, a 28-year-old former *Sunday Times* storeroom clerk who, jobless and suffering from depression but unable to get a hospital bed, threw himself out of his flat window to his death.

Times' chapel members met again at Keith's memorial service a year after the strike had ended. There we also remembered all those who had died during the Wapping dispute: Sarah Johnson; Les Hill; Jimmy Stanton; Joe Paul; and Michael Delaney.

The Hope of Resurrection

As I grieved over their deaths and the dissolution of our chapel, it seemed to me, as a Christian, that only a faith in resurrection could give ultimate hope. 'Theology . . . is the hope that this injustice by which the world is characterised is not permanent, that injustice may not be the last word.'

But this hope, which comes from trusting to the reality of the Kingdom of God, goes beyond seeing justice only in terms of rewards in the next world for afflictions suffered here: justice has to be striven for in this world. As Donald Senior puts it, the Kingdom, or Reign, of God 'is not an abstract, individualistic ethical concept as some 19th-century theologians presumed. Nor, as liberation theologians have rightly insisted, can it be divorced from social and political transformation'.

It is because liberation theology chooses the option for the poor and the historical transformation this entails that it appeals to me as an authentic expression of Biblical Christianity for our day. I found liberation theology even more relevant after my involvement in major industrial disputes because it links the political and religious in a way that proved true to my experiences, and it has largely accepted the socialist critique of capitalism 'as a correct way of explaining the increasing inequality between an owning class of people and those who possess nothing but their labour to sell, and who are dependent on a job-market which is manipulated in the interests of depressing wages and curbing the power of working people to organise themselves'. (Andrew Kirk, *Theology in the City*.)

As a trade unionist sacked after 20 years I experienced at first hand the power of the employer and why the ownership of the means of production has been historically important to Labour; how the institutions of the state are shaped by the interests of capital and the differential justice accorded to employers and workers.

To the right-wing Christian, the left's attempt to get more social justice and create a better world is optimistic and naïve because man's fallen nature prevents this. But it was my experience that the right were being naïve in the belief that unhindered market forces best promote the general good – a position which endorses the status quo and conveniently leaves the power and privilege of the rich intact.

I do believe the doctrine of the fall represents an aspect of truth and that humankind's fallen nature is reflected in a fallen world order with its structures of domination and exploitation which we have to try continually to reshape if, as Christians, we align ourselves with the values of the Kingdom.

Nor do I imagine trade unions are exempt from 'fallenness'. To me they are a 'secondary' or 'relative' good – only God is the ultimate good – but marked by the flaws and failings of our fallen society. So I can acknowledge that the print unions might have got into Wapping at an earlier stage but for their own divisions about 'who followed the job' to Wapping; that there were tensions between chapels and the national union during the dispute and that we were not always generous to those we differed from in our own movement – let alone our opponents.

At a personal level, I found that the crisis of the strike showed me, as in a magnifying mirror, my frailties and fears, my selfishness and lack of faith. And it is difficult to take part in such a prolonged conflict without sometimes sinning against charity.

For the quietistic Christian this is a reason to avoid conflict.

But this is not always desirable – justice-seeking often involves conflict – or even possible. For when a strike is called, you either go outside with the workers, or you throw in your lot with the management. There is no hovering above the strike, like an angel, no middle way beloved of Anglicans. A picket line makes you choose. More creative in my view are such Anglo-Catholic practices as confession, absolution and discussing the ethical issues with a sympathetic confessor or friend. 'Forgive us our trespasses', took on added meaning for me during the dispute.

The acknowledgement of human 'fallenness' can lead to political conservatism, but has not done so in my case. Rather the political conclusions I draw are: the desirability of democratic accountability, the independent scrutiny of the police and constitutional checks and balances; that the rich are powerful enough and don't need a Government specially looking out for them; and the distinction between a socialist vision and a practical political programme in the here and now.

In the here and now Christians may see signs and experience foretastes of the Kingdom, sacraments of the present moment which point to a future where we all flourish. Such moments I sometimes experienced in the solidarity of the chapel with its fellowship and equality; the blossoming of the talents of ordinary workers and the selfless sympathy action of others, like the trade unionists who put their jobs on the line to support us.

Solidarity, as Ken Leech has pointed out, is a deeply Christian concept: 'solidarity is an expression of our rootedness in God, and our common bonds one with another, by virtue of our creation and of the strengthening, transfiguring and recreation of that rootedness by Christ's incarnation, death and resurrection'. An early Christian example of solidarity was that of the apostles, 'And all that believed were together and had all things common . . .' Another is the sharing and equality of the Holy Communion ('though we are many, we are one body, because we all share in one bread') when the transformation of the material elements of bread and wine are a foretaste of personal and social transformation.

Solidarity is at the heart of trade unionism: 'an injury to one is an injury to all'. As we discovered in the strike, it was not simply a pious aspiration, it was all we had; Rupert Murdoch had the Government and its resources on his side. No wonder then if 'it is easier for a camel to go through the eye of a needle than for a rich man to enter the Kingdom of God'! Why trust a hypothetical God when Mammon delivers so much?

We got solidarity from many quarters including local authorities that banned Murdoch's papers from their libraries, Scottish dockers who boycotted newsprint supplies, postal workers who would not deliver *Sun* bingo cards – all then threatened with legal restraint and damage costs – as well as readers who boycotted Murdoch newspapers (*The Sun* and *News of the World* lost 150,000 and 300,000 copies per issue that year).

But we failed to get solidarity in certain key areas and this was the principal factor in our defeat. For Murdoch could not have moved to Wapping leaving us behind without the collaboration of other trade unionists, especially the EETPU. The extent of that collaboration has been revealed in a recently published autobiography by Eric Hammond, the EETPU's retiring General Secretary, in which he comes clean about his meetings with Murdoch before the dispute when they came to an unofficial understanding that electricians would do print-workers' jobs at Wapping (Hammond claims in a letter to the *Guardian*, published 19 March 1992, that this applied only to the proposed *London Post*). To their great credit, Fleet Street electricians led by Sean Geraghty, vigorously contested their union's Wapping policy, ultimately breaking away from the EETPU (when it was expelled from the TUC in 1988 over another issue) to join Sogat and form an electricians' branch.

In the Britain of the 1980s solidarity was costly; not only did unemployment mean workers scrambling to compete for jobs, but sympathy action had been outlawed. In answer to the question, 'Am I my brother's keeper?' Tory industrial law said only if he is at the same workplace – and not necessarily even then.

It is because solidarity is costly that it is so precious. At the end of the strike, Carmel Bedford and I interviewed a dozen women strikers for a possible book and the majority pinpointed solidarity as the best thing about the strike. They used different words, but the meaning was the same: 'the comradeship', 'the fellowship', 'the camaraderie'.

As a Christian I believe this solidarity has ultimate meaning. We lost the strike and dispersed – but all that was good about our self-sacrificing struggle will not be lost, but will, I believe, be recovered and incorporated into the future of God's Kingdom.

For the Christian and socialist, the solidarity we learn in the school of struggle must grow in inclusiveness, so that it becomes a basic solidarity with all humankind – solidarity confined to one's own group can become a form of tribalism. It is this wider human solidarity we affirm when we pray 'Our Father'. In the strike I found that saying 'Our Father' and then letting my mind range over everyone involved in the dispute was the way I could with sincerity pray for our 'enemies': Murdoch's management and its Tory allies and the strikebreakers. And saying 'Our Father' confirmed my feeling that the kinship we experienced in the strike demanded a better social system for its expression, for the prevailing world system of widespread hunger and oppression has to be radically changed if the words 'Our Father' are not to be a mockery.

Jean Sargeant, *Liberation Theology on the Wapping Picket Line*, London, Jubilee Group, 1992, pp. 22–8.

Promoting industrial change – the workforce seeks to innovate

In the late 1970s, the trade unions at Lucas Aerospace, a major manufacturer of armaments for the government and for export, attempted to put forward a plan for radically reshaping their industry in order to diversify into non-military production. There were many roots to this experimental venture, including a political revulsion from the escalating arms race and the recognition that people employed in the arms industries were frequently disturbed by the implications of their trade. The Lucas Shop Stewards' plan achieved extensive publicity, although ultimately rejected and undermined by the company, and provided an important impetus for later ventures in arms conversion and diversification in the brief period when the end of the Cold War suggested the possibility of a 'peace dividend' for the economies of the West.

However, this extract is important also because of the insight it gives to the way industrial missioners went about their work in the 1980s. Anthony Dalling, for many years an Industrial Missioner in Kent, wrote this article as an attempt to enlist wider interests within IM in the Lucas project at a time when it was under considerable fire from the company. The article reveals how IM at its best could get very close to what was going on at a critical time for a company and its staff, and could grasp – and communicate – the central complexities in a way which refused to yield to the oversimplification usual in the national press. But Dalling also exposes something of his personal journey into involvement with, and championship of, the project. This is not overt theology of the kind exemplified in other texts in this chapter (although Dalling moves in that direction in his final paragraph), but it shows the serious and conscientious engagement with the realities of other people's lives for which IM justly became proud and which, in the end, provide the root of all good inductive theology. This essay is quite typical of Industrial Missioners' reflections on industries caught up in radical change during the period under review.

> Those of us who are on the mailing list of the Lucas Aerospace Combine Shop Stewards Committee know from the latest circular from the secretary that they are at a critical stage in their struggle to combat continuing redundancies by proposing alternative socially useful work. I am writing to urge that those who believe that the initiative of the stewards at Lucas is one of the most creative developments in our Industrial

Democracy should use their influence, through whatever contacts and channels they may have, to develop awareness and support for this campaign. There are powerful forces of tradition, bureaucracy and self-interest – in the management, in the government and in the trade union movement – which would be only too happy to kill off this whole enterprise but the idea is spreading and it is important that more people should catch the vision and the hard common sense of what the Stewards are saying.

I will give a brief account of my own commitment to the Corporate Plan, mention some of the latest developments and say why I find the so-called 'Independence' of industrial chaplains increasingly hollow. I helped to organize two meetings about the plan when I was in Hemel Hempstead, one connected with my Trade Union Branch and one with the Trades Council. Since I have been in Kent I have proposed resolutions of support which were passed at my Trade Union Branch, at two local Trades Councils and at both the Kent and Greater London Associations of Trades Councils.

In September 1978 I wrote to Bernard Scott, the Chairman of Lucas Industries, when Michael Cooley, one of the founders of the plan, was under threat of dismissal for his continued work on the plan. Later in the year I received a copy of the Company's Annual Report and again I wrote to the Chairman as there was no reference at all in the report to the original and constructive research done by the Combine Committee. In January 1979 I received a letter from Alan Read, the Personnel Director of CAV Acton, a subsidiary of Lucas, inviting me to meet him, so that he could talk through with me the points I had made in my letters to the Chairman.

Initially my thoughts about this invitation were rather negative. I either pictured myself being lectured on the economic and industrial facts of life or engaged in a confrontation in which there was too much emotion and not enough reason. What I found it difficult to believe in was the possibility of expressing deep and serious concern in a rational and open way, quite clear about my own commitment, but at the same time understanding just how big a change in management attitudes and values is being demanded by the Stewards. I was persuaded of the possibility of this by the Stewards themselves, who have offered to take part in public debate with the management. In the event, I found that such a meeting was possible and Alan Read and I met for 2½ hours in April at CAV Acton.

Not one of the 150 products mentioned in the plan has yet been produced but the idea has caught on in other companies and a group of technicians from Vickers, who went to India to set up a Chieftain tank factory, came back asking, 'Why can't we set up a tractor factory instead?' The Vickers' National Combine Committee of Shop Stewards have produced a pamphlet, 'Building a Chieftain Tank and the Alternative' and 'Alternative Employment for Naval Shipbuilding Workers'. . . .

The Lucas idea has caught the imagination of people abroad, perhaps more than in this country and several groups of people have nominated the Stewards for the 1979 Nobel Peace Prize . . .

The latest publication by the Stewards is called 'Turning Industrial Decline Into Expansion – A Trade Union Initiative'. The proposals in this report, dated February 1979, are an extension of those in the original Corporate Plan but the important step forward is that the group presenting them is now an official CSEU (Confederation of Shipbuilding and Engineering Unions) working party. . . . 'The report is based on an analysis of the Company's proposals to reduce the existing Lucas Aerospace workforce in the UK from its present approximate 12,000 to 10,000 employees.' It puts forward radical proposals for the restructuring of the Liverpool and Bradford sites.

There is now a Technical Working Party, set up as a result of a tripartite meeting in February 1979 between representatives of the CSEU, Lucas Aerospace Management and the Minister of State for Industry, to consider a limited number of alternative products, some to be nominated by the CSEU and some by Lucas Management. Alan Read claimed that one of the biggest difficulties for the management since the plan was presented in 1976 was Trade Union Bureaucracy – the Combine was unofficial and the Company did not want to upset the Trade Union officials. This phase was now over, he said, and the Company wanted to work through the proposals. Evidence of this was the appointment by the Company of the Chairman of the Technical Working Party. What I was able to tell Alan Read was that the Chairman of this working party was not acceptable to the Stewards Negotiating Committee, because he was known to have declined an association with the North East London Polytechnic (NELP), precisely because it had given facilities there for the Stewards to establish the 'Centre for Alternative Industrial and Technological Systems' (CAITS). In other words, his objectivity and impartiality could not be trusted.

Two years ago the Company started to set up separate Shop Floor Committees in opposition to the Combine, which it referred to as a 'maverick' organization and today it still continues to harass individuals closely associated with the plan. Whether the Company's participation in the Technical Working Party represents a partial change of attitude therefore or whether it is playing an elaborate cat and mouse game, the outcome of which is just a matter of time, remains to be seen. Clearly there are huge differences of philosophy and perspective

[. . .]

The changes which (they) are demanding are big changes and at the heart of their philosophy is a vision of a different sort of society. This comes across in their various pieces of writing. They speak of 'social need', 'humane technology', the need 'to minimise or eliminate the alienation and frustration that can so easily lead to social conflict', 'A gentle and caring society' and their faith in what they are doing is expressed in their quotation from Victor Hugo, 'There is one thing more powerful than all the armies of the world and that is an idea which has come of its time'.

If the initiative of the Lucas Stewards is a sign of the

Kingdom, a breakthrough of new life, new ideas, into a jaded, alienated, depressed society, then we are either for it or against it. We must judge it, but it will also judge us, and if we say we are 'independent' of it, this means we are against it. When I attended the conference 'Alternatives to Unemployment' in November 1978 organized by the Stewards and CAITS and attended by hundreds of people, there was a quality of excitement in the air that I have not experienced at any other conference.

What we have done in Industrial Mission is to take the word independence, which has relevance in particular contexts and situations, and exalt it into a universal attitude towards society. This, I believe, is phoney. It means that we are guilty, along with the rest of the Church, of privatizing and neutralizing the Gospel, which is about the transforming power of God at work in Society, encouraging people to take hold of their lives and to challenge the values and power structures which dehumanize and enslave. Can we legitimately talk of 'doing' theology if we are not similarly engaged in the struggle towards a more just and human society and committed to particular policies and particular courses of action?

Anthony Dalling, 'Lucas – Which Side Are We On?'
Industrial Mission Association Newsletter, June 1980.

An economy dominated by armaments – the case of the churches in South Hampshire

If Anthony Dalling's article on the Lucas Aerospace conversion project represents a good example of an individual Industrial Missioner's involvement in an issue of national significance, the following extract demonstrates the involvement of IM and others at a more local level in an attempt to mobilize the churches to address a major economic aspect of the life of their region.

South Hampshire is – or was in the 1980s – dominated by arms-related industry. Portsmouth naval base was a major employer and had acted as a magnet for manufacturers of defence equipment, armaments and high-tech products geared to military use. As the country grew increasingly alarmed by Mrs Thatcher's belligerent approach to international relations and her determination, in cahoots with the US President Ronald Reagan, to accelerate the arms race, members of South Hampshire Industrial Mission (an ecumenical body which embraced the south of the county from Portsmouth to Southampton) understood that the economic dependence of the region on arms-related manufacture was a profound ethical issue for every citizen, since the prosperity of the region, and not just of individuals, rested on this morally contentious trade.

The following is an extract from their report, which exemplifies IM's willingness to engage in serious empirical research before ever launching into theological imperatives. In this venture, IM was joined by Social Responsibility officers and others from the churches of the region, demonstrating that IM was not always the isolationist body that some church people supposed. The report was written on behalf of, and was introduced by, the heads of the churches in Hampshire. Their foreword is included here for the hints it gives of the discomfort which this kind of research, and its associated moral and theological reasoning, generated among those who were the very public faces of the churches at a time of deep social conflict and unease.

Foreword by The Heads of Hampshire Churches

We welcome the publication of this well written and passionately felt report. It is particularly useful in calling attention to the extent of Hampshire's dependence on military spending and to the moral pressures to which those who work in weapons-related industries may be subject. These matters cannot but engage the concern of the Churches.

In some respects we believe the Report is open to criticism. For example, there is no examination of the right of defence against aggression. Except in Appendix 2, where an alternative view is propounded, non-violence is assumed to be the overriding principle not only for the individual Christian but for society as a whole. Thus, so far as the arms trade is concerned, the Report simply wants it brought to an end; the authors do not see it as within their brief to consider how this trade is at present controlled or how such control might be improved.

Nevertheless we are grateful for the work that has been done on these momentous issues, and we hope very much that the Report will further encourage that honest debate in the Churches and in the community at large for which the working party has pleaded.

Laurence Ashman
Peter S Chesney
Anthony Emery
Ronald Portsmouth
Geoffrey Reynolds
John Winton

May 1983

Introduction

In the spring of 1980 the Heads of Churches in Hampshire set up a Working Party with the following terms of reference:

To consider ethical issues in the manufacture and sale of armaments, with special reference to enterprises in this area.

The Working Party was established in response to an awareness that, since the mid 1960s, there has been a rapid expansion of international trade in conventional weapons. The volume of trade was increased, and the number of countries participating in the arms trade has grown. Weapons systems have become increasingly sophisticated and expensive. The countries of the South are rapidly developing their own arms production industries.

But the manufacture and sale of arms is also a local issue. Within the County of Hampshire, there are believed to be at least 120 firms manufacturing arms and components. And in Portsmouth and Aldershot, the Ministry of Defence, in collaboration with the Defence Sales Organisation and the arms producers, engages in annual events designed to promote arms exports. It was one such event – the 1979 Royal Navy Equipment Exhibition in Portsmouth – which prompted the Heads of Churches to establish the Working Party.

[. . .]

The nature of this response is two-fold. In the first place, the growth of the international arms trade is a cause for Christian concern because of its implications for human dignity, peace and social justice. And secondly, there is a pastoral concern for individuals who depend on the arms industry for employment but who may be conscientiously compromised by the work they do.

[. . .]

Local Involvement In The Arms Trade

In Hampshire, according to the County Corporate Planning Unit, one in every five pay packets is dependent on military spending – about 136,000 in all. There are nearly 35,000 service personnel based in the county, supported by a further 33,000 civilians working for the armed forces. These 68,000 Ministry of Defence workers were matched by as many who are employed by firms manufacturing and supplying arms or components.

Nationally, there are about a third of a million people employed in each of these three sectors: service personnel; civilian support; and arms manufacture. This represents 3% of the economically active population. So Hampshire with 20% of its workforce dependent on military spending has a critically large stake in this area of activity.

But what of involvement in the arms trade itself, as distinct from national defence. Precise information is not available. But three indicators are worth noting.

1. 25% of British defence products are sold abroad. It is reasonable to suppose that Hampshire firms have a proportionate share of this trade.

2. 119 Hampshire firms have exhibited at recent British Army and Royal Navy Equipment Exhibitions – annual events staged in turn at Aldershot and Portsmouth (see Appendix for full list). Among the counties, only neighbouring Surrey has more exhibiting firms. These Exhibitions, sponsored by the Government's Defence Sales Organisation, are set up specifically to promote the sale of British defence equipment abroad.

3. Only some of the individual deals between foreign governments and firms based or operating in Hampshire are known about.

[. . .]

The Effects of The Arms Trade In Hampshire

We have already pointed to the relatively high proportion of people in Hampshire who are dependent on military spending in general.

In particular, there are industries and companies which are very dependent on arms manufacture, there may be individual plants which are completely devoted to defence and armaments. For these plants, the loss of a contract could lead to their closure. Such pressures are especially powerful in Hampshire for companies like British Aerospace, British Shipbuilders, GEC and Plessey. As recession bites deeper and as successive Governments make cuts in expenditure on national defence, companies will be seeking to gain more foreign orders.

An alternative reaction to these pressures might be, however, that industry (both management and unions) begins to consider conversion from arms manufacture to products which are potentially profitable and socially more useful. In an environment of full employment and growth such conversion might not present too great a difficulty, particularly in view of the skills of the workforce. Now, clearly, it would present more problems.

But it is worth noting that after World War II enormous

numbers of working people were transferred from military to civilian occupations with virtually no increase in unemployment.

[. . .]

It is argued within industry in Hampshire that arms sales are good for the economy of the county and that any move towards conversion will cause major economic problems. But there seems little evidence for this view, though some communities, dependent on arms sales to a considerable extent, would be very vulnerable (Vospers of Woolston and Portchester).

[. . .]

The Effects on Individuals

The effects of the Arms Trade on those who work within it are inevitably difficult to assess. Such effects are hard to measure. But conversations with people who work in weapons-related industries indicate experience of stress, anxiety and confusion which take a significant toll in terms of human happiness. A general picture can therefore be built up on the basis of this individual experience.

People working in weapons-related jobs are, of course, subject to the same personal pressures that are felt in most industries in the present economic climate – the threat of redundancy and uncertainty about the future. But jobs in weapons industries are at greater risk still since they are particularly vulnerable to the unexpected ups and downs of international relations and these industries, more than some others, are increasingly capital-intensive.

An additional pressure is felt by men and women, Christians and others, who try to live by moral principles but find these principles denied and themselves compromised by the jobs they do. This experience again is not unique to people in weapons industries, but here it is felt with particular clarity and intensity.

For many people, the necessity of paying the mortgage and feeding the family on the one hand is matched on the other by a profound sense of moral discomfort at being involved in, for example, the production of warships or missile-control equipment. And people often find themselves in this dilemma through no choice of their own. The firm they joined some years ago, making pleasure-craft or domestic radios, has perhaps been taken over or restructured and their skills are now being used to an entirely different end.

Even people in senior management protest that they feel powerless to redirect the company away from military work. How much more helpless the individuals on the shop-floor. Collective action occurs rarely, with trades unions often more concerned with defending present jobs than with taking new initiatives.

The obvious solution to this personal moral dilemma is to resign and find less morally sensitive work. But this, for most people in the present economic conditions, is not a real option. Although many people in the weapons industries have particular technical or craft skills which could easily be transferred to different work, in this part of the country it is hard to find a company, particularly in engineering or electronics, that is not already involved in military work directly or indirectly.

Most people have no option but to live with the dilemma. They learn to become deaf to the moral questions. They become pragmatists. If they are Christians, they are forced to resort to a double standard – the high ideals of their faith in one compartment of their mind, the necessities of practical day-to-day reality in another. Living with this polarity causes for some a kind of schizophrenia which desensitises and disintegrates them as people, driving some to cynicism and despair, or more often making them live with the nagging knowledge that they are avoiding an issue of great importance in their lives.

Any job which subjects people to this kind of moral dilemma, forcing them to become indifferent to their own convictions and values, is guilty of attacking their very humanity – and of course it is the most morally sensitive who are the most vulnerable. The weapons industries impose this pressure in a particularly violent way.

[. . .]

But there are those for whom this is a keenly felt moral and religious issue. Every Christian congregation in this part of the county must contain people who are in this predicament. What is the Church's proper response? Does 'pastoral care' require us to help someone to live with his compromise? Does the unmistakeable ethical thrust of the Christian Gospel require us to challenge people to resolve their dilemma with integrity? Is it possible to do both?
[. . .]

The Ethical Issues

The Criteria for Ethical Judgement

In considering 'the ethical issues in the manufacture and sale of armaments', this Working Party wishes first of all to affirm its allegiance to what we believe to be a fundamental ethical and theological principle of both Judaism and Christianity – that human life is a gift of God in creation and has a share in the sanctity of God himself.

The Church has often made exceptions to this principle and condoned the taking of life – under a variety of names. We believe this to be a violation of that sanctity. We are not convinced that expediency, pragmatism or strategic necessity constitute ethical justification. We do not believe that in God's world it can ever be *right* for man to become the victim of man. In this report, therefore, we are not concerned to make minute distinctions between those occasions when armed violence may be justified and those when it cannot. Nor do we attempt to tailor our ethics to suit our needs. Rather, we wish to state radically our conviction that human life is God-given and that respect for life stands as an unqualified imperative for Christians.

We also believe that Christ's teaching and example require us to extend our understanding of what violence means. We are prompted to add to a prohibition on killing a further condemnation of oppression and exploitation, both military, economic and political, which result in men, women and children being forced to live in fear, poverty or ignorance. And we believe that the present world-wide trade in arms must take a major share of responsibility for the continuing oppression and exploitation of much of the developing world.

It is argued by some that a controlled arms trade makes a contribution to world peace, giving vulnerable nations the means to defend themselves and deter aggressors. From the evidence assembled in Chapters 1 and 2, we would reply that the proliferation of weapons has destabilised many nations, has increased the number of military governments who have come to power by violence and has greatly intensified human fear and anxiety. This we do not consider to be a contribution to peace. For peace is not an acceptable level of violence, but a positive state. 'It is the condition of a just world, responsive to God's purpose and law.' (Danus Skene 'Development and Disarmament'.) We do not see the arms trade making this just world more of a reality in our time.

[. . .]

Assumptions Which Need To Be Tested

1. That 'rights' should be exercised regardless of the cost or the consequences. The arms race is based on a concept of rights and of man's right to defence, to retaliation and, in the case of arms exports, to a slice of the market. 'The pursuit of rights implies the maximising of one's own potential position' (Skene). But a peace-maker has to try to give up the practice of what is understood as a right if the exercise of that right impedes peace. Arms salesmen and generals may be important in promoting arms sales, but they are not as essential as the politicians and industrial policy-makers who decide whether or not to exercise their political and economic rights.

2. That disarmament and the running down or conversion of military industries will lead to massive unemployment.

Certainly a major change of attitude would be required within industry, but the arms industries, increasingly capital intensive and vulnerable to the whims of international relations, are at present far from being the source of secure employment.

3. That weapons proliferation makes the world safer. Recent absence of armed violence in Europe is untypical of the world as a whole. It is noticeable that the wars of the last 30 years have occurred between the customers not the suppliers in the international arms trade.

4. That the Government's existing sales policy is acceptable and that checks, security procedures, export licensing, etc are adequate, particularly when dealing with repressive regimes and potentially hostile countries.

5. That the arms industries should enjoy a higher degree of economic protection and encouragement from the Government than the non-military sector.

6. That the only way of meeting research and development costs of military hardware needed for our own national security is through arms exports.

Our Ethical Judgement

[. . .]

We believe that the international arms trade, both as it is currently practised and by its very existence is contrary to the demands of the Christian Gospel and to the will of God. And we urge the leaders of the Churches to commit themselves energetically to a process of change.

Now . . . Thrive the Armourers, A Report to the Heads of Hampshire Churches by a Working Party on the Manufacture and Sale of Armaments, 1983, pp. 1–24.

5 Continuing the spiritual journey

Since 1965, the Industrial Mission Association has offered a place for practitioners to come together for sharing ideas and reflections. Periodically, it has sponsored groups to pursue particular areas of concern, the most prolific of which was the Theology Development Group, which existed through various incarnations from the 1970s to the end of the century. In the ferment that surrounded the social changes of the early 1980s, the Group was a focal point for exploring the theological foundations of IM and the potential of alternative theological approaches to inform changing practice. Meetings of the Group typically revolved around papers prepared by members and many of these were subsequently published by the William Temple Foundation on behalf of the Industrial Mission Association.

The collection of papers 'Spirituality and Necessity' took its title from the paper by Rodney Ward from which the following extract is taken. Ward was a Baptist minister whose work involved lengthy spells in IM and in higher education chaplaincy. While IM had traditionally eschewed anything that smacked of pietism, the consciousness of its own theological weakness in the 1980s, and the obligation to rethink its relationships with the churches, brought the question of spirituality and IM's place within the Christian community to the fore. There was little further exploration of the theme, however, and it has never been possible to say with any confidence that Industrial Mission is at all clear about its own spirituality or that which it promotes for others.

> This paper involves looking at the concept 'necessity'. The main thesis is that necessity is inbuilt in a work-based society, and that it is in encounters with necessity that man's spiritual development takes place.
>
> We find the concept 'necessity' in a variety of contexts. One is art. For instance, Stravinsky in his book *Poetics of Music*, sees unrestricted freedom as an abyss, the enemy of creativity.

Deliverance from the abyss comes only by turning to the concrete, which is the realm of necessity. In Stravinsky's case, the concrete is 'the seven notes of the scale and its chromatic intervals'. He writes, 'What delivers me from the anguish into which an unrestricted freedom plunges me is the fact that I am always able to turn immediately to concrete things that are here in question. I have no use for theoretical freedom. Let me have something finite, definite – matter that can lend itself to my operation only insofar as it is commensurate with my possibilities. And such measure presents itself to me with its limitations. I must in turn impose mine upon it. So here we are, whether we like it or not, in the realm of necessity . . . In art, as in everything else, one can only build upon a resisting foundation: whatever constantly gives way to pressure, constantly renders movement impossible. My freedom thus consists in my moving about within the narrow frame that I have assigned myself for each of my undertakings'.

This idea is applied more widely to culture which is the product of work, by the artist Eric Gill. Krishan Kumar quotes him inveighing against the leisure state with its notion 'that matter is essentially evil and therefore work essentially degrading . . . Culture if it is to be a real thing and a holy thing must be the product of what we actually do for a living – not something added like sugar on a pill'.

Of course, what we actually do for a living may also be degrading not because it is caught up in the material world but because as Simone Weil says, it fails to reflect eternity.

[. . .]

In different periods of history there have been whole classes which have known the despair of having no purpose in life either because they had no work or because the work they had provided them with no role. Tchehov in his play *The Three Sisters* portrays the Russian aristocracy of a provincial town in such a state of despair. Irina, one of the sisters of the title, confesses her yearning for work and Tusenbach responds: 'The yearning for work, oh dear, how well I understand it! I have never worked in my life. I was born in cold, idle Petersburg, in a family that had known nothing of work or cares of any kind . . . I was guarded from work. But I doubt if they have succeeded in guarding me completely. I doubt it! The time is at hand, an avalanche is moving down upon us, a mighty clearing storm which is coming, is already near and will soon blow the laziness, the indifference, the distaste for work, the rotten boredom out of our society. I shall work, and in another twenty-five or thirty years everyone will have to work. Everyone!'

Sometimes one encounters places without a role. For instance, a visit to the Esk Valley railway takes us to the village of Grosmont, Cleveland. Now a quiet village nestling in the hills it was once the scene of an important railway junction built to bring the coal necessary for the production of iron ore. At the height of its prosperity its population in 1881 was 1,581. Now the population of 350 consists mainly of elderly retired folk. The local Church guide wistfully remarks, 'one hears from time to time folk deploring the destruction of the countryside for industrial purposes, but one wonders if it is not better to have decently planned industry with its life and vigour, rather than areas such as ours being denuded of its young people for lack of work'.

Linking these various experiences of necessity together we see that whether it is the realm of art, or work, or society, creative freedom is found within a framework, a discipline which provides resistance against which the will is pitched, but is a resistance which is not blind, but purposeful enough to provide meaning. Bit parts are no good. What is required is a role.

[. . .]

For Simone Weil obedience to necessity is the supreme virtue, remembering that God makes himself necessity. This obedience to necessity must be distinguished from obedience to force. Obedience to force creates a terrible void, as in the case of slaves. Thus whilst Simone Weil has a keen sense of the mysticism of work this does not mean she is sentimental about it. 'Man's greatness is always to recreate his life, to recreate what is given to him to fashion that very thing which he undergoes.' But as we have seen, work without light from eternity is slavery. Simone had herself worked in a Renault works and on the land. She recognises that work is monotonous. 'Monotony is the most beautiful or the most atrocious thing. The most beautiful if it is a reflection of eternity – the most atrocious if it is a sign of an unvarying perpetuity. It is time surpassed or time sterilised.' For Weil, 'Manual labour is either a degrading servitude or a sacrifice'. We see then that work presents a terrible face. But for Weil it is not to be avoided but accepted in a spirit of obedience, seen in the light of eternity and so turned into a sacrifice. 'The spirituality of work makes us experience in the most exhausting manner the phenomena of finality rebounding like a ball; to work in order to eat, to eat in order to work. If we regard one of the two as an end, or the one or other taken separately, we are lost. Only the cycle contains the truth.'

Of course, as Krishan Kumar points out, if paid employment decreases on a substantial scale there will still be work 'in making, maintaining, and remaking ourselves, our families, our homes, our environment, our world'. Whether that will by itself sufficiently provide an encounter with necessity is to be questioned. The presence of large groups in society such as housewives and school children is a reminder that a challenging way of life can be found outside the area of paid employment. But these groups are not such exceptions as at first appears. Both roles provide a structure for living. If millions of people dropped out of paid employment it is not clear that they would find similar alternative structures. Although many people like to retire a third of them are far from happy to do so according to a survey carried out by Age Concern in 1974.

We are not trying to absolutise one particular segment of history, namely the period since the industrial revolution. The well-known existence of other societies where work is seen in a different perspective prevents us from doing that. But we ought to remember that in the case of other societies like the aboriginal and tribal, they depend on small populations, wide spaces and a closeness to nature, which we cannot duplicate.

There seems little doubt that we cannot think of a spirituality apart from necessity. Religious create their own realm of necessity by surrounding their lives with rules, as to when to eat, pray, work, sleep. Radical Christians find the realm of necessity in the struggle for justice. As J M Bonino writes, 'Spirituality is a total way of life which grows out of and surrounds any deep commitment'. Mostyn Davies talks about the necessity of doing a job (running a training workshop) along with others in which is discovered 'a spirituality about struggling on with something through every kind of setback'.

If we are right in what we have said about the encounter with necessity and the place of work as an avenue for this then we come back to the original point that visions of a society without work need challenging. But on the other hand, if we have a society in which people on the whole can't have a confrontation with necessity through work as paid employment, it is not very realistic to think that many will enter the monasteries to find it, or will feel inclined to enter the political arena. How then will they have an encounter with necessity out of which a spirituality may be formed? Will work in the informal economy of the household economy provide it? There is some reason to doubt that. In any case a society which is a sort of 'Disneyland of leisure-time pursuits' cannot provide it. As far as I know a spirituality hasn't emerged out of the casinos of Monte Carlo. That may not get us very far along the road, but at least it clears the ground, and in so doing challenges thinkers like W H Vanstone to give more content to their vision of a society based on something other than man's activity.

Rodney Ward, 'Spirituality and Necessity' in Industrial Mission Association, Theology Development Group, *Spirituality and Necessity*, Manchester, William Temple Foundation, 1985, pp. 19–25.

6 Individual authors

This book draws its material principally from texts that are not easily accessible and that reflect the churches' practice as well as theological thinking. Nevertheless, the writings of academics and others made their own contribution to the life and work of the churches in their engagement with the economy. The list below is not intended to be exhaustive but gives some insight into the range of writing in this field in the period.

P. D. Anthony, *The Ideology of Work*, London, Tavistock Publications, 1977.

Not itself a work of theology, and written slightly before the period of this chapter, Anthony's book nonetheless proved influential among Industrial Missioners and others in clarifying the issues and underlying ideas as unemployment soared in the early 1980s.

Anne Borrowdale, *A Woman's Work: Changing Christian Attitudes*, London, SPCK, 1989.

The growth of feminist theologies and gender studies coupled with the increasing participation of women in the workforce, was reflected in a new attentiveness to the theology that lay behind attitudes to women at work. Anne Borrowdale, a former Industrial Missioner, was an early contributor to this field.

Roger Clarke, *Work in Crisis: Dilemma of a Nation*, Edinburgh, St Andrew Press, 1982.

Drawing on his work with the Scottish Churches' Industrial Mission, Clarke (who later joined the staff of the William Temple Foundation) contributed one of the most thoughtful analyses and theological reflections on unemployment and the nature of work to emerge from the churches in this period.

Ulrich Duchrow, *Global Economy: A Confessional Issue for the Churches?* Geneva, World Council of Churches, 1987.

Duchrow, a German Lutheran scholar, has been immensely influential in the WCC for his attention to global economic issues and his arguments that the depredations of global capitalism require no less than a confessionally based rejection by the Christian churches.

Gordon Hewitt (ed.), *Strategist for the Spirit: Leslie Hunter, Bishop of Sheffield 1939–62*, Oxford, Becket Publications, 1985.

Hunter's name, as the founding genius behind Industrial Mission, has already arisen. This collection of essays marks his many achievements, including an article by Michael Atkinson, one of the early Industrial Missioners in Sheffield.

Margaret Kane, *Theology in an Industrial Society*, London, SCM Press, 1975.

Written before the period in question, but deeply influential through the 1980s, Margaret Kane's work draws strongly on her work as one of the early Sheffield Industrial Missioners and is an excellent example of a lay theologian's concern for work and the economy.

5

Consumption 1985 to the Present

Part 1 Making sense of where we are now

'The Age of Extremes' by the historian Eric Hobsbawm is subtitled 'The Short Twentieth Century'.[1] For Hobsbawm, the twentieth century lasted, in effect, from 1914, with the outbreak of the First World War, until 1991 and the final collapse of Soviet-style communism. The periods before and after those dates were qualitatively very different times. There is, of course, an interesting debate about whether history can be usefully studied as if significant dates mark out distinctive eras about which it is possible to make any generalizations at all. But the mid-1980s certainly marked a period in the life of the churches in which a changing context made 'business as usual', in terms of ministry and mission, an impossibility.

So while the last chapter traced the struggles by the churches to engage through their familiar instruments – boards, Industrial Mission, the hierarchy – with a new and rapidly changing political and economic context, this chapter tries to discern the strands of thinking that had already grasped that changing times required a very different kind of response, and it then brings the story full circle with accounts of contemporary developments that seem in many ways to be reassertions of old practices. During the late 1980s, two stories – the institutional struggle and local innovation – were evolving side by side; hence the overlap in the time periods covered in these two chapters.

By 1985, the illusion that the radical realignment of British industry wrought by the Thatcher governments' economic and social policies could be unravelled was beginning to fade. 'Industry' no longer conjured up images of mass workplaces staffed by men in overalls. The understanding of the scope and significance of economics, too, was changing as the focus on domestic economic management through rival parties' ideologically driven policies was eclipsed by a growing realization that global economic forces, transnational institutions and footloose capital were severely constraining the ability of national governments to decree the direction of policies and outcomes. Very high levels of unemployment were changing the profile of the labour market as part-time and casualized work burgeoned and women's participation in the labour force rose to almost 50 per cent. The trends that were to mark the way the economy would be conceived in the early years of the twenty-first century were laid well before the end of the twentieth.

Church workers involved in workplace ministries or other engagements with economic issues are often asked 'What do you do?' They frequently find that a description of their activities only elicits the further question, 'So why do you do things like that?' In a rapidly, and fundamentally, changing context, the churches' practitioners had, perforce, to attend to both questions – revising and reconsidering the nature of their activities and addressing the underlying questions of theological and missiological rationale. The readings in this chapter are broadly divided into those that address the practicalities of ministry and mission in a radically changed economic climate, those that seek to develop a viable theoretical understanding of engagement, and those that epitomize the churches' engagement with economic issues today.

Of all the trends that have challenged the churches in the economic field, the multifaceted phenomenon known as globalization is, perhaps, the most far-reaching and, as yet, hardest to comprehend. There are competing theories about the extent and the trajectory of the global market, but it is not contested that many old assumptions about the management of national and local economies no longer hold good. And with the loss of that shared framework, the interventions of the churches become problematic. The Church of England, in particular, which prided itself on the access to power afforded by establishment, has had to reassess its position.

Nevertheless, the fall of the command economies of the Eastern Bloc, and the burgeoning of the 'Washington Consensus' economic model of markets throughout the world, has changed the balance of power and, hence, the nature of the debate about concepts such as economic justice, to which the churches once felt called to respond. Where once there had been attempts to establish the proper Christian position regarding two opposing economic systems, now the lack of alternative models (except at the fringes) has largely marginalized serious moral debate about the virtues and vices of capitalism. Even in the mid-1980s, a few Industrial Mission teams and others were earnestly discussing with pastors in (for example) the German Democratic Republic the implications of standing in 'critical solidarity' with their respective systems. The very notion of such a dialogue became inconceivable within only a few years.

Not surprisingly, a dominant – even hubristic – economic system has generated critics in the churches. In a way, this is uncontroversial, since it must be a theological truth that no system can approach the perfection of God's Kingdom. However, far more divisive has been the debate about how a critique of the global market system might be taken forward. And, here, differing theological traditions have begun to move apart.

It is not, perhaps, surprising that some in the Lutheran and Reformed traditions of Germany (and other parts of Continental Europe), with their all-too-recent experience of living under totalitarian regimes, should find echoes of that history in the global presumptions of the market economy. Nor, given the wild divergence of outcome for the market 'winners' and 'losers' across the globe, is it unexpected that theologians in the developing world should seek to resist the onslaught of this economic leviathan. The work of the German theologian Ulrich Duchrow who called for the churches to declare a *status confessionis* on the global economy (reflecting the *status confessionis* against apartheid agreed by the Lutheran World Federation in 1977) was taken up strongly in the World Council of Churches where a theology focused on the injustices and sufferings that global capitalism has imposed on the poor remains a dominant theme.[2]

Among churches with a less recent history of confronting a dominant or malign culture, and where the perceived impact of global capitalism was not wholly uncomfortable, a more cautious approach was predominant. The legacy of a middle-axiom methodology continued to inform church responses in England, the appeal to inter-disciplinary dialogue – especially with economists – and the hope that consensual positions would emerge, being underpinned by a theology that saw ambiguity as a more authentic human response to complexity than counter-cultural, or prophetic, stances. Between these positions, a fundamental theological divide was revealed. Is the task of the Church to witness boldly to the imperatives of a Kingdom ethic, or to work with the paradoxes of a complex world inhabiting the theological interim – the age between Pentecost and the Parousia in which grace abounds but sin persists? Is the Church called to compromise in the interests of helping the powerful to exercise their power more justly, or to eschew compromise with power in the name of God's preferential option for the poor and marginalized? And is the Church called to participate in effective, if worldly, politics, measuring its impact by policies changed and lives improved, or to speak of another politics and another justice, informed by the divine economy rather than the limitations of a finite creation?

Most of the British churches have found themselves caught on the horns of this fundamental theological dilemma. But in terms of the churches' engagement with the most pressing set of economic constructs of the day, the theological issues and questions of practical action have not yet, in our opinion, been brought into an adequate dialogue.

The continuing difficulty of establishing an analysis of globalization echoes the impasse faced by the authors of *Perspectives on Economics* and, perhaps, represents the shape of debates to come. But, while exactly the same theological and ecclesial questions may be seen to lurk not far below the surface, the integration of social and theological analysis on other matters of economic life has appeared less problematical. Throughout the last fifteen years of the twentieth century, the churches maintained – often against the odds, given their own increasing marginalization from national life – a significant role in keeping the lives and concerns of the marginalized and the neglected somewhere in the national consciousness. In the absence of a challenge from any easily grasped alternative economic system, the market economy came to dominate aspects of life that had rarely, hitherto, been conceived of as economic issues at all. And the fundamental market assumption of competition as a governing metaphor left an inevitable legacy of losers as well as winners – and it was in few people's interest to highlight the losers' situation.

Here, it might be said, the inheritance of a middle-axiom approach to Christian ethics – with its insistence on an interdisciplinary conversation in search of 'the facts' of the situation – demonstrated its continuing usefulness. Where some voices are deliberately neglected or silenced in order to maintain illusions of unflawed economic success, it remains important to hold to a concept of objective truth and to utilize methods of research that are incontrovertible according to the mores of the day in order to enable them to be heard. Alison Peacock's work in statistical analysis as a vital building block for missiological decision-making is a good example.[3]

But, in contrast to much that passed for middle-axiom ethics in earlier decades, the latter years of the twentieth century saw a modest resurgence of theological seriousness in social action circles. The influence of liberation theology remained in places, but with less slavish devotion to Latin American precedents and a greater awareness that transferring theological models from oppressed base communities to the more socially ambiguous structures of western Christianity could not be undertaken in one jump.

The problem that theology and Christian action now had to contend with was that of facing its own social marginalization. The word of the Church no longer carried political clout. A more self-consciously plural society did not react to imperatives derived from the traditions of a faith community to which, on the whole, people did not belong. Yet the appeal to common values that had been the grounding of much church witness in the 1960s and '70s had served only to marginalize Christian theology still further by consigning its contribution to that of an optional appendix. A significant, though under-recognized, contribution to theological method was found in the pamphlet called *Hearing the Cry of the Poor* from the ecumenical research and lobbying group Church Action on Poverty. Here, an appeal to fairly generalized common values ('It cannot be right that ...') echoed Temple's famous middle axioms from his *Christianity and Social Order* (1942) while avoiding complex and disputatious questions of whose conception of right and wrong was being appealed to here. But the paper went on to identify some key, theologically grounded, notions which (it was confidently assumed) most Christians could embrace, thereby making an implicit but unavoidable connection between theology and the imperative of social action.

Nor were the victims of change identified solely in terms of material poverty. There was a growing sense of social dislocation throughout much of the middle class as economic change, driven by a politics of conviction, began to bite at the professions and commercial classes. Christians who had entered the so-called 'caring professions' as an expression of personal vocation found that the human caring that had drawn them into that sector was now explicitly subordinate to the financial bottom line and that people's concerns and well-being were of only instrumental value. One Industrial Missioner, active in the late 1980s, clearly recalls lengthy conversations with a workplace nurse who believed she could make a greater impact for good by retraining in personnel management, only to arrive in such a post at a time of radical revision when human resources management became driven mainly by the financial imperatives of cost-cutting through workforce reduction – a task she had to carry out from her first day in the new post. And while many of the people affected by the reorientation of professional concerns were to be found in typical Christian congregations, their experience made little if any impact on the concerns of the churches, locally or nationally, except, perhaps, by default as over-stressed professionals found Sundays invaded by paperwork or sheer exhaustion and began to opt out of congregational life.

One point at which church interventions were both prominent and modestly effective was in the debate about Sunday trading. Indeed, this episode, which had a long history but which might be traced in its most recent manifestation from the unsuccessful Witney Bill of 1983 to the final success of deregulation in 2001, reflected a number of trends in the churches' concern with economic life. First, a good deal of informed evidence was a by-product of the trend in Industrial Mission away from the traditional, male-dominated factory as the site of workplace visiting and the gradual deployment of chaplains among the largely female, predominantly non-unionized workforce of the big retail groups. Traditionally paternalistic, some of the big retailers gladly took on chaplains in the expectation that they would offer a (free) additional pastoral service to staff. Sometimes this was all they got. But the Sunday trading debate, driven as it was by the financial ambitions of only a few sectors of the industry such as do-it-yourself chains, found chaplains embroiled in complex roles in which the interests of the churches tended to cohere with those of management, workers and some unions.

This time, the extent of the churches' concern for an essentially economic issue ran far further than the established groupings like Industrial Mission, although IM made a prominent contribution. For the first time in recent memory, prominent evangelical groups mobilized their increasingly impressive battalions in opposition to a Conservative government's policies. And, as with the contributions from IM, their interventions focused not directly on the commandment to keep the Sabbath day holy (despite the slogan 'Keep Sunday Special') but on the threat to the social infrastructure of losing the established rhythms of work and leisure. Indeed, the combined lobbies against Sunday trading succeeded in defeating the government in a Parliamentary vote for the first and only time in the Thatcher regime (although cosmetic changes to the Bill saw it passed later).

It seemed, for a short while, as if traditional partisan campaigning models of Industrial Mission had successfully gained a foothold in the usually non-confrontational world of the service sector. But, in truth, this was a unique issue which, far from validating old models, represented an early realignment of political and economic interests on utilitarian rather than class-based grounds. And it was in the early days of this seismic realignment that IM and others began a process of self-examination and analysis of the theology and practice of economic engagement.

What was beyond doubt was that the landscape of industry and economics was becoming fragmentary and fluid. Workplaces looked and felt different – offering few opportunities for pastoral 'loitering with intent'. The growth of part-time and sessional work, the rise of sub-contracted labour and the increasing participation of women changed the ways in which workers and managers conceived the role of work and the workplace in forging their personal identities. The pastoral model of chaplaincy, which had never gone away, inexorably yet quietly supplanted the model which had seen IM as a vehicle for radicalizing the churches. IM practitioners started to speak of entering the 'Fourth Generation' of IM – the old navvy missions having given way to the Wickham model in the 1960s, which in turn evolved into a role as instigator and sustainer of project work in the 1980s. So IM had become, to some degree, the handmaid of the very government whose policies and their impact on the poor it deplored, ecclesial energy being directed to government-funded ameliorative programmes. And when the voluntary sector, including the churches, found itself pushed out of such work by shifting political priorities, the movement appeared to be in want of both a theology and a new practice.

Fourth-generation IM sought to capture something of the

fluid mood of the moment by making the local economy as a whole the object of its concern, attempting to embrace through 'networking' the cumulative contributions of large-scale industry, the public and voluntary sectors and those on the margins of the economy. Implicitly, it retained a rationale of engaging with economic life as a kind of research project geared to educating the churches in their mission, even as chaplains and churches made some practical contributions of their own to voluntary-sector activity. But it was at this point that the churches' own existential crisis took centre stage.

The 1990s might be said to be the decade in which the British mainstream churches first began seriously to face the fact of their own decline. One measure of this might be the increasingly frantic efforts by the Church of England to find new ways of measuring church attendance that could convey a less bleak message than the raw statistics implied. It is certainly the case that patterns of churchgoing changed in this decade, even as membership declined, and factors such as Sunday working, constricted leisure time for those in work and geographically scattered networks of family and friends all contributed to a certain irregularity of attendance even among the faithful. But no amount of statistical spin could conceal the downward trends and the Methodist and Free Churches, with fewer cushions of expectation and inherited wealth, faced this much earlier than the Anglicans.

Ironically, for those involved in mission in the workplace, one consequence was that the churches turned to secular management methods for models of how to control costs and focus endeavours. Whether this borrowing was well advised is another question, since it is not immediately obvious that churches are analogous institutions to commercial companies. But by turning to the jargon and mind set of managerialism, the churches were quick to adopt concepts such as 'downsizing' and 'core business activity'. What, after all, were churches for? That is a question that would elicit very different answers in different ages. The saying, attributed to William Temple, that the churches were unique in being institutions that exist for the benefit of those who are not their members, perhaps summed up the expansive and confident years of social consensus. But it assumed that the members existed in sufficient numbers to resource ministry and mission on that scale. Not surprisingly, the 1990s was the decade in which the concept of mission became interpreted much more in terms of building up the Church numerically and financially than in terms of offering pastoral services or prophetic witness to the world at large. To be sure, there was much agreement that the Church needed radicalizing, but this was conceived more in terms of a purge of practices and approaches that were deemed responsible for decline. Engagement with the structures and institutions of the economy, battered as that work already was by rapidly shifting patterns of economic life, was profoundly out of favour in such an environment since it could give no convincing account of how it could build up the Church, restore the institution's confidence or draw in new material resources.

One facet of financial stringency in the churches was a largely unforeseen shift of power from the centre to the local. National structures faded. In 2000, the Anglican Board for Social Responsibility was disbanded – residually present within a new Mission and Public Affairs Division, but a shadow of its former confident self. And in church structures generally, resentment in local congregations at the levies that funded central or regional functions grew, perhaps perceived as a kind of taxation in an age where the discourses of national politics had turned taxation into an incubus.

In terms of their theology, the churches through the 1990s saw a tremendous resurgence of evangelicalism in various guises. Some evangelicals, notably those associated with the Evangelical Coalition for Urban Mission, maintained an energetic presence in hard-pressed communities and embraced, within their social analysis, a clear grasp of the significance of economics for human well-being. But the bulk of the evangelical revival was far more strongly committed to a socially conservative stance which viewed anything reminiscent of the 'Social Gospel'[4] with profound suspicion. Large, and often wealthy, evangelical congregations became increasingly suspicious of delegating areas of mission policy to centralized bodies which did not, or might not, share their particular theological approach. In consequence, they found ways to utilize their resources to set up their own mission activities, grounded in their own theology, and withdrew (or begrudged) funding for wider church initiatives.

It has to be said that some agencies, not least some IM teams, did themselves few favours by reacting defensively against the trend towards greater management accountability within the churches. The echoes of Sheffield IM's traumas in the 1960s, when capricious episcopal power sought to disband Ted Wickham's creation, reverberated for a long time.

So, with a perplexing industrial and economic context, a mistrustful, theologically triumphalist yet socially beleaguered Church, eking out declining resources, the early years of the twenty-first century have seen some interesting mission ventures in the economy that would have puzzled earlier generations in Industrial Mission and the churches' social outreach bodies.

One response was to seek direct funding for chaplaincy from the businesses visited. An early example of this was the chaplaincy at Manchester Airport, a post originally funded by the Baptist Union and held by a Baptist minister whose retirement in the mid-1990s coincided with a large-scale withdrawal of Baptist resources from sector ministries. The ecumenical Greater Manchester Industrial Mission, however, recognizing that the companies on the airport site had valued the chaplaincy presence, managed to generate sufficient funds through direct donations to renew the post. The new chaplain, Mike Vincer, alludes to this in his article (quoted in this chapter) about airport chaplaincy. It may be too soon to evaluate how the dynamics of mission have changed with the shift in funding and, hence, accountability. But, by 2005, Manchester Airport is far from being a unique example of the direct funding of chaplaincy by business. It will be instructive to observe how the theological language of such chaplains evolves. One suspects that the emphasis on prophetic ministry calling for tangible social and structural change – a rhetoric that got more than one chaplain excluded from a workplace in the 1980s – will not be dominant. Instead, a more overtly pastoral theology seems to inform the churches' current engagement with institutions in the economy at local level. The recruitment of voluntary chaplains – and not just Christians – by Asda supermarkets is an example, and it seems certain that the pastoral nature of ministry, rather than the desire for a theological critique, is what drives this trend. The Church, it seems, is recognized to 'add value' in the area now known generically as 'spirituality'. The precise Christian theological rationale for this, however, has yet to emerge.

Allied to this, and again connected with the trend away from manufacturing industry toward jobs in the service sector and retailing in particular, has been the provision of worship opportunities in commercial settings. This trend – mainly seen in the large out-of-town shopping centres – has an interesting story. In the early 1980s, the Church Commissioners invested heavily in new retail developments and their flagship was the Gateshead MetroCentre – one of the first of the vast out-of-town sites. The venture generated much local opposition at a time when the depressed North East was mourning the loss of male employment in traditional industry and was deeply sceptical of the kind of jobs the service sector had to offer. For reasons now obscure, the Commissioners responded to local scepticism by funding the appointment of a chaplain to the MetroCentre, and the first person in post did much to build links between the Centre and the local communities. By the time the deregulation of Sunday trading came in, a new chaplain was continuing this work. She saw at first hand the gloom with which shop staff anticipated the advent of seven-day trading and the caution of managers who doubted its commercial justification but knew that the laws of competition meant that, once one company traded on Sunday, all would have to follow. The churches had joined battle over the legislation, and lost. Should the churches' representative on site now roll over and accept the development as an inevitability, reinforcing, perhaps, an image of a God powerless before the imperatives of Mammon? It seemed that some small act of rebellion or defiance was called for to demonstrate that God, and the people of God, had not simply sold the pass to secularism but retained an incarnational concern for the lives of the workers and shoppers of Gateshead. So, on the first trading Sunday, the chaplain got together a small group from a local church and, with the permission of the Centre management, held a short, informal act of worship in the main atrium. Many passed by; others stopped; some joined in. Staff in nearby shops heard the singing and the prayers. In subsequent days, the chaplain heard many appreciative comments. The service was repeated, and before long, local churches had formed a rota of different denominations to lead the weekly worship. Other chaplains, in other shopping centres, heard about it and set up similar services. The press cottoned on and the churches were once again news. The church hierarchies, and the people in the pews, saw something they could recognize, and supported it. A gesture, a political statement addressed to an issue of the day had rather quickly become something regular, 'churchy' and, it seemed, politically neutral.

That may be a good story on which to end the introduction to this chapter. It reflects the shift away from manufacturing and into services, from men's work to that of women and from full-time work to part-time hours at times that respond to consumer demand. It reflects a shift in understanding from humanity defined by work to humanity defined by consumption. It emerged as a reaction to a political philosophy that placed choice at the apex of human ambition and celebrated the fluidities of a geographically mobile population. Yet it also required Christians to exercise their mobility and ability to choose. It leaves many questions in the air. What is the place of worship and prayer in a theology of economic engagement? Whose mission is it anyway? The churches do not agree about the objectives or methods of mission – can their different approaches be brought together in a venture like this, or must the varied agendas inhibit real engagement with economic realities? Can the churches ever sustain a serious political engagement with economic policies for the sake of the world itself, or must they always turn work in the economy to their own ends and translate innovative mission back into the familiar vocabulary of church-centred concerns? And, perhaps most importantly, for whom is the Church doing all this? For its members? Those marginalized within the economy? For those seeking to ameliorate the rough edges of capitalism, or those who challenge its legitimacy?

There remains much serious theological work to be done before it will be possible to speak of the British churches having, once again, any coherent approach to ministry and mission in the economy.

Part 2 Readings

1 Globalization

A theological and spiritual perspective

Much work – secular and ecclesial – has been expended in analysis of the phenomenon known as Globalization, with its combination of economic, political and cultural facets. Robin Morrison is Church and Society Officer for the Church in Wales, a post to which he came with past experience in Industrial Mission and university chaplaincy. Morrison's theological consideration of globalization takes a generally positive view of the trends and movements it entails, and a consequently cautious approach to protest that resists all that globalization stands for. In this, Morrison is attempting to reflect a recognition that economics, whatever its ill effects at particular moments in history, is at the heart of human relations and should be taken much more seriously by Christians and by the churches than has often been the case.

At the very end, written after the substantive text was complete, Morrison makes an early reaction to the terrorist attacks on New York and Washington on September 11th 2001, effectively acknowledging that the arguments about globalization and protest had, at that moment, entered a new era.

GLOBALISATION

Theologically, a global if not cosmological perspective should be right at the heart of the churches' attitude to local, national and international disputes and to issues of identity and diversity. More than any other group in society we have a spirituality that enables us to wonder at the works of God in the cosmos and around the globe. Cosmology should be a mainstream theological subject. More, the incarnation enables us to affirm the local, ordinary and particular in relationship to the cosmological and global. We seek to hold together the transcendent and imminent truth of God. We of all people should never allow national or party concerns and agendas to have priority or to be the basis for any kind of exclusion. For the Christian the stranger and the 'other', from whatever background and nationality, has divine significance. Christianity, therefore, rejoices in globalisation per se, as it contextualises and qualifies all our narrower and partial concerns, even as it seeks to understand our personhood and humanity – a humanity God has entered in the incarnation and taken into the very heart and nature of the divine to redeem and perfect it in theotic union and communion. The Anglican and other Churches rejoice in their universality (catholicity). They are not only corporate but global. It is from this perspective that we enter the debate about globalisation with something distinctive to contribute.

Globalisation is not a cause of inequality or poverty or the destruction of the environment or the transformation of human relations into mere utility or the lack of democratic process. All these things pre-date the 21st century versions of globalisation and can be found in different kinds of society and stages in human history. It is also a mistake to see globalisation as a recent invention. It is clear that there have been significant points in the history of the world when we have drawn closer together. At every point in world history where travel became easier and the exchange of human goods and services developed beyond our own immediate family, tribal, regional, and state boundaries we can then say that we were turning our faces in the direction of a wider and closer world.

[. . .]

Globalisation can be described as universal access but not equal access. It is possible (and probable) for everyone on the planet to have access to certain goods, eg Coca Cola. It is not possible (or probable) that everyone can afford it. It is likely that everyone will be able to afford Coca Cola as globalisation increases economic opportunity even for the most poor. It is questionable whether everyone should or does want to use a particular product. While the rich majority get disproportionately richer, the poor will also get richer. New access to globalised employment means higher wages for the poor than local economies can usually provide, even though those wages are lower than they would be in developed countries. However, it may never be possible for everyone on the planet to have access to other kinds of goods and services, eg an opera at La Scala, Milan, even if they could afford it

[. . .]

Globalisation performs a useful function in civil society if it demonstrates inequalities and encourages actions to address them. The messenger is different from the message. We have always lived in social systems that have struggled to achieve social and economic justice (the Old Testament period witnesses to that) as it presents itself in different ways and for different reasons. If globalisation has made us more aware of global and local inequalities, then globalisation in this sense is the messenger rather than the message.

It seems that this one word 'Globalisation' has accrued to itself particular subtexts. Each, in its own way, contains a matter of legitimate and urgent concern and debate. Subsumed under the one concept, negatively interpreted, it is not, however, surprising that a negative spin appears in each subtext. The following is no more than a brief, headline series of comments and questions about some of them and the way they have accumulated an approach to the argument about globalisation. It's as if this argument has been subsumed within an ideological package or jigsaw puzzle that requires each piece to be placed pointing in the same direction. In reality many of the individual pieces have more than their own integrity, but should not perhaps be forced so simplistically to make up the whole.

In the Globalisation debate, we face many moral dilemmas. Spiritually, isn't it immoral to criticise others, if we do not pass the test ourselves? On the other hand, should we reduce our commitment to ask profound questions about economic and political systems, because our own behaviour isn't perfect? Wouldn't that of itself be immoral if the systems were causing harm? Don't all systems cause a measure of harm? If we took a snap shot of any organisation, at certain points in its history (not always at the beginning), wouldn't we see mistakes and difficulties? This is not to claim that organisations improve automatically with time, but they do change and there is much moral pressure internally and externally for that change to be positive.

[. . .]

There may be much in our present economic and political life that needs improving. It would be strange if this were not the case and complacency has its own moral implications. It would be a great tragedy if the idea of 'globalisation' were simplistically dismissed or undermined, as it surely carries many positive dimensions and realities. It would be a tragedy if we ignored or dismissed the positive effects of those economic organisations which bring new hope to the poor throughout the world. Certainly, the moral, cultural, environmental and other content of economic progress needs to be examined rigorously. Rather than pretend we can or should stop the world because everything is wrong, let's now ask for the wisdom and discernment, the humility and the perception to identify the real causes of the symptoms that trouble us and the grace to celebrate and enjoy the many positive aspects of our economic and social life in a common search for global community well-being.

Robin Morrison. July 24th 2001

POST SCRIPT

[. . .]

'THE NEWS IS JUST BREAKING . . .' TODAY, 11TH SEPTEMBER, 2001 2.30PM UK TIME

Today, as I finished off the design of the cover for this book and was talking to the printer, the news came in. In a book about Globalisation, these hasty words are added at the last minute to express something of the horror that can only grow over the next days, weeks and months and the many questions that will follow.

Our thoughts are firstly with the people of America and the thousands who must have died (as the Mayor of New York said – 'more than any of us can bear') and with the bereaved; for every family and work place affected by this unprecedented and horrific tragedy. It is already being described as a 21st Century Pearl Harbour right at the heart of American society – the Twin Towers of the Trade Centre and the Pentagon.

Tomorrow we will all wake up to a changed globalised world; the skyline of New York will never look the same again; Americans will have tasted the horrors of terrorism on a scale that is beyond anything imaginable; the Global Stock Exchanges will have dipped further into shock and recession, affecting ordinary people and companies around the world; leaders will call for 'Business as usual' in a situation that is far from normality; Liberal Societies will increase their security measures and so change aspects of their 'libertarian' values and practice; Americans, in their shock and fury will wonder why the Muslim or at least the Muslim fundamentalist world hates them so much and all of us will wonder who is the real enemy and where and what kind of response is possible or appropriate.

We live in a globalised world where there is no guaranteed security against a handful of terrorists who can take over domestic flights. No missile defence shield would have prevented this. We live in a world increasingly divided by a new enmity – that between the so called 'free democratic world' in the West and elsewhere and the so called Muslim world. Many Arab countries will distance themselves from this horror and already the Palestinian leadership have done so, but many Muslims will rejoice. How can this be? How can anyone want to kill innocent civilians on this scale anywhere in the world? We live in a globalised world where host states will be accused of the crimes of individual terrorists; where, as in the Israeli–Palestinian conflict, increased 'security' measures, let along revenge, only escalate the violence and that violence reaches out from the streets of Jerusalem to the streets of New York. How will America now react? Will they over-react? Will their response not just escalate the motivation of Muslim terrorists and extremists for future atrocities? What is the way out of this vicious spiral of violence? Certainly to look at the causes and address those. The long term security of us all is not enhanced by ever greater military strikes, but by facing the enmity and changing that.

At the heart of the Gospel is the Christian belief that Jesus came to heal the 'enmity' between us and the divisions that separate us; to break down all the dividing walls and to bring restoration and reconciliation. Whatever else the 'free world' now calls for in response to this terror, let us pray that it calls for that and acts to achieve the abolition of the enmity and all its global and local causes.

Robin Morrison, *Globalisation, Democracy and Protest*, The Church in Wales, 2001, pp. 14–58.

Different approaches in tension

Whereas Morrison's work for the Church in Wales represents the thinking of an individual holding a key remit within a denomination, other approaches have sought (in a return to earlier models of working) to enable a whole church or denomination to declare its position. The Church of England's Board for Social Responsibility set up a working group to do just this in 1997–98 and their report, *Faith in a Global Economy*, was received (without much debate or contention) by the General Synod in the latter year. The lack of contention at Synod belied the difficulty the working group had experienced in reaching a shared position itself. The group had included members of the Board's Social, Economic and Industrial Affairs Committee (SEIAC) and its International and Development Affairs Committee (IDAC) and, from the world of the non-governmental organizations (NGOs), members of Christian Aid and the pressure group for international debt relief, Jubilee 2000. There were significant divisions between those members of the group who represented the 'traditional' discipline of economics and those who argued for a major shift in the paradigms of global economic relations. And this was essentially a theological, as well as a practical, dispute, since it turned on the extent to which Christians are called to work with the created order as it is, including a realistic view of the persistence of human sin, or the calling of Christians to embody in earthy relationships the new dispensation of the Kingdom of God inaugurated, but not yet fully realized, in Christ. Echoes of these tensions remain in what was, in the event, a compromise document. Nevertheless, the extent of the disputes within the group may be one explanation for the greater prominence given here to theological reasoning alongside social analysis.

Part 3. The critical dialogue between faith and world

Addressing the challenge of poverty in a global economy therefore requires Christians to enter into arguments about the nature and importance of:

- economics and the market
- the global dimension
- change itself

3.1 Engaging with economics and markets

Economics as a discipline is now entirely autonomous. However it grew up in a Christian society, alongside the processes of industrialisation and urbanisation, Adam Smith was a moral philosopher as well as an economist. It can be seen as developing from a Christian conviction about the importance of stewardship – the very name of economics links it with that tradition. Christians have long recognised the economy, alongside the family, politics and so on, as an order of God's creation and as a possible means of providence. Nevertheless, the economy is a social and political construct and sadly imperfect. It is open to reform by human initiative. Its structure is not something that we have to accept as being ordained by God.

The concern of Christians for justice and human rights is rooted in biblical teaching, and Christian social thought has used justice as its main criterion in judging economic systems. It has been particularly concerned with distributive justice – the equitable distribution of goods which is central to the debate about poverty in a global context. More recently the concept of 'productive justice' has emerged. It is not merely about a just distribution of resources but justice in the way resources are generated.

We cannot simply say that economics is about efficiency and theology is about justice. There is a complex relationship between justice and efficiency. Efficiency means the best use of resources to meet our aims and objectives. It needs other values and purposes, for until we know the purpose of economic life, we cannot say what is meant by efficiency. Justice depends on economic and other circumstances. What is just depends on what is possible. It has to be understood in the context of a particular social and economic system in which particular expectations and norms of behaviour are embedded. Often concern for justice will appear to conflict with concern for efficiency. For example high rates of taxation and social security benefits may improve the distribution of income. They may also reduce incentives to work and hence result in a lower level of national income. On the other hand justice and efficiency in other circumstances may reinforce one another. Workers who are well treated will often work harder and produce more. Economists are increasingly recognising that trust and equity improve productive efficiency. Good relationships are part of what is now called 'social capital'.

There is, however, a deeper issue in the relationship between Christian faith and economics. Economists make certain assumptions about human behaviour. They usually assume that all good comes from the satisfaction of individual preferences; that resources are scarce and the human appetite for consumption is, in effect, insatiable. In a given state of knowledge and technology some wants will have to go unsatisfied. Christians recognise the reality of scarcity as a constant factor in economic life. Jesus' challenge of the Kingdom of God means that the market system must always be questioned in terms of its values and objectives. The challenge is to include those who can easily be forgotten and excluded because they do not appear to be economically significant.

Within Christianity there can be tensions between justice and compassion. In the Hebrew scriptures (Old Testament) the God of inflexible justice is also the God of mercy. In the New Testament Jesus challenges the belief of his followers with a call to respond to the values of the Kingdom of God. It was left to the Church that emerged after his death to work out the implications of this challenge for everyday economic life.

3.2 Engaging with the global

The world is moving remorselessly to a global economy as the logical consequence of those processes of industrialisation which began in the UK. The Christian tradition supports the move to 'global' with its commitment to the ecumenical, to the whole inhabited world. Yet we have seen how that commitment challenges the very processes of globalisation for their exclusion of people and nations from it. The ways forward, like arguments about globalisation, are therefore complex.

They will not be single, simple, solutions. We are seeking new and overlapping systems of responsibility and control. It is significantly an affirmation of the political task and vocation, facing up to the following arguments:

- The need to recognise the three orders of creation (the political, economic and cultural) as relatively autonomous realities in an interactive relationship with each other, and requiring appropriate forms of citizen participation in each.
- The need to refashion the practices and procedures of democracy, given the tendency of majorities to exclude minorities, especially the marginalised. This argument over the culture of contentment applies within Western societies but equally between them and the least developed countries. How can the marginalised be given a proper stake in society and world?
- The need to rethink the function and influence of the nation state and regional nation-state groupings, as a counterforce to harmful tendencies in globalisation processes.
- The need to affirm the growing importance of those civic groups such as NGOs, as counter-movements to the power of international interests and lobbies' harmful global processes, and as effective partners in collaboration with public and private sectors, at all levels, not just the local. The Christian involvement in the historic campaign against slavery, and the contemporary campaign of Jubilee 2000 for debt remission, illustrate this need and potential, linking as they do with the Roman Catholic stress on subsidiarity, and Protestant social teaching on intermediate associations.

[. . .]

Part 4. Promoting change

The preceding parts of this Report have indicated the tension between what is and what could be. Some might say there appears to be some ambiguity between our acceptance of what is realistic ('living in the real world') and the vision of a New

Creation and of the Jubilee. We have identified four possible responses to the global economy:

1. Simply accept it because there is no alternative.
2. We must stop it! This is the other extreme to 1.
3. Try to slow it down.
4. Try to reshape it.

In Part 4 we will focus on the attitudes expressed under 3 and 4 above.

Many of the problems outlined above will find partial solutions in the economic and political policies of Least Developed Countries (LDCs). Land reform, cuts in spending, greater investment in education and the provision of credit to the poor are just some of the policies that are likely to produce benefits. The issue of addressing corruption must also be faced.

Much can also be done by the richest (OECD) governments to create a favourable economic and political climate: a substantial forgiveness of debt for the jubilee; a better targeting of aid spending within an expanding aid budget; more coherent foreign policy and better trade deals for the products the Least Developed Countries have to sell are some of the immediate needs.

As we have seen, we live in a world where economic relations are becoming ever more globalised. But political decisions and the social underpinnings have not kept track. Economic integration has run ahead. There is a need for new forms of regulation and global governance to cope with the new challenges outlined about: codes of conduct for international business; measures to stabilise regulation of currency flows; new forms of economic co-operation and planning.

We cannot, however, just wait for governments to act. There is much that churches, congregations and individual Christians can do. Corporations already operate globally. Civil society – the churches, NGOs and trade unions will also have to work with their global neighbours, looking for new forms of partnership and solidarity.

It is necessary to take note of:

- A changing culture of more market and less state, with a growing reorganisation of partnerships across all three sectors (private business, public and voluntary).
- The need to seize the moment '*Kairos*' by concentrating on sharply focused targets as representative interventions.
- Facing up to structural issues but without neglecting care for those who suffer from their effects.
- The pervasive and insidious impact of the 'culture of contentment' which colludes with those who benefit from increased globalisation. To combat the culture of contentment requires a robust rejection of some economic myths: that the scientific and technological knowledge of the West is the key to world survival; that the techniques of business and trade should be imported into the running of every human activity; that if something is not quantifiable it either does not exist or is simply a matter of private, individual taste.

We are aware of the need to restore and enlarge the understanding of oikonomia – the community of the whole inhabited world. The Anglican Church must also recognize the importance of the worldwide Anglican Communion and international ecumenical bodies in addressing these issues.

There are a number of areas where change has already begun where concerned people can make a difference by taking action. These may seem small in themselves but they are not irrelevant and they point the way in which we wish to go. Thus, for example, a congregation deciding only to drink fairly traded coffee may seem to be a 'drop in the ocean' but it does call to mind those who grow the coffee and make a conscious link between the congregation and the growers – as well as the economic benefit of the producers. Furthermore, the relationship between structural change and individual concern must be maintained. The former Roman Catholic Archbishop of Recife, Brazil, Dom Helder Camara, was once asked why he had feeding schemes for poor people, since these were typical of the charitable approach criticised by many liberation theologians. Camara affirmed the importance of structural change, since there would otherwise always be more people being made destitute, but did not write off this generation in a hard-hearted way. He likened them to wounded soldiers, casualties in the war against the poor. They too needed care – and now, since it would otherwise be too late for them when structural change had been achieved. So representative or symbolic actions, symbols which 'ring true' make a real difference now and point the way to greater change. They should be consistent with the overall goal to be achieved and inspire others to consider 'going and doing likewise' – as Jesus put it at the end of his story of effective love, the parable of the Good Samaritan.

4.1 Affirming fair trade in a global economy

A number of initiatives can be cited as illustrations of what is happening and what can be done:

- Fair Trade campaigns set up by churches encourage church members to take the issues seriously and to take action within their own spheres of influence.
- Shared Interest which enables people to buy equity in companies that are selling fairly traded goods.
- The Micro Enterprise Development Movement which makes credit and other financial services available to people running very small businesses and, although it does not change the larger picture, these can make a big difference in the economy at the local level.
- Ethical Trade Initiatives bring together a range of companies who are taking a lead in developing more ethical trading, including supermarkets, clothes retailers, telecommunications and DIY retailing.
- Campaigns that put pressure on multinationals, as witnessed by Christian Aid's campaigns with supermarkets and the sports industry and CAFOD's work with the toy industry.

Other initiatives are needed including a critical assessment of the policies and practices of agencies like the International Labour Organisation and the World Trade Organisation. This implies that it is necessary to encourage recognition of minimum standards for workers and the dignity of labour as part of Fair Trade.

Ethical investment policies contribute to these aims and need to be developed and broadened to include these considerations. The Church Commissioners have begun to examine these issues in greater depth than previously, with the establishment of the Ethical Investments Working Group. This is a welcome development which should be encouraged.

4.2 The need for redistribution of wealth

We have seen that inequality is increasing as a result of globalisation – within countries and between countries. The market is good at encouraging production, but is not able, uncorrected, to protect the weak and vulnerable. There will thus continue to be the need for policies of redistribution to offset the concentration of wealth.

Foreign aid is one essential part of international redistribution. But the effectiveness of aid is heavily compromised by the massive debt burden of the poorest countries. A priority for redistribution must therefore be the campaign for debt remission, which must be realistically motivated both by altruism and self-interest. The glaring inequalities of life chances and distribution of wealth call urgently for redistribution.

4.3 Promoting Jubilee

As we approach the Millennium celebrations, Christians, together with people of other faiths and none, are coming together around the world, under the banner of the Jubilee 2000 movement, to pressure the G8 (main industrialised countries) creditors to release the most indebted countries from the bondage of international debt.

The essential element of the Old Testament Jubilee Year of Release was the remission of debt. At the very heart of the Good News which Jesus proclaims is the declaration of Jubilee

Release from sin and debt. In the Jubilee Year, the same release that redeemed the land for the people of Israel also redeemed the people themselves. As Bishop Laurie Green has noted, '*When we read the New Testament with Jubilee eyes, we see the Release which is brought by the Sabbath Year of the Lord's favour writ large in the parables and beatitudes and in many aspects of his teaching and ministry.*'

The remission of debt demonstrates the essence of mercy in that it draws a line under indebtedness, and brings it to an end. Because of the absence of an international insolvency procedure, it is not possible to draw a line under international debts and bring them to an end, as can be done under domestic insolvency laws. As a result poor country debts are allowed to grow remorselessly. These countries then fall into arrears and have the interest on debts compounded. Poor counties then find themselves on an endless treadmill of borrowing to pay off old loans, while the interest on old debts builds up relentlessly.

[. . .]

4.4 Developing a new polity: making accountability effective internationally

There is a pressing need to develop appropriate political structures that are responsive to the complexities of the modern world. Whilst not arguing for world government, there needs to be reliable, clearly understood structures for dealing with inter-national issues.

There is a need for independent monitoring of Transnational Corporations in response to consumer pressure, and indeed pressure from environmental labour/worker and development groups. Stakeholding needs to be recognised and fostered on the broadest possible basis. The Multi-lateral Agreement on Investment (MAI) is an international treaty under negotiation by the twenty-nine member countries of the OECD aimed at minimizing the extent of government regulation of foreign investment. But although it purports to produce a 'level playing field' for investment by transnational corporations and national companies in different economies, it does so at the expense of removing a degree of national sovereignty over investment decisions with potential threats to environmental and labour regulation.

International institutions like the International Monetary Fund, the World Bank and the World Trade Organisation need to be reformed in order to become more representative, more open and more transparent. They need to operate in the right relationship with regional groupings like the European Union and NAFTA (North Atlantic Free Trade Area) and both in turn need to acknowledge the role of 'local' institutions at national level and below.

In other words the economic order should not be subordinated to the political order but the proper relationship and interaction between the two must be promoted. The role of NGOs and the so-called third sector needs affirmation. Increasingly aid organisations such as Christian Aid and other NGOs are campaigning for international Codes of Conduct and independent monitoring to prevent child labour and attempting to insist that multinational companies adopt the same standards on issues such as environmental measures in developing countries as they would in the industrialised world.

The key concept of subsidiarity has implications for the protection of human dignity in a global economy. Subsidiarity requires that decisions affecting the lives of people be made at the lowest possible level appropriate. However it must be recognised that on some issues the lowest appropriate level may be the global level.

In summary, then, there should be support for moves towards:

- Subsidiarity – that the decisions which affect people's lives should be made as close as possible to them – and, where practicable, with their active involvement.
- Democracy, although many feel that voting gives them little control over their lives – and virtually none over economic issues either national or international, participation must be encouraged.

- Transparency – since economic decisions which have dramatic effects on people's lives are made without people's knowledge or involvement, and
- Accountability – since those who make these decisions can rarely be called to account.

In this context, civic society and NGOs have an important role to play.

4.5 Defending the environment

No other issue has moved so quickly from the periphery of human social concern to the centre as environmental awareness. It has also become clear that environmental concerns are not a luxury for the North; global warming will affect everyone. To make a vastly expanded and integrated global economy sustainable is a massive challenge. It requires active and vigorous responses from all sides – governments, business and consumers. It will require a fundamental shift in values, which currently ignore or belittle local knowledge of environments, with a decentralisation of decision-making alongside. The environmental costs of trade need to be considered explicitly.

Clean industrialisation and sustainable agriculture will require incentives and regulation that work but do not destroy much-needed growth in poorer countries. Finally, the endless expansion of consumption in already wealthy countries needs to be questioned and examined.

Faith in a Global Economy, London,
Board for Social Responsibility,
1998, pp. 31–41.

2 The professions under fire

In a period of social division and growing material inequality, few commentators in the churches broke out of a straightforward typology of rich and poor, comfortable and marginalized.

Nevertheless, by the end of the 1980s, many were becoming aware that the Conservative government's antipathy to special-interest groups extended far beyond the trade unions and constituted a considerable threat to cherished practices in the professions and middle classes. The wider cultural reconfiguring of human relationships on an essentially business-based model accelerated this process.

Rachel Jenkins's study, conducted through the William Temple Foundation in Manchester with grant support from the Audenshaw Foundation (with its historic concern for lay issues in the churches) sought to track the changes to the underlying values in the professions, especially for lay Christians who had entered their profession as an outworking of their sense of God's calling, but who now found the values they had espoused turned upon their heads. Working with a reference group of people thus affected, and conscious that practical considerations militated against rousing battle cries to resistance and rebellion, Jenkins coined the term 'unquiet endurance' as a spiritual and practical response for those who recognized their own impotence to change a whole culture yet who had few, if any, sources of support in the churches. Indeed, one of the key findings of this work was the incapacity of local churches to grasp the human significance of the cultural revolution being wrought in British institutions and the cost borne by ordinary, often churchgoing, people.

With the ending of the grant funding for this project, Rachel Jenkins became an Executive Secretary of the William Temple Foundation and went on to join the teaching staff of the Northern Baptist College.

INTRODUCTION

This research is based on a concern first expressed by the William Temple Foundation in 1986:

> 'We are concerned about new pressures on Christians emerging in industrial and commercial organisations and in the

> public sector. Lay people caught in these frontier situations need support and sustenance at an individual level if they are to be obedient to the distinctive value systems of the Christian faith. But even more so do they need help and encouragement if they are to attempt to carry those values into the very heartland of industrial, commercial and public life, so that the value systems, and practices and policies of our institutions show signs of transformation, as well as the lives of ordinary people.'

As a commemoration to the lifelong work of Mark Gibbs, who worked to promote the importance of lay people in the church and their influence in the world, the work on which this paper is based has been funded by the Audenshaw Foundation, which Mark Gibbs set up.

The starting point is this question: What can Christians do when they discover that the values to which they are committed are challenged and undermined by the policy of the organisation within which they are working?

It is not surprising that many Christians feel confused and anxious. They talk in terms of feeling powerless and not knowing what to do for the best. Those who are committed to treating their colleagues and clients with respect feel under threat. Compassion, encouragement, the sharing of power and social justice are now rejected as guiding principles. People committed to them find the competitive, individualistic context alien and in conflict with the way they believe that things should be done. However difficult it may have been in the past to work on these principles they were at least recognised as having some validity. They now appear discredited in public debate and as principles for the setting of policy.

In the following paragraphs I am using examples (with one exception) from people with whom I have worked to illustrate the kind of pressures that they feel and the questions with which they are faced.

The first is a bank employee who has worked for the same company for over twenty years. Her last post was that of

Assistant Branch Manager, which she had held for some time. She enjoyed her work, was good at it and took particular pride in making financial affairs accessible to those who were somewhat mystified by them. She believed that this was an integral and important part of her work and encouraged those who were working for her to be helpful and to respect all customers. The changes in central policy, especially the shift from customer to share-holder interests, were a threat to the way in which she believed the job should be done. She perceived the new insistence on charging for every piece of extra work or advice as detrimental to the customer and in the long run detrimental to the bank, which would eventually lose many customers. She anticipated the time when she would be faced with the necessity to act against her principles or refuse to do as directed. If she chose the latter course, she would almost certainly put her position at risk.

As Assistant Branch Manager, she was too low in the chain of command to make any significant difference to the policies that she was required to implement. As an employee of twenty years' standing, she believed she owed loyalty to the company and felt ambiguous about the possibility of leaving. If she stayed on, she did not know how to handle the conflict of values in her own work and felt unhappy about future relations with colleagues, especially those who apparently were undisturbed by the changes. The possibility of voluntary redundancy caused her to feel guilty. Was not this an easy way out? At the same time, her church congregation believed that she should remain 'to provide a Christian presence', yet she was convinced that she had no influence in any significant way over the new changes. The idea of a 'Christian presence' needed to be explored to give it meaning.

She therefore faced difficult questions of personal integrity and compromise. She was concerned about the potential isolation and lack of support. In her own assessment her level of influence was too little in terms of policy to make any significant difference. She was unsure of her influence over colleagues.

This case study raises other than individual questions.

Companies developing policies along these lines are making staff redundant who have considerable experience. What does this mean for the future of the firms who are losing an experienced band of middle management? In terms of efficiency they may be losing expensive staff; in terms of the quality of the service provided the effect has yet to be seen, but both staff and customers anticipate little improvement.

A second example is derived from the continual pressure placed on doctors regarding hospital admissions. This particular case is now more than three years old but it serves to highlight many of the problems which professionals face. In a psychiatric unit in a general district hospital beds had been closed. This meant that on one day the doctors were faced with one bed to offer to three patients in urgent need of hospital care. One was a young mother with severe post-natal depression, who was threatening to kill herself and her baby. The second was a man well known to the unit, who was showing early signs of deterioration. On previous experience they knew that a short admission at this stage (up to two weeks) would arrest the trend and return him to his family. If he was not admitted at this point he would grow increasingly ill until he would have to be admitted, but this time the stay would be several months. Thirdly, an elderly lady who lived alone was in a depressed state and needed treatment to alleviate distressing symptoms. The doctors felt the first case to be most urgent, but were unable to get another unit to accept the second, because he was not an emergency case.

The elderly lady was accepted for a bed some 40 miles away, which she refused because of the distance, but because of the urgency of her case they felt obliged to use the law to compel her to be admitted. The relationship of trust developed between the staff of the in-patient unit and its patients, their relatives and the community was being eroded. The distress which this caused patients and their relatives was considerable. It is a situation which the doctors and nurses found extremely difficult to accept. While the support within the medical team and from other hospitals was helpful, management tended to say to the staff that 'they would have to do their best' and at the same time protest to the public that they were spending more money than ever before on these particular services. Meanwhile, the suffering of the patients and their relatives continued, and the medical staff, although professionally capable of helping them, lacked the resources to carry out the task.

A third example. This is a Christian working in the private sector as a financial director in a manufacturing firm. He articulated very clearly the pressures he felt. He recognised that his own motives, which he describes as 'loving and sharing', were very different from, and at odds with, the majority of his colleagues, whom he saw as essentially self-seeking and self-centred. He felt continual pressure from the firm and as an energetic and conscientious person he was conscious that there were times when the work pulled him away from his family responsibilities.

His commitment to more collaborative ways of managing the firm led him to persuade his colleagues to hold management team meetings (a remarkable development for this old-fashioned organisation). He had succeeded at this level in developing the firm according to his principles rather than an internally combative style. His hope was to extend the principle of team meetings to lower levels of management, although the initial discussions had been discouraging. However, he was prepared to keep working along these lines.

His commitment to keeping the firm profitable and to maintaining jobs for the employees was an important part of his work. During times of recession there were inevitably redundancies, which he found distressing. He felt the context of his work was essentially alien to him. At times he seriously thinks of working in the voluntary sector, where he could expect the work context to be more congenial to his motives. However, as an observer commented, it would be sad if the private sector lost a person of his integrity, skill and commitment.

For him questions arise about areas of professional influence, about patterns of support in this firm and about the constraints laid on him by his personal commitments outside work. Also important is the level of energy he can maintain for fighting what is essentially a lone battle.

The fourth example is again from the Health Service. This person is a professional but not a medical employee, deeply disturbed by the structural changes in the NHS.

For him the proposals for hospital trusts seriously eroded the nature of the National Health Service where sophisticated resources based at the hospital would no longer be available to all in the Region. He had other profound objections to their establishment.

The logical step would appear to be to make some kind of protest. However, this was ruled out for several reasons. Protest would be futile because in certain hospitals, including his own, there were sufficient people of influence arguing for the establishment of a hospital trust. Despite his professional status, he saw his own position as carrying very little influence and therefore any protest he made would have minimal effect. Moreover, protest would be risky. He could lose what little influence he had, which would be detrimental to his department, and he might lose the respect of people with whom he worked. Finally, public criticism of policy was dangerous. It had led to suspensions in other health districts of doctors and nurses resulting in two cases of unexpectedly early retirement. Yet, as a Christian who throughout his adult life had been actively committed to justice, he felt frustrated with a sense that he was not being true to his principles.

This case raises questions again of personal and professional integrity. As a person with family responsibilities he could not risk losing his job. As someone who saw very clearly what the new developments would mean he found himself depressed and deeply regretting the changes he envisaged. The situation was further complicated by the knowledge that improvements were needed but the proposed changes would not bring about those improvements. He asked himself whether he could continue to work in a context which he saw as being deeply flawed in principle but where his own particular role was not significantly altered. Once the changes were made, he would be working in a system which failed to live up to his ideals. Would his participation be seen as condoning the changes?

ISSUES ARISING FROM THE CASE STUDIES

A recent publication reviewing the considerable changes occurring in schools suggests that there are four possible positions a Christian might take in relation to developments like the Education Reform Act or any other major new policy. The positions Hill has identified indicate different levels of active involvement. Where the level of resistance is low, I recognise people may be acting sometimes out of despair or sometimes out of a theology which divides Christian faith from the difficulties of the world.

People may react by *abdicating*, or retreating from a wicked world into a Christian ghetto. There is no attempt to bring any kind of influence to bear in the structure or policies of work.

Rather more engagement with the world is suggested by *conservation* where there is, however, a desire to return to times when all was thought to be well. This reaction acknowledges the values of a previous era even if there is no engagement with the present.

Values are also acknowledged in *acquiescence* because in Hill's terms this indicates a need for change but the responsibility for it is left to others. I believe these are times when professional and personal constraints, either from the family or from the level of one's own energy, makes engagement difficult and I do not wish to criticise those who fail to engage without considering these factors.

His final option is *transformation*, which means to provide 'a visible Christian presence' to make an impact on policy and structures.

I think it is right to add a fifth possibility – *transferral*, where it is time 'to shake off the dust from your feet' and move to another role to use one's energy and commitment.

Transformation is a general term which encompasses a range of alternative strategies. To identify the alternatives open to any group or individual is a painstaking task. As the case studies indicate, the areas for influence may be limited and, in the Health Service in particular, the possibility of a visible presence is subject to restrictions.

Neither transferral nor transformation are easy options and the people who have the courage to face these decisions deserve to be supported by the churches as they struggle with ethical issues involved.

Where people are faced with decisions about transformation or transferral, I have found them working in several levels to help them make their decision. These are summarised below in a set of questions about the right action to take – in a series of interlinking, but not necessarily consistent issues. In each course of action, I find people weighing up answers to the following:

What would be the responsible action for me and for my family?

What would be responsible action for me as an employee (or employer) and for my colleagues?

How will my decision affect my friends and my support group?

How would the decision affect my firm/department/employing organisation?

How would the decision affect the environment?

Will the decision promote or diminish social justice?

These are such profound and far-reaching questions it will be impossible to be sure of all of the answers.

They are questions, however, that I find many people recognise as important, not simply in personal terms but in their long-term effect on the situation in which they work.

SECTION 5: TOWARDS A THEOLOGICAL FRAMEWORK

A PROPHETIC MINISTRY

The theological framework in which I am working assumes that the church exists on behalf of the world and should be concerned for the world in its 'lostness'.

The 'lostness' of the world presses closely on the church as a gathered community through the members who are engaged in conflicts of values. The people who are thus involved are in a pivotal position. They search for ways to promote Christian values in situations of confusion and conflict and so they can offer their church communities insights into their struggles and the struggles of many people beyond the churches. At the same time, it is reasonable for them to expect support and encouragement from the fellowship of the church.

As the work has progressed it has become clear that many of the people I have worked with are engaged in a prophetic ministry. As they work through their experiences of ideals and values being lost, they begin to form an awareness that the values on which their organisations are based need to be challenged.

The establishment of an alternative consciousness is an integral part of the prophetic ministries of Moses, Jeremiah, Isaiah and Jesus.

All four share the determination to declare that alternative understandings are possible. In writing about these men, the American theologian Brueggemann argues very powerfully that the first step is to *imagine* that the world and life can be ordered differently. Moses challenged the oppression of slavery which had created in the Israelites a sense of the inevitability of their condition and declared liberation was possible and was the will of Jahweh. Jeremiah faced the self-serving powers of a monarchy which refused to acknowledge the suffering it caused, and spoke eloquently of the grief of the people who were too numb to grieve. To the Israelites in exile, Isaiah

40–55 takes their overwhelming despair and talks of hope. Jesus of Nazareth challenged the oppression of religious authority, removing the exploitative traders from the Temple courtyards and breaking the Sabbath, particularly to heal people. In his teaching, he turned standards upside down in the Beatitudes and in his ministry he acknowledged the pain of the poor and the marginalised. His resurrection declared a totally unexpected new future for God's people.

Imagining alternatives challenges the accepted norms. This imagination is based on grief and mourning for loss, which challenges the statements of the powerful that 'all is well'. Judgement can lead to hope, and hope to energy. It is this process which I believe illuminates the experiences of the people with whom I am working, and my own. Their suffering is a challenge to the denial by people in authority that pain and suffering exists. A few years ago a government minister denied that there was poverty in Britain – contrary to the findings of reputable research organisations. More recent examples come from the way in which Health Service Managers argue against the experiences of patients and staff. The positive action of acknowledging pain counteracts the numbness and despair of people who believe nothing can be changed.

Thus the pain can be seen as part of building a vision or an alternative consciousness which challenges the existing powers. Keeping alternative values alive may not change the value structures immediately or even in the foreseeable future, but it does keep open the possibility that these structures can be changed. The process of mourning or regretting is integral to the building of visions, and we are committed to finding ways of maintaining that vision.

This is particularly important to the people who feel that they are virtually powerless to affect the situations in which they work. They face a long period when their commitment may develop as a kind of 'unquiet endurance'. Through this kind of spirituality their awareness of the pain and short-comings does not cause the paralysis of despair. It rather confirms a faith in the future but not one which abdicates all responsibility to an interventionist God.

'Unquiet endurance' means mourning the values which are rejected and living in the tension between the ideal of what one hopes for and the limitations of what is possible. One person concluded that it was always possible to find some aspect of work in which to pursue Christian principles as a contribution to building a new consciousness. At the same time, he recognised that there is always a danger of becoming complacent if the focus becomes too short term and the wider vision is lost.

When people share in the formation of alternative visions based on alternative values, they challenge the dismissive authorities which exile or tame God to meet their own purposes. They present a challenge in the formation of their vision. They need help to develop a spirituality to match their situation and skills to meet the demands of their challenge.

THE RESPONSIBILITY OF THE CHURCH

The failure of the church by and large to minister to the people engaged in prophetic ministry is noticeable.

For many of these people the church fails to handle the complexities and lack of clarity they face. The issue of compromise is rarely talked about and examples all too often demonstrate clear cut decisions of right and wrong, rather than the complicated ethical relationships noted in this paper.

Many of my contacts are people who do not expect a great deal of support from the church. They are, however, resilient people who are strong enough to face the issues in isolation. How many more people might be empowered to do the same if the churches were to find ways of supporting them?

It is clear from the work of the last three years that the church has a responsibility to the people engaged in this ministry. They need to be recognised as carrying this responsibility. The church also needs to develop a sensitive understanding of their situations. It is through the church that they may be offered an opportunity to diminish their sense of isolation, and support and encouragement for the difficulties they face.

Perhaps we also need to face the difficulties of working with

New Testament texts which were written in expectation of an imminent second coming. Nearly two thousand years later that basis of theology sits uneasily with a lengthy struggle to make sense of living in the world.

Rachel Jenkins, *Changing Times, Unchanging Values?*
Manchester, William Temple Foundation,
1991, pp. 1–25.

3 Economics, social trends and the churches

Patterns of work

One mark of the separation between internal church concerns and a theological engagement with the economy has been the dearth of material exploring the links between the practices of Christians and their location within, and experience of, economic life. This short paper, presented to a conference convened by members of the Methodist Church in Scotland, is an exception. Alison Peacock was Research Officer for the European Contact Group on Urban Industrial Mission but was here exploring a personal interest in the use of statistical data linking church concerns with wider social trends. A Methodist, and later a member of the URC, Peacock went on to be Mission Planning Officer for the Anglican Diocese of Manchester where she pioneered the use of Geographic Information Systems in the development of church policy.

As the provenance of statistical data is crucial in assessing its validity, we have retained Peacock's extensive referencing and bibliography.

The changing face of work has been hotly debated throughout the 1990s. The nature, extent and consequences of change may be contested but the need to respond to the reality is recognised by, among others, academics, employers and Trade Unions. In September 1995 another interested party, the Council of Churches for Britain and Ireland (CCBI), entered the debate with the launch of an ecumenical enquiry into 'unemployment and the future of work'. It aimed to produce a report which would 'analyse the various emerging trends, and evaluate the policy options from a Christian standpoint' (CCBI 1997: 199). This was eventually published during the General Election campaign of 1997, and – on the whole – met with a respectful reception from policy-makers.

Unemployment and the Future of Work, as the title suggests, is primarily concerned with unemployment, although the topics of increasingly deregulated employment and the pressures upon those 'working still' are also addressed. The third section of the report examines the contribution of the churches: as actors in the policy debate, as holders of resources; as organisations responsible for employment projects and mission to the world of work; and as worshipping congregations committed to engaging with social questions. However, Elaine Graham, in a paper on the ecclesiology of *Unemployment and the Future of Work*, comments that the report presents two models of church – 'advocate' and 'community of expertise' – which, taken together, present 'one particular model of who and what (sociologically and theologically) the church is: drawn from the privileged and powerful, seeking to address those in government and authority who are similar to themselves' (Graham 1998). This, she argues, may be politically realistic, but unintentionally gives the impression that 'church' is somehow separate from the issues addressed in *Unemployment and the Future of Work*. I would also add that this leaves the churches open to complacency: if the report is to be 'of real service to both Church and Society' (CCBI 1997: 199), the churches need to reflect upon the implications of its findings for their own survival.

I do not suggest that employment is the only, or even the most important, factor affecting membership trends. However, changing patterns of employment do have implications for the churches, as they struggle to respond not only to questions of Christian social responsibility, but also to those raised by their own depleted numbers and resources. My aim in this paper, therefore, is to open up the issues. It is divided into two sections: a presentation of three key employment trends, and an identification of emerging challenges for the churches.

A. Key Trends

The three inter-connected trends selected for discussion – rising female employment; part-time working; and changing working hours – are all noted as significant developments in *Unemployment and the Future of Work*. Individually, each is already affecting the churches as well as wider society. Together they point to a profound social change which poses a more serious challenge to their organisation, mission and identity.

1) The increasing economic activity of women

Between 1971 and 1996 the percentage of economically active men over the age of 16 dropped from 80.5% to 71.9%; in Scotland during the same period the percentage of economically active men over the age of 16 dropped even further from 80.5% to 70.9%. By contrast the economic activity rate for women in the United Kingdom has risen from 43.7% in 1971 to 53.5% in 1996; the rate for women over 16 in Scotland has also risen, peaking at 53.5% in 1995, and dropping to slightly below the UK rate in 1996.

Why is female employment an issue for the churches? The most important reason is that existing church-goers tend to be female: women represent 58.0% of church-goers (Peter Brierley quoted in Richter and Francis 1998: 172), and the 1991 British Social Attitudes Survey found that they constitute nearly two-thirds of those who described themselves as 'frequent' attendees (quoted in Bruce 1995: 42–43). The statistical returns for this church in October 1997 tell a similar story: 61.5% of attendances recorded were by women (Peacock 1997). It follows, therefore, that any change in women's employment is likely to impact disproportionately on the churches: not only is there more pressure on the time of the majority, and most committed, of church-goers, but also on that of the social group which is most likely to express an interest in religious activities. Certainly, studies consistently report a higher level of religious belief in women than men (Davie 1994: 118–21).

2) The expansion of part-time working

The increased economic activity of women is closely associated with another key trend in employment: the growth in part-time working in the 1980s and 1990s. . . .

The number of men working part-time more than doubled between 1984 and 1997, although the number of men working full-time, despite fluctuations, has not altered greatly over the same period. The number of women working part-time also rose by nearly 25.0%. However, although the percentage rise is greater for men than for women, the rise in the number of part-time workers is greater for women than for men. Women still represented 85.0% of all part-time workers in spring 1997.

Part-time working, together with self-employment, is commonly considered to be a key indicator of labour market flexibility (Spencer 1996: 76–77). It is argued that flexibility benefits workers as well as employers, enabling the former to combine paid employment with family responsibilities, study and personal development, community activities and voluntary work. However, although the majority of women part-timers consistently report that they do not want a full-time job, the most frequent reason given is pressure of domestic responsibilities (quoted in Methodist Church Division of Social Responsibility 1995: 12). It is therefore unwise to assume that part-time working, although it clearly has the potential to do so, automatically frees time for other activities.

The freedom afforded by part-time working is also called into question by a Trade Union survey, which noted that between 1990 and 1995 the proportion of women working part-time involuntarily rose from just over 5.0% to nearly 10.8% (TUC 1996). It also found an increase in the number of women workers with second jobs: although the number of women working part-time in their main job in 1995 was 20.0%

higher than in spring 1984, the number of women with second jobs rose by 132.0% (TUC 1996). The most likely reason for both these trends is low pay, as an analysis of 91 part-time posts advertised in Stirling Job Centre by a new supermarket shows. They offered an average working week of eleven and a half hours, and the average income, calculated at the higher rate of pay, was £39.05 (Low Pay Network quoted in CCBI 1997: 239–40).

3) The use of weekends, shift and night-working

Part-time workers, according to recent research from the European Commission, are being used to promote unsocial hours working – specifically weekend, shift and night-working – in the United Kingdom (European Commission. DG-V Employment and Social Affairs 1997).

[. . .]

In a snap-shot of the situation in spring 1996: 14.0% of men, and 12.2% of women, describe themselves as 'usually' involved in Sunday working; 28.7% of men, and 22.1% of women, as 'usually' involved in Saturday working; and 15.9% of men, and 12.2% of women, as 'usually' involved in night and other shift-working. In all but one category (males working Saturdays), the percentage of workers in Scotland who are involved in weekend, shift and night-working is higher than the percentage for the United Kingdom. In fact, the proportion of women involved in permanent night and other shift-work is higher in Scotland than in any other part of the United Kingdom. However, again with one exception (night shift work in Scotland), the proportion of men involved in weekend, shift and night-working is still higher than the proportion of women.

[. . .]

Sunday working is, of course, of particular interest to churches, but trends in Saturday and shift-working also deserve their attention: evenings and weekends, after all, are times for house groups, Bible studies, meetings, social activities and community service. Some commentators have argued that Britain is fast becoming a 'twenty-four-hour society', in which shops, sports and leisure facilities, financial and other services, increasingly operate outside '9 to 5' from Monday to Friday (Vidal 1997). The decision of the Halifax to pilot Sunday working in 200 of its 900 branches for three months from this weekend is the most recent example of the trend (Incomes Data Services 1998). Yet, if this is the case, the degree to which the workers who service the 'twenty-four-hour society' may exercise choice is likely to be limited. Certainly, there is already evidence of compulsion: shopworkers are already under pressure to work Sundays (GMLPU 1996), and the case of two lone mothers dismissed from their posts in a Belfast filling station for resisting their pressure to work longer and more flexible hours suggests that flexibility can be double-edged (Labour Research 1998). Managers and professionals who are expected to be instantly available, as the CCBI enquiry observes, may also in practice exercise no choice over their working hours (CCBI 1997: 163).

B. Key Challenges

Before addressing the challenges raised, I want first to consider the degree to which churches are already affected by employment changes I have identified. The recent survey of church leavers by Richter and Francis (1998) indicates that trends in Sunday working are already having an impact: one in seven of the respondents cited 'having to work on Sunday' as a reason for ceasing to attend. This reason was more common among younger people, many of whom relied upon part-time work to see their way through college, and one interviewee considered that this accounted for the 19.0% loss of under-25s from the Methodist Church between 1992 and 1995 (Richter and Francis 1998: 71–72). However, the same reason was also cited by managers and professionals who found that they were coming under increasing pressure to work on Sundays. In addition, some found that mounting responsibilities at work were tending to compete with church participation on weeknights, and at least one interviewee had decided that his role as a parent needed to take priority over his role as a churchgoer in increasingly restricted leisure time (Richter and Francis 1998: 16).

One of the most interesting findings from the survey of church-leavers is that the respondents who ceased to attend for work-related reasons were also among the most likely people to return (Richter and Francis 1998: 136–38). Yet the suggestions offered in conclusion – changing the times and even the venues of services and activities – miss the heart of the problem: namely, that the rise of the flexible society, driven by the increasing use of women and part-time labour, is gradually eroding the concept of common time. To cite a specific example, the very language used to describe weekend, shift and night-working in *Social Trends* suggests that such work is no longer considered unsocial: the neutral terms initially used are soon referred to, complete with inverted commas, as '*unsociable*' (*Social Trends* 1990). Four years later they are referred to as '*so-called "unsocial" hours*' (*Social Trends* 1994). I would also argue that unemployed people, who may place fewer and fewer restrictions on the days and hours they are available for work, are already experiencing these changing expectations of working time.

The erosion of both the concept and experience of common time is, I believe, a trend of profound significance for the churches, since it calls into question a fundamental assumption upon which much contemporary church life in Britain is based. For, without common time, how may the common life be created and nurtured? Or, to return to a key concern of *Unemployment and the Future of Work*, how may the churches re-affirm and express in practical action a sense of inclusive community in an employment context which appears to deny the need for '*shared recreation as part of the basis of society*' (CCBI 1997: 197)? Yet, as the report also argues, '*the future cannot be a return to the past*' (CCBI 1997: 172). Now that change appears to be here to stay, new strategies are required.

First, there is a need to understand how employment trends impact upon congregations: although research is already concerned with the social class of church-goers, perhaps their working arrangements and conditions could be incorporated into the analysis, at least at local level. This may yield some surprises: when I attempted an informal experiment in a church meeting, I found that only 9 of the 18 people present were in paid employment; that only 6 of these were in full-time employment; and that only 3 of these had anything approaching a permanent contract (one member of this group has since been made redundant). More systematic case studies of employment patterns within individual congregations might prove insightful.

Second, as I suggested with reference to *Unemployment and the Future of Work*, greater interaction between social responsibility and membership studies is needed. The study guide to the Methodist report, 'Consumerism and Employment', includes a question on '*the competing claims of our paid employment, our family and friends, the church and the local community*' (Methodist Church Division of Social Responsibility 1994: 32), but this is the only occasion in the study guide (or in the original report) where these issues are explicitly addressed. However, at national level, the information on employment issues found in denominational and ecumenical social responsibility reports could be used more extensively to develop an understanding of the implications for membership trends.

Finally, as understanding of both the working lives of congregations and the wider context develops, the churches nationally and locally need to begin to address the hard questions. How might the churches organise themselves to relate to a flexible, but increasingly fragmented, society? What are the implications for their own identity and self-understanding? There are no easy answers. Yet, if the churches wish to maintain both their own sense of community, and their commitment to addressing the needs of wider society, such questions should be attempted.

Bibliography

Bruce, Steve (1995) *Religion in Modern Britain*, Oxford: Oxford University Press

Council of Churches for Britain and Ireland (1997) *Unemployment and the Future of Work. An Enquiry for the Churches*, London: Council of Churches for Britain and Ireland

Davie, Grace (1994) *Religion in Britain Since 1945. Believing Without Belonging*, Oxford: Blackwell

European Commission. DG-V Employment and Social Affairs (1997) *Women and Employment in the European Union. Gender and Working Time in the 1990s*. Supplement to Issue No. 3 of the quarterly Magazine of the medium-term Community action programme on equal opportunities for women and men, December

Graham, Elaine (1998) 'The ecclesiology of *Unemployment and the Future of Work*' in *Putting Theology to Work*, edited by Malcolm Brown and Peter Sedgwick, London: Council of Churches for Britain and Ireland/The William Temple Foundation

GMLPU (1996) 'It doesn't pay to work Sunday', *The Bottom Line. Magazine from Greater Manchester Low Pay Unit*, Autumn, pp. 3–4

Incomes Data Services (1998) 'Halifax pilots Sunday working in the branch network', *IDS Report*, 756, March, p 6

Labour Research (1998) 'Flexibility causes concern for parents', *Labour Research*, Volume 87, Number 3, March, p. 6

Methodist Church Division of Social Responsibility (1994), *Our Daily Labour. A Methodist Reflection on Employment, Growth, Consumerism and the Environment*, London: The Methodist Church Division of Social Responsibility

Methodist Church Division of Social Responsibility (1995), *Part-time working. The full text of a summary paper debated at the Methodist Conference in June 1995*, London: The Methodist Church Division of Social Responsibility

Peacock, P Gordon (1997) 'Attendance at worship at a Methodist Church: A case study' (unpublished paper)

Richter, Philip and Francis, Leslie J (1998) *Gone But Not Forgotten*, London: Darton, Longman and Todd

Spencer, Peter (1996) 'Reactions to a flexible labour market' in *British Social Attitudes: the 13th report*, edited by Roger Jowell, John Curtice, Alison Park, Lindsay Brook and Katarina Thomson, SCPR/Dartmouth

TUC (1996) *Women on the Edge: Women, Jobs and Insecurity in the 1990s*. Prepared by the TUC's Economic and Social Affairs Department for the 1996 TUC Women's Conference

Vidal, John (1997) 'Welcome to the 24-hour society', *The Guardian*, 24 September

Alison Peacock, 'Employment and The Future of Church', paper presented at 'Soundings: A Day Conference on Church Membership', Stirling, 14 March 1998.

The United Reformed Church (URC) and the quality of work

Worth working for?

This interesting project illustrates a dimension that has always been present but hidden. Local churches and IM teams have often been engaged in small research projects as part of their planning. At the same time these are also one way of getting church members and others involved in and conscientized about the socio-economic dimension of Christian witness. In 2000 the URC sponsored a national survey of jobs available through job centres throughout Britain. This was to be taken up by local congregations and the data collected was processed by David Luckin of the Greater Manchester Low Pay Unit and Gabrielle Cox of the Church and Society Committee of the URC. The report, published in 2002, set out the findings in terms of such matters as types of job, pay, full or part time, regional differences. It did not reveal any surprises but underlined some of the issues facing those who are unemployed and seeking work. But, as an exercise, it had very definite uses. The full report was accompanied by a summary designed for use in study groups and congregations.

Why this survey is important.

Although only about a third of all vacancies are processed through Jobcentres, a survey such as this is important for two reasons:

- it gives information about jobs which are likely to be available to unemployed people in their area, and therefore shows the kind of opportunities which are open to them; and
- it provides a wealth of detail about a part of the labour market which is under represented in the official statistics on earnings, and can throw light on the likely impact of particular government labour market policies. . . .

The aim of the survey.

The report set out to

- help shed light on the frequently limited opportunities available to unemployed people;
- inform debate about policies such as welfare to work, increased 'targeting' of benefits and the use of in-work benefits to top up low income employment; and
- contribute to debates surrounding the effectiveness and appropriate level of the national minimum wage.

[. . .]

What churches can do.

Local churches can play an important part in bringing this data to the attention of policy makers and opinion formers in their own area, as well as supporting the Church and Society Committee as it seeks to make the report known nationally.

Meet to discuss the report and to decide what you can do. Here are some suggestions, and you may have lots of other ideas. . . .

1. . . . issue a press release and try to get local newspapers and radio stations to cover it.
2. . . . send the report to other groups in your area . . .
3. . . . send the report to your MP and invite him/her to a meeting . . .
4. . . . send the report to your local council and ask for comments . . .
5. . . . raise the issue during a local or general election . . .
6. . . . send the report to your local Jobcentre and ask them about the quality of information they take on vacancies . . .
7. . . . discuss the report . . . at District or Synod level . . .
8. . . . find out if there are any organisations which represent or support unemployed people in your area. Is there any way in which you can help them?
9. you could consider other events and ways of raising and focussing awareness on issues . . .
10. . . . write to relevant ministers . . .

A Summary of 'Worth Working For?: Job Opportunities in 21st Century Britain, London, United Reformed Church, 2002. pp. 2–12.

4 The challenge from the activists

Poverty

The ecumenical church pressure group Church Action on Poverty became, during the 1980s and 1990s, one of the most authoritative voices expressing concern for the growth of poverty and marginalization in British society. This short document, here reproduced in its entirety, is noteworthy for its methods of argument, attempting both to establish a consensus of dissatisfaction with the status quo and to demonstrate the authentically Christian theological grounds for seeking to overcome poverty in all its forms.

HEARING THE CRY OF THE POOR

A DECLARATION BY CHURCH ACTION ON POVERTY

This declaration springs from the urgent concern of Christians across all the Churches. We have heard with our own ears the cry of the poor. We have seen with our own eyes our society being driven in a direction that contradicts the Gospel. Wounding effects are witnessed and experienced daily. **They challenge us to seek a new social order** founded upon that vision and possibility of human wholeness which is contained in the Christian message and which speaks to all human experience.

As we survey our society, our inescapable conclusion is that many are being hurt in Britain today, damaged and discounted by public policy. This is the story that emerges from the pastoral experience of teachers, social workers, community workers, doctors, clergy and others in urban and rural areas. Over recent years, social divisions have widened and community life has been gravely eroded. These trends and the suffering they cause diminish everyone. They must cease.

As we enter the 1990s, our lives are being reshaped radically by a changing technology. The economies of whole continents are increasingly interlocked and we grow more conscious of our global reliance on natural resources that are neither infinite nor indestructible. Choices have to be made concerning the way we want to live together and our vision of a future society.

How poor people are treated is a touchstone for the values that inform all our thought, policies and actions. It is central to our Christian faith. It is central to our political challenge.

Church Action on Poverty is asking all concerned about our common humanity to share in bringing to birth a vision for a new social order.

WHAT HAS HAPPENED TO OUR COMMON LIFE?

We acknowledge that many people are enjoying new opportunities and living more comfortably. **However,** it must be asked how far their financial security requires others to be deprived, how far their freedom of choice curtails what is available to others.

It cannot be right:

- That some have to survive on less than £60 per week while others receive pay rises of £3,000 per week.
- That benefit levels are so low that loans are needed for essential items.
- That more people are begging in the street.
- That young people are living in cardboard boxes.
- That over one third of a million are homeless and the number of homeless households has nearly doubled in the last ten years.
- That hospital wards are being closed but waiting lists grow.
- That the mentally ill are discharged from hospital without adequate support.
- That children are sent home from school because they have no teachers.
- That people are demoralised by long term unemployment and short term job schemes.
- That for black people disadvantage is compounded by racism.

It cannot be right:

- To cut taxes as an incentive to the rich but reduce incomes to spur on the poor.
- That economic growth is paid for by those excluded from its benefits.
- That public services are so seriously under-funded and the commitment of their staff so undermined.
- That local government is being weakened and public accountability becoming more remote.
- To pass community assets and essential services into private control.
- To impose restrictions in spheres such as education, broadcasting and trades union organisation that curtail democratic freedoms.

It cannot be right:

- To deny our interdependence.
- To dismiss the possibility of social justice.
- To measure individual value in terms of economic success and use value for money as the yardstick for all spheres of human activity.
- To foster a self-serving individualism centred on getting, owning and consuming.
- That whole communities can be disrupted by decisions taken in distant offices or multi-national boardrooms.
- To learn from experience that market forces favour the rich and dispossess the poor **and yet** do nothing about it.

WE BELIEVE . . .

We believe that God, in whom we live and move and have our being, has chosen to reveal the meaning of our human story.

God so loved this world as to send us his Son Jesus Christ and in him the true story – the Kingdom that he preached – is both revealed and made possible. It was in proclaiming this Kingdom, to which we are all invited and in which the poor have a special place that Jesus was rejected. But through his death and resurrection – the story's climax – the Kingdom is made present and we are invited to celebrate and live this new reality.

We believe that when we pray 'Thy Kingdom come, thy will be done on earth', we commit ourselves to be part of this story-in-the-making and we bind ourselves to work for a social order which mirrors, realises, and incarnates the realities of the Kingdom.

Our human tragedy is to set our hearts on mirages or look-alikes of the real Kingdom. We turn God's gifts into idols which promise life but cannot deliver it. When we enthrone money, power, privilege and pleasure, God's gifts become God-substitutes.

We believe that God's Spirit speaks through the cries of the poor and the vulnerable to expose our illusions and break their power over us; calling us to our proper task of working for the emerging Kingdom, restoring us to the human story's authentic theme.

FROM FAITH TO ACTION

The true end of any social order, therefore, is to embody the Kingdom of God in human affairs. Signs of the Kingdom will be:

- When the basic needs of every child, woman and man are given priority.
- When the experience of the poor can contribute to the transformation of society and therefore to its salvation.
- When full citizenship is not dependent on wealth, race, gender, status or educational privilege.

- When all are open and hopeful and joyful about the future and move towards it sharing the costs and benefits of social and economic change.

Two stories have been told here. One describes what **is**, the other what **might be**. It is because of the contrast between them that we believe a new social order is needed in Britain. Christians have a contribution to make. We seek a social vision:

- Which is rooted in experience and especially in the hopes and struggles of those hurt by our society, who have been ignored and who have no voice.
- Which is grounded in our faith – the Good News that new life is possible – which calls the Churches to be a sign and a foretaste of a new order which invites and enables us all to live in accordance with God's story.
- Which is informed by the practical wisdom of those individuals and groups who try to base their lives on principles of mutual responsibility, respect and justice.
- Which can generate feasible policies for the renewal of our wider society.

Church Action on Poverty invites individuals and groups

- To endorse this statement.
- To use it in worship, in reflection, in preparation for action.
- To work with people of other faiths – and none – to bring about a new social order.

Employment

Employment Forum (UK) – Chris Beales

In recent years a new model of Christian engagement with the economic social reality has become prominent. The illustrative example given here is Employment Forum (UK). This is a self-supporting organization, independent of the churches, yet working very much from a Christian base and in collaboration with the churches at national, regional and local levels. Chris Beales, a former IM chaplain and an active and effective Secretary to the Anglican Board for Social Responsibility, is the dynamic behind this particular initiative. It was set up deliberately to take forward the concerns of *Unemployment and the Future of Work* in practical ways. The excerpt sets out its aims.

Employment Forum (UK), together with similar enterprises such as Community Action Network (CAN), which was set up by Andrew Mawson and Adele Blakeborough, and other local initiatives, represent an entrepreneurial approach to social development, reflecting the model of collaborative initiatives between Government, business and the voluntary sector favoured by New Labour. For Beales and others this is a logical development from *Faith in the City*, IM, work with the unemployed, and with community development, though perhaps with an echo of community organizing. Further, it responds to the interest in involving 'faith communities' in social regeneration. The favoured way of working is through creating networks between interested parties in a project, including other 'faith communities' to provide a 'critical mass' of energy and resources to support local initiatives, drawing on funding from statutory and other sources, until they can maintain their own momentum.

So far Employment Forum (UK) has acted as consultant in a number of regional initiatives, notably in the North East, the North West, the Midlands and London. These have largely been concerned with inner-city regeneration. This has included collaboration with Muslim, Black-led churches and other groups in relation to financial, small businesses and other entrepreneurial activities. Employment Forum (UK) is now known as Employment Focus.

> Employment Forum (UK) is a small, innovative agency that has developed unusual new networks and employment initiatives, particularly across the range of faith communities in the UK. . . . Our approach is to bring together people from the public,

private and voluntary sectors, to enable creative networks to develop, to 'mobilise' people and give them a distinctive voice. And especially to involve people of faith – Christian, Hindu, Jewish, Muslim, Sikh and others.

[. . .]

Our broader aim has been to breathe fresh life into the engagement with politics and economics of Churches and faith communities. We link employment with social exclusion, poverty and regeneration, with debt and finance, and with regional government and hopes for greater democracy. We have worked to build bridges between people of different faiths and have shown the practical possibilities of working together with shared values and solidarity.

A DISTINCTIVE APPROACH

We believe that Employment Forum has the track record, the practical experience of fund raising and project development and expertise to engage the churches in a dialogue not just about social engagement – or about employment and industrial mission – but about future ways of 'being and doing Church'. We help churches and faith communities to act as 'brokers'; after all, they have extensive networks and contacts and can play a pivotal role in bringing together disparate people to explore ideas and make things happen. We are keen to work alongside local people and we bring considerable experience of organising events and fund-raising with them.

We actively seek the involvement of those who often do not get invited to events on employment, training, regeneration and enterprise – like unemployed people or young people – and bring them together with policy makers and others. Our style is to encourage extensive participation from the floor of our events. Everyone's view matters.

GOOD NEWS

This distinctive approach has an underlying theological understanding of Good News based on the following key values and insights. Our work is incarnational and action-based – it makes things happen! It involves people directly in concerns relating to their daily experiences, and their economic and social circumstances. It does so from a distinctive (but not exclusive) Christian perspective.

It reinforces, supports and builds on what is already happening, and deliberately sets out to spread models of good practice. It takes power seriously, seeking to help people to take greater responsibility for control over their own personal and collective destinies. It recognises the constraints under which people have to live and work.

It takes the Church seriously; . . . [and] has deliberately set out to build strong relationships with people of other faith and from diverse ethnic groups. . . .

We are committed to action – not just talking shops – but believe that talking through our visions can affect and create change.

Chris Beales, draft of 'Chapter 1: Introducing Employment Forum (UK)', for a book on Employment Forum (UK), 2002.

5 In the name of the churches

By the 1990s, the flow of denominational church reports on social and economic issues had slowed to a trickle. Many reasons for this might be proposed: the growing nervousness within the churches about their declining numbers, resources and roles; the apparent triumph of the market model and collapse of serious alternatives; the signs of political apathy, or at least the loss of confidence in the mainstream processes of democracy. The resignation of Margaret Thatcher and the unexpected General Election victory of her successor John Major in 1992 began to create conditions in which an alternative to Conservative governments could once again be conceived and, as the next election loomed, the churches began to consider where and how their voices might once again be heard.

Two major church interventions on economic themes appeared in the run-up to the 1997 General Election. The first, from the Roman Catholic Bishops' Conference of England and Wales, entitled *The Common Good and the Catholic Church's Social Teaching*, was a succinct but authoritative expression of Catholic social teaching on social issues. Only 35 pages long, the report was accompanied by a study guide for use in parishes and small groups and was clearly designed as an affirmation of a theological tradition, which implicitly but firmly, stood in opposition to the naked individualism and social divisions of the Tory years.

The Common Good

Introduction and Guide to the Document

[. . .]

Anyone who studies [this] document will quickly see that these ideas are not solely Catholic property. Their aim is to bring about a good and fair society, for the benefit of everyone. Most people feel that society ought to be organised in such a way as to improve the lot of all its members. They will find much to agree with in this document. Anyone who doesn't feel that way, won't.

This is what social teaching calls the idea of 'the common good'. . . .

These are issues about which people feel strongly. If they misunderstand what is intended, they might resent an intervention by the Catholic bishops or any other religious body. People do not want to be told how to vote. That is not what this document does.

[. . .]

As at the end of the 19th century, Catholic Social Teaching is concerned to protect the poor and vulnerable from the chill winds of economic forces. The defeat of Communism should not mean the triumph of unbridled capitalism.

[. . .]

The social dimension of faith

[. . .]
19. It is a distortion of human nature, therefore, to suppose that individuals can exist independently of society, as if it had no demand on them. Members of society are individually subject to moral principles in their own lives, and these implicit and explicit moral demands are not of their own invention. The same is true of societies. They too have demands and those demands are not arbitrary. There are ways of structuring society which are inimical to human progress and personal development. The Church calls them 'structures of sin'.

Morality in the Market Place

76. The Catholic doctrine of the common good is incompatible with unlimited free-market, or laissez-faire, capitalism, which insists that the distribution of wealth must occur entirely according to the dictates of market forces. This theory presupposes that the common good will take care of itself, being identified with the summation of vast numbers of individual consumer decisions in a fully competitive, and entirely free, market economy. Its central dogma (as expressed by Adam Smith, the founding father of capitalist theory, in his *The Wealth of Nations* 1776) is the belief that in an entirely free economy, each citizen, through seeking his own gain, would be 'led by an invisible hand to promote an end which is not part of his intention', namely the prosperity of society. This does sometimes happen; but to say that it invariably must happen, as if by a God-given natural law, is a view which can amount to idolatry or a form of economic superstition. Smith himself did not appear to think the rule was inevitable, for he also observed 'By pursuing his own interest he *frequently* promotes that of society. . .' *(italics added)*.

77. The Catholic Church, in its social teaching, explicitly

rejects belief in the automatic beneficence of market forces. It insists that the end result of market forces must be scrutinised and if necessary corrected in the name of natural law, social justice, human rights, and the common good. . . .

78. The Church recognises that market forces, when properly regulated in the name of the common good, can be an efficient mechanism for matching resources to needs in a developed society. No other system has so far shown itself superior in encouraging wealth creation and hence in advancing the prosperity of the community, and enabling poverty and hardship to be more generously relieved. . . . In a market economy the existence of a wide variety of consumer choice means that individual decisions can be made according to individual wants and needs, thus respecting certain aspects of human freedom and following the principle of subsidiarity. Moreover the good functioning of the market requires ethical behaviour and the embodiment of certain ethical principles within a regulatory and ethical framework. This reflects the corresponding principle of solidarity.

79. The distinction has always to be kept in mind between a technical economic method and a total ideology or world view. Catholic Social teaching has constantly been aware of this tendency of free market economic theory to claim more for itself than is warranted. . . . Christian teaching that the service of others is of greater value than the service of self is sure to seem at odds with the ethos of a capitalist economy.

80. . . . Those who advocate unlimited free-market capitalism and at the same time lament the decline in public and private morality, to which the encouragement of selfishness is a prime contributing factor, must ask themselves whether the messages they are sending are in fact mutually contradictory. People tend to need more encouragement to be unselfish than to be selfish, so it is not difficult to imagine which of the two messages will

have most influence. A wealthy society, if it is a greedy society, is not a good society.

The Common Good and the Catholic Church's Social Teaching, Catholic Bishops' Conference of England and Wales, 1996, pp. 2–19.

Unemployment and the future of work

The second major church report that sought to enter the social and economic debate in the run-up to the 1997 General Election was not from any one church or denomination but from the ecumenical body, the Council of Churches for Britain and Ireland (formerly the British Council of Churches, but reconstituted as CCBI in 1990 with Roman Catholic participation and currently named Churches Together in Britain and Ireland). The genesis of this report is interesting in the light of the changing dynamics of Christian social intervention noted in the previous chapter.

Of all the cities of Britain, Liverpool had perhaps been hardest hit by the massive, and seemingly inexorable, rise in unemployment since the 1970s. The Anglican Bishop of Liverpool, David Sheppard, and his Roman Catholic counterpart, Derek Warlock, had formed a unique ecumenical partnership whose commitment and leadership had earned the intense respect of the people of Liverpool and beyond. For Sheppard in particular, combating unemployment became something of a crusade and, looking back to *Faith in the City*, he envisaged a church report on a similar scale and with a commensurate potential to change the political climate in church and society alike.

Although he was at the time Chair of the Board for Social Responsibility, Sheppard realized that there were limitations to a single-denomination project that had not pertained ten years before. Robert Runcie had retired from Canterbury and his successor George Carey, an evangelical like Sheppard, nevertheless did not share the Bishop of Liverpool's confidence in the Church's political role. Resources were tight, the BSR was being squeezed financially and, after almost twenty years of high unemployment, Anglican opinion was perhaps not ready to be galvanized by this seemingly intractable issue. So, for pragmatic reasons as well as his own convictions, Sheppard convened an ecumenical group to produce the report on unemployment, with an economist, Andrew Britton, as its Executive Secretary.

Britton had just left the National Institute of Economic and Social Research, a think-tank not especially in tune with Tory policies, where he had been Director. His economic credentials were of the best but although he had served for many years on the Church of England's BSR, he was not especially well grounded in the tradition of theological enquiry that the Board had epitomized, nor alert to the growing ranks of critics of that method in the academy. Perhaps also, the ecumenical nature of the project, bringing together a number of traditions of Christian social action and engagement, did not have the resources to explore an appropriate theological method as well as to undertake a formidable programme of fact-finding and analysis.

The result is a document of impressive gravitas on the economic and social case for tackling high unemployment, but which relegates overtly theological material to a series of short papers appended to the main report without any attempt at integration with it. It was feared by some at the time that this refusal to make the theological case for economic and political intervention by the churches would weaken the report's impact. Indeed, fear of the political impact of issuing such a report in the immediate run-up to a General Election caused George Carey to attempt to delay or suppress it – fortunately in vain. His anxieties were misplaced. The report entered the public arena at a moment when it was becoming clear that the Conservative government was on its way out and Tony Blair's New Labour landslide was widely anticipated. The report won the dubious accolade of being welcomed warmly by Conservative ministers such as Peter Lilley and Labour leaders alike. Only the *Daily Telegraph* warned darkly of a church in thrall to Marxism. In general, the ecumenical nature of the report was not understood by the media for whom the image of Anglican bishops at loggerheads with governments was too familiar to abandon. The commitment of New Labour to reducing unemployment by means not wholly at odds with the recommendations of the report, and its subsequent limited but far from negligible success in so doing, was both the report's vindication and its consignment to history.

The report ended with an enumeration of a range of practical church responses to unemployment and a call to better coordination and greater effectiveness in this work. The extract below has been chosen from this section of the report for its value in showing something of how much, largely unpublicized and unpublished, work was sponsored by British churches in order to engage with the pressing problems of unemployment through the 1980s and 1990s.

> The churches themselves are deeply involved in the world of work and with the social issues which have been the concern of our enquiry. We will concentrate in this chapter on employment projects and industrial mission in Britain, but many other Christian activities and organisations take part in mission to the world of work. We should also mention the Catholic Young Christian Workers, the Social Responsibility Boards, the Justice and Peace Committees, the William Temple Foundation, the Industry Churches' Forum, the Von Hugel Institute, the Jubilee Centre, the Hinksey Centre, St George's at Windsor, St William's at York and too many more to list them all. There is a great deal of excellent work going on, indicating a high level of interest and commitment.
>
> We are also conscious that these efforts need some coordination to make them fully effective. Someone remarked to us that the churches' activities to help the unemployed were impressive but patchy, In some places churches seem to be falling over one another to obtain support for employment projects; in others no-one is doing very much at all, so far as we could tell.
>
> [. . .]
>
> The activities which we have seen, or heard about, cover

a wide range. They include counselling and pastoral care of the unemployed, training and careers guidance, community development and organisation, care for the homeless and ex-offenders. Often it is difficult to draw the line between help with employment problems and help with related problems of education, morale or discrimination. Christian organisations are concerned with the whole person, not just with their potential contribution to the workforce.

We have been able to observe industrial mission, in which several members of the working party are involved, in action at local level. This also encompasses a wide variety of activities . . .

Employment Projects

The **Peckham Evangelical Churches' Action Network** (PECAN) in South London is a good example of a Christian-based employment project. It began in the late 1980s with the observation that shortages of skilled and reliable staff persisted in an area with up to 30 per cent unemployment. The answer was to go from door to door personally inviting unemployed people to attend an employment preparation course. PECAN now trains over 1000 local residents each year . . .

Also in London we visited **New Life Electrics**, one of several projects run by Quaker Social Action. . . . It provides training and work for unemployed people and at the same time reconditions cookers and other electrical equipment for families in need.

We obtained a more comprehensive picture from the London Churches' **Employment Development Unit,** an ecumenical body, funded by the London Borough Grants Committee, which provides advice to churches on how to set up and manage church projects for unemployed people. . . .

Special mention should be made of the **Christians' Unemployment Group** in South Yorkshire (CHUG) which in 1995 was in contact with over 20 community projects in that area related to unemployment, poverty and community development. . . .

As an example of Christian involvement in vocational training we visited Training for Employment Ltd, in Exeter, a subsidiary company of **Christian Care Training**. . . . It grew out of an initiative by local church leaders in the 1980s . . .

To illustrate the link between pastoral work and employment advice we could quote the example of the **St Ignatius Housing and Advice Centre** in South Tottenham. The project was set up about twelve years ago, and grew out of the help given by a Catholic parish church to people who were homeless and asking for food or money. It became clear that there was also a need for advice in seeking work and a volunteer was found with experience of working for the Employment Service. . . .

Right at the beginning of our enquiry we were told that one of the organisations we must certainly visit is **Respond!** on Teesside. . . . It was established in 1984 as the response of the major church denominations in the region to the crisis of unemployment. It was asked to discover 'new patterns of living and working'. . . . It has organised workshops, national conferences and meetings between church leaders and successive Secretaries of State for Employment.

[. . .]

Our main concern is that the world of work should be taken right into the heart of Christian life, which is the main Sunday service that most church members attend. This is when we all pray together, every week in most churches, for peace and justice in the world, for those who are sick in body or mind and for the coming of God's Kingdom here on earth. We should also pray, every week as a matter of course, for God's help in our daily work, for economic justice and prosperity, and for the poor, the overburdened and the rejected.

Unemployment and the Future of Work: An Enquiry for the Churches, London, Council of Churches for Britain and Ireland, 1997, pp. 180–194.

The Methodist Church

Employment and consumerism

This publication from the Division of Social Responsibility, 1994, invited Methodists and others to reflect on what was happening to the economy and the labour market at a time of considerable social change. There are two, interlinked, themes: the advantages and snares of affluence and the problem of unemployment and a widening poverty gap.

4. Work and consumerism.

We inhabit a society in which it is increasingly difficult to live modestly. . . . Ours is a culture of consumption. We are experiencing marked changes in contemporary culture; a decline in the capacity to take things seriously, to pay attention, to listen to difficult argument, to face up to hard choices. This decline is associated with a totally commercial society, in which advertising and the values of entertainment are all pervasive.

What we have here are quite new features of the affluent society. In general, over many decades each generation has found itself more prosperous than the previous one. But this generation is experiencing more hardship than the last. The problems began with mass unemployment. Young people lack the prospects, and the hope, that sustained their parents. Whole sections of society suffer from idleness and low pay that afflict the less skilled. Middle-aged middle managers find their careers at an end. The elderly find survival more costly and themselves more isolated.

Yet all this misery is wrapped in a synthetic tissue of false well being. The affluent society is marked not only by a growth in prosperity, but also by the construction of a huge variety of institutions which help us to belong together. But the very same affluence has created an entertainment-based culture which threatens to undermine our ability to belong together and to shape a common future. We are in danger, as one commentator has put it, of *'amusing ourselves to death'*.

We need also to consider the extent to which we now consume not only goods and services but one another. We expect more of life and more of one another than reality can sustain. . . . [T]he corruption of the intimate sphere by the commercial does seem to be a feature of our age.

[. . .]

. . . Either way, the features of a consumer society are unlikely to disappear, except in the wake of some terrible catastrophe. Creating a higher level of employment in a growing, environmentally conscious society is one thing; managing our fantasies of consumption is quite another.

[. . .]

5. An Employment Policy for Britain.

It is rare for a modern economy to contain no unemployment at all. For a labour market to operate, there has to be a pool of available employees prepared to work at the wages offered. Unemployment tends to act as a downward pressure on wages and therefore inflation, since the threat of being laid-off is often enough to persuade people in work to accept modest pay rises. Thus, to an extent, a certain level of unemployment is acceptable, so long as no single individual is unemployed for very long. . . .

The unemployment that has caused most concern in recent years is the huge growth in the number of people who have been unemployed for over a year, the long-term unemployed. . . . The long-term unemployed stop affecting the labour market and the level of wages altogether. They simply become a cost to the state and hence the taxpayer.

[. . .]

Although levels of unemployment have tended to stay above two million over the last thirteen years, the total number of jobs has actually increased. Many of the jobs created, however, are part-time and taken by women whose partners are already working. This had led to increasing divisions between households which are 'work rich' and those that are 'work poor' and usually dependent on benefits. Another feature of today's labour market is the increase in temporary employment and short-term contracts. From an employer's point of view these can be useful in reducing costs and avoiding expensive redundancy payouts should the need arise. Unskilled men, however, are left on the dole with no prospect of long-term full-time employment.

[. . .]

Britain has been said to have an employment culture similar to the 'hire and fire' practices of the United States. Compared with the rest of Europe it is easy to get a job, and easy to loose it too. In contrast, continental European culture tends to emphasise a degree of consensus between employers and their workforces in which experience and loyalty are valued. Both approaches have good and bad points. There is evidence that shows that the US has been much better at creating jobs than Europe, but that many of them are low paid and poor quality. European workers tend to be better paid and have greater security, but often at the expense of the unemployed.

Ideally we need to take the best of both systems. There has to be flexibility and low costs that encourage firms to take on new employees, rather than manage with existing workers. But we also need the political commitment to a system in which employees are valued for their skills and experience. Short-term success is often measured solely in terms of dividends which can squeeze out the longer-term benefits of building co-operative and creative working teams.

New jobs are being created, but unless they are in industries that are 'sustainable' the country will not benefit in the long term. . . . [T]here is a good deal of scope for more investment in new 'green' technologies. Service industries, particularly in health and personal care, also have the capacity to employ large numbers of people. In order to succeed, though, they need to be providing a service which is to some extent 'essential' if they are not to fold at the first sign of a recession. A healthy job-creating business culture makes provision for long term investment capital. It also consists of people who are equipped and able to take the jobs available, even if these are part-time.

Our Daily Labour: A Methodist Reflection on Employment, Growth, Consumerism and the Environment, Methodist Division of Social Responsibility, 1994, pp. 20–5.

A vision for the city

In line with Methodism's long interest in the city and its people, a major report was published in 1997 on the future of the city. This necessarily included some reference to the economic viability of the city and the effects of globalization. In this passage, having set out the pessimistic prognosis for Britain's cities' continuing decline in the face of global economic movements and the optimistic view that sees Britain's cities regenerating through economic change, there is an evaluation of what the future could be.

> Whichever version of the future comes to pass, the optimistic or the pessimistic, or something in-between, the reality is that some British cities are clearly better placed to take advantage of current economic trends than others.
>
> London is in a quite different position economically to all other British cities because it is the only British global city; in the first rank of European cities . . . and also probably one of the three major world cities in economic terms. . . . Furthermore, London is particularly fortunate among British cities because it is a major hub in world airline networks, a feature which is increasingly important in the global economy.
>
> It has already been suggested that Salford [linked in to Greater Manchester] and Glasgow are successfully regenerating themselves, each by maximising their competitive advantages. . . .
>
> However, by no means all British cities are so fortunate in having this potential for growth, in terms of the current

European prescription for economic prosperity. Not all, for example, have . . . a stimulating 'learning environment' of interest to new businesses or a well preserved, historic city centre, to attract tourists. If cities become increasingly competitive, there will be losers as well as winners. . . .

A further difficulty is the obvious lack of balance in terms of economic growth and prosperity within cities. If cities do succeed in attracting new investment and employment, how can they ensure that all the people living there are able to benefit equally?

[. . .]

As has been observed, the process of city regeneration itself unfortunately tends to produce stark contrasts between adjacent districts. . . . [The central business district] is the centre of political power and economic growth. Nearby may be the homes of the 'new elite'. . . . In some cities these areas are bordered by ghetto districts of acute deprivation. In these places however, and indeed scattered across the city, are pockets of economic vitality. These are often produced by immigrants from Asia and elsewhere. . . . Small businesses have an important role to play in enriching the commercial life of cities, and often provide a valuable service to local communities. . . .

Further away from the city centre, suburban sprawl is concentrating business services and other office and retail functions into 'Edge Cities', economic sub-centres which are often larger and busier than more central areas. . . . One of the attractions of these shopping environments is that they are highly sanitised. Shopping malls are private property, with their own conditions of entry.

[. . .]

Projections make it clear that some people are much better placed to benefit from current labour market trends, than others. Over the next two decades, employers will place a higher premium on flexibility, solid educational attainment, computer literacy and good communication and social skills, even than they do today, and this can only enhance the competitiveness of already advantaged groups in the labour market. People who are less well endowed with these attributes are likely to lose ground, rather than gain it, and they are especially likely to be concentrated in the most disadvantaged areas of our cities.

The Cities: A Methodist Report,
Methodist Church and NCH Action for
Children, 1997, pp. 94–7, 101.

6 Industrial Mission reinvents itself

Entering the service sector

During the 1980s, the general trend away from manufacturing as the mainstay of Britain's wealth, and towards the service sector, led a number of Industrial Mission teams to establish chaplaincies in large department stores where substantial workforces (predominantly female) were at the forefront of the consumer revolution. In many ways, the origins of employment in retailing lay in the model of domestic service rather than that of factories, and one consequence was that chaplains were often welcomed as a branch of the staff welfare provision. Nonetheless, many chaplains developed strong analyses of the power relationships at work in retailing and saw their role as one of raising concerns about values, policies and fairness. One such chaplain was Wendy Brooker who was part of the London Industrial Chaplaincy team working in stores in London's Oxford Street. The article below, by Catherine Treasure, originally appeared in *Marxism Today* (at a time when that journal was extending its scope well beyond the tightly drawn bounds of Communist Party orthodoxy). There, it attracted little attention. But when the piece was reprinted in a free magazine for shoppers it came to the notice of the management of the store where Wendy visited. Her chaplaincy was summarily terminated.

CHRISTIAN SHOPPING

Beyond the toy counter over the drooping heads of jaded present-seekers or through the branches of slowly turning electric plastic Christmas trees, you may glimpse a red-haired figure sporting a dog collar, black pullover and Black Watch kilt. It is a Tuesday and this is the Reverend Wendy Brooker, Anglican Deacon.

She took up her post last January, as one of Oxford Street's two industrial chaplains. 'Previous chaplains had kept a low profile and worn plain clothes, but that's not my way. When I first began, one of the assistants exclaimed, "You're one of those women priests!" and I thought, "I should be so lucky!"'

As a deacon, Wendy has reached the end of the line for women in the Church of England, able to do all that a priest may do, barred only from pronouncing priestly absolution and the blessing of sacraments. It is six years since she first protested at the offensive male exclusivity of the Church; faced with this, like many other women in her position, she realised she must develop her own kind of ministry, parallel but different. As a woman, she'd done a lot of shopping in her time, so she began as a store chaplain in her local shopping centre in Harrow, north-west London, which led to her placement on Oxford Street.

She also helps with Sunday services in a Harrow church, but feels this is a comparatively small ministry, divorced from the wider world. 'My ministry is to those for whom organised religion is largely irrelevant. I'm trying to build bridges between the Church and the workplace by being a spiritual presence where most people see God as being shut up in churches.'

Though much of her work in the store is pastoral, she hopes it is also much more than that: 'It is involvement of the theology of God in the workplace, which automatically brings in issues such as seven-day trading, racism, the effects of out-of-town shopping centres, the morality of credit.' Present by permission of the store, she is paid by the Church, and her status, independent of the management, makes her a better confidante: staff would rather discuss their problems with someone outside the organisation, with whom confidentiality is assured.

She roams the store, encouraging people of all faiths and

of none not to give in to a system which relies on employees' goodwill and low wages, to take the time off to which they are entitled, reminding them that overtime is not compulsory. 'I also spend a lot of time affirming that employees are doing their best in a difficult situation, when they feel management takes them for granted and that profit is more important than their well-being.'

She is a listening ear. 'In a shop this size, assistants can become numbers.' The youngest come straight from school and have concerns ranging from loneliness on leaving home to how to work alongside gay colleagues. 'Language is very important because Church jargon alienates. I'm not evangelising; we might not even mention God.'

The store chaplain can be a bridge between the management and the shop floor, monitoring the climate of feeling on matters such as pay and equal opportunities. Wendy sees the women there as a 'living expression of the female in God'. When management bewail the decline in the workforce, she asks when they are going to provide crèches for working women. 'These stores would fall apart without married women. What sort of career structure are they providing for them?' It's true that the top management is currently always male, but since it's assumed that women *will* soon have equal opportunities, she finds the store more comfortable than the Church. And she finds many of the women and men about her are pleased to see her in a traditionally male role: 'They're rooting for me, regardless of theology.'

The rest of her week is spent on the other part of her work, as an industrial chaplain developing an understanding of tourism, especially in London, and trying to pass on grassroots opinion when the opportunity arises. Sadly, she finds the Church at large shows little interest in her work; most people see spiritual and secular matters as entirely separate. She and the ten other chaplains in the London Industrial Chaplaincy regularly hold seminars on topics from shopping-hours to the effects of the Channel Tunnel development. She is part of a nationwide network of chaplains in the retail trade and hopes to develop a chaplaincy in tourism, which will soon be Britain's largest industry.

Though not formally involved in the store's Employment Training Scheme, she takes an interest in its trainees. In the carpet department she stops to talk to one of them and enquires as to the progress of his current project. He in turn unrolls the latest delivery, an Afghan rug featuring up-to-the-minute motifs from local life: machine guns, tanks and helicopters.

Wendy admits there is a certain moral dilemma in being a store chaplain, comparable to that of a military chaplain: how does the Christian message of simplicity find a place in a store full of such opulence? Even those retailing expensive clothes need pastoral care. So too do the customers, but they are not her primary concern here. They periodically ask her for directions for the loo, and she doesn't mind, but it does make her wonder: 'I mean, how many shop assistants do you see wearing a dog collar?'

Catherine Treasure, 'Christian Shopping', *Marxism Today*, December 1989, p. 43.

The persistence of the pastoral model

As traditional manufacturing industry waned as a 'central determining reality' within the British economy, new arenas began to be perceived as places where an effective engagement between church and working lives might take place. Among these were the rapidly growing international airports – source of employment to thousands and part of the common experience of an increasingly mobile population. Here, ministers could combine a presence among a disparate and sizeable workforce with a pastoral role among passengers centred upon the provision of worship and prayer facilities. In this way, airport chaplaincy took on a distinctive character of its own, which is well captured in this piece by the Manchester Airport chaplain, Mike Vincer. He outlines something of the history of the chaplaincy at the airport and the way in which the work is now funded by the companies operating on the site – arguably the most important shift in the relationship between industrial missioner and the workplaces they visit since the Industrial Mission movement established itself on a principle of independence from industry in the 1940s. Vincer makes the case for seeing this shift in positive terms and it is certain that, without the funding from the industry, the pioneering work of his predecessor would not have been continued as the resources, and the approach to mission, within the churches moved away from the older IM model during the 1990s.

Pie in the Sky . . . or Faith on the Ground?

Chaplaincy at Manchester Airport

1 The Chaplaincy – its role and establishment

'To raise awareness of dignity for all people in their work' is one of the objectives of The Chaplaincy, Manchester Airport. It is both grand aspiration as well as awesome challenge, a task that is at times as daunting as it is wondrous! Daunting because of the 'size and complexity' of the place: wondrous because of the acceptance and welcome The Chaplaincy receives. Of course, we have other objectives: to encourage understanding and mutual responsibility in the workplace, and to explore the relationship between life and faith . . . and faith and life.

There has been a Chaplaincy here since 1980, a period during which the Airport, in both staff and passenger numbers, has grown virtually 5-fold. We are a team of three: two Chaplains, Major Ian Field SA and myself, and a Pastoral Co-ordinator, Jenny Wright. We seek to achieve our objectives through visibility, availability, and engagement, and I guess a Spirit-motivated determination (or should that be doggedness!). Like all aspects of a pilgrimage there are occasions for joy as well as moments when the view is bleaker.

Optimism and hope are often difficult to sustain with purpose when the conditions that many colleagues face lack the elements of life that affirm their role and value. Of course this is not unique to the Airport, nevertheless it makes us aware of a general malaise about working life – its purpose, direction and fulfilment – not only here but across the country, if not beyond. Curiously, for such an influence on life's potential *Shalom*, this is something which appears to be notably absent from the Church's agenda and public proclamation.

A comprehensive review of Chaplaincy activity conducted some time ago highlighted the distinction between service to passengers (entirely *re-active* in its operation), and work amongst staff (with a potential for pro-active development). The review also pointed the way towards a sustainable Chaplaincy in a complex and rapidly developing industry.

Support, care and counselling for all who work here (around 18,500) are the basis of our activity. This develops our involvement with companies in terms of training and support for staff in the fulfilment of their duties. Such association naturally leads to a comprehensive commitment to passengers (currently some 19 million annually).

We have adopted the Airport's philosophy of Service Partnership, a principle encouraging all companies, and their employees, to see their role as being of mutual benefit to both the Airport and its customers, as well as each other. In that respect airports are unusual places: they have a specific and singular identity that transcends that of the individual company, despite the fact that many of those companies have their own well-established identities in the commercial world.

It was the principle of service partnership that encouraged the evolution of The Chaplaincy from a 'one-man-band' with doubtful management, accountability and engagement, to a company limited by guarantee and a registered charity. The overriding objective was a conviction that a Chaplaincy serving an 'institution' should take both risk and opportunity to be managed more by the place it sought to serve, than by the Church in which it has its origin. We had to 'stake a claim' here whereby our standard of service and professional operation was up to that expected of all companies.

Ideally, this should work itself out creatively as a partnership between the Church and the workplace. It should also be a means of two-way communication. Perversely however, it is our experience that while the 'workplace' has little difficulty in accepting our role, for the Church it is more 'problematic'. Many Church members, and ministers, do not readily perceive the relevance of workplace involvement, or make the connection between faith, and the ordinary and peculiar, or mundane and shocking, aspects of daily life.

We have plans to address specific opportunities of comprehensive and ecumenical representation, counselling development, and relationships with other faiths and the wider community. However, resources are limited and efforts to attract denominational personnel and extra funding have so far failed. However, we are adequately supported for the staff we have, but there is no room for development.

The Chaplaincy in its present form has been entirely enabled by the groundwork undertaken by the first Chaplain, the Revd Arthur Grimshaw who, during his twelve year ministry, was wholly funded by the Baptist Church. Funding could not be sustained at that level, and there were other pressing priorities. However the concept of an engaged workplace Chaplaincy had been established, and to such an extent that a number of companies were prepared to provide sustainable funding. Since 1992 Manchester Airport plc has been a key player in the Chaplaincy's developing service. Indeed, if it hadn't been for the Airport's willingness to provide financial support for this Chaplaincy, then it would have ceased its work in the early 90s. Today, other companies have shared in this process, and local denominations make valuable contribution.

Two overriding principles of our operation direct our activity and spirituality:

- that the mission of the Church is to be with people *where they are* and primarily *on their terms*
- that work, in ideal terms, presents us with the opportunity to use our talents (the developed skills and abilities we have) in the service of others.

The first point requires us to be mindful of the fact that our speciality has roots in the theological, pastoral, liturgical and prophetic activity of the Church. It does not require us to become experts in civil aviation. It does require us to understand what people do, the abilities they put into practice, the nature of their work, their commitment and dedication, and the pressures they are under. It should prompt us to ask of people 'What does your work do to you?' It should inspire us to question policy, practice and procedure particularly where there appears to be conflict between the principles of justice, dignity, integrity, honesty, and morality as manifested in the workplace and at odds with the principles of faith and responsibility to God and Neighbour.

The second point is extremely idealistic and no doubt more than a little sensitive when one considers the large number of mundane jobs and repetitive tasks that people undertake, and on which the Airport relies. (Arguments equally true of the functioning of society as a whole.) However, it should allow for the *celebration* of work as a creative activity for the benefit of community, society and, potentially, all people.

In actual fact I believe the above to be true of any ministry, wherever it is undertaken. To be engaged with people where they are is the essence of Jesus' ministry, and we should not become distracted by fleeting attractions and diversions we will inevitably encounter. Operating in a City renowned for its proliferation of football teams, an appropriate analogy would be that of keeping one's eye on the ball. Strategic thinking, and an engaged Chaplaincy management, together with other insights and wisdom gained from the workplace, will encourage regular appraisal to make sure both that the ball is still there and that we are on the pitch. In this context we are managed by a Board of seventeen people: thirteen being senior managers from a variety of representative companies, three nominated by the Church leaders of Greater Manchester, and one by the Council of Greater Manchester Industrial Mission.

[. . .]

It is in this tension that The Chaplaincy stands and it is here that we seek to reflect the requirements and aspirations of faith and responsibility. To respond to the commands to Love God and Love Neighbour is a perpetually challenging task wherever a ministry is exercised.

More Generalities and some Specifics

The Chaplaincy does this in a variety of ways, each activity often presenting us with further opportunities. It is, I think, unfortunate that our presence raises more queries in the minds of 'Church' people than it seems to of 'others'. The question '*What do you do?*' is asked of us, just as it is, I imagine, of other Industrial Chaplains. I suspect however, it is rarely if ever asked of the parish or congregational minister. People make assumptions about what *they* do and cannot seem to perceive that the nature of a ministry in a community, be it rural, urban or workplace, is essentially the same as any ministry, whether ordained or not.

To be involved with people on their terms and where they are, while at the same time being confident about what you are taking with you in faith, trust, hope and calling, is what any minister should seek to do. I have yet to decide whether the poser of such a question is either too unimaginative to see the challenge and relevance of faith in a setting other than a settled community, or lacks the perceptions and insights that are the diet of any ministry. Or maybe I'm having a bad day.

Trying to encourage a sense of dignity in the workplace, and greater value for the skills and abilities of all workers is something of which we continue to raise awareness. For over ten years The Chaplaincy has produced a weekly Newsletter addressing workplace issues that frequently comes back to the themes of attitude, value, relationship and responsibility. This sits nicely with the idea of *Mutuality, Transparency and Accountability*, a theme in the early 90s of a Year Book of The United Society for the Propagation of the Gospel. It's a theme as relevant to the workplace as it is for relationships between Churches around the world.

Mike Vincer, 'Pie in the Sky . . . or Faith on the Ground?', *Faith in Business Quarterly*, 6: 4, Winter 2002–03.

Struggling with church structures across Europe

The international dimension to church engagements with economic affairs remained strong through the last decades of the twentieth century. However, in other parts of Europe as well as Britain, changes to the industrial context and an increasing sense that the churches' commitment to socially engaged mission was waning in favour of a revived emphasis on personal pietism, led to a desire to restate the foundational principles and continuing rationale for industrial missions. A joint consultation, convened by Dr Bernt Fechner of the German Industrial Mission movement, KDA (Kirchlicher Dienst in der Arbeitswelt), at the Hamburg Missionsakademie in 1995 was one attempt to reinvigorate an engagement with economic affairs as part of a European approach to church life and economic trends. The consultation brought together a group of practitioners from the UK and Germany who represented some of the most innovative areas of work concerned with economic matters. It was, however, surprising that there was little analysis here of why the churches' interests were turning in other directions, and almost no consideration of how such a grouping might make its voice heard. Even at this late stage, it seemed as if the practitioners remained locked into a world where agreeing a statement between those concerned was, in itself, an act of political import. Although the Hamburg Declaration was circulated among IM and KDA practitioners and their associates, it was never treated as the basis for any sustained lobbying of church, or secular structures. It remains, however, an interesting example of how the churches' activists in economic affairs, in two European countries, saw themselves and their work in the late 1990s.

THE HAMBURG DECLARATION

INDUSTRIAL MISSION AT THE CROSSROAD

[. . .]

The conviction remains that the nature of economic life, which determines so much of our social existence and the nature of so many of our relationships with our brothers and sisters locally, nationally and globally, is too important to be overlooked by the churches. Yet the theology and methodology of the churches' engagement with the economic is problematical and new pressures on the churches are essential. Consulting together has shown us some of the ways we must change. Britain and Germany are not the same, yet the similarities in our situations are profound. Western Europe is not the world – yet our analysis of our situation makes sense only in a global context. We have moved beyond moaning and know at least that the arguments about faith and the economy are fluid, that there remains a need for groups and alliances within the churches to grapple with economic complexities in the light of faith, and that – in an age that is 'post modern' and unclear about the identity of his own spirit, the need for spiritual discernment in the structures and institutions of our society will not go away.

The work we are called to is more important than the organisations historically set up to do it. But can the work continue without either these organisations or new, dedicated bodies with a clear mandate to engage with economic life? In all reshaping and restructuring of IM-work and its relation both to the churches and secular agencies it should be important to keep in mind: This mission of the church is not necessarily synonymous with God's mission.

II Signs of crisis in the economy – common challenges for IM/KDA

Both Germany and UK have experienced rapid economic and social change in recent years. In Germany, reunification has heightened the gap between rich and poor, those with jobs and prospects, and those whose skills are unwanted or who live in the 'wrong' place. In UK, the massive exodus of manufacturing jobs in the early 80s has been followed by cutbacks in banking, insurance and the whole service sector. In both countries, even the middle classes feel insecure as companies 'downsize' their management structures and shift production to cheap labour areas in the Far East and elsewhere, a process of globalisation which has run out of control. A three-tier society is developing with highly paid core workers, more marginal employees in insecure, lower-paid jobs and a growing underclass without access to regular employment. Work is no longer a unifying social experience and the former consensus in society has long since been replaced by conflicting interest groups and a sense of fragmentation.

III Signs of crises in the churches – reformulating the theological identity of IM/KDA

In the face of such enormous upheavals in society, the institutional churches in Germany and the UK are in danger of turning inwards. Financial crises and a renewed but exclusive focus on the local and parochial dimension of the church have led to increasing pressure to disengage from a strategic involvement with industry and economy – and to withdraw support from industrial mission-type activities. But the churches are not simply the institutional and power structures. Many church members and unaligned Christians are struggling to make sense of the changing social and economic context. In local and national groupings as diverse as community work, the peace movement, the ecological movement, research institutes and economic literacy movements they are developing their own spiritualities, liturgies and life-styles which contribute to the formulation of a new economic ethic. Their relationship with the institutional churches will vary widely but among such groups IM and KDA have already found many partners and allies.

This withdrawal takes place at a time when the resources of KDA in Germany are being stretched by the requirement to respond to increasing social need resulting from high unemployment and other structural stresses of economic change. In the UK IM is not required to be a service provider in quite this way, but British IM has a strong track record in projects for supporting the economically disadvantaged and the need for such work, supported by knowledge, understanding and analysis, has not diminished although resources for IM are contracting. Thus the reformulation of the theological and missionary identity of IM/KDA needs to take place both within the broadened framework of relations to new social movements and partners of IM's work and within a growing awareness of the ecumenical dimension of the worldwide church and its need for mutual correction and enrichment.

IV Visions of hope – objectives for the future task of urban industrial mission

Despite the crises in the world of economics and in the traditions of social engagement by the churches, Christians, in IM, KDA and elsewhere are regaining their confidence in tackling questions of economic morality – those who have always maintained a commitment to the task of presenting faith and society to one another are finding a renewed articulacy.

The signs of a new coherence are to be found in new alliances between people and groups – Christian and other – who, from different starting points, agree that economic change can be affected by human choices, political movements and value-based action. Much of this action takes place in local, negotiated, alliances, but is strengthened and given 'critical mass' through networking in European and international agencies for the churches' social concern. For us and our partners and allies, pointers are emerging towards new work ethics with moral foundations in elements of the Christian traditions.

New ethical understandings do not emerge out of nothing but are discovered in the processes of engagement with the powers and principalities of the world – whether in lobbying, campaigning or building coalitions for limited, but concrete, social change.

In the process, the economic concerns of IM and KDA are making common course with, for example, the ecological and two-thirds-world movements, and signs are emerging of a more holistic approach to issue-based social and economic engagements.

Most of all, the relationship between the concerns of KDA and IM, and the missionary strategy of the churches including their other agencies for mission, is being redefined. IM/KDA claims its place as mainstream and orthodox within the churches and as a vital and irreplaceable part of the missionary history of the churches in the ecumene.

Engagement with changing economic realities must be matched by a responsiveness to the changes faced by the structures of the churches. A mutual journey with sisters and brothers of faith is as essential as our journey into partnerships and alliances in the economic world. Industrial missioners in both countries who learned to be wary of liturgical and spiritual traditions founded in 'church theology' are becoming more and more exposed to the liberating potential of other traditions of spiritual life, personal devotion, and corporate worship, discovering a wealth of insight from the two-thirds-world, the feminist movement, the Celtic tradition, etc. We are learning that our practice and political action may be strengthened by an understanding of the effectiveness of symbolism and symbolic acts of resistance . . . .

V Some Practical Suggestions

The consultation was felt to fulfil a vital need for mutual exchange and enrichment on both sides and therefore should be seen as a strategic step in a continued process of mutual co-operation between German KDA and British IM in the future. Particularly the following recommendations should be considered:

- **That regional partnerships between IM workers and networks in Britain and KDA offices in the various regional churches in Germany should be strengthened,** [to] increase the chances of mutual learning and practical exchange. Regular exchange of publication material between KDA and IM could enhance this.
- **That specific co-operative initiatives should be taken** with regard to the formation of transnational labour unions in enterprises which are working in both countries and should act together on the issue of codes of practice for TNCS operating from the UK or Germany in the two-thirds-world.
- **That the issue of cheap UK labour in construction work in Germany could form an entry point for further discussion and workshops** between IM and KDA in which the conflicting interests are brought to a common forum. Another example for further exchange may be around experiences and models of inter-faith dialogue and co-operation in the areas of unemployment, marginalization and social exclusion because this is increasingly important in urban priority areas both in Germany and in Britain.
- **That existing channels of European co-operation should be strengthened** and more used from both sides, namely the European Contact Group, the Work and Economy Network and relations to EECCS (European Ecumenical Committee on Church and Society).
- **That a joint initiative should be started to work out a common 'mission declaration'** of UIM-networks in Europe, reformulating both the theological understanding of the missionary and diaconical dimension in IM as rooted in a specific notion of Missio Dei and its new task in a rapidly changing context of European social policies and economical decline ('Kairos-document for IM in Europe').
- **That more ecumenical exchange of personnel should be developed** for limited periods of exposure involving practitioners of IM in local regions (short term exposure

programmes for German KDA workers on British IM fields and vice versa).

- **That the URM office in the WCC should be asked to enable a working process towards a common 'mission declaration of IM in Europe'** (Kairos-Papier) in the way towards the world missions conference in Brazil at the end of 1996 through its adviser for the European region.

Industrial Mission – losing its way?

One of the longest-serving, and also the most widely read, practitioners in British Industrial Mission was Mostyn Davies whose work in Peterborough spanned almost thirty-five years from 1969. Davies constantly attempted to bring contemporary thinking – whether in theology, the theory of knowledge, management theory or other fields – to bear on a social and theological analysis of the changing economic scene and the churches' missiological response. Here, Davies argues for the need to react to the socio-economic changes and the pressures on IM not merely by structural adjustment but more profoundly on the basis of values and commitment. Reflecting on the important thesis on IM by Lillemor Erlander, Davies appeals for a recovery of mythology and quest, for courage and vision. The challenge is to dare to exist as witness to the importance of the unity of culture and commerce, of the private and the public, of the spiritual and the material, when these are so often regarded as opposites and antagonists.

The Deeper Crisis

So far, the argument has been largely historical, rational and organisational. It will seem a sudden and unpredictable jump to plunge into the world of spirituality and mythology. Because it is easy to handle and argue about, organisation and method can claim excessive attention but mission is ultimately about the human soul and its individual and corporate relationship with God. It would be convenient to define the crisis of IM in terms of organisation because then it could be easily solved but the problems run much deeper. As Erlander points out, there is a mystical dimension to IM: it is not just a particular school of business ethics. If IM is to be true to itself it has also to be true to the realities pointed at by myth and scripture and these are the product of different and more primitive ways of knowing than are accessible to pure reason and scientific investigation. When Erlander speaks of IM's *secular spirituality* she describes its spiritual understanding of the world; she does not mean to imply reductionism or the stripping away of the mystical; on the contrary, it is the *official Church's* current grasp of the spiritual tradition which she regards as heretical and lacking.

> The secular spirituality to which IM is committed means refusing to upgrade the spiritual, which has to do with God as the important part, only to degrade the secular as material without interest to him. This process downgrades work, democracy, political activity and trade union solidarity; the very activities in which IM has discovered many modern men and women finding that which is holy.
>
> Erlander, *Faith in the World of Work (paraphrased)*

Her thesis pleads for IM not to let go of its most precious gift and the reason for its existence, its spiritual insight into the redemptive work of God in the world. She points to an all too worldly motivation in the official church; it has a vested interest in attacking those who affirm the activity of God outside its formal structures and controls. This is the deeper crisis which IM faces; all the church's instincts are to suck IM resources back into itself and to silence the challenge of its spirituality. It has very nearly succeeded. Like Christian Socialism before it, IM is being heavily institutionalised in the name of giving it place and voice. If IM is to have any future as a prophetic ministry, if it is to go on having something distinctive to offer the church, it has to recover and renew its distinctive spirituality. This means resisting the process by which it is being bureaucratised and manipulated into a safe, uncritical, undisturbing servant of the Establishment. Erlander is right; IM is in terrible danger of losing its soul by colluding with those who want to secularise it by turning missioners into executives, and replace the turbulence of spiritual animation and heroism with the neat orderliness of management by objectives, performance appraisals and five-year employment contracts.

The Redeemer-Hero

The late Joseph Campbell analysed what James Joyce called the *monomyth* of the hero. This is a cross-cultural framework which can be seen underlying mythical stories with a thousand different origins. Campbell was writing in 1949, before inclusive language became politically correct, but he means the word *man* to be taken inclusively. Mythologically, male and female stand as knower to that which is yet to be known; the universe, especially the unknown universe and the mystery of the future, is feminine; the act of penetrating these mysteries and venturing into new worlds, is masculine. A woman can act as or with a hero, either in the manly, physical sense, or in the more womanly ways of secret knowing; so, Medea lacks physical strength but knows how the Golden Fleece can be taken; Jason has the strength and courage but not the knowledge. The heroic act requires the union of Jason and Medea before it can be accomplished. Later, when the couple separate, all collapses. The relationship between masculine and feminine is treated with extreme subtlety in mythology and we are meant to draw distinctions and explore relationships which inclusive language exists to destroy. The bare bones of the monomyth are these . . .

> A hero ventures forth from the world of the common day into a region of supernatural wonder: fabulous forces are there encountered and a decisive victory is won: the hero comes back from this mysterious adventure with the power to bestow boons on his fellow man.
>
> *The Hero with a Thousand Faces* (1949)

At one level, this conjures up Michael Jackson's attack on Wickham's heroic view of IM; a protestation at the hero figure striding into the world of Hercules and Vulcan to encounter strange wonders and supernatural forces, to fight great mystical battles and return to the mundane reality of the church with the power to bestow boons. It smacks of all the Gnosticism, Pelagianism and *folie de grandeur* which Jackson couldn't take in IM, as he saw it. Of course, put this way, to see the industrial chaplain as a redemptive hero or heroine would be gross pretension and Wickham would never have entertained such an idea. Much better, much safer, to see the chaplain as Chaplin; the anti-hero, the fool; though the irony is that this turns out to be the same story. In practice, this is the role which industrial chaplains have actually taken because it is the only one they can sustain. Maybe Jackson rightly identified a shadow side to Sheffield IM in the sixties; every missioner has feet of clay and all missionary activity has its downside. This is the human condition. But, at another level, central to Wickham's IM theology was his recognition that the redeemer-hero is there at the heart of the industrial and commercial process. His IM fools, like children in the market place, were trying to make people dance to the redeemer-hero's tune and cry to his lament. Jackson tried to create an altogether more ecclesiastical and structured link between the redeemer and his people by trying to relate the local congregation with the world of work. The historical fact is that this latter approach has never really worked. IM has been upheld by its heroic Fools.

In the sixties, both Wickham and Jackson were still able to work with Christendom assumptions about the role of the established and mainstream churches in ways that are no longer possible in today's multi-racial, plural society. To be truthful, they were even then out of their time. Secularism was already too far advanced. Later IM practitioners had to learn to hold within themselves the mythic language of religious belief and their commitment to the redeemer-hero. Outwardly, they spoke in secular language and argued a Christian humanitarianism. This was a very conscious and deliberate process often misunderstood as loss of faith or what a former Archdeacon of Northampton referred to as *going native*. In fact, very few industrial chaplains have abandoned their ministry or lost their faith; the reverse is true. But IM did have to try and create its own *applied* theology to bridge between the *pure* theology of the tradition and the secular culture of the industrial world. Chaplains had to be able to forge a link between what they were doing and saying in industry and the doing and saying of the redeemer-hero of the Gospels. But great difficulties arose in trying to do this. Generally speaking, the Church could not follow the steps IM made between the tradition and its application in secular terms. This was mainly because the church in general wasn't making the effort itself. Church people heard and understood the secular language spoken by IM as disconnected from the tradition and thought it too radical and left-wing; their redeemer-hero was a conservative creature of the status quo. On the other hand, although secular people could understand what IM was saying, they couldn't relate it back to the old religious language and liturgy and felt little need to try too hard anyway. The redeemer-heroes they recognised were politicians, executives, trade-union leaders and the new wave of management gurus. This split between the religious and secular, which IM has had to embrace and hold within itself, has been a critical problem both for it and for the whole Church.

[. . .]

At the neck of the Bosphorus floated two stone islands, the wind-driven Clashing Rocks, *The Symplegades*, which crushed any ship daring to try and pass between them and enter the Euxine Sea of Marvels. They picture *hard and unremitting competition for material supremacy and resources* to perfection, not just as crushing threat but as the very barrier standing between us and the better world we wish to enter. Jason was at first defeated by these terrifying obstacles but Phineus told him to fly a dove between them; he did so and the bird's wing beats held the rocks apart so the Argo and her crew could sail through unscathed. This is the mythic root of much salvation theology. In psychological terms, when the ego faces and flies free of its dread, what was terrifying becomes impotent. This is the spiritual struggle demanded of the redeemer-hero; he has to make the shamanic journey and fly his soul through fearful situations to show that the way through dread lies open. Only a Fool has the strange combination of redemptive courage and humility to resist overwhelming physical power with the wing-beat of a dove. In Christian theology this is depicted in the journey Christ makes from God into man, through the crushing gate of death and back to God again.

But how can IM make visible in commercial life the forms of heaven when a terrible gulf has been opened up in the culture so that heaven and earth, the Sea of Marvels and the world of competitive materialism and war, are utterly separated? This is the deeper crisis. If IM tries to recover anything of its priestly, shamanic witness in the world of economic-political organisation it looks incomprehensible, out of place and time, and unacceptable in a plural society. Establishment and the vestiges of our Christian past may still permit of chaplains dispensing pastoral care and giving ethical tone to the workplace. A skilful chaplain with something intelligent to say about moral and relationship issues can earn the right to a hearing. But a safe, pastoral, mainstream chaplain is one thing; an Industrial Imam, or shaman, who *would* keep bringing religion into things and require commercial submission to divine law, is quite another. IM is acceptable in industry only when it has safely shed its religious role and adopted a secular, professional role as counsellor and ethicist. As Campbell says, society no longer supports the world to which the gods belonged.

[. . .]

The foolishness of IM is that it still believes in the possibility of the whole social order being transmuted so that the Christ within it is made known to consciousness; indeed, IM believes it is the work of the god-man who is made immanent and effective in all of us to make it so. This is what the Kingdom theology of the sixties and seventies was all about. Why IM then had such trouble with the Church was because it confronted what Campbell calls 'monkey-holiness', by which he means parody. We repeat the rituals in church but they no longer have the power to make the forms of heaven live again for us in society so that our culture is transformed and reconnected with the source of its fertility, creation and redemption.

It is not the language or the signs of the traditional church which are at fault. The deeper problem is that the capacity of most people to understand the nature of the truths liturgy expresses has been culturally repressed. The receivers do not work on that wavelength any more; such signals, however transmitted, are as jammed as if any reference to the mystical had been electronically censored; culturally speaking, this is exactly what has happened. Both Wickham and Jackson were, in their differing ways, trying to rebuild this fallen bridge. Later IM came to realise this may not be possible; certainly it is not a problem which can be addressed through the token gestures and 'monkey-holiness' of Unemployment Sundays or Industrial Services at Rogationtide. We cannot consciously design and deliver a new set of symbols which will relate heaven and earth any more than we can design tonight's dream.

Through The Crisis

All ministry is crisis ministry these days. It doesn't take a genius to see that there is a titanic battle going on out there as a physical projection of the titanic battle going on within us. There is the technical projection, weaving magical networks of communication to screen our edited highlights of world events; but there is also the projection of our avarice and plundering as we fell our forests, destroy species and poison the land, sea and air; the violent projections of atavistic tribal conflicts in racism and civil war; and the hysterical projection of our need to be saved which drives fundamentalism and nationalism into irrational excess. There are Symplegades enough to be going on with in our generation and they all threaten to paralyse us with despair.

This, at last, pinpoints the contemporary location of IM and begins to collect and shape the framework of symbols which are evolving to allow all of us to begin sharing common dreams and nightmares again. It couldn't happen without the forming of a world information system to act as its medium; nor without the scientific, economic and political analysis which tells us what is happening; nor without the world sporting, trading, educational and tourist exchanges which bring us into cross-cultural contact; nor without war and migration. We are being heaped up against the Symplegades, pressed together, competing both to pass through and to escape. Campbell's term is no exaggeration; there is a titanic evolutionary battle going on and the air is full of the passionate, urgent calling of the redeemer-hero who is struggling at the heart of it all and who *must* be followed as he makes passage through the most dread-inducing situations.

At its best, IM has always understood this. Historically, it located itself at the focal points of the industrial revolution where sparks flew and anvils rang. But, if IM was romantic, it was saved from sentimentality by the practical realities to which it was exposed; moreover, its romanticism was saved from becoming vacuous by the rich resonances it found with the theological truths preserved by myth. Above all, what has made IM strong has been its *being out there*, as viewed by the church, but *here with us* as viewed by the world it dares to penetrate. IM has tried to relate to the world as *knower* to she who is to *be known*; a very sexual, personal encounter which seems to me to be a thousand miles away from holy huddles trying to build bridges between the ecclesiastical and the secular in order to save the church. It is this same intuitive feeling which, I am sure, makes committed lay-people shy away from attempts to create some kind of ecclesiastical structure for IM. It does not seem to be one of the things which the redeemer-hero is yelling for! In contrast, networks build up naturally wherever IM is working, whether a lay person or a chaplain is the catalyst. This is the reason why there is ground for scepticism about whether Peterborough's *People and Work Programme* will burgeon. It will if it can capture the necessary romance and energy which gives people the sense of travelling to the Sea of Marvels via the Clashing Rocks of Dread. People know intuitively that this is the mark of the real thing.

It is the romantic impulse, so shunned by rationalism, which senses and responds to the truths which mythology expresses; it is inconceivable to think of following the redeemer-hero and being part of a salvation drama in anything but romantic, mythological language. It is so much more than dispassionate analysis and logical restructuring; it is about boarding the Argo and facing every kind of physical, moral and spiritual danger. In short, it is heroic. If it is not, how can it have anything to do with responding to the redeemer-hero who wrestles at the heart of everything? So, IM is primarily to be located and defined in this existential way. What put IM into steel mills and shipyards was a romantic instinct to be where hard, unremitting interests clashed and ground in the forging of industrial society. To be there, was to experience the full force of the commercial elements at work and to make the breathtakingly Foolish attempt to Christianise them. Whatever intellectualising IM did about itself it is this heroic foolishness which has always marked its real strength and integrity. What worries me is that this foolishness may be lost because without it IM is dead.

Mostyn Davies, *IM: The Anatomy of a Crisis*, Manchester, William Temple Foundation, 1992, pp. 39–47.

Industrial Mission – seeking a new focus

In another of Mostyn Davies's papers (this time, unpublished, but written for the IMA's Theology Development Group and circulated widely among IM teams) he explores the future of Industrial Mission in terms of its history, developing a typology of 'four generations' of mission. The concept of 'fourth-generation IM' gave some impetus to the work of established IM teams who were seeking to respond to the loss of major manufacturing plants and the new fragmentation of the labour force in the local economy.

The four generations of Industrial Mission – seen as overlapping in time and often coexisting within the work of IM teams – were seen as follows:

- First generation – the Navvy Missions, the Missions to Seamen, and so on. This was the oldest-established work of the churches among people defined by their work; often based on the rationale of taking the church to those whose work precluded regular attendance, but sometimes developing a strong concern for issues within particular industries and communities.
- Second generation – Wickham's Sheffield experiment and the IM ventures that consciously followed this model. This was conceived as a movement reforming the churches through engagement with industry and working life, and tending (especially in later years) to see workplace visiting as its distinctive activity.
- Third generation – the move away from workplace visiting towards projects with unemployed people, job-creation ventures and community-based action.
- Fourth generation – focusing on the local economy.

It was this fourth generation that Mostyn Davies was keen to explore. The idea that IM should locate its work in the realities of the local economic network and the ethical issues it presents would now be accepted by most chaplains. In places like Sheffield, Liverpool and Greater Manchester, collapsing traditional industries long ago forced IM to start relating to what was happening in the local economy as well as inside the particular factory, dock or steelworks. However, although our analysis of IM into four co-existing generations would be quite familiar within IM, we think few IM teams have as yet clearly articulated a strategy, organisation and methods for fourth generation IM. At present, the tendency is for IM to work intuitively and, in changing times, to follow where opportunity leads. The variety of IM models described in the Appraisal shows this very well.

Nevertheless, a pattern is emerging and we set ourselves the task of trying to define it, beginning with these random points:

> The erosion of so many key IM bases has a liberating effect to it. IM now has a window of opportunity in which it is free to rethink its work and reset its priorities for ministry and mission.
>
> IM's experience of third generation IM (MSC projects) has led it to see the value of making more broadly based alliances in the local economic community and in the church.
>
> Many chaplains now have up to ten years' executive experience in MSC projects and have greatly extended their management and planning skills. As such chaplains replan their ministry, they will be looking for purposeful, well-applied and well-structured approaches to fourth-generation IM.
>
> Principle and practice from earlier models of IM can often be carried forward into fourth generation IM by re-applying them to the local economic community rather than particular factories and projects.
>
> If fourth generation IM is to be effective, it will need to work with others in making detailed action plans and establishing secular and church partnerships for their delivery.
>
> IM's primary work is to apply Christian moral theology to the ethical and spiritual questions posed by the way the economy runs. The World Council of Churches' work on 'Justice, Peace and Integrity of Creation' conveniently summarises this theology.
>
> The local economy is far more complex than even a very large company. Trying to work within the local economic network is like trying to find one's way about a maze. The problem is to make the work trace out a 'purposeful track'.

By a 'purposeful tracking' we mean carefully designing a path of action leading through the local economic network so the person following it can achieve definite results. For example, if IM wanted to examine particular ethical questions arising in the local financial sector, it could decide on a list of financial interests, identifying people to meet, send them letters setting out precisely what IM wanted to know and discuss, and then make purposeful visits. Chaplains could share this visiting with lay, clerical or trainee colleagues. The output from such visits should give IM new contacts, a clearer understanding of the ethical issue being studied, and indicate options for responding to it. Sample financial topics might relate to inward investment, small business development, consumer credit, mortgaging and home ownership, or the consequences of entering the European Single Market.

This idea of 'purposeful tracking' shows up the key differences between fourth generation IM and its predecessors. The visiting field is now the economic area, not the individual factory; and a variety of ethical issues may be treated, not a single issue as in the case of unemployment projects. This doesn't exclude factory visiting or single-issue project work, but priorities and resources for these have now to be set by IM's strategy for the whole area. Of course, once IM looks on the whole local economy as its field, it must become highly selective about what it actually does. This 'selection process' becomes the most important but also the most difficult corporate task for IM management groups. The whole viability of fourth generation IM depends upon its management team being capable of analysing the local economic situation, discerning the key ethical questions posed for Christian conscience, planning and resourcing practical action in response to those questions, reviewing the effectiveness of that response and then repeating the process over a period of several years. IM has very limited resources, so effective work would have to be collaborative both with Christian and secular interests sharing its values and concerned to see its practical objects fulfilled.

Expanding these points and putting them into a logical pattern gave us the following framework for fourth generation IM.

AN OUTLINE MODEL FOR LOCAL ECONOMY BASED IM

OBJECTIVE:	To provide well-informed, committed, Christian ethical inputs to the local economic community.
FIELD:	The local economic community and its industrial, commercial, agricultural, local and national government organisations.
ETHICAL BASIS:	The biblical ideals of justice and peace which are expressed in the term 'Shalom'; the values of the Kingdom as we have them expressed in the New Testament; the theologies of creation, liberation, redemption and consummation as they have been developed in the ecumenical Christian tradition.
METHOD:	→ ANALYSE → PRIORITISE → ACT → REVIEW → A fourth stage process undertaken in alliance with lay, clerical and secular colleagues.

Mostyn Davies et al., 'Towards a Strategy for the Fourth Generation of IM', from *Local Economy Based Industrial Mission*, a paper produced by the Theology Development Group (TDG) of the Industrial Mission Association, 1991.

7 Reconnecting with theology, ecclesiology and spirituality

Rebuilding a public theology

Consideration by the churches of economic issues has frequently, but perhaps erroneously, been compartmentalized as if the economy existed independently of wider cultural and political considerations. Andrew Shanks is a theologian who has maintained an interest in engagements with economic matters, while focusing the majority of his theological work on wider questions of civil society. Strongly influenced by the revolution in the Czech Republic in the 1980s, Shanks envisages the churches contributing in new alliances to a reconfigured civil society in which Christians are full participants concerned to discover their identity in an engagement with others and not through a closed, world-rejecting piety. In his book *Civil Society: Civil Religion* (Blackwell, 1995), Shanks develops these themes at length and calls, among other things, for the churches to sponsor more industrial missioners, not as pastoral outreach workers but as raisers of critical questions. Here, in a shorter piece written for the Christians in Public Life programme based at Westhill College, Birmingham, Shanks usefully condenses his argument. The relevance of his work to a Christian engagement with the economy is that it re-casts the workings of the economy in a wider social and cultural context, working with an analysis of the flaw lines of contemporary public life in ways that are suggestive of new connections to the Christian theological traditions. As such, Shanks's work offers a pointer to new directions in the churches' consideration of economic affairs. Andrew Shanks is now Canon Theologian of Manchester Cathedral; successor in that post to John Atherton and Ronald Preston.

Lessons from corporate trauma

1. Christianity is part of the family of religious traditions stemming back, in terms of its earliest written records, to the great eighth century BCE Hebrew poet-prophets. But have we Christians ever, in fact, fully appropriated the latent truth-potential of that primary inheritance? There is some reason to doubt it.

2. The genius of those prophets may be said to have consisted in their poetic ability directly to convert the **shaking** power of great corporate trauma into a religious **saving** power. Their

most urgently abiding insight lies in their vivid mistrust of ordinary routine thoughtlessness. Against the sheer deadly inertia of which, they mobilised everything they could: conjuring up the most disturbing memories of historic disaster from the past, or the most terrible presentiments of historic disaster to come. Theology that was true to this heritage would in essence surely be a sustained meditation on the great catastrophes in recent history, to the same end.

3. For us, at the turn of the millennium, arguably the most important such memories are those of twentieth century **totalitarianism**. For here we have what Václav Havel has called a 'distorting mirror', in which liberal modernity may contemplate some of its own very deepest tendencies, for cautionary purposes grotesquely accentuated. Totalitarianism, after all, is simply the conformist logic of industrialised bureaucracy and mass-media propaganda carried to its ultimate extreme. But the culture of liberal modernity is also deeply permeated by that same logic. And so it is only right and proper for us beneficiaries of liberalism to remember the enthusiastic crowds and anaesthetised collaborators of those nightmare regimes with a vivid sense of 'there but for the grace of God go we'.

The new purpose of prayer

4. Indeed, this sense of danger has become what perhaps most fundamentally defines the present generation's specific need for salvation, in religious terms. There is today a whole new rationale and necessity for prayer – it has been developing over the past two centuries or so. Namely: to serve as a medium of therapy, for both individuals and whole communities, from the encroaching corruption of a human spirit by the proto-totalitarian impulses of modern bureaucracy and propaganda.

5. A theology properly focused on the newness of this new state of affairs would however be one with an equivalently new

set of socio-political loyalties. And the traditional exclusivism of Christian theology's loyalty-ties to the institutional church, as such, has now become a major obstacle to what is required. If we give the general name '**civil society**' to everything unbureaucratic and non-propagandistic that totalitarianism by definition seeks to repress, then is not Christ – the crucified dissident free spirit – pre-eminently made present, in our world, by the activities of the most free-spirited, (anti-)politically critical and active elements within civil society? In which case, though, the church is only truly 'the body of Christ' in so far as it too serves to articulate that more than merely ecclesiastical ideal.

6. Therefore, we need a form of theology whose chief avowed purpose would be the systematic liberation of the gospel from its traditional entanglement with mere church-ideology; by which the church continually sets itself apart from the rest of civil society.

Another centre of gravity

7. The problem to be tackled goes right back to what might be termed the primal paradox of Christian history. Thus, on the one hand, there could be no more vivid symbolic affirmation of dissident individual free-spiritedness, in general, than the Christian confession of faith in a solitary crucified saviour. And no doubt only a community like the early church, fired up by its own ongoing experience of suffering under a persecutory regime, could ever have invested such a revolutionary insight with sufficient emotional conviction to disseminate it at all effectively. But, on the other hand, the survival of a persecuted community largely depends upon its unity, and hence on strict group-discipline. **As regards its internal life** it just cannot afford to leave any real space for such dissent. So that, in many ways, the dictates of church-survival ran clean contrary to the original freedom of the gospel.

8. Christianity is a religious tradition grievously abused in its childhood, which to this day has still not altogether recovered. The institutional church began as a set of strategies for surviving persecution. It derives its most fundamental instincts from that formative context – many of them retained long after their original justification has disappeared. Unity demanded a clear canon, creeds, a clerical hierarchy to police them, the expulsion of heretics, glorification of martyrs. And this was also what compelled the church to insist on an exclusive loyalty to itself: deprecating family loyalties and glorifying celibacy; deprecating civic loyalties, as such.

9. Theology today urgently requires an alternative centre of gravity, outside the resultant heritage of collective neurosis. Since the Enlightenment, some have thought to find it in a Christian adherence to secular liberalism; or to secular socialism. Both of these however are projects belonging to **political** society: in other words, they aim at becoming ideologies of government. And so they tend to get directly tangled up, themselves, in all the banalities of party-political bureaucracy and propaganda. Jesus said, 'My kingdom is not of this world'. Surely, Christ's kingdom does not belong to this world of political society – but, on the contrary, to that of **civil** society.

Calendar reform?

10. Civil society differs from political society in that it is a world of enterprises not aiming at coercive power, but only to entertain, support, instruct, persuade. And from a theological point of view the great glory of the twentieth century has been the development, above all over the past forty years, of a whole range of new consciousness-raising movements, conscientiously committed to remaining part of civil, not political, society: peace movements, civil liberties movements, feminist movements, green movements,

anti-racist movements, economic justice movements of every sort. It is (I think) theology's calling today to place itself, unequivocally, within that current.

11. The creative theology of the future would then, more and more, become a constant process of negotiation between two basic loyalties:

First, a loyalty to the emergent ethos of free-spirited civil society as a whole – understood to be the primary medium of Christ's **practical** presence in the world;

And second, a loyalty to the church, simply as guardian of the rich communicative resources necessary to give proper religious depth to civil-society debate.

12. Theology, though, is most effective where it most immediately impacts upon liturgy. And perhaps the most promising actual focus for this negotiation-process would be a thoroughgoing project of liturgical **calendar reform**. That is to say: a systematic reshaping of the church's year by the introduction of a new set of 'civil religious' observances. At present, the church's calendar basically just invites us to ponder who we are as church-members; so we commemorate the founding of the church, its prehistory and later development. It is as though, before God, that was the only one of our many social identities which really mattered. But there are also a great many other public memories helping shape who we are as members of civil society – some of them, moreover, still raw and painful. And surely we should be working at these too, the rawest and most painful first: honestly confronting, and so struggling to dissolve, all the more conventional and superficial propaganda-interpretations of our past, so as to learn from it.

Andrew Shanks, *Twelve Theses on Theology and Civil Society*,
Christians in Public Life programme, 1999.

The multiple identities of 'the Church'

In many of the texts we have drawn upon so far, 'the Church' has featured both as the sponsor of mission and as part of the problem that mission addresses. The very nature of the Church, as a flawed human institution with divinely ordained calling, is a source of potential confusion and discontent among its members and others, but it is perhaps, surprising that there has been little sustained ecclesiological study among those engaged with mission in the economic context. Although studies of Industrial Mission, such as that by Shigeko Masumoto, and the Church of England's report *Industrial Mission: An Appraisal* (both already quoted), comment on IM's predicament in its relationship with the institutional churches, the lack of clarity about the nature of the Church goes much deeper. IM, it might be argued, had a contradictory ecclesiology built into it from the start, since Ted Wickham's understanding of the movement as a radical and prophetic attempt to reorientate the Church's social identity required the sponsorship and patronage of the very institution he sought to radicalize. But IM's confusions become more easily understood when the lack of ecclesiological clarity within more central church institutions is exposed.

In the following piece, Elaine Graham analyses the numerous models of church which appear implicitly in the report (sponsored by the Council of Churches for Britain and Ireland) on *Unemployment and the Future of Work*, which appeared just before the 1997 General Election. This report enjoyed the affirmative support of numerous church leaders and was the product of a working party which not only demonstrated ecumenical breadth but had access to all kinds of sources: academic, practical and grass-roots. Yet, the numerous, and not wholly compatible, models of church which underpin the report's findings are not simply the result of divergent views being echoed in an ecumenical setting, but seem to stem from a lack of awareness that understandings of the Church are complex and often in tension with one another.

This passage is taken from a paper that Elaine Graham

delivered to a symposium on the *Unemployment and the Future of Work* report, organized by the William Temple Foundation in July 1997. The symposium papers were later published in book form as *Putting Theology to Work*. Elaine Graham is the Samuel Ferguson Professor of Social and Pastoral Theology in the University of Manchester.

If theological values have any substance, they will exist in primary form as faithful practices – pastoral care, worship, social action – and only derivatively as doctrines and concepts. So it is thus in the dynamics and practices of faithful community that Christians embody their truth claims.

So if we actually look to see what models of 'being Church' and of '*praxis*' are actually present in this Report, I think we would find an amazing kaleidoscope of practical engagement from which some important criteria for effective and faithful Christian intervention and involvement might be derived. But we have to understand, I think, that such evidence conceals a wide variety of implicit assumptions about why Christians should be involved in society, to what ends.

Firstly, although the prospect of individual witness and ministry is mentioned, it is hardly developed; we have little idea of what the Christian is witnessing to. So personal evangelism does not feature in this model of the Church in the world. More firmly rejected is the idea of Church as 'sanctuary or haven' from social and moral issues. '*In times of rapid social change and insecurity, churches and other religious institutions are often seen as places of refuge in which people can shelter and find comfort.*' But the Church has a responsibility to embrace the future and foster the Kingdom. '*It is all too easy for the Church to retreat into a private sphere, to become an escape route from the world and not a means of redeeming it.*'

So here we seem to have a fundamental understanding of the Church which is the vehicle and source of Christian activity as institutional presence at many points of the world of work, industry, unemployment and politics. But clearly, the Church of this report is not content with words; actions feature prominently, for example, in the section '*Mobilising our Resources*'. So, for starters, the Church is seen as 'service provider': practical provision, such as Employment Projects, counselling or rights and advice work. The churches here engage with the wider community primarily as voluntary organisations. . . . We are also reminded that, historically speaking, the churches have always been providers of training and education.

Another model is that of 'presence': the Church in the local neighbourhood, or represented in the workplace via kinds of sector ministry such as Industrial Mission (IM). However, there is an ambivalence over IM as there is within the wider church which further suggests that the ecclesiology of the Report – the relationship between 'Church' as committed congregation, sector chaplains, Diaspora of lay ministers and so on – is underdeveloped.

Another model is that of 'advocate', on behalf of the unemployed or poor. But the impression given is that 'Church' and 'unemployed' are separate constituencies: not the intention of the report, I know, but a trap into which it falls nonetheless. '*Church leaders have been able on occasion to speak in national policy debates on behalf of the powerless . . . people living in poverty . . . had the opportunity to describe their way of life to an audience of leaders in Church and community.*' A similar emphasis emerges from the model of Church as 'community of expertise', containing many people with power and influence in society. '*The churches also have influence because they include in their membership many in positions of power and responsibility in government, business, trade unions and other organisations.*' However, if these two models are to be taken together, they present one particular model of who and what (sociologically and theologically) the Church is: drawn from the privileged and powerful, seeking to address those in government and authority who are similar to themselves. . . .

This . . . reflects an ecclesiology of a Church which is aware of its marginal place in the hearts and minds of many, but is confident still of its seat at the table of power. But are there not alternative ecclesiologies, of dissent and non-conformity, of solidarity with the powerless? Where do we hear traditions of Church as suffering servant, of struggle against powerlessness and oppression, of the importance of 'holiness' amidst hardship, characteristic of some Black-majority traditions?

The Church is also conceived of as *Guardian* or *Repository*: of values, insights and perspectives from '*the Christian tradition*' . . . However, diversity and disagreement in tradition is not considered; rather, theological tradition appears to be homogeneous and uniform. The strands of teaching alluded to in *Unemployment and the Future of Work* – the common good, inclusive community and the work ethic – owe a great deal to their Christian origins, but these are assumed to be normative and definitive. This is therefore a tradition which is self-evident and unproblematic . . .

The Church is also portrayed as a teller of stories: linked with guardian of tradition and insights, but it is interesting to note how Biblical and historical narrative is inserted to illustrate a point, e.g. the story of Israelites captive in Egypt forced to make bricks without straw as an illustration of unfair employment practices! So not only is the Church a source of particular values, but a resource for telling the stories from a particular body of wisdom.

The model of Church as worshipping congregation is also given a fair degree of attention. This is particularly relevant in relation to references to Unemployment Sunday, but emerging, significantly, towards the very end of the Report in some very different reflections on the importance – or even primacy – of worship. There are two particularly interesting strands to this: firstly, we see a model of Church as local congregation focussed on the ministry of the Word . . . Secondly, we have a much more Eucharistic and sacramental understanding of Church – again, arguing that it is at its gathering for worship that the Church most authentically enacts its truth-claims . . .

Now, those two models of Church reflect very different emphases. In practice, they would be representative not of one uniform tradition, but hold in tension a wide spectrum of theological and ecclesiological understandings: but I don't think that the diversity and heterogeneity of Christian experience is fully acknowledged or valued.

[. . .]

So, although we are presented with a number of models of 'Church' within this Report, and of not one but many Christian experiences of involvement with the world, the Working Party does not properly address or engage with that diversity.

[. . .]

In not wishing to privilege any one particular Christian denomination, the Working Party fails to speak from any clear tradition, grounded in the specific activities or practices of the churches.

Elaine Graham, 'The Ecclesiology of *Unemployment and the Future of Work*', in Malcolm Brown and Peter Sedgwick (eds.), *Putting Theology to Work: A Theological Symposium on 'Unemployment and the Future of Work'*, London and Manchester, Council of Churches for Britain and Ireland and William Temple Foundation, 1998, pp. 42–7.

Putting spirituality back on the agenda

Not many of those involved in church-related engagement with the economy have had much to say about spirituality, apparently preferring to leave that element of the life of faith to individual conscience as if it had no bearing on corporate life or social issues. The Industrial Mission publication *Spirituality and Necessity*, already mentioned, was an honourable exception but generated little further material. Perhaps surprisingly, the spirituality associated with the liberation theologians did not seem to make the transition to the British context very easily. Only in the last few years has the Industrial Mission movement, in its journal *IM Agenda*, included prayers, liturgical materials and a number of articles touching on the spirituality of work.

In many ways, it has been the secular world that has set the pace in this respect. When industry and commerce started using the term 'mission statement' in the early 1980s, it felt to many like an encroachment of the secular into the vocabulary of faith. But it did not stop there, and an interest in spirituality, usually divorced from any adherence to established religion, has become widespread, in the commercial world as much as anywhere. A great deal has been written on the 'secular' world's interest in spirituality (see, for instance, Grace Davie, *Religion in Britain Since 1945*, and *Europe: The Exceptional Case*) which is not within the scope of this book. However, there have been a number of attempts by church practitioners to make sense, in terms of Christian theology, of the way concepts like spirituality were being used in a context of rapid economic and social change where meanings and relationships seemed increasingly fluid. The following extract, by Robin Morrison, is one example. Perhaps typically of the genre, it is excited by the new vocabularies emerging in the world of commerce and impatient for the churches to respond positively. In this, the extract is consistent with Industrial Mission's self-understanding as a movement recalling the Church to its vocation through an engagement with secular realities; but it seems simultaneously to lack solid theological grounds for judging the coherence of the 'new vocabulary' against Christian notions of truth and authenticity. It is, nevertheless, one example of a new direction in theological reflection on the economy and the discourses of commerce.

At the time this was written, Robin Morrison was a member of the South Hampshire Industrial Mission team, later becoming Social Responsibility Officer for the Church in Wales.

> Now the traditions and cultural concordats of different forms of Christendom through the ages can no longer be taken for granted. Yes, they were exploited and exploiting, mistakes were made by too much identification. The pattern seems to be that inevitably the church speaks 'out of the age' and is in that sense always secular. Then comes new knowledge and insight and we then have to dig the church out of its embedded framework. Sometimes it takes centuries to do that viz. Galileo and the Catholic Church. But is there an alternative, even when forewarned, we still cannot see what can only be discerned

through the filter of new knowledge? The key thing is to try and avoid making idols of our worldview and good theology helps by keeping our horizons broad and our eyes fixed on a transcendent God of mystery who calls us forward even when we have climbed the mountaintop of achievement. The point is that in every age the only way to learn is through discourse and dialogue, engagement and reflection.

In a pre-industrial age early capitalism was given spiritual roots, indeed grew out of them. Postmodernist values have their own spirituality. Self-interest and greed are not enough to explain the drive to work hard and well, to achieve quality results and fulfilling work relationships. Organisations are forging and discovering a new spirituality. The Church could be an obvious tool for enabling this, recognising, valuing celebrating and developing this in the next century.

Now economic and organisational language embrace new science, technology and the knowledge revolution. They are the new frameworks within which the world forms its myths and its self-understanding. It is from within these arenas that theology will blossom and become real for today. Organisational self-awareness is only a recent phenomenon appearing mostly after the 2nd WW. It is time for theology to recognise God in this growing awareness and to search with others for an 'ontology' of organisations. Something quite extraordinary is happening. From different roots and starting places, something to do with 'spirituality' in organisations and the spiritual resources of Christianity seem to be capable of exchange and mutual learning.

It has taken the whole of human history and consciousness to evolve organisations to their present state of sophistication. Fukuyama's work has documented the story of their development through Adam Smith, Hobbes, Locke, Hegel, Hayek and others. Through much of that time, they have grown within the nourishment of a sacred cosmology, knowing that the handling of matter and processes is also a spiritual, sacramental thing. The pre industrial work ethic had spiritual roots. People were motivated, as Fukuyama describes it by an irrational 'thymos' or 'spiritedness' as well as by 'Reason and Desire'. The desire to 'maximise utility' often hides a deeper search for purpose and meaning. Hegel's State of Recognition in work and relationships is one way of describing this. In other language, human beings require something almost mystical to glue Reason and Desire together and make sense of them.

We still sense this truth in some parts of rural industry, in crafts and skills. Why not in strategic process, management theory, technical research and development, industrial and commercial production? New language in organisations is already way beyond the Church's apparent reluctance to translate its spirituality into the arena of work. As organisational language reaches for new thinking, and practices in leadership change, and people management discovers new ways of relating to local communities and external customers, it is having a social affect way beyond economic transactions. It is increasingly difficult therefore to separate economic and social processes and to ignore the spiritual if not the moral fibre-optics deeply embedded in the connections. Triggered by a drive for short-term competitive success, many organisations have discovered the importance of longer-term vision, confidence building and collaboration. Japan's organisational culture has taught us that product confidence in the market place is of real long term value that gives competitive edge. Cutting short-term corners makes sustainable development and success difficult. The new language includes the ideas of 'confidence', 'trust' and 'relationship'. These are keywords to explore in our learning and exchange together. These are immensely important issues and discoveries.

This is a 'language' the church must learn to speak – not simply for the sake of communicating with an alien culture, but to learn something new of God.

Robin Morrison, 'The Economy in Relation to Issues of "Salvation"', in Malcolm Brown and Robin Morrison, *Church, Change and the Economy*, Manchester, William Temple Foundation, 1999.

8 Comfortable with consumer capitalism?

This final text, from a national broadsheet newspaper, gives a flavour of where chaplaincy in the workplace has come to in the early years of the twenty-first century. The location is in retailing, the contact is with staff and with customers. The ministry is present as an initiative of the company's management at national level and appears to be directed to the welfare of staff and customers rather than to policy and structure in the institution itself. The tone is that of religion and ministry as another service that can be made available, sitting comfortably within the world of consumerism, marketing and the job-structures of the industry. As for the Church, there is no hint here that mission in the workplace is part of a process of changing, let alone radicalizing, the ecclesiastical institutions. The Church has become a service provider in a context where fundamental challenges to the ways the world is ordered have been largely written out of the script. It is, in its way, a parable for a depoliticized, individualized and consumerist new century which seems to have little place for encounters between big ideas.

SUPERNATURAL POWERS AT THE SUPERMARKET

Walking down the aisle with a priest in attendance used to happen only when you were getting married in church. Now it can occur when you're selecting the frozen veg.

Virginia Matthews on the advent of walkabout 'retail chaplains'.

'I see myself as a spiritual maintenance man', says Mark Houghton. 'I'm a sympathetic listener for when a problem is too personal to be discussed with colleagues, spouses or family. I'll talk to anybody who needs it – checkout personnel, managers, customers – and even if the conversation is about little more than the price of bread, I feel that I am building up more trust every day.'

It's the atheist's nightmare, but God and Mammon are joining forces to provide a free portion of spirituality in every shopping trolley at the cheap 'n' cheerful supermarket chain Asda. The Rev Doctor Mark Houghton, to give him his full title (pictured on cover and above), is the workplace chaplain at Asda's Longsight store in Manchester, and last November became the first minister ordained specifically to work in the retail sector. A patent lawyer by day, he spends his spare time working his spiritual magic in the supermarket aisles and hopes one day to go into the ministry full-time.

Asda first hit upon the idea of enlisting so-called 'retail chaplains' in 2003. Since then, spurred on by the enthusiasm of many staff, the firm has installed volunteer men and women of the cloth at more than 160 of its UK stores; providing what it calls a 'friendly shoulder' for employees and, in some cases, providing succour to the chain's 13 million weekly customers. While any out-and-about Bible-thumping, evangelising or loud hymn-singing is strictly forbidden in-store – where it would clash with the infinitely more popular religion of shopping – the brief of the so-called 'pasta pastors' is to act as a sounding board for people with problems and to redirect them to professional counsellors where necessary.

Although their chief role is to listen to dissatisfied or distressed employees – something that would once have been the remit of personnel or HR – the unpaid supermarket God Squad say they like to pack bags, stack shelves and direct shoppers to own-brand baked beans or unsalted cheese biscuits while they work.

Despite the fact that most of the checkout clerics wear C of E dog-collars, Asda is keen to stress that its service – which in time will be rolled out in all 271 of its stores – is both multi-denominational and ethnically diverse. Most stores are widening their search for God to include rabbis, imams, Roman Catholic priests, Buddhist monks, Black Majority church pastors, Methodists and Baptists – all of whom tend to work different shifts on a kind of buy-one-get-one-free basis. In one case, shoppers were surprised to find a Haiti bishop hovering around the frozen food in search of business.

One of Houghton's trickiest problems concerned a young Muslim woman – an Asda employee – whose parents had discovered she was seeing a white boy and had chucked her out. 'I like to feel that one of the reasons she turned up for work every day during this really difficult time was in part because she was getting support from me', he says.

Professor Nigel Nicholson, head of organisational psychology at the London Business School, says that the Asda deal helps 'justify the existence of what would otherwise be a whole army of under-employed vicars', but he warns that it could be dangerous for them to act as untrained counsellors. He adds that he is sceptical of the notion that 'salvation comes at a discount'.

While Asda claims that the staff are largely in favour of the scheme, not all shoppers feel comfortable about it. 'It's bad enough that our vast supermarkets already control what we buy and where we shop without introducing God into the equation', grumbles Elliott Relf, a regular shopper at Asda's Eastbourne store on the south coast.

'I dislike having a man in a dog-collar watching me shop and I feel particularly wary if I'm buying booze or cigarettes that day. If I want to go to church, I'll do so, but I don't want church when I'm buying groceries and I don't want to discuss personal issues in a shop. The directors might think it's good for business, but to me, it's just as unpleasant as being watched by those supermarket security men, who at least have a proper job to do.'

But Houghton is well aware that not everybody puts spirituality high up on their shopping list. 'The hardest people to strike up conversation with tend to be white people with no religious background and middle managers', he reveals, adding 'they tend to be suspicious or who worry that I'm going to pass on confidential information.'

Professor Suzan Lewis, professor of organisational psychology at Manchester Metropolitan University, sees the initiative as a positive thing. 'If Asda really has tackled some of the fundamental problems that affect workers – such as the intensification of work and the blurring of work and home life – then I think it's fine to offer spirituality on top', she judges, adding that she is concerned with the firm's possible ulterior motive. 'If, like so many of these initiatives though, the retail chaplains are simply there to make the company look good and to avoid tackling the real problems of the staff, then they will not ultimately create a happier workforce', she says.

'Industrial missionary', as it is properly called, grew up amid the old smokestack manufacturing industries of the 1940s at a time when clerics were accused of being remote from the realities of industrial life. More recently, mobile chaplains have deserted factories and offices for hospitals and prisons.

Today, there is a marked resurgence in the notion of workplace chaplaincy, says Ed Watson, co-ordinator of the Asda programme. Employee pastors are now in place at Parker Pens, Norwich Union, Nestlé, John Lewis, the government technology research agency Qinetiq, the City of York and other local authorities as well as a number of airports and football clubs.

While Marks & Spencer and Sainsbury have no official policy on chaplaincy, a number of their stores operate their own local pastor schemes. Such is the scale of the chaplaincy job at the Bluewater shopping complex in Kent that the task of offering spiritual solace to the 7,000 staff is now shared between 12 different volunteers. 'The Asda scheme began when two colleagues were lost to cancer', says Watson, 'and although there was a surge in interest in the aftermath of 9/11 and the Harold Shipman case' – the death doctor's infamous surgery being right across the street from an Asda store in Hyde, Greater Manchester – 'we are seeing a steady growth in custom regardless of news headlines.'

'Whether all we do is discuss last night's telly or some really pressing personal or world problems', he says, 'the important thing is to become a familiar sight to shoppers who may not have been in a church since they got married or buried parents.'

To the Rev Dick Johnson of the Kent Industrial Mission, the Asda experiment reflects the clear need among many of us for a more spiritual dimension to our work. 'We are not evangelists and we cannot be considered professional counsellors', he says, 'but we are there, during working hours and without an appointment, to discuss the really important things that are happening in our working and personal lives.'

'Whether it is helping people with their specific bereavement or debt problems, talking about a bullying colleague or world famine, real ministry does tend to happen outside the confines of church.'

While Johnson applauds the renewed interest in workplace chaplaincy by employers, he says that the motives of a small number of firms may be less than honourable. 'On odd occasions, we have suspected certain companies of wanting to turn us into spies for management or an additional management tool, but that is something we will resist at all costs. Industrial chaplaincy works because it is informal, impromptu and totally confidential and that must never change.'

The Guardian, Officehours Section, 24 January 2005,

9 Individual authors

Books from this later period show the growing interest among Christian ethicists and other academic theologians in the deep moral questions raised by economic life. Where the 1980s spawned a considerable amount of writing from practitioners and relatively little from the academy, this trend was reversed through the 1990s.

John Atherton, *Christianity and the Market*, London: SPCK, 1992; *Social Christianity: A Reader*, London, SPCK, 1994.

Two important books from the leading contemporary British Christian ethicist concerned with economic issues. In the first, Atherton considers the moral and political arguments for and against the market economy. In the second, he draws together the tradition of Christian social thinking in Britain and the USA since the beginning of the nineteenth century, showing how economic and other concerns have figured within that tradition.

Grace Davie, *Religion in Britain Since 1945*, Oxford, Blackwell, 1994.

A seminal work in the sociology of religion, charting the fortunes of the churches since the war and coining the much-adopted phrase 'believing without belonging' to describe the prevalent British attitude to faith.

Timothy Gorringe, *Capital and the Kingdom: Theological Ethics and Economic Order*, New York, Orbis; London, SPCK, 1994.

A serious, and essentially communitarian, approach to Christian ethics and the global market economy.

Donald A. Hay and Alan Kreider (eds.), *Christianity and the Culture of Economics,* Cardiff, University of Wales Press, 2001.

An excellent collection of essays from theologians and economists, including Donald Kraybill's fascinating study of Amish economics.

David Jenkins, *Market Whys and Human Wherefores: Thinking Again about Markets, Politics and People*, London, Cassell, 2000.

Following his retirement as Bishop of Durham, Jenkins maintained his interest in theology and the economy. This passionate book is one of the fruits of his studies.

Hans Küng, *A Global Ethic for Global Politics and Economics*, London, SCM Press, 1997.

The well-known Roman Catholic scholar argues that a global economy demands a concerted response from all faiths.

Michael Novak, *The Spirit of Democratic Capitalism*, London, Institute for Economic Affairs Health and Welfare Unit, 1982.

A US Roman Catholic theologian's apologia for market economics – published by a market-oriented think-tank in the UK and therefore influential in forming opinions in Britain during the 1980s and 1990s.

Ronald Preston, *Religion and the Ambiguities of Capitalism*, London, SCM Press, 1991.

The last major book by the doyen of British Christian ethicists whose engagement with economics dated back to his undergraduate years as a pupil of R. H. Tawney at the London School of Economics.

Peter Sedgwick, *The Enterprise Culture*, London, SPCK, 1992; *The Market Economy and Christian Ethics*, Cambridge, Cambridge University Press, 1999; and Andrew Britton, *Economic Theory and Christian Belief*, Oxford, Peter Lang, 2003.

Three works by a theologian who, with John Atherton and others, has maintained an engagement with economic issues and Christian ethics. With the economist, Andrew Britton, the dialogue between the disciplines of theology and economics becomes the focus.

6

Where Now?

When we set out to write this book, it was with a conviction that the history of the churches' engagement with economic issues since the Second World War was not only worth telling for its own sake but that it pointed towards an area of mission that the churches are today in danger of neglecting. We have examined our own consciences and are not convinced that this belief stems merely from anxiety that the legacy of our own work in those fields, and our own areas of academic interest, are being marginalized by current trends! However, if we are right that the activities and ideas that we have explored in the previous chapters are of current relevance, we need first to plot some of the significant changes that have happened to the British – and, to a great extent, the global – economy since the end of the twentieth century.

The British economy in 2006

Just as it took the popular imagination some time to recognize that the Thatcher 'Revolution' was not to be quickly or easily reversed, so it has taken a while to be clear that Tony Blair's New Labour project was not going to undermine Thatcherism's central economic tenets. Blair and his Chancellor Gordon Brown remain committed to market economics as intrinsically preferable to government-directed public spending. The principles, well established by 1997 when they came to power, that (almost whatever the evidence) the public sector is inefficient, the private sector is virtuous and the voluntary sector is to be courted as a major player in the contract culture, have been retained as articles of faith. Nevertheless, New Labour has been committed throughout its time in office to the reform of the welfare state and to overcoming the inherited legacy of millions of people in poverty. To do this within the strictures of a market ideology has involved a degree of sleight of hand but has been quietly successful – helped, perhaps, by a generally favourable world economy.

So to try to sum up the state of the economy today in terms of categories familiar in the preceding sixty years is an awkward task. What the government stands for in its rhetoric (the market, a burgeoning private sector and a diminished public sector) are, to a degree, contradicted by its achievements, which have been led by innumerable government initiatives frequently involving private-, public- and voluntary-sector partnerships. One interpretation of all this is that New Labour has restored the politics of consensus, since debate about economics between the main political parties no longer turns on questions of ideology but involves issues of relatively small-scale management.

This is not, however, a return to the consensus politics of the 1950s to 1970s. Or at least, if it is a consensus around a mixed economy, the proportions of the public/private mix have been changed considerably. And one consequence of extending the market – whose outcomes are directed by the 'hidden hand' rather than by central diktat – into so many areas of life has been that more and more aspects of human existence are becoming understood in terms of economic paradigms (at a relatively trivial level, expressions such as 'the bottom line' are almost ubiquitous). Yet at the same time, with the market's insistence that government interventions are inevitably harmful or distorting, the scope for legitimate government action in economic life – and hence, for political or democratic debate – has been significantly reduced. It is not easy to discern whether the lower public profile of big economic issues compared to the ferment of the Thatcher years is a sign of broad consensus or of apathy and frustration that there is so little debate about alternatives. Gordon Brown's early decision to leave interest rate policy solely in the hands of the Bank of England not only absolved the government of responsibility for potentially unpopular decisions but was a signal that the government itself believed that its proper and legitimate range of powers was constrained by the primacy of market forces.

But now, in New Labour's third term of office, a very big economic question indeed is beginning to be articulated more frequently. In terms of culture, and certainly in terms of economic policies, Britain since the Second World War has been equivocal about its identity and its most important world partners. In 1973, Edward Heath's Conservative government had taken Britain into the European Community (not, incidentally, a subject about which the churches had much to say). The next Conservative leader, Margaret Thatcher, turned her scepticism about Europe into a shibboleth of the Tory Right. New Labour has proclaimed a commitment to the European Union which has sometimes felt distinctly uneasy. Yet governments of all stripes have, since 1945, sought to build and maintain a 'special relationship' with the United States of America. Once, this was expressed largely in terms of defence policy, although the dominant role of defence spending made it a highly significant economic relationship also. But since the collapse of the Soviet bloc in the late 1980s, the rationale has become more concerned with seeking influence with the last undisputed global economic superpower. In short, is Britain, culturally and economically, more like the USA or more like the rest of the European and Nordic countries? The shared English language and the relatively recent history of major conflict between European nations suggest the primacy of one relationship. The post-war project of rendering European wars unthinkable, the burgeoning of European holiday destinations among the British and the commensurate size of many European economies points the other way. At such times, it is a moot point whether the Channel or the Atlantic is the wider expanse of water.

The election in 2000 of a somewhat isolationist Republican President in George W. Bush has brought US policy more overtly into tension with the economic priorities of the European Union or the Nordic countries. The so-called 'Washington model' based on low taxation, labour-market flexibility, the removal of trade barriers (except where some US products are concerned) – that is, free trade, supply-side 'liberalization' – has long been dominant in the USA and its client nations but, with the rapid opening up of global markets, is presented as a condition for other countries, especially in the developing world, to become players on the global economy at all. It is a real, and as yet largely unanswered, question whether the economic power of the USA is such that any other nation can effectively operate a significantly different economic model on its own.

Meanwhile, many member states of the European Union continue to espouse a greater governmental economic role and a significantly larger welfare budget. In the Nordic countries (not all of which are EU members) welfare expenditure – and benefits – remain vastly greater than the British welfare state ever achieved. Different countries have distinct histories, of course, and the relatively classless Swedes and Finns, with a massive popular commitment to social equality, seem largely unswayed by the claimed advantages of the Washington market model; but whether this stems from unique elements in their social history or whether their model is replicable in other countries remains debatable.

Of all the European leaders, Tony Blair has been the most vociferous supporter of George W. Bush's international policies. Domestically, he has led Britain – almost by stealth – towards greater social inclusion but without making equality a political lodestone. This may represent a skilful negotiation of a 'Third Way' between a European and US economic model. But the absence of a well-expressed ideology, or any moral case for the desirability of this course of action, has left Blair vulnerable to two charges: that he stands for nothing more than managing the margins of the economy, and that his policies are informed by no coherent moral compass. Yet the tension between European and US models is unlikely to go away and may prove to be a defining question, the answer to which signals the end of the current era of economic consensus in Britain.

The British churches today

The steady marginalization of the Church within everyday life in Britain continues, apparently unstoppably. This is not the place to explore the data on this subject, but it is worth noting that the evidence of decline, and the inferences to be drawn from it, is contested. What may be more significant is the extent to which a mentality of decline and marginalization has become rooted in the consciousness of British Christians. None of the mainstream denominations is exempt. Some have had to face the prospect of effective extinction within a generation, should current membership trends continue (although trends rarely follow straight lines on a graph). Many would agree that, in the last fifteen years or so, the churches have become more introspective; more concerned with their distinctiveness than with their participation in wider society; more divided within denominations and yet, perhaps paradoxically, less concerned with denominational distinctions along the old structural lines. This has had a significant effect on the ways in which the churches now approach questions of economic ethics, working life and issues of wealth, poverty and social justice.

When New Labour came to power in 1997, many socially active Christians expected a revival of interest in their concerns and new possibilities for partnerships between the churches and government agencies. Blair was the first Prime Minister for decades – perhaps since Gladstone – to wear his Christian faith so openly on his sleeve. Gordon Brown (a Church of Scotland minister's son) loudly welcomed the report on *Unemployment and the Future of Work*, which the Council of Churches for Britain and Ireland had published during the 1997 General Election campaign and, while he had his own policy agenda for attacking unemployment, the government's actions were largely congruent with the report's recommendations. The years of frosty relations between the Tory administrations and the churches' social action agencies were almost immediately transformed by New Labour's early desire to consult widely on almost every topic of public interest. The Church of England's

Board for Social Responsibility had rarely been so busy responding to consultative initiatives from government.

Yet there has been no renaissance of the heady days when church leaders like Temple played an important part in the debate about the economic future of the country. Internal church pressures – shortages of money, a concern for building up the membership (rather than influencing society and hoping people would get the message), the re-emergence of more aggressive theologies that stressed Christian distinctiveness – meant a highly significant shift of the churches' interests and resources towards issues which the Church, rather than the wider world, had defined as central.

Today, the departments and boards that had led the engagement with economic issues have either been disbanded or are shadows of their former selves. The once-prolific Church of England Board for Social Responsibility has been subsumed into a Division for Mission and Public Affairs, largely dominated by an understanding of mission that is concerned to build up the church as a community of holiness, rather than to radicalize its engagement with social issues. On the other hand, the Industrial Mission movement has not (contrary to some predictions from within and beyond IM) been annihilated by unsympathetic church leaders but remains an active presence in many parts of the country. The movement has certainly had to become more accountable to the churches, and church structures have had to become more accountable to their members, for power has shifted from the central to the local. One aspect of increasing material inequality since 1979 has been that financial power within the churches has become concentrated in the wealthier congregations such that, in one Anglican diocese, four large suburban parishes contribute some 25 per cent of the diocesan budget. The reality of financial power has allowed such congregations a disproportionate influence on policy, and IM has had to come out from under the patronage of benevolent bishops and make its case to the local churches. But this in itself is not new. The Free Churches have always been governed from the local level much more than the Church of England ever was, yet they had been staunch supporters of IM in its heyday. Nor is shortage of church funds the simple cause of IM's lower profile. In 2005, the Church of England Diocese of Manchester (never one of the wealthier dioceses) decided that up to 5 per cent of its clergy should be 'roving missioners' without a parochial brief. In the 1980s, Manchester had supported a large IM team along with community workers and other social activists, most of whose posts had been wound up, apparently on grounds of cost, by 2005. But now there appear to be equivalent funds for new missioners who will, it seems, direct their work to 'mission' in the church-centred evangelistic sense rather than to social action.

IM's practitioners are more likely now to be part time, combining IM work with a parochial or congregational responsibility. The freebooting Industrial Missioner to whom the institutional church was a part of the problem (but one which happened to pay his or her stipend) has joined the dinosaurs, but so too, it seems, has the Industrial Missioner whose involvement with economic agencies was concerned to identify and assert the claims of the Kingdom of God on the structures of secular society. IM today has a more comfortably pastoral focus and works more with the grain of contemporary economic assumptions. In the absence of an articulate political debate about economic models and priorities it could hardly be otherwise.

Of the denominations, the United Reformed Church has maintained its commitment to addressing economic issues, and to innovative models of ministry, more effectively than most. Its Church and Society Committee, and successive secretaries, have helped the church to avoid excessive introspection and have continued to regard economic matters as germane to Christian ethics and discipleship. The URC's acceptance of church-related community work as a distinctive order of ministry has allowed it, in a small but significant way, to retain and develop its roots in local communities and hard-pressed areas where local issues, rather than the church's needs, drive the agenda. Never a large or particularly financially secure denomination, the URC experience suggests that loss of interest in social, political and economic issues is not inevitable in the current ecclesial climate.

In ecumenical relations generally, it is still the Church of England whose greater resources tend to dominate other denominations. Not infrequently, the Anglicans' residual tone of effortless superiority, which can imply that all other Christians in the country are invisible, hinders effective co-operation both at local and at national levels. But it remains, in terms of the public consciousness, that the denominations are playing on a much more level playing field than was the case for most of the period of this book. When the public at large is so widely ignorant of most matters of faith, and where religion of all kinds is seen as mysterious, outmoded and odd, the niceties of denominational difference count for little. On matters where the churches wish to address the wider world, the task of speaking on behalf of the Christian faith does not devolve exclusively on Anglicans as often as it did.

The ecumenical bodies – Churches Together in Britain and Ireland and the 'Churches Together' agencies for the separate countries of the UK and for local areas – are at something of a crossroads. Never particularly well resourced, or especially popular with the bigger denominations, they have nonetheless retained a concern for the churches' engagements with the wider context. A big report, like *Unemployment and the Future of Work*, showed that it was only with considerable practical and staffing support from the better endowed denominations (in that case, the Church of England) that major new work could be completed in the name of the ecumenical bodies. They have, nevertheless, continued to act as facilitators, bringing groups together to work on key issues. The emergence from Churches Together in Britain and Ireland of the collection of essays *Prosperity with a Purpose* (2005) is a good example and suggests a number of ways in which the churches may continue to address the questions posed by the dominant economic models.

But, as noted above, the relatively low profile of formal ecumenical structures does not signify a return to a strident denominationalism. Groupings such as the Evangelical Alliance bring together Christians from a wide variety of churches and denominations who nonetheless share a particular theological stance. What unites members of the Evangelical Alliance is frequently far more extensive than that which its members share with others in their denomination. And while this is true for such large, doctrinally oriented groupings, it is also true to some extent for the churches' action for social justice.

The churches and the economy today

The *Church Times* for 9 July 2005 carried a front page colour photograph of Princes Street, Edinburgh, teeming with demonstrators marching on a day when the leaders of the G8 nations met at Gleneagles. The marchers' banners carried the slogan 'Make Poverty History' and their demand was for the leaders of the industrialized world to write off the vast debts of the developing world – especially Africa – and commit themselves to policies that would reverse the deepening polarization between rich and poor in a global economy. For months before, the white wristbands of the Make Poverty History campaign had been worn by Christians and others as an outward sign of their commitment. Many churches and cathedrals joined in the campaign in very public ways – Chelmsford cathedral was encircled by a white cloth band, by now the instantly recognizable symbol of the campaign. The prominence given to the campaign in the church press is an indication of the high level of involvement of Christians and churches in such campaigns for global economic justice.

But Make Poverty History was not a campaign for Christians alone. Nor, although supported by many church leaders, was it the initiative of any institutional church body. Instead, like the earlier Jubilee 2000 campaign, which we have already met, it showed that popular movements are still capable of mobilizing large numbers around a single issue straightforwardly presented. Many of those people are Christians for whom such actions are intrinsic to their discipleship and vocation, and it is obvious that involvement in such campaigns has been energizing for many local congregations and groups.

The emergence of campaigns like Make Poverty History makes it harder to speak of 'the churches' in their engagement with the economy. It is as if the denominations have franchised this aspect of their work to autonomous, and not overtly faith-based, organizations that mobilize Christian opinion independently of church structures. At the same time, it becomes difficult to quantify the levels of Christian involvement or to evaluate the extent to which such activity is changing the way the churches work.

What is also becoming clear is that, in a global economy, the focus of moral and ethical engagement with economic issues has also acquired a global perspective. A Christian understanding of economics that confines itself to domestic issues and has nothing to say about the scale of world poverty or the imbalances of global trade protocols could never, now, connect with the way the majority of people feel. In this, perhaps, the churches' longstanding internationalism has helped to lead the way.

It still needs to be said, however, that moral and ethical issues in domestic economics have not gone away. The way the economy is ordered, and especially questions of employment, are of profound importance in shaping the ways in which people relate to one another, value themselves and understand the nature of 'good living'. If the depredations of unfettered global markets are now the subject of concerted Christian action and lobbying, it is important to ask where similar questions about the dominant market model and the spread of consumeristic approaches to life are being asked in the domestic and local context.

It is not a wholly bleak picture. Church Action on Poverty remains a leading Christian campaign group in relation to national policy, and many of the think-tanks and research units already noted, such as The London Institute for Contemporary Christianity and the William Temple Foundation are very active players. But in terms of wider church life, questions of global economic justice can seem rather safely remote from day-to-day decision-making. Sometimes the gross poverty of Africa can seem more visible and easier to address than the intractable issues of poverty close to home. It may also be the case that the grotesque imbalances in global economic affairs deflect attention from the ambiguities and complexities of sustained ethical engagement with practical economic questions. Certainly there seems to be a growing tendency for church leaders and theologians alike to prefer the sweeping ethical imperative ('We must change the rules of trade!') to the difficulties of forging practical and local solutions with all the ethical grey areas that such steps entail.

To some extent, the eclipse of the middle-axiom approach to doing theology is both a cause and a symptom of wider contextual changes and shifts of theological emphasis. We have already traced the problems of that approach as the easy consensus of like-minded people, which had allowed dialogue between disciplines to seem straightforward, crumbled in the 1980s. Without that careful attention to other ways of knowing, theology can quickly become abstract, utopian and unworldly, as Ronald Preston so frequently commented. But this is not a world where the narrow definitions of expertise, with which Temple or Preston worked, can be sustained – doing social theology must now embrace an immense diversity of perspectives if it is to reflect the ways people think and feel about the world they inhabit.

And here there is an issue in which the changing context in which the churches do their theology, and the ethical questions surrounding economics, come together in a way that has yet to be fully explored. For the market economy, as we noted in the first chapter, is to a very great extent the creature of social plurality; a system that is explicitly designed to address a world in which simple moral agreement is increasingly hard to attain. Even today, more than twenty-five years since Mrs Thatcher began to enact her economic experiment, many Christian writers, thinkers and practitioners continue to ignore the extent to which rival conceptions of justice and of moral behaviour mean that challenges to market economics are obliged to give a better account of plurality.

This more self-consciously plural context is reflected in developments in academic theology also. We have touched briefly on the rise of radical orthodoxy and other challenges to liberal theological positions, and it is true that the dominant voices speaking of theology in the academy are more concerned to explore the distinctiveness of the Christian revelation, the counter-cultural nature of the Church and the centrality of liturgy and practice, than to reason from experience to policy and to seek to influence the activities of secular institutions. We have largely avoided the term 'postmodernity' in this book, since it is such a contested concept, but in so far as the term marks a more self-conscious alertness to difference, a stronger awareness of identity as something malleable, and the relativizing of ethical narratives, then the questions exercising contemporary Christian ethicists are largely framed by the terms of postmodernity. Inevitably, the whole approach to theology in the public arena has come to reflect this and so it is unsurprising that the agencies of the churches whose calling was to enact a widely held understanding of public theology have had to adapt or flounder.

The continuing relevance of the economy to the churches

But the response of the churches and of theology to postmodernity has been ambiguous and here, perhaps, lies the beginning of a debate that may yet bring questions of economic ethics back into the forefront of Christian ethical enquiry. In short, it is unclear what, in postmodernity, is compatible with, or contrary to, Christian understandings of God, humanity and the world. In particular, the place of consumerism is hotly contested. For some, the implication that human beings can choose so much of their identity as to live by essentially self-chosen life stories is an appalling prospect, which threatens to drive the notion of a creator God, whose actions are part of the given context for life, out of the picture. Others embrace consumerism as the harbinger of a new freedom for Christians to choose ways of faith that need no longer conform to established structures – distinctive Christian communities serving the increasingly fragmentary and differentiated human community.

Yet while consumerism as a concept is frequently drawn upon by both academic theology and church strategists, the essential connection between consumerism and economics – specifically the market system – is rarely explored. While this may reflect the general political consensus referred to earlier, it leaves unexamined many of the ethical questions that arise in the practical out-working of market principles. It is our contention that the churches would understand more about themselves, as well as about the social context in which most Christians live out their lives, if they were to take a more critical interest in the workings of the economy.

The growing awareness of the ubiquity of consumerist thinking, coupled with the increasing public profile of popular dissent from the global market and its international repercussions, may well be two factors that prompt the churches in Britain to a renewed engagement with the complexities of economic issues at different levels.

The texts on which we have drawn in this book were all significant in their day. They represent an immense amount of serious theological and missiological endeavour by the churches and by their members. They are well worth recording for the picture they paint of churches that saw their calling as one of service and 'critical solidarity' with the worlds of politics, economics and secular work, rather than focus on the distinctiveness and separateness of faith. The world of today looks very different, so it is inevitable that much of our material will now appear as of more historical than contemporary relevance. Nevertheless, we would argue that through much of the period since the Second World War, the churches in Britain had, in their agencies, like Industrial Mission and Social Responsibility, examples of an approach to mission which, while much more muted today, represents an essential element in any serious theology of mission.

Shigeko Masumoto (see Chapter 4) argued that all mission is

concerned to address a 'gap', but that there were three distinct gaps waiting to be addressed. There was the sociological gap, between the Church and the world. Bridging this gap means addressing the way the wider world understands the Church and how the Church can appeal to the world. Mission in this gap seeks primarily to attract people to join the Church and profess the Christian faith – and it is, of course, this version of mission that is today in the ascendancy.

But there is always the danger that Christians will mistake the finite and flawed institution of the church for the Kingdom of God in all its fullness. Thus another missiological gap opens up – the ecclesiological gap between the church and the Kingdom. This was the gap which, in the days of Leslie Hunter and Ted Wickham, Industrial Mission was founded to address. Wickham believed the church to be apostate because of its tendency to mistake bourgeois values for Christian virtues, and the remedy was to be found in an attentive dialogue with working-class people in the place where they found their most distinctive identities as men and women – the workplace. Thus IM was conceived as a project to call the Church back to its true vocation instead of acquiescing in its captivity to narrow class-based interests. And it is fair to ask where, today, are there serious endeavours in the 'ecclesiological gap'? Class in Britain now takes on a rather different set of profiles, but social stratification remains prevalent. The churches have not been significantly successful in escaping their middle-class strongholds. IM's contention was that the hidden issues behind the reality of class were the economy and work. It has not been established that, in this, the diagnosis was wrong, but the Church now gives itself fewer opportunities for sustained and respectful listening to parts of the economic world that it does not always understand.

And the third gap in Shigeko Masumoto's analysis was the theological gap – the gap between the Kingdom of God and the world as it is. It is the gap that is addressed every time we pray for the Kingdom to come on earth as in heaven; but the enacting of that prayer has often entailed the conviction that God is at work in the world beyond the Church and not solely through the communities of the faithful. If IM was felt, at times, to be at best semi-detached from the institutional churches, a positive reason was that the movement held to the belief that God's Kingdom could be brought nearer by the actions of men and women in their secular lives, creating change through the 'central determining realities' of the economy. A church that has become anxiously concerned for its internal workings will find it harder to hold to such a belief. But such a church is in grave danger of hubristically regarding itself as the present fulfilment of the Kingdom of God.

Bodies like Industrial Mission, for all that they were the progeny of a very different economy and a very different sort of church life, helped keep the churches honest by broadening their conception of mission to consider all three of the gaps. One would probably not set out to address the theological or ecclesiological gaps today through a medium akin to IM as it was between the 1940s and 1990s. But the economy, with its concern for the finite, material world, for human creativity and for the structural relationships between people, still offers a fruitful point of entry for considering mission in those particular three dimensions.

It is not yet possible to say what form such a multi-dimensional approach to mission might take in the future, or how the workings of the economy might become the focus of Christian social action in a way that informs and enriches the churches' mission. But few useful movements have succeeded by being oblivious to their history. We believe that the activities and thinking explored in the pages of this book might yet provide a basis for a reappraisal of the churches' mission and a renewed seriousness about Christian engagement with the economic issues that none of us, in the course of our lives, can avoid.

Notes

Foreword

1 A discussion document entitled 'Prosperity with a Purpose' was produced by The Conference of Irish Bishops of the Roman Catholic Church in 1999 but not formally published.

1 The Economy as a Site of Christian Mission

1 Given Temple's enormous, and very public, commitment to ecumenism, it seems justifiable to refer here to the churches in the plural. While Anglican dominance of public life remained extensive in the 1930s, the public perception of Temple included his good relations with other denominations and churches. Today, and throughout this study, we will refer wherever possible to the churches in the plural since engagement with economic issues has been an ecumenical as well as a denominational activity throughout our period.

2 For instance, alcohol-related crime against the person is believed to increase during periods of economic prosperity, while crime against property rises in times of recession.

3 See Donald B. Kraybill, 'Amish Economics: The Interface of Religious Values and Economic Interests' in Donald A. Hay and Alan Kreider (eds.), *Christianity and the Culture of Economics*, Cardiff, University of Wales Press, 2001.

4 For more on these arguments, see Raymond Plant and others, 'Conservative Capitalism: Theological and Moral Challenges' in Anthony Harvey (ed.), *Theology in the City*, London, SPCK, 1997.

5 This argument is explored at greater length in Malcolm Brown, *After the Market: Economics, Moral Agreement and the Churches' Mission*, Bern, Peter Lang, 2004.

6 See, for example, D. Stephen Long, *Divine Economy: Theology and the Market*, London and New York, Routledge, 2000, in the 'Radical Orthodoxy' series.

7 Cynthia D. Moe-Lobeda, *Healing a Broken World: Globalisation and God*, Minneapolis, Fortress Press, 2002.

3 Consensus 1945–79

1 See David L. Edwards, *Priests and Workers*, London, SCM Press, 1961.
2 See: John Mantle, *Britain's First Worker Priests*, London, SCM Press, 2000.

4 Crisis 1979–90

1 Julian Barnes, *Letters from London, 1990–1995*, London, Picador, 1995, pp. 242–3.
2 Francis Wheen, *How Mumbo-Jumbo Conquered the World: A Short History of Modern Delusions*, London, Fourth Estate, 2004.
3 For the text of this address, and a critical analysis of it, see Jonathan Raban, *God, Man and Mrs.Thatcher*, Chatto & Windus, 1989.
4 F. A. Hayek, *Law, Legislation and Liberty Vol. 2: The Mirage of Social Justice*, London, Routledge & Kegan Paul, 1976.
5 For an excellent exposition of the philosophy of market economics – and a tentative rebuttal – see Raymond Plant and others, 'Conservative Capitalism: Some Theological and Moral Challenges' in Anthony Harvey (ed.), *Theology in the City*, London, SPCK, 1997.
6 See Digby Anderson, *The Kindness that Kills: The Churches' Simplistic Response to Complex Social Issues*, London, SPCK, 1984.
7 *The Church and the Bomb*, London, Church Information Office, 1982.
8 See Elaine Graham, *Theology in the City: Ten Years After 'Faith in the City'*, Bulletin of the John Ryland University Library of Manchester, 78:1, Spring 1996. Also Malcolm Brown, 'Some Thoughts on Theological Method' in *Unemployment and the Future of Work: An Enquiry for the Churches*, London, Council of Churches for Britain and Ireland, 1997.
9 Grace Davie, *Religion in Britain Since 1945*, Oxford, Blackwell, 1994; *Europe: The Exceptional Case*, London, Darton, Longman & Todd, 2001.
10 For Jenkins's account of his involvement in this and other controversies, see his book, *The Calling of a Cuckoo*, London, Continuum, 2002.
11 Harvey Cox, *The Secular City*, London, SCM Press, 1965.
12 Alasdair MacIntyre, *After Virtue: A Study in Moral Theory*, London, Duckworth, 1981.

13 The French worker-priest movement had enthused a number of British Anglican priests to emulate the model. See John Mantle, *Britain's First Worker Priests*, London, SCM Press, 2000.
14 Catholic Bishops' Conference of England and Wales, *The Common Good and the Catholic Church's Social Teaching*, 1996.
15 Published in *The Listener*, 18 April 1984.
16 For a more detailed exploration of this argument see, Malcolm Brown, *After the Market: Economics, Moral Agreement and the Churches' Mission*, Bern, Peter Lang, 2004.
17 See Peter Selby, *Grace and Mortgage: The Language of Faith and the Debt of the World*, London, Darton, Longman & Todd, 1997, for an interesting exploration of the social, political and theological implications of global and personal debt.
18 Board for Social Responsibility, *Church and Economy: Effective Industrial Mission for the 1990s*, 1989.
19 For instance, Michael Northcott, whose doctoral thesis was published later as *The Church and Secularisation: Urban Industrial Mission in North East England*, Bern, Peter Lang, 1989.
20 Lillemor Erlander, *Faith in the World of Work: On the Theology of Work as Lived by the French Worker-Priests and British Industrial Mission*, Acta Universitatis Upsaliensis, 1991.
21 Shigeko Masumoto, *A Critique of British Industrial Mission*, Industrial Mission and the Church in Britain Today, Paper 1, Board for Social Responsibility, 1987.
22 See Sedgwick's article, 'Refusing to Despair over Families', *Church Times*, 30 July 1995.

5 *Consumption 1985 to the Present*

1 Eric Hobsbawm, *The Age of Extremes: The Short Twentieth Century 1914–1991*, London, Michael Joseph, 1994.
2 Ulrich Duchrow, *Global Economy: A Confessional Issue for the Churches*, Geneva, World Council of Churches, 1987.
3 Peacock currently (2006) is developing models of statistical research as Mission Planning Officer for the Anglican Diocese of Manchester – perhaps one of the most sophisticated examples of a church basing its mission policy on empirical analysis.
4 Interestingly, 'the social gospel' is a term familiar in the USA since the late nineteenth century but almost unheard of in Britain except among those seeking to attack it as a concept. Such usage suggests that conservative or evangelical opponents of Christian social engagement often draw their ammunition from across the Atlantic. This may constitute one small piece of evidence for another trend that we have

not examined here: the strong links between evangelical Christianity in the USA and Britain. In contrast, the more liberal stances that dominated the British churches' work in economic affairs and workplace ministry in the twentieth century were much more strongly committed to the European project and sceptical of US power and dominance.

Bibliography

Economics, church and theology

Anderson, Digby, *The Kindness that Kills: The Churches' Simplistic Response to Complex Social Issues*, London, SPCK, 1984.

Atherton, John R., *Faith in the Nation: A Christian Vision for Britain*, London, SPCK, 1988.

——*Christianity and the Market: Christian Social Thought for our Time*, London, SPCK, 1992.

——*Social Christianity: A Reader*, London, SPCK, 1995.

——*Public Theology for Changing Times*, London, SPCK, 2000.

——*Marginalisation*, London, SCM Press, 2003.

Bagshaw, P., *The Church Beyond the Church: Sheffield Industrial Mission 1944–94*, Industrial Mission in South Yorkshire, 1994.

Ballard, Paul H., *Towards a Contemporary Theology of Work*, Cardiff, HOLI 4, Faculty of Theology, Cardiff University, 1982.

——*In and Out of Work: a Pastoral Perspective*, Edinburgh, St Andrew Press, 1987.

Banner, Michael, *Christian Ethics and Contemporary Moral Problems*, Cambridge, Cambridge University Press, 1999.

Barrow, Simon and Smith, Graeme (eds.), *Christian Mission in Western Society*, London, Churches Together in Britain and Ireland, 2002.

Bartholomew, Craig and Moritz, Thornton, *Christ and Consumerism*, Carlisle, Paternoster Press, 2000.

Bevans, S., *Models of Contextual Theology*, (revised and expanded edn), Maryknoll, Orbis, 2002.

Biggar, Nigel, *The Good Life: Reflections on What We Value Today*, London, SPCK, 1997.

Bonhoeffer, Dietrich, *Letters and Papers from Prison*, London, SCM Press, 1953.

Borrowdale, Anne, *A Woman's Work: Changing Christian Attitudes*, London, SPCK, 1989.

Britton, Andrew and Sedgwick, Peter, *Economic Theory and Christian Belief*, Bern, Peter Lang, 2003.

Brown, Malcolm, *After the Market: Economics, Moral Agreement and the Churches Mission*, Bern, Peter Lang, 2004.

Brown, Malcolm and Sedgwick, Peter (eds.), *Putting Theology to Work*, Manchester, Council of Churches for Britain and Ireland and William Temple Foundation, 1998.

Brown, Malcolm and Morrison, Robin, *Church, Change and the Economy*. Manchester, William Temple Foundation, 1999.

Catherwood, H. F. R., *The Christian in Industrial Society*, London, Tyndale Press, 1964.

Cavanaugh, William T., *Theopolitical Imagination*, London, Continuum, 2003.

Charland, William A., *The Heart of the Global Village: Technology and the New Millennium*, London, SCM Press, 1990.

Childs, James M., *Greed, Economics and Ethics in Conflict*, New York, Fortress Press, 2000.

Claringbull, Denis, *Front Line Mission: Ministry in the Market Place*, Norwich, Canterbury Press, 1994.

Clark, David (ed.), *Changing World, Unchanging Church?* London, Mowbray, 1997.

Clark, Henry, *The Church under Thatcher*, London, SPCK, 1993.

Clarke, Roger, *Work in Crisis: Dilemma of a Nation*, Edinburgh, St Andrew Press, 1982.

Clements, Keith, *Learning to Speak: The Church's Voice in Public Affairs*, Edinburgh, T & T Clark, 1995.

Cobb, John, *The Earthist Challenge to Economism: A Theological Critique of the World Bank*, Basingstoke, Macmillan, 1999.

Cockin, F. A., *Faith and Work*, London, Mowbray, 1955.

Conway, Ruth, *Choices at the Heart of Technology*, London, Continuum, 1999.

Cox, Harvey, *The Secular City*, London, SCM Press, 1965.

Davies, J. (ed.), *God and the Market Place: Essays on the Morality of Wealth Creation*, London, Institute for Economic Affairs, Health and Welfare Unit, 1978.

Dean, J. M. and Waterman A. M. C. (eds.), *Religion and Economics: Normative Social Theory*, Boston, Kluwer Academic Press, 1999.

Demant, V. A., *Religion and the Decline of Capitalism*, London, Faber and Faber, 1949.

Dimmelen, R. van, *Faith in the Global Economy: A Primer for Christians*, Geneva, World Council of Churches, 1998.

Dommen, Edward, *How Just is the Market Economy?* Geneva, World Council of Churches, 2003.

Duchrow, Ulrich, *Global Economy: A Confessional Issue for the Churches?* Geneva, World Council of Churches, 1987.

Edwards, David L. (ed.), *Priests and Workers*, London, SCM Press, 1961.

Elliott, Charles, *Inflation and the Compromised Church*, Belfast, Christian Journals, 1975.

——*Praying the Kingdom*, London, Darton, Longman & Todd, 1985.

Erlander, Lillemor, *Faith in the World of Work: On the Theology of Work as Lived by the French Worker-Priests and British Industrial Mission*, Uppsala, Acta Universitatis Uppsaliensis, 1991.

Ferguson, Ronald, *Technology at the Crossroads*, Edinburgh, St Andrew Press, 1994.

Fergusson, David, *Community, Liberalism and Christian Ethics*, Cambridge, Cambridge University Press, 1998.

Forder, Walter, *Christian in the Market Place*, Galway, Campus Press, 1999.

Forrester, Duncan B., *Christianity and the Future of Welfare*, Peterborough, Epworth Press, 1985.

——*Beliefs, Values and Practices: Conviction Politics in a Secular Age*, Oxford, Oxford University Press, 1989.

——(ed.), *Theology and Practice*, Peterborough, Epworth Press, 1990.

——*Christian Justice and Public Policy*, Cambridge, Cambridge University Press, 1997.

Fraser, Ian, *Reinventing Theology as the People's Work*, Glasgow, Wild Goose, 1988.

Fuller, John and Vaughn, Patrick (eds.), *Working for the Kingdom: The Story of Ministers in Secular Employment*, London, SPCK, 1986.

Gorringe, T. J., *Capital and the Kingdom: Theological Ethics and Economic Order*, London, SPCK, 1994.

Grelle, Bruce, and Krueger, David A., *Christianity and Capitalism: Perspectives on Religion, Liberalism and the Economy*, Chicago, Center for the Scientific Study of Religion, 1986.

Griffiths, Brian, *Morality and the Market Place*, London, Hodder & Stoughton, 1982.

——*Monetarism and Morality: An Answer to the Bishops*, London, Centre for Policy Studies, 1985.

Grundy, Malcolm, *An Unholy Conspiracy: The Scandal of the Separation of the Church and Industry Since the Reformation*, Norwich, Canterbury Press, 1992.

Habgood, John, *Church and Nation in a Secular Age*, London, Darton, Longman & Todd, 1983.

Harries, Richard, *Is There a Gospel for the Rich?* London, Mowbray, 1992.

Harvey, Anthony (ed.), *Theology in the City*, London, SPCK, 1997.

——*By What Authority? The Churches and Social Concern*, London, SCM Press, 2001.

Hauerwas, Stanley, *The Peaceable Kingdom: A Primer in Christian Ethics*, London, SCM Press, 1983.

Hauerwas, Stanley, *With the Grain of the Universe*, London, SCM Press, 2002.
Hay, Donald A., *Economics Today: A Christian Critique*, Leicester, Apollos, 1989.
Hay, Donald and Kreider, Alan (eds.), *Christianity and the Culture of Economics*, Cardiff, University of Wales Press, 2001.
Heslam, Peter, *Globalization: Unravelling the New Capitalism*, Cambridge, Grove, 2002.
——(ed.), *Globalization and the Good*, London, SPCK, 2004.
Hewitt, Gordon, *Strategist for the Spirit: Leslie Hunter, Bishop of Sheffield 1939–62*, Oxford, Becket Publications, 1985.
Hill, Alexander D., *Just Business*, Leicester, InterVarsity Press, 1997.
Hollenbach, David, *The Common Good and Christian Ethics*, Cambridge, Cambridge University Press, 2002.
Hoogstraten, Hans-Dirk van, *Deep Economy: Caring for Ecology, Humanity and Religion*, Cambridge, James Clark, 2001.
Hunter, Leslie S., *Church Strategy in a Changing World*, London, Hodder & Stoughton, 1949.
Hybels, Bill, *Christians in the Market Place*, London, Hodder & Stoughton, 1986.
Jarl, Ann-Cathrin, *In Justice: Women and Global Economics*, Minneapolis, Fortress Press, 2003.
Jenkins, Daniel, *Equality and Excellence*, London, SCM Press, 1961.
Jenkins, David, *God, Politics and the Future*, London, SCM Press, 1988.
——*Market Whys and Human Wherefores: Thinking Again about Market, Politics and People*, London, Cassell, 2000.
——*The Calling of a Cuckoo*, London, Continuum, 2003.
Jenkins, Rachel, *Changing Times, Unchanging Values?* Manchester, William Temple Foundation, 1991.
Jeremy, D. J., *Business and Religion*, Aldershot, Gower, 1988.
——*Capitalists and Christians*, Oxford, Clarendon Press, 1990.
Kane, Margaret, *Theology in an Industrial Society*, London, SCM Press, 1975.
——*Gospel in Industrial Society*, London, SCM Press, 1980.
Keiser, Jack, *Men at Work: A Christian Approach to Business and Industrial Ethics*, London, Epworth Press, 1978.
Küng, Hans, *A Global Ethic for Politics and Economics*, London, SCM Press, 1997.
Legood, Giles (ed.), *Chaplaincy: The Churches' Sector Ministries*, London, Cassell, 1999.
Long, D. Stephen, *Theology and Economics: Values, Protests, Virtues*, London, Routledge, 2000.
——*Divine Economy: Theology and the Market*, London, Routledge, 2000.

MacLeod, George, F., *Only One Way Left*, Glasgow, Iona Community, 1956.
Mann, Adrian, *No Small Change: Money, Christians and the Church*, Norwich, Canterbury Press, 1992.
Mantle, John, *Britain's First Worker Priests*, London, SCM Press, 2000.
Maurice, F. D., *The Kingdom of Christ*, Cambridge, Lutterworth Press, 2003.
Meeks, M. D., *God the Economist: The Doctrine of God and the Political Economy*, Minneapolis, Fortress Press, 1989.
Milbank, John, *Theology and Social Theory: Beyond Secular Reason*, Oxford, Blackwell, 1990.
Moberly, Walter, *Crisis in the University*, London, SCM Press, 1949.
Moe-Lobeda, Cynthia D., *Healing a Broken World: Globalisation and God*, New York, Fortress Press, 2002.
Munby, Denys, *Christianity and Economic Problems*, London, Macmillan, 1956.
—— *God and the Rich Society*, Oxford, Oxford University Press, 1961.
Nankivell, Owen, *All God's Gifts: A Christian View of the Affluent Society*, Peterborough, Epworth Press, 1978.
Nesbett, Paula, *Religion and Social Policy*, Walnut Creek CA, Alta Mira, 2001.
Neuhaus, Richard J., *The Naked Public Square: Religion and Democracy in America*, Grand Rapids, Eerdmans, 1986.
—— *Confession, Conflict and Community*, Grand Rapids, Eerdmans, 1986.
Newbigin, Lesslie, *The Gospel in a Pluralist Society*, London, SPCK, 1994.
Niebuhr, H. R., *Christ and Culture*, New York, Harper & Row, 1951.
Niebuhr, Reinhold, *Moral Man and Immoral Society*, London, SCM Press, 1963.
Northcott, C. H., *Christian Principles in Industry*, London, Pitman, 1958.
Northcott, Michael, *The Church and Secularization: Urban Industrial Mission in North East England*, Bern, Peter Lang, 1989.
—— *Urban Theology: A reader*, London, Cassell, 1998.
Novak, Michael, *The Spirit of Democratic Capitalism*, London, Institute of Economic Affairs, Health and Welfare Unit, 1982.
O'Donovan, Oliver, *Principles in the Public Realm: The Dilemma of Christian Moral Witness*, Oxford, Clarendon Press, 1984.
—— *Resurrection and Moral Order: An Outline for Evangelical Ethics*, Leicester, InterVarsity Press, 1986.
Oldham, J. H., *Work in Modern Society*, London, SCM Press, 1950.
Ormiston, H. and Ross, M., *New Patterns of Work*, London, SCM Press, 1990.

Oslington, Paul, *Economics and Religion*, Cheltenham, Elgar Reference Collection, 2003.

Parvis, Peter J., *God and Globalization*, London, Continuum, 2001.

Pattison, Stephen, *The Faith of the Managers: When Management Becomes Religion*, London, Cassell, 1997.

Percy, Martyn, *Power and the Church: Ecclesiology in an Age of Transition*, London, Cassell, 1998.

Phipps, Simon, *God on Monday*, London, Hodder & Stoughton, 1966.

Preston, Ronald H., (ed.), *Technology and Social Justice*, London, SCM Press, 1971.

——(ed.), *Industrial Conflicts and their Place in Modern Society*, London, SCM Press, 1974.

——(ed.), *Perspectives on Strikes*, London, SCM Press, 1975.

——*Religion and the Persistence of Capitalism*, London, SCM Press, 1979.

——*Explorations in Theology 9*, London, SCM Press,1981.

——*Church and Society in the Late Twentieth Century, The Economic and Political Task*, London, SCM Press, 1983.

——*Religion and the Ambiguities of Capitalism*, London, SCM Press, 1991.

——*Confusions in Christian Ethics: Problems for Geneva and Rome*, London, SCM Press, 1994.

Preston, Ronald H. and Barker, Edwin, *Christians in Society*, London, SCM Press, 1939.

Raban, Jonathan, *God, Man and Mrs. Thatcher*, London, Chatto & Windus, 1989.

Reader, J., *Local Theology: Church and Community in Dialogue*, London, SPCK, 1994.

Richardson, Alan, *The Biblical Doctrine of Work*, London, SCM Press, 1952.

Roberts, R., *Religion and the Transformation of Capitalism: Comparative Approaches*, London, Routledge, 1995.

Rogerson, John (ed.), *Industrial Mission in a Changing World*, Sheffield, Sheffield Academic Press, 1996.

Schluter, Michael and Ashcroft, John, *Jubilee Manifesto: A Framework Agenda and Strategy for Social Reform*, Leicester, InterVarsity Press, 2005.

Schumacher, Christian, *Small is Beautiful: Economics as though People Mattered*, London, Vintage, 1993.

——*To Live and Work*, Eastbourne, MARC, 1987.

Schweilker, William, *Theological Ethics and Global Dynamics*, Oxford, Blackwell, 2004.

Sedgwick, Peter, *Not Ceasing from Exploring*, Industrial Mission and

the Church in Britain Today, Paper 2, London, Board for Social Responsibility, 1987.
——(ed.), *The Enterprise Culture*. London: SPCK, 1992.
——(ed.), *God in the City*, London, Mowbray, 1995.
——*The Market Economy and Christian Ethics*, Cambridge, Cambridge University Press, 1999.
Sedgwick, Peter and Britton, Andrew, *Economic Theory and Christian Belief*, Oxford, Peter Long, 2003.
Selby, Peter, *Grace and Mortgage: The Language of Faith and the Debt of the World*, London, Darton, Longman & Todd, 1997.
Shanks, Andrew, *Civil Society, Civil Religion*, Oxford, Blackwell, 1995.
Sheppard, David, *Built as a City*, London, Hodder & Stoughton, 1975.
——*Bias for the Poor*, London, Hodder & Stoughton, 1983.
Sider, Ronald, *Rich Christians in an Age of Hunger*, London, Hodder & Stoughton, 1977.
——*Living More Simply*, London, Hodder & Stoughton, 1980.
Siefer, G., *The Church in Industrial Society: A Survey of the Worker Priest Movement and Its Implications for the Christian Mission*, London, Darton, Longman & Todd, 1964.
Simons, Robert G., *Competing Gospels: Public Theology and Economic Theory*, Alexandria NSW, Australia, E J Dwyer, 1995.
Stackhouse, M. L., *Public Theology and Political Economy: Christian Stewardship in Modern Society*, New York, University Press of America, 1991.
——(ed.), *On Moral Business: Classic and Contemporary Resources for Ethics in Economic Life*, Grand Rapids, Eerdmans, 1995.
Stapleford, John, *Bulls, Bears and Golden Calves: Applying Christian Ethics in Economics*, Leicester, InterVarsity Press, 2002.
Storkey, Alan, *Transforming Economics*, London, SPCK, 1986.
Storrar, William and Morton, Andrew R., (eds), *Public Theology for the Twenty-First Century*, Edinburgh, T &T Clark, 2005.
Sugden, Christopher, *Fair Trade as Christian Mission*, Cambridge, Grove, 1999.
Suggate, A. M., *William Temple and Christian Social Ethics Today*, Edinburgh, T & T Clark, 1987.
Symanowski, Horst, *The Christian Witness in an Industrial Society*, London, Collins, 1966.
Tawney, R. H., *Religion and the Rise of Capitalism*, Harmondsworth, Penguin, 1938.
Taylor, M. H. (ed.), *Christians and the Future of Social Democracy*, Ormskirk, G. W. and A. Hesketh, 1981.
Taylor, Richard, *Christians in an Industrial Society*, London, SCM Press, 1961.

Temple, William, *Christianity and Social Order*, Harmondsworth, Penguin, 1942.
Todd, John M. (ed.), *Work: Christian Thought and Practice*, London, Darton, Longman & Todd, 1960.
Tracy, David, *The Analogical Imagination: Christian Theology and the Culture of Pluralism*, New York, Crossroad, 1981.
Velten, George, *Mission in Industrial France*, London, SCM Press, 1968.
Visser t'Hooft, W. A. and Oldham, J. H., *The Church and Its Function in Society*, London, Allen & Unwin, 1937.
Ward, Graham (ed.), *The Postmodern God: A Reader*, Oxford, Blackwell, 1997.
Wells, S. and Hauerwas, S. (eds.), *The Blackwell Companion to Christian Ethics*, Oxford, Blackwell, 2004.
Wickham, E. R., *Church and People in an Industrial City*, London, Lutterworth Press, 1957.
——*Encounter with Modern Society*, London, Lutterworth Press, 1964.
Wilkie, George, *Thinking about Industrial Life*, Edinburgh, St Andrew Press, 1980.
Wilson, Rodney, *Economics, Ethics and Religion: Jewish, Christian and Muslim Thought*, Basingstoke, Macmillan, 1996.
Wogaman, J. P., *Christians and the Great Economic Debate*, London, SCM Press, 1977.
——*Economics and Ethics: A Christian Enquiry*, London, SCM Press, 1986.
——*Christian Perspectives on Politics*, London, SCM Press, 1988.
Wolf, Miroslav, *Work in the Spirit: Towards a Theology of Work*, Oxford, Oxford University Press, 1991.
Young, Frances, *Dare We Speak of God in Public?* London, Mowbray, 1995.
Zinborg, Edward D., *Faith, Morals and Money*, London, Continuum, forthcoming.

Background

Alcock, Peter, *Social Policy in Britain*, Basingstoke, Macmillan, 2003.
Alcock, Peter and May, Margaret: *Students' Companion to Social Policy*, Oxford, Blackwell, 2003.
Anthony, P. D., *The Ideology of Work*, London, Tavistock Publications, 1977.
Askonas, P. and Frowen S. F. (eds.), *Welfare and Values: Challenging the Culture of Unconcern*, Basingstoke, Macmillan, 1997.

Bibliography

Askonas, P. and Stewart, Angus (eds.), *Social Inclusion: Possibilities and Tensions*, Basingstoke, Macmillan, 2000.

Barnes, Julian, *Letters from London 1900–1995*, London, Picador, 1995.

Baylis, John and Smith, Steve, *The Globalisation of World Politics*, Oxford, Oxford University Press, 2001.

Bell, D., *The Cultural Contradictions of Capitalism*, London, Heinemann, 1976.

—— *Communitarianism and Its Critics*, Oxford, Clarendon Press, 1993.

Bellah, R. N., *The Broken Covenant: American Civil Religion*, Chicago, University of Chicago Press, 1992.

—— et al., *Habits of the Heart: Individualism and Commitment in American Life*, San Francisco, University of California Press, 1995.

Blake, Robert, *The Decline of Power, 1915–1964*, London, Paladin, 1986.

Booth, Alan (ed.), *British Economic Development since 1945*, Manchester, Manchester University Press, 1995.

Boswell, J., *Community and the Economy: The Theory of Public Cooperation*, London, Routledge, 1990.

Brittan, S. and Hamlin, A. (eds.), *Market Capitalism and Moral Values*, Aldershot, Edward Elgar, 1995.

Bruce, Steve, *Religion in Modern Britain*, Oxford, Oxford University Press, 1995.

Childs, David, *Britain since 1945*, London, Routledge, 1992.

Cook, Chris and Stevenson, John (eds.), *Britain since 1945*, London, Longmans, 2000.

Daly, H. E. and Robb, J. B., *For the Common Good*, Boston, Beacon, 1989.

Davie, Grace, *Religion in Britain since 1945*, Oxford, Blackwell, 1994.

—— *Europe: The Exceptional Case*, London, Darton, Longman & Todd, 2001.

Dorey, Peter, *British Politics Since 1945*, Oxford, Blackwell, 1995.

Etzioni, A., *The Moral Dimension: Towards a New Economics*, New York, Free Press, 1988.

Field, Frank, *Stakeholder Welfare*, London, Insititute for Economic Affairs, Health and Welfare Unit, 1996.

Galbraith, J. K., *The Culture of Contentment*, Harmondsworth, Penguin, 1992.

Giddens, A., *Runaway World*, London, Profile, 2002.

Gray, J., *Beyond the New Right: Markets, Government and the Common Environment*, London, Routledge, 1993.

—— *False Dawn: The Delusions of Global Capitalism*, London, Granta, 2002.

Hastings, Adrian, *A History of English Christianity, 1920–85*, London, Collins, 1986.

Hastings, Adrian, *Church and State: The English Experience*, Exeter, University of Exeter Press, 1991.

Hay, Donald, *Economics Today*, Leicester, Apollos, 1989.

Hayek, F. A., *The Road to Serfdom*, London, Routledge, 1944.

——*The Constitution of Liberty*. London, Routledge and Kegan Paul, 1960.

——*The Mirage of Social Justice* (vol 2: *Law, Legislation and Liberty*), London, Routledge & Kegan Paul, 1976.

Held, David and McGrew, A. (eds.), *The Global Transformation Reader*, Cambridge, Polity Press, 2000.

Hobsbawm, Eric, *The Age of Extremes: The Short Twentieth Century, 1914–1991*, London, Michael Joseph, 1994.

Hunt, Stephen J., *Religion in Western Society*, Basingstoke, Palgrave, 2002.

Hutton, Will, *The State We're In*, London, Cape, 1995.

Keegan, W., *Mrs. Thatcher's Economic Experiment*, Harmondsworth, Penguin, 1984.

Lloyd, Roger, *The Church of England in the Twentieth Century* (vol 2: *1919–39*) London, Longman Green, 1950.

MacIntyre, Alasdair, *After Virtue: A Study in Moral Theory*, London, Duckworth, 1981.

——*Three Rival Versions of Moral Enquiry: Encyclopedia, Genealogy and Tradition*, London, Duckworth, 1990.

Middleton, Roger, *The British Economy since 1945: Engaging with the Debate*, Basingstoke, Macmillan, 2000.

Rawls, J., *A Theory of Justice*, Oxford, Oxford University Press, 1972.

——*Political Liberalism*, New York, Columbia University Press, 1993.

Richter, Philip and Francis, Leslie J., *Gone But Not Forgotten*, London, Darton, Longman & Todd, 1998.

Rose, M., *The Post-Modern and the Post-Industrial*, Cambridge, Cambridge University Press, 1991.

Scruton, Roger, *The West and the Rest: Globalization and the Terrorist Threat*, London, Continuum, 2005.

Stewart, Michael, *Keynes and After*, Harmondsworth, Penguin, 1991.

Stiglite, Joseph, *Globalisation and Its Discontents*, Harmondsworth, Penguin, 2003.

Taylor, Charles, *Sources of the Self: The Making of Modern Identity*, Cambridge, Cambridge University Press, 1989.

Thomson, David, *England in the Twentieth Century, 1914–1963*, Harmondsworth, Penguin, 1965.

Vallely, Paul, *The New Politics*, London, SCM Press, 1998.

Wesby, P. A., *A History of the Church of England, 1945–80*, Oxford, Oxford University Press, 1984.

Wheen, Francis, *How Mumbo-Jumbo Conquered the World: A Short History of Modern Delusions*, London, Fourth Estate, 2004.

Reports, pamphlets etc.

British Council of Churches/Council of Churches for Britain and Ireland/Churches Together in Britain and Ireland

The Church and Industry, 1958.
Work or What? 1977.
Understanding Inequality, 1977.
The Consumer Good Society, 1978.
Unemployment and the Future of Work: An Enquiry for the Churches, Council of Churches for Britain and Ireland, 1997.
Longley, Clifford (ed.), *Prosperity with a Purpose: Christians and the Ethics of Affluence*, 2005.
Skinner, David, *Prosperity with a Purpose: Exploring the Ethics of Affluence*, 2005.

The Church in Wales

Morrison, Robin, *Globalisation, Democracy and Protest*, The Church in Wales, 2001.

The Church of England

Malvern 1941: The Proceedings of the Archbishop of York's Conference, London, Longman Green, 1941.
Towards the Conversion of England, London, Church Assembly, 1945.
The National Church and Social Order, London, Church Information Office, 1956.
The Task of the Church in Relation to Industry, London, Church Information Office, 1959.
Work in Britain Today, London, Board for Social Responsibility, 1969.
Adams, Kenneth, *Ethical Choice and Business Responsibilities*, London, Board for Social Responsibility, Church Information Office, 1975.
Gilbertson, Geoffrey, *Power Sharing in Industry*, London, Board for Social Responsibility, Church Information Office, 1975.
Wickham, E. R., *Growth and Inflation*, London, Board for Social Responsibility, Church Information Office, 1975

Understanding Closed Shops, London, Board for Social Responsibility, Church Information Office, 1977.

Work and the Future, London, Board for Social Responsibility, Church Information Office, 1979.

Winters of Discontent, London, Church Information Office, 1981.

The Church and the Bomb, London, Board for Social Responsibility, Church Information Office, 1982.

Transnational Corporations: Confronting the Issues, London, Church Information Office, 1983.

Perspectives on Economics, London, Church Information Office, 1984.

Growth, Justice and Work, London, Church Information Office, 1985.

Faith in the City: A Call for Action by Church and Nation, London: Church Information Office, 1985.

Not Just for the Poor, London, Church House Publishing, 1985.

All That Is Unseen: A New Look at Women and Work, London, Board for Social Responsibility, Church House Publishing, 1986.

Shigeko Masumoto, *A Critique of British Industrial Mission*, Industrial Mission and the Church Today, Paper 1, London, Board for Social Responsibility, 1987.

Muir, Kevin, *Industrial Mission – Catholic Style*, Industrial Mission and the Church in Britain Today, Paper 4, London, Board for Social Responsibility, 1987.

Industrial Mission – An Appraisal: The Church's Response to the Changing Industrial and Economic Order, London, Board for Social Responsibility, 1988.

The Ethics of Acquisition, London, Board for Social Responsibility, 1989.

Church and Economy: Effective Industrial Mission for the 1990's, London Board for Social Responsibility, 1989.

Something to Celebrate: Valuing Families in Church and Society, London, Board for Social Responsibility, Church House Publishing, 1995.

Faith in a Global Economy, London, Board for Social Responsibility, 1998.

The Church of Scotland

Baillie, John (ed.), *God's Will for Church and Nation: Reprinted from the Reports of the Commission for the Interpretation of God's Will in the Present Crisis*, London, SCM Press, 1946.

Francis, J. and Swann, N., *Scotland in Turmoil*, St Andrew Press, 1973.

——*Scotland's Pipe Dream*, 1974.

Page, Ruth, *Theology and Industrial Mission*, Scottish Churches Industrial Mission, 1994.

Bibliography

Industrial Mission

The End of Work? Working Papers from Industrial Mission, Manchester, William Temple Foundation, 1980.
Thinking in Practice, Manchester, William Temple Foundation, 1980
Changing Industrial Mission: Models and Hopes, Manchester, William Temple Foundation, 1985.
Spirituality and Necessity, Manchester, William Temple Foundation, 1985.
Davies, Mostyn, et al., *Towards a Strategy for the Fourth Generation of IM*, Theology Development Group, 1991.
——*IM: The Anatomy of a Crisis*, Manchester, William Temple Foundation, 1992.

The Methodist Church

The Methodist Approach to Industrial Mission, Occasional Paper 5, Home Mission Department, 1968.
Hill, Clifford, *Renewal in the Inner City*, Occasional Paper 27, Home Mission Department, 1977.
Our Daily Labour: A Methodist Reflection on Employment, Growth, Consumerism and the Environment, Division of Social Responsibility, 1994.
Part-Time Working, Division of Social Responsibility, 1995.
The Cities: A Methodist Report, Methodist Church and NCH Action for Children, 1997

Roman Catholic Church

Encyclicals
Rerum Novarum, 1891.
Quadragesimo Anno, 1931.
Mater et Magistra, 1961.
Pacem in Terris, 1963.
Populorum Progressio, 1967.
Octogesima Adveniens, 1971.
Redemptor Hominis, 1979.
Laborem Exercens, 1981.

Second Vatican Council, 1962–65
Gaudium et Spes (*Pastoral Constitution on the Church in the Modern World*), 1965.

Others

The Common Good and the Catholic Church's Social Teaching, Catholic Bishops' Conference of England and Wales, 1996.

Compendium of the Social Doctrine of the Church, Pontifical Council for Justice and Peace, London, Burns & Oates, 2005.

The Salvation Army

The Paradox of Prosperity, 1999 (in conjunction with the Henley Centre).

Burden of Youth, 2001.

The Responsibility Gap, 2004.

A Home for All, 2005.

The Society of Friends (Quakers)

Quaker Faith and Practice, London, The Yearly Meeting of the Religious Society of Friends (Quakers) in Britain, 1995.

The United Reformed Church

Luckin, David, *Worth Working For?*, 2002.

World Council of Churches

The Churches Survey Their Task, Oxford Conference on Life and Work, 1937.

Christian Faith and the World Economy Today, Geneva, WCC, 1992.

Other bodies

The Beveridge Report, HMSO, 1942.

Hearing the Cry of the Poor: A Declaration by Church Action on Poverty, (undated).

Now . . . Thrive the Armourers, A Report to the Heads of Hampshire Churches by a Working Party on the Manufacture and Sale of Armaments, 1983.

The Creation of Wealth, Occasional Paper 14, Manchester, William Temple Foundation, 1985.

Sargeant, Jean, *Liberation Theology on the Wapping Picket Lines*, London, Jubilee Group, 1992.

Clark, David, *A Survey of Christians at Work and Its Implications for the Churches*, Birmingham, Christians in Public Life, 1993.
Social Justice: Strategies for National Renewal, Report of the Social Justice Commission, 1994.
Ballard, Paul, *Christians at Work: A Welsh Survey*, Cardiff, HOLI 8, RELIG, Cardiff University, 1998.
Baker, C. and Skinner, H., *Regenerating Communities: A Theological and Strategic Critique*, Manchester, William Temple Foundation: *I. Mapping the Boundaries* (2003); *II. Telling the Stories* (2005).
Graham, E. and Baker, C. (eds.), *Religious Capital in Regenerating Communities*, Manchester, Manchester Centre for Public Theology and William Temple Foundation, 2004.
Parker, Caroline, *Social Ethics in the Post-Modern City: Local Churches as Urban Planners for Multicultural Communities*, Manchester, William Temple Foundation, 2004.

Journals

The following journals and newsletters carry material relevant to the study of the churches and the economy.

Contact – Practical Theology and Pastoral Care.
Crucible, founded as the house journal of the Board for Social Responsibility of the Church of England, now published by the *Church Times*.
Faith in Business, Quarterly, Industrial Christian Fellowship and the Ridley Hall Foundation.
Frontier, published by the Christian Frontier Council 1950–75.
IM Agenda, Industrial Mission Association.
Modern Believing, Modern Churchpeople's Union.
Political Theology, London, Equinox Press.
Theology, London, SPCK.
Urban Bulletin, ECUM Urban Bulletin.

Sources and Acknowledgements

We are grateful to the following individuals and bodies for allowing us to use extracts for which they hold copyright. Every effort has been made to trace the copyright owners of material included in this book, and any omissions will be corrected in future editions on receipt of information.

The Archbishops' Council, for permission to use extracts from: *Towards the Conversion of England*, 1945; *The Task of the Church in Relation to Industry*, 1959; *Growth and Inflation*, 1975; *Power Sharing in Industry*, 1975; *Understanding Closed Shops*, 1977; *Work and the Future*, 1979; *Winters of Discontent*, 1981, *Transnational Corporations*, 1983; *Perspectives on Economics*, 1984; *Growth, Justice and Work*, 1985; *Faith in the City*, 1985; *Not Just for the Poor*, 1986; Peter Sedgwick, *Not Ceasing from Exploring*, 1987; Kevin Muir, *IM Catholic Style*, 1987; Shigeko Masumoto, *A Critique of British Industrial Mission*, 1987; *Industrial Mission: An Appraisal*, 1988; *The Ethics of Acquisition*, 1989; *Faith in a Global Economy*, 1998.

Chris Beales, for permission to use extracts from *Introducing Employment Forum (UK)*, 2002.

The Catholic Bishops' Conference of England and Wales, for permission to use extracts from *The Common Good*, 1996.

Church Action on Poverty, for permission to use the pamphlet, *Hearing the Cry of the Poor*.

Churches Together in Britain and Ireland, for permission to use extracts from: *The Church and Industry* (BCC), 1958; *Work or What?* (BCC), 1977; *Understanding Inequality* (BCC), 1977; *The Consumer Goods Society* (BCC), 1978; *Unemployment and the Future of Work* (CCBI), 1997; *Putting Theology to Work* (CCBI/WTF), 1998.

Mostyn Davies, for permission to use extracts from: *Towards a Strategy for the Fourth Generation of IM*, 1991, and *Industrial Mission – Anatomy of a Crisis*, 1992.

Guardian Newspapers Limited, for permission to use the article by Virginia Matthews, '*Supernatural Powers at the Supermarket.*'

Richard Higginson, for permission to use an extract from the Mission Statement of the Ridley Hall Foundation and an extract from Mike Vincer, 'Pie in the Sky . . . Or Faith on the Ground?' in *Faith in Business Quarterly*, Winter 2002–3.

The Industrial Mission Association, Central Co-ordinating Committee, for permission to use an extract from Anthony Dalling, 'Lucas – Which side are we on?' in *The IMA Newsletter*, 1980.

The Rt Revd David Jenkins, for permission to use extracts from his enthronement sermon at Durham Cathedral, 21 September 1984.

The Jubilee Group, for permission to use extracts from Jean Sargeant, *Liberation Theology on the Wapping Picket Line*, 1992.

The Methodist Church Publishing House, for permission to use extracts from: *Our Daily Labour*, 1994; *The Cities – A Methodist Report*, 1997; *Home Mission Reports*, 1954 and 1956; *Home Mission Occasional Paper 5*; *Home Mission Occasional Paper 27* by Clifford Hill; Jack Keiser, *Men at Work*, 1978.

Robin Morrison, for permission to use extracts from *Globalisation, Democracy and Protest*, 2001.

Orbis Books, for permission to use an extract from S. B. Bevans, *Models of Contextual Theology*, 1992.

SPCK, for permission to use extracts from: Henry Clark, *The Church under Thatcher*, 1993; John Atherton, *Christianity and the Market*, 1992.

Alison Peacock, for permission to use extracts from *Employment and the Future of the Church*, 1998.

The Saint Andrew Press, for permission to use extracts from *The Church of Scotland, Church and Nation Committee Reports to Assembly*, 1956, 1973, 1974, 1976; and *Home Mission Board Reports to Assembly*, 1958, 1959, 1961, 1962, 1971, 1976.

Andrew Shanks, for permission to use extracts from, *Twelve Theses on Theology and Civil Society*, 1999.

The United Reformed Church, for permission to use an extract from *A Summary of 'Worth Working For? Job Opportunities in 21st Century Britain'*, London, The United Reformed Church, 2002. pp. 2–12.

The William Temple Foundation, for permission to use extracts from: Rodney Ward in *Spirituality and Necessity*, 1985; Ronald Preston in *Occasional Paper 14*, 1985; *Changing Industrial Mission: Models and Hopes*, 1985; Rachel Jenkins, *Changing Times: Unchanging Values*, 1991; Mostyn Davies, *Industrial Mission: Anatomy of a Crisis*, 1992; *Religious Capital in Regenerating Communities*, 2004; Malcolm Brown and Peter Sedgwick (eds.), *Putting Theology to Work*, 1998; Malcolm Brown and Robin Morrison, *Church, Change and the Economy* (1999).

Index of Names and Subjects